FEMINIST CATHOLIC THEOLOGICAL ETHICS:
Conversations in the World Church

Edited by

LINDA HOGAN

AND

AGBONKHIANMEGHE E. OROBATOR

ORBIS BOOKS
Maryknoll, New York 10545

Library of Congress Cataloging-in-Publication Data

Feminist Catholic theological ethics : conversations in the world church / edited by Linda Hogan and Agbonkhianmeghe E. Orobator.
        pages cm. — (Catholic theological ethics in the world church ; 2)
    Includes bibliographical references and index.
    ISBN 978-1-62698-078-5 (pbk.)
    1. Women in the Catholic Church.   2. Feminist theology.   3. Christian ethics—Catholic authors.   I. Hogan, Linda, 1964– editor of compilation.
BX2347.8.W6F45 2014
241'.042082--dc23

                                                                2013039977

Feminist Catholic
Theological Ethics

CATHOLIC THEOLOGICAL ETHICS IN THE WORLD CHURCH

James F. Keenan, Series Editor

Since theological ethics is so diffuse today, since practitioners and scholars are caught up in their own specific cultures, and since their interlocutors tend to be in other disciplines, there is the need for an international exchange of ideas in Catholic theological ethics.

Catholic Theological Ethics in the World Church (CTEWC) recognizes the need to appreciate the challenge of pluralism, to dialogue from and beyond local culture, and to interconnect within a world church not dominated solely by a northern paradigm. In this light, CTEWC is undertaking four areas of activity: fostering new scholars in theological ethics, sponsoring regional conferencing, supporting the exchange of ideas via our website (catholicethics.com), and publishing a book series.

The book series will pursue critical and emerging issues in theological ethics. It will proceed in a manner that reflects local cultures and engages in cross-cultural, interdisciplinary conversations motivated by mercy and care and shaped by shared visions of hope.

To Margaret Ogola and Ada María Isasi-Díaz

Contents

Acknowledgments

This volume on feminism in the world church is the outcome of a truly global collaboration in Catholic theological ethics. Special thanks to all the contributors representing different parts of the globe for their prompt submission and diligent revision of the essays for publication. The Planning Committee of *Catholic Theological Ethics in the World Church* (CTEWC) conceived the original idea of a book series, following two successful cross-cultural conferences in Padua (2006) and Trent (2010). This volume is the second in the series. We owe a debt of gratitude to members of the Planning Committee for their insight and suggestions. Special thanks are due to Celia Grace Kenny for her editorial assistance. We are grateful to the publisher, Orbis Books, and editor James Keane for their commitment to the timely publication of this volume.

Introduction:
Of Feminism and
Conversations in Church and Society

Agbonkhianmeghe E. Orobator

According to a contemporary myth, feminism has run its course, and feminist discourse has reached a saturation point. While the first half of this perception confines feminism to the margins of irrelevance in church and society, the second claims that nothing new can be expected of or added to the existing body of feminist discourse. The essays in this book invalidate both theses on two counts. First, it is erroneous to take a static view of feminism and treat it as a monolithic edifice hermetically encased in a historical-temporal framework. Second, it depends on where one looks to hear new voices, discover fresh insights, and engage creative imagination. Considered as discourse, process, methodology, or movement, feminism is globally variegated, contextually multilayered, and methodologically polyglot. The essays in this book aim to demonstrate all three claims.

The body of feminist literature in the late twentieth and early twenty-first centuries demonstrates the phenomenal growth of feminist thought and movements in the global context of church and society. Characteristic of this growth is the relocation of issues from the global North and broadening of focus to include voices from the global South. The themes and topics addressed in feminist discourse are as intense and controversial as they are pertinent and critical, both in the realm of faith and in the public sphere.

In the context of globalization, new vistas and voices are emerging that trace alternative directions and seek to rephrase the central questions advanced in feminist discourse. Thus, while analyses converge around enduring "traditional" themes, there are emerging voices articulating new issues and challenges, and identifying opportunities for deepening and expanding the conversations. These conversations contain distinct perceptions, analyses, and interpretations that are all held in an ongoing tension.

This book also aims to highlight the changing face, color, themes, and locus of feminist theological discourse; to recognize innovative research in the field; and to facilitate a global conversation among feminists engaged in theological ethics in the world church. One can raise an objection as to whether or not such a global conversation is possible at a time when local identity is gaining ascendancy and

1

seeking increased recognition. The complementarity or compatibility of purposes
between global and local perspectives constitute a unique feature and nature of the
investigation undertaken by contributors to this book.

The contributors come from Africa, Asia, Latin America, Europe, and North
America. In considering their accounts, it is important to note that they do not
exhaust the feminist conversations happening in these geographical contexts. The
issues they raise, the context they describe, the challenges they surface, and the
strategies they propose account for a fraction of a much wider process of theological and ethical conversation in church and society. Rather than present a closed
debate, they open possibilities for conversation around issues that matter in church
and society, but that may question established models of ecclesial management
and political governance. Besides, the geographical location of the contributors
need not be taken as neat and rigid boundaries. Geography represents a useful
criterion for ease of identification, but the contributors' locations, or, better still,
their spaces, are "fluid" or "porous," a fact demonstrated by their capabilities to
traverse continents and interact in academic circles, engage in scholarly encounters,
and undertake joint research projects that maintain and promote a global outlook
regarding the issues under investigation. To cite but a few examples, if Gerard
Mannion is European by nationality, the context and content of his contribution
is North American; if Anne Arabome and Lilian Dube are Nigerian-American
and Zimbabwean-American, respectively, their conversations draw on narratives
from the far-flung continent of Africa; if the location of Nichole Flores is North
America, her analysis focuses on Latin America; and Anna Perkins bridges North
America and Latin America. We can multiply examples, but the important thing
is to avoid imposing geographical boundaries or territoriality as determinants of
the quality, orientation, and value of feminist conversations in the world church.

The Voices

To begin the contribution from Africa, **Anne Arabome** paints a portrait of
the African woman and her quest for what Elizabeth Johnson has christened "the
living God." By Arabome's account, this quest is laden with passion and compassion, driven by reflective depth and insight, and colored with song and joy—all of
them gifts at the service of the community called church and the African society.
Yet, in church and society, formidable barriers and factors militate against the
flourishing of these gifts. More significantly, however, the African woman is not
merely a victim, as she is oftentimes characterized in Western scholarship. By right
she is a prophet that feminist critique and hermeneutics need to take seriously
in order to overcome oppressive patriarchal and theological mind-sets, harmful
cultural biases, and internalized oppression, of the kind that Shawnee Daniels
Sykes denounces in her essay. A particularly provocative idea is the argument that
African women's perceptions of God transcend and bridge the gender divide simultaneously; they reveal an inclusive vision of God in worship, ritual, prayer, and

celebration. Arabome's idea advances or resembles a unique type of anthropomor-
phism that names and images God in the creative and resilient life-giving capacities
and joy-giving genius of African women.

Within the same African context, **Lilian Dube** undertakes a phenomenology
of contrasting images of Mary in a local church in Zimbabwe, where a women's
devotional group's predilection for pre–Vatican II colonial Marian images conflicts
with post–Vatican II-inspired inculturated artistic rendition. This situation reveals
the tension between missionary Christianity and postcolonial Christianity. In
the course of this analysis, Dube's appreciation of papal documents on women
is perhaps more complimentary than most in this book. One implication of this
positive appreciation emerges in the difference between feminist theology and
hermeneutics in the global North and in Africa. This difference evokes old fissures
and tension between racialized images and universalized models. Opting for a
mutually exclusive approach fails to resolve the tension. Dube's preferred route
or means for diffusing this tension is the path of hybridity that transcends and
reconciles the black-white divide. In the end, her analysis leaves more questions
than it answers: Why do African Marian devotees (women) prefer white images
of Mary to inculturated black images? Who is to judge the motives and validity
of their preference—theologians or the women themselves, who obviously do not
perceive (contrary to the claims of theologians) any evidence of racially tinged
hermeneutical dissonance or the need for deconstruction of their preferred images
of Mary? Who really speaks for African women? Who embodies or incarnates the
"spirit" of Mary? What is the color of feminist discourse?

Veronica Rop reviews the culture, context, and scriptural hermeneutics that
shape the image and experiences of African women. Her argument for greater
access to education in order to enhance their contribution to church and society
is irrefutable. Her narrative of the experience of African women in an oppressive
culture corroborates those of Arabome and Dube as well as Kochurani Abraham
and Shaji George Kochuthara (in India). Here education must be conceived of
in a wide, inclusive sense to include formation in theological knowledge, critical
analysis of culture, and sensitivity to human rights. The goal is to give voice to all,
including women—to empower their equal and full participation in church and
public life, in full recognition and validation of their dignity grounded in widening
circles of relationality. Without denigrating the importance of the other components of education in what concerns church, theological education plays a vital
role in opening social and ethical contexts to the revelation of the divine in order
to build a more just, peaceful, and reconciled church and society, inspired by the
teaching and praxis of Jesus.

The name of **Alison Munro** is practically synonymous with the response of
the Roman Catholic Church in South Africa to the AIDS pandemic. The church
stands out as a leader and credible partner in its involvement in programs for
providing lifesaving antiretroviral drugs to people living with HIV/AIDS. This
program, which benefits a large number of women, faces multiple challenges of

rising costs, funding constraints, sustainability, viability of public-private partnership, and relationship with the church on some contentious ethical issues. The
questions that Munro raises are crucial: How can the church guarantee sustainability of treatment programs with limited resources and infrastructure? What
ethical criteria should the church programs use in the selection of patients for
antiretroviral therapy? As the structure of care evolves and patients are transferred
to government facilities, what commitment does the church owe health care and
counseling workers facing redundancy? How is the neuralgic question of condom
use dealt with in this context?

At face value, it may be hard to see the relevance of this essay to the conversations in this book. There is nothing explicitly feminist in this essay. The value can
be glimpsed only if we pay attention to the fact that, globally, women and girls
continue to bear the brunt of HIV/AIDS inordinately and disproportionately
on account of various kinds of gender-based structural injustice, similar to what
Kochuthara and Abraham uncover in India. Whether as caregivers or people living
with AIDS, women are far more vulnerable as infected and affected. There is no
room to doubt the gender quotient of HIV infection and the care of people living
with AIDS.

Sharon Bong introduces the conversations in Asia by painting in broad
strokes a decade of Ecclesia of Women in Asia (EWA), a network of Asian Catholic
women theologizing from the womb of Asia.[1] The feminist account of *ecclesia* in
Asia reverses the invisibility of women and confirms their role as generators of
theological knowledge. Their feminist approach prioritizes a contextualized methodology that recognizes and affirms the inclusivity of truth and bodies from the
epistemological, socioeconomic, and political margins of Asia. This approach exists
both as successor and subjugated knowledge, continuity and discontinuity, that
ultimately liberates theology from its patriarchal stranglehold for an embodied and
engendered universal mission at the service of the church.

A founding member of EWA, **Agnes Brazal** undertakes a fascinating historical
and postcolonial phenomenology of power-beauty dialectic in the contemporary
Filipino context. She poignantly demonstrates how this dialectic is skewed by a
dualistic gender ideology and a feminist epistemology that prefers discoursing
"body" to validating "beauty" as worthy of serious feminist epistemological investigation and integration. Power is not exclusively male; it is beautiful, as well. Nor
is beauty exclusively female; it is powerful, as well. The fluidity of gender construction offers a potent tool for decolonizing entrenched patriarchal structures in
church and society and for reconstructing sociocultural relational frameworks
that honor the dignity of women and men created in the beautiful *and* powerful
image and likeness of God. Like Elizabeth Marie Bucar, Brazal offers convincing
examples from scripture of iconic female personalities who holistically integrate
this power-beauty dialectic.

Focusing on the Roman Catholic Church in the Philippines, **Aloysius Lopez
Cartagenas** maps the shift in feminist discourse in Asia from gender polarities

to gender fluidities. The assumed cohort of this empirical study is composed of diocesan priests, though it does not exempt religious priests. This shift in feminist discourse causes unease and reinforcement of barriers and bastions of clericalism in the church. Cartagenas dissects the sociological archetypes, prototypes, and typologies, as well as socioeconomic stratification, incarnated in clericalism in the church. These gender-biased and male-structured categories are deeply imbedded in imbalanced models and processes that take place in the family, society, parish, and seminary formation. The focus of this formation and socialization not only serves to enhance and consolidate the status of the male but also the construction of the female self as subservient and subordinate to and a perpetuator of male clergy and privilege. Notwithstanding this process, transitions and ongoing nego- tiation of masculinity are compelled by demographic and socioeconomic factors such as the migration of Filipina women to work outside of the country. There are deep echoes here of Arabome's analysis of the African context.

Considering the issues raised in this essay, the following question can be asked: What can provoke and sustain change in attitudes, behavior, and institutions in order to create a more balanced gender typology? The complex of solutions and strategies is varied and includes the following: first, providing theological educa- tion for women and men without restricting this to the circle of clergy and male religious; second, creating spaces where gender-biased structures and assumptions are challenged and alternative, inclusive, and liberating models are reconstructed, as Bong shows in the case of Ecclesia of Women in Asia; third, engaging in a balanced hermeneutic that validates the intrinsic value, dignity, and mystery of the human person, male and female, as *imago Dei*.

The disturbing experience of sexual gender-based violence against Indian women rooted in a distorted and exploitative gender socialization and indoctrina- tion is the prompt for **Kochurani Abraham's** characterization of Indian women as contemporary progenies of the fourteenth-century icon of resistance, Janabai. In such a context, passivity or acceptance of the status quo is anything but a virtue. Abraham deconstructs the insidious ideological mechanisms used to construct the "ideal Indian woman" and that entrench class, caste, and religion as instruments of exploitation and oppression. Abraham's deconstruction of so-called feminist virtue in the Indian religio-cultural setting unfolds along the same critical axis as Brazal's reinterpretation of a power-beauty dialectic and ethics in the Filipino context. Quite clearly, religion plays a key role in the social construction, exploitation, and indoctrination of the "ideal" woman. To counter this move, Abraham appeals to a virtue ethics that resists the temptation of naïve deference to patriarchal imposition of gender norms and expectations. The essential ingredients of a liberating femi- nist ethics combine a multiplicity of interior processes and concrete praxes: first, a critical consciousness that recognizes and denounces the status quo for what it is—oppressive and exploitative; second, a critical agency that allows the oppressed to query and transform the status quo; third, the emergence of critical voices that aims to liberate the oppressed; and finally, political resistance that not only aim at subverting the status quo but also strives for the affirmation of the dignity and equality of human beings.

Shaji George Kochuthara's vivid and incisive analysis of the oppressive system of dowry in India and the associated horrific crimes of harassment, torture, murder, female feticide, malnutrition, and sex trafficking, should carry a health warning: "Some Readers May Find the Situations Described in this Essay Shocking." They are revolting. There are resonances and illustrations here of Daniels Sykes' point about internalization of oppression and perpetuation of the cycle of violence and bullying by women. Kochuthara categorizes the system of dowry in India as a structural sin that reduces the value of women to material calculation of monetary or material gain and, therefore, easily makes them subject to violence, torture, and murder. Similar to what Abraham argues about the construction of the ideal Indian woman, this system is supported by a larger cultural, religious, legal, and patriarchal network operated by males. There is no denying the urgency for moral theology to address such structural sin in order to reverse the inferior status and commodification foisted on women and girls and the violence perpetuated against them in the name of sacrosanct cultural norms and venerable religious traditions. Particularly disturbing is the timidity and complicity of the Catholic response to this structural sin, especially because the practice of dowry glaringly undermines and contradicts the meaning of marriage as a sacrament of love, mutuality, and reciprocity. Kochuthara's essay delivers a damning indictment of a church that has become too distracted by the usual cluster of issues in sexual morality—abortion, contraception, and homosexuality—while the system of dowry continues to blight the lives of countless women and girls in India and elsewhere.

Using a contextual analysis of Hong Kong, **Mary Yuen** alerts us to the complacency that relative and partial gender equality can occasion. The story is far from complete. Nor is this mission of feminist discourse accomplished—judging by the accounts of other contributors to this book and considering the socioeconomic, religious, and cultural diversities that mark Asia and the lives of Asian women. The problem is particularly acute in the context of globalization, especially when the negative impact of this phenomenon is narrated through the voices of its victims and casualties, notably women. Yuen's analysis of Catholic social teaching in the context of Hong Kong indicts the government of Hong Kong for failing to uphold the dignity and protect the rights of women. It should be said, as other contributors show, that pointing accusing fingers at public and political institutions and systems constitutes a partial approach and yields limited results. The church bears a fair share of the blame for not practicing sufficiently what it preaches vociferously in regard to equality, dignity, and workers' rights. While, in general, church teaching adopts an inductive methodology, in contrast the Federation of Asian Bishops' Conferences adopts a deductive approach that accords a stronger voice to women's opinions and experiences. The gap between magisterial rhetoric and ecclesial practices is a space that several Hong Kong women are filling via ministries and initiatives that focus on the promotion and recognition of women's rights and dignity.

Several essays in this book extol the value of theological education as a tool for overcoming gender-based oppression. **Maria Clara Lucchetti Bingemer** stands out in her effort to retrace the historical trajectory of the theological in-breaking of women in ecclesial and public space in Latin America. Her account shows that this protracted struggle has gone beyond a narrow feminist agenda to frame the discourse in the wider context of human rights. Her appreciation of theological education as a catalyst for seismic ecclesial and social changes jibes well with Rop's position in the African context and Yuen's in the Asian context. Bingemer lays out a theological tableau, at once holistic and contextualized, encompassing rights, liberation, ecology, sexuality, body theology, and ministry in the church. There is a striking resemblance to Bong's survey of Ecclesia of Women in Asia. That there is a body of knowledge known as women's theology lies beyond doubt; but her analysis explodes narrow conceptions of the purposes and methodology of theological inquiry. Properly conceived, this inquiry embraces and holds in dialectical tension the trinity of divinity, humanity, and nature. In the final analysis, what should concern us is not to construct a theology of, by, and for women; it is to do theology—fair, just, and whole!

Emilce Cuda continues Bingemer's analysis of women doing theology in Latin America, an enterprise that places them at the heart of momentous political shifts, events, and movements. This historic development reconfigures the shape of the entire region. The election of three women presidents in Argentina (Cristina Fernandez de Kirchner), Brazil (Dilma Rousseff), and Chile (Michelle Bachelet) creates a new phenomenon that is not merely political but has profound ethical implications. Among other developments, this event renders audible the voice of the feminine "other" that hitherto has been silenced by political and religious androcracy, that is, the rule of men. As in Dube's essay, Mary appears here as the catalyst for the newfound audibility of the woman's voice in theology and politics. If Cuda's analysis of this political trend is correct, the woman's voice is no longer silent in ecclesial, theological, and political spaces. Her voice is constitutive of these spaces; they do not exist in the absence or silence of her word. This is a hard lesson for a church and a society theologically and politically attuned only to the jarring noises of androcracy and patriarchy.

Anna Perkins presents a two-pronged analysis: first, a critique of the exclusion of religious feminists from feminist discourse originating from the Anglophone Caribbean; second, a sampling of the contributions and narratives of committed religious feminists via the works of two Caribbean religious women theologians. She demonstrates that what they say is important not only for the local church but for the world church. Their narratives reveal helpful methodological tools of feminist discourse and conversation: connecting theological ethics with *le cotidiano*; embracing and including women's experiences as material for theological analysis and reflection, a process long entrapped in the underworld by knight guardians of patriarchal theological orthodoxy; and naming the space of violence, suffering, and entrapment foisted on humanity by a constellation of injustices in church and society. In this space, friendship emerges not only as a strategy for reconciliation, restoration, or healing, but also as a theological hermeneutics of just relationship, liberation, mutuality, overcoming of segregating boundaries, dialogue, inclusiveness, and edification of the Body of Christ. Creating this space of friendship represents a task for women inspired by wisdom/Sophia and wielding critical theological tools of honest inquiry, prophetic imagination, celebratory actions, and healing praxis for church and society.

Turning to voices from Europe, the Congregation for the Doctrine of the Faith Notification against eminent feminist theologian Margaret Farley serves as a case study for **Gerard Mannion's** critical examination of the role and contribution of Catholic feminist theologians and their authority in the exercise of magisterium. His analysis alerts us to the danger of the exercise of power/authority that thrives in an all-male enclave, as James Keenan also shows, the result of which is an ecclesial political rhetoric that ignores history, overlooks context, and tramples upon the faithful witness of women as moral theologians at the service of the people of God. The Notification raises significant problems for how we understand the concept of magisterium. Reading Mannion's unflattering catalog of what is wrong with the Notification offers us a clearer sense of how magisterium (ought to) function, that is as conversational, multivoice, historical (because it develops and evolves in time), compassionate, and persuasive rather than absolutist. Under present circumstances, what Vatican II defines as "the living teaching office of the Church" (*Dei Verbum*, no. 10) has progressively become stifling, exclusionary, manipulative, and remote rather than becoming life giving and competent. A change in mentality is one option for transforming the status quo, that is, by recognizing feminist theologians, especially moral theologians like Farley, as pioneers, teachers, innovators, and fellow workers of the church's magisterium.

Teresa Forcades i Vila describes the pioneering theological breakthrough of Saint Gertrude and the exclusively female theological school of Helfta, which was unique for its theological positions, notably that reciprocity, mutuality, and receptivity characterize divine-human relationship via (not beyond or in spite of) gender, sensuousness of bodily affection, and emotional intimacy. Besides, vulnerability is not alien to God's self-revelation; it is, rather, a condition for *embracing* this revelation. Her analysis recalls Brazal's power-beauty dialectic that eschews dualistic and binary formulations of gendered relations. In sum, Forcades's analysis summons theological ethics to rethink theology, especially sacramental theology, in all its concrete and embodied expressions, along the path of inclusivity, mutuality, and reciprocity.

Stefanie Knauss focuses her analysis on the question of religious leadership of women through the lenses of film/cinema. Through the medium of three feature films she reveals a culture clash—when women achieve leadership positions—between social gender roles and expectations and actual performance, especially where, as in the case of the Philippines, power is associated with the male/masculine, and thus reinforces stereotypes. She debunks the idea of a "natural" feminine leadership style and highlights social factors that shape positive and creative exercise of leadership by women. Transposed into a religious context, the gender quotient of leadership rises to a critical level, where authority is often gender-ascribed rather than earned and in a way that permanently excludes women from positions of sacramental leadership, albeit allowing them to exercise subordinate roles in other areas. The result is that women develop new and creative models of leadership at variance with entrenched authoritarian and hierarchical models, even as doubts persist about the authenticity of these models.

Without contradicting the views held by some contributors regarding the agency of women in the internalization and perpetuation of oppression, **James Keenan** shifts the focus to the contribution of women in prosecuting child abusers in the context of North America. The immediate context is a study of a notorious child abuse case in the United States of America that exposed how an all-male culture of deceit and cover-up excludes the voices of women as outsiders. While highly placed members of this all-male-club culture attain a frightening level of sophistication in committing and covering up heinous abuse of minors, women take a contrary stand. They open our eyes to the culture of abuse that targets both girls and boys. Their ethical stance sunders the veil of silence that shrouds and protects the sexual perversion and malevolence of the high and mighty in church and society. Keenan's argument offers new strategies for addressing this problem. First, instances of all-male exercise of power and authority should arouse suspicion, precisely because the absence of women is a deliberate part of the plot to abuse with impunity while hiding behind the wall of perverse male privilege. Second, a simple rule (named after Margaret Gallant, who courageously called on church leadership to pay attention to and act decisively in instances of sexual abuse) should apply: at gatherings of social responsibility, the absence of women should automatically trigger an alert in regard to the motives and intentions of an enclave of male privilege and complicity, self-preservation, and deception that could cause grave harm to others. Third, a strong invitation is needed to all manner of people to enlist under the banner of feminist vigilance in order to dismantle an abusive culture of ascribed (unearned) male privilege.

Nichole Flores performs a multilevel analysis of the notion of justice in Latino contexts that draws on classical Thomistic tradition and engages with contemporary exponents and proponents. The result is an incisive and penetrating concept of justice that accords priority to personal, political, communal, and relational dimensions of justice. Here we see strong echoes of and notable resemblances to the African ethical, communicative, and relational anthropology that Arabome unveils in her analysis, lending credence to the universal quality of this feminist conversation, albeit rooted in contextual realities and local particularities. Anthropologically and ethically speaking, the just person is both relational and political. Public policies and institutions can claim the designation "just" to the extent that they consistently promote the personal and public dimensions in formulating and actualizing the common good. In simple terms, there is no justice without relationality.

More importantly, justice embodies a component of resistance and struggle against suffering, a thesis that Flores demonstrates in engaging Isasi-Diaz, Bucar explores via Diana Hayes, and Abraham illustrates using the situation of Indian women.

Elizabeth Marie Bucar examines the unintended consequences of rhetoric and warrants originating from patently clericalist, authoritarian, and patriarchal structures. The politics and logics of exemplarity of female biblical personality creates an arena wherein flag bearers of divergent ecclesiastical, ideological, and ethical-theological camps (Blessed John Paul II, Diane Hayes, Helen Hull Hitchcock, and more) have clashed with gladiatorial and Amazonian rhetorical intensity and ferocity. Yet rhetoric is important. The malleability of rhetoric allows for creativity not only in regard to moral knowledge and discourse but also an ecclesial praxis for women, while widening and somewhat leveling the field of play for laywomen theologians/activists and male clerics. At least at the level of rhetoric and moral knowledge, the claim of the exclusion of women from the production of ethical knowledge in society represents a complex issue and bears deeper nuances.

The analyses of Keenan and Bucar each highlight the perverse consequences that arise within the church as a result of the exercise of unaccountable power and privilege. **Anne Patrick** is highly attuned to this problematic and in her essay suggests that feminist women and men have the option of either challenging injustice in our institutions, leaving these institutions, or "shriveling up" within them. Patrick is ultimately concerned with developing an "ethics of church participation," and to that end highlights the negative effects of the contemporary tendency to idealize spirituality at the expense of religion. In fact, she argues, secular forms of spirituality and those associated with traditional religious faiths each need to be challenged by the demands of justice.

Shawnee Daniels Sykes offers an analysis of the mechanism of succession and perpetuation of patriarchal systems and attitudes. As expected, they are self-replicating and self-perpetuating. The surprise is that this process is not genetically engineered: women and girls perpetuate and replicate oppressive systems and attitudes through a process of internalization of oppression. The result is the active agency of women and girls as oppressors in their own right of other women and girls, albeit guided, as Daniels Sykes claims, by the invisible hand of patriarchy. Examples of women's complicity and agency in the oppression of other women are not hard to find: multiple forms of bullying, trafficking of human persons, and female genital mutilation. Thus rebirth or conversion toward restoration of ruptured human relationship is as urgent for women and girls as it is for men and boys.

Lessons from Feminist Conversations in the World Church

An African proverb says that if you listen carefully, you can hear a crab coughing. Listening to the conversations in this book allows us to hear voices, discern movements, and perceive insights of significant value for the world church and global society. Without intending to prejudice the reader's own opinion and position, we can summarize some lessons of the conversations in this book in the following terms.

The language of conversation is constructed from a vocabulary and sustained by a grammar as diverse as there are conversation partners. Its key words form a multifaceted and multicolored composition that confers beauty and charm on this conversation. From *lakas-ganda* and *gandang loob* to *Janabai* and to *mujerista* and *mestizaje/mulatez,* this conversation speaks of globalized and universal realities grounded in localized and contextualized narratives. In this sense, contrary to popular belief, as Bucar notes, "women" (and their voices) do not designate and circumscribe a "cohesive group." The lure of gender reductionism lies at the root of systemic gender injustice in church and society. It is to be avoided at all times.

To call this exercise a conversation means that it is anything but abstract: it is an assemblage of themes, topics, and purposes; it has interlocutors and partners; and it happens in time and space. Simply put, it is ethically grounded and theologically contextualized. As several contributors demonstrate, the conversation is about real cases (Cuda, Mannion, and Keenan), true life situations (Abraham, Arabome, and Kochuthara), and concrete issues (Brazal and Daniels Sykes).

Authentic conversations do not adopt a simplistic and dualistic apportioning of blame—or an Orwellian "four legs good, two legs bad" caricature—that casts women as victims and men as oppressors. Whether in India (Abraham) or North America (Daniels Sykes), Africa (Arabome and Dube), or Latin America (Flores), women and men are part of the problem of a gender-biased culture and part of the solution toward inaugurating gender justice in church and society. A subtext of this consideration shows that mechanisms and methodologies of gender construction do not only exist or function at a subconscious level. Gender is not constructed in spite of ourselves. The processes are deliberate, structural, and largely self-preserving. By implication, a transformation of the status quo cannot happen accidentally or haphazardly. It involves a deliberate option to resist harmful gender stereotypes and practices and promote life-affirming and empowering models and paradigms.

As we see in Abraham, Brazal, Bucar, and Dube, the biblical figure of Mary remains a fascinating personality and character in feminist theological and ethical discourse. The question is what to make of her. Traditional icons casting her as a hapless "handmaid" in a remotely controlled human-divine drama irk radicals, just as much as iconoclastic or subversive typologies unnerve traditionalists. On the basis of the conversations presented in this book, Mary straddles the gaping chasm between both worlds, confined to neither, but ally to both. She hardly cuts the figure of a divisive personality; yet not every contributor relies on her to construct her or his hermeneutical and ethical discourse.

Scripture retains a unique status in this conversation as an inexhaustible and profound font for feminist discourse. If, as Vatican II claims, scripture is the soul of theology (*Dei Verbum*, no. 24), it is no less so for feminist theology, without contesting or limiting the latter's legitimate and necessary warrant to undertake a critique of cultural prejudices and patriarchal tailoring of the word of God expressed in limited human language (*Dei Verbum,* no.12).

Speaking of sources of feminist conversations in the world church, something interesting catches the eye of the careful reader of the essays presented in this book. What does it imply that many of the major references are male authors—Paulo Freire, Thomas Aquinas, John Paul II, Amartya Sen, and more? There are many ways of interpreting and understanding this fact. We choose to put a positive interpretation on it. It reaffirms the inclusivity of the conversational methodology central to feminist analyses—not just women to women, women against men, but a conversation of equals and partners in mutuality. We can single out John Paul II for the multiple positive references to his writings and proclamation regarding the dignity of woman and her role in the church. Inarguably, he wrote and spoke good and inspirational words. Yet, as seen in the conversations in this book, his approach also contains examples of dissonance between rhetoric and praxis.

Related to the question of sources is the status of religion as it emerges in these conversations. The naïve would find disturbing the apparent trial of and negative portrayal of religion. For good or for ill, religion and its associated practices account for some of the instances of gender-based injustice depicted in this book. In reality, the ultimate objective of feminist conversations is to expose the side of religion held captive by patriarchal traditions, clericalist practices, and ecclesial androcracy. Where these aberrations exist and impact the lives of the Disciples of Christ, feminist conversations demonstrate that religion stands in need of liberation and redemption, and offer us tools for undertaking this enterprise.

Furthermore, the enthronement and supremacy of theological and ecclesial androcracy or the rule of the church exclusively by men has a long history and tradition; its dethronement represents an ongoing task. Judging by the multiple voices and accounts collected in these conversations, the mission is far from accomplished. There are indications of what constitutes effective methods and tools, realistic goals and purposes, and insightful focus and motivation. In regard to the first, the method is dialogical, inclusive, and contextual. In regard to the second, the objective is the renewal of humanity, celebration of difference, and affirmation of equality. And in regard to the third, the tone is holistic, relational, and life affirming.

Conversations in the world church define the unifying purpose of the essays presented in this book. They offer narratives, clarify assumptions, investigate issues, confront challenges, and propose new ways of perceiving gender and its implications for how we understand church and society. These conversations expand and subvert this understanding in equal measure. As one would expect, conversations of this kind generate proponents and discontents. It is important to keep talking and listening across ideological and doctrinal divides in view of achieving a holistic, liberating, and life-affirming ecclesiology.

Notes

1. See C. S. Song, *Theology from the Womb of Asia* (Maryknoll, NY: Orbis Books, 1986).

Dreams from My Mother, Prayers to My Father: Rethinking the Trinity of God, Woman, and Church

Anne Arabome

Introduction

"It is I" . . . I am the power and the Goodness of the Father, I am the Wisdom of the Mother, I am the Light and the Grace which is blessed love, I am the Trinity, I am the Unity, I am the supreme Goodness of all kind of things, I am the One who makes you love, I am the One who makes you desire, I am the never-ending fulfilment of all true desires.

—Julian of Norwich

These words of Julian of Norwich have a striking resonance with the African woman's innate experience of God. In the context of the rich religious traditions of Africa, the cry of the African woman and her comprehension of who-God-is could offer new insights and shed new light on some African concepts of God for theology in the world church. For theology to develop further in a way that honors the African understanding of God, theologians must take into account the way that ordinary people see themselves and their societies.[1] Not surprisingly, Africans have ways of viewing God that may seem alien to Western thinking. To "do theology" in Africa, one must come with a curious and open mind.[2] Pope John Paul II encouraged this reflective attitude when he invited the Catholics in Malawi to "look inside yourselves. Look to the riches of your traditions, look to the faith . . . here you will find Christ who will lead you to the truth."[3] This is the yearning of African women, because "our salvation as Africans lies in achieving unity in our diversity and in being thankful for the gift the 'other' brings."[4]

The worldview of the African woman embraces unity. She experiences God as one who is in communion with all. She sees herself as transmitter and promoter of life. Neither seeking fame nor ambitioning power, she seeks the dignity that is accorded her and the rest of God's creation. She is very earthy and frequently communicates with her God and the ancestors, both living and dead. She is highly intuitive. She sees herself as a presence that is synonymous with life. She knows that she is brave and beautiful. Although some traditions fabricate negative images of woman, she does not perceive herself in a negative light.

The African woman shares an affinity with the prophetess of the Hebrew scriptures. Like Miriam, she raises her hands in praise and song, and she beats her tambourine. Like Deborah, she rouses the people to follow God's lead and inspires men to fulfill God's promises. Like Huldah, she reaches out to other women in compassion and support. The prophetic tradition has never been closed to women, though at times there have been struggles to preserve this understanding. Throughout the centuries, and especially at Pentecost, the presence of the prophetic Spirit has been acknowledged as being possible in women as well as in men. "Patriarchal Christianity . . . never denied that God might send prophets, and that women were equally able to exercise prophetic gifts."[5]

The African Christian woman knows Christ in a very personal way. She speaks of the Son of God as one who has come to save and liberate her from the shackles of sin and death. Her songs and her language about God reflected in Jesus Christ are tangible and relate to her daily life. She may not possess a sophisticated theological education or hermeneutical tools for assessing the scriptures, but she knows the Word of God from lived experience; although "the holy mystery of God is beyond all imagining . . . at the same time God is not less than personal, and many of the most prized characteristics of God's relationship to the world, such as fidelity, compassion, and liberating love, belong to human rather than the nonhuman world."[6] My mother and her African sisters understand this.

Toward a New Feminist Hermeneutics

A cliché of modern scholarship is that Africans, on the whole, are notoriously religious. This religiosity is alive and active in the daily happenings and events of people's lives. The question posed for women, then, is why would societies that are so highly religious be so highly oppressive of women at the same time? Sadly, the dominant religions in Africa—Christianity, Islam, and African Religion—have not helped the plight of women. Ancient traditions, combined with the patriarchy of these religions, have ensured the continued oppression of women. In spite of the religiosity of Africa, women remain unequal. The gifts of the African woman are not sufficiently recognized or celebrated. Since the patristic era, the Christian church has expressed its identity through patriarchal elements of domination. In the rituals and beliefs of African Religion, oppressive and degrading attitudes toward women are expressed in myths, proverbs, stories, and customs. These cultural and religious vehicles shape and mold negative perceptions and mentalities. Because of this, women often do not realize that they are oppressed. They take on the mind-set of the dominant class.

This oppression is mimicked in recent scholarship, especially by some in the global North, where the African woman is portrayed as powerless, uneducated, voiceless, and needing to be rescued or saved from her woes and afflictions. She is portrayed as suffering from patriarchy's oppression, from disease, poverty, illiteracy, and all the negativity associated with the "dark continent." While these perceptions might have some truth, this scholarship overlooks the strength of the African woman. Even though she is "tired, emotionally neglected, socially stressed," she is brave in her resiliency against the difficulties present in her life.[7]

In a similar fashion, "in most Euro-American discourses about women, the term 'women' in Europe often refers to middle class, educated white 'women' while 'women' in Africa refers to illiterate, peasant, working class or poor 'women' or perhaps to a dark hole named 'women'—a primitive mass that manifests pristine, incomprehensible behavior in ignorance and speechlessness."[8] It is quite obvious then, that,

> the middle class educated African women are not somehow included in this referent African women; neither are they equivalent to Euro-American women of the middle class. Therefore in discussing Africa, there is usually a "rural Africa" where that pristine, undifferentiated, ahistorical mass of "real" African women inhabit, in which context all theories about "African women" are tested. No one can speak to this process, to this knowledge of this atavistic womanhood, not even African women from the continent themselves, but only Euro-American theorists and experts.[9]

The African woman cannot be defined by the woes and misery that are often projected about her in the Western media. I have often pondered the lives of my remarkably strong and assertive maternal grandmother, my mother, my aunties, cousins, and sisters in my lineage, as well as the women in my extended family and my friends. Are they the same women referred to in modern scholarship? Inclusivity defines the first task of a new feminist hermeneutics:

> In order to be truly a women's liberation movement, feminism needs to include all women; women of all classes, races and cultures. This means that Afro-American women, African women, Hispanic women, Asian women, Jewish women, Muslim women, working-class women, women in every social context, must develop self-defined movements that critique patriarchy within their situation. Feminism (womanism, or whatever other terms women prefer to use) would then become a network of solidarity among these many women's movements. White western middle-class women (and we must remember that middle-class is not synonymous with white and western) would then be able to define their own particular issues in solidarity with these movements of less privileged women, rather than feminism being defined normatively in terms of this one class and cultural context.[10]

This is particularly important for two reasons. The first has to do with self-definition. Women the world over must be the subject of their own reflection and their own decision making about themselves as subject. The second is that women must then share their reflections with one another—one cultural group to another—so that new definitions of femininity may develop.[11] This is a formidable challenge.

What, then, accounts for the oppression of women in Africa—especially in societies in which women are valued as the center of family life and seen as those who hold the values and virtues of the nation? How can it be that women are treated as second-class citizens by the Christian churches that pride themselves on embracing the Beatitudes of Jesus Christ? There are at least three systemic realities that cause this disjunctive situation: a patriarchal theological mind-set, cultural biases, and the contribution of both women and men to this oppression. On the first cause, Elizabeth Johnson notes that

> the precise ideal from the world of men that has provided the paradigm of God is the ruling man within a patriarchal system. Divine mystery is cast in the role of monarch, absolute ruler, King of Kings, Lord of Lords, one whose will none can escape, to whom is owed total and unquestioning obedience. This powerful monarch is sometimes spoken of as just and harsh, threatening hell fire to sinners who do not measure up. But even when he is presented as kindly, merciful, and forgiving, the fundamental problem remains. Benevolent patriarchy is still patriarchy.[12]

Sadly, while the oppression of women is the most major form of oppression, it is mirrored in other forms as well: white over black, middle class over indigenous people, and straight over gay, to name but a few examples. The exploitation of the dominator over the subjugated "others" continues.[13] Whether this subjugation is toward women or toward persons of color or toward sexually frowned-upon individuals, patriarchy reigns supreme. Yet antidotes exist within religion.

In African Religion, some of the myths about the divine speak of deities that are both masculine and feminine. For example, in Nigeria, "God as *Oduduwa* is considered by the Yoruba to be the original and great ancestor of man. Therefore, embedded in the concepts in *Oduduwa* are the notions of an Entity closely associated with the power of creation and with the original, great, and grand ancestor of man, and who is considered to be female and the 'essence of cosmic totality.'"[14] Sadly, not infrequently, narratives of the nature and being of God hide this powerful theological insight on God and femininity. As Mary Daly notes with distress, "if God is male, then the male is God. The divine patriarch castrates women as long as he is allowed to live on in the human imagination."[15] Over the years, women, especially African women, have been "castrated" by the long-held belief that women are less than human.

In precolonial times, African women were leaders in the community. These women exercised authority through the gift of service. They held the life of the family and community together through generous self-giving. Theirs is a liberating love, encouraging fullness of life for all, and transmitting life in all its forms. It is no surprise, then, that African women theologians often embrace the image of Christ as One who opens doors to freedom; as One who delivers the people from the woes and miseries of starvation and provides cleansing water. This is a Christ who leads to human ways of living.[16] Understandably, "African women's experiences lead them into a Christological language that does not come to African men."[17] The African woman knows a God who is very close to her, an intimate God who loves and frees her from the shackles of a patriarchal Christological discourse.

Cultural biases are particularly rampant in Africa. At the fifth conference of the Ecumenical Association of Third World Theologians held in New Delhi in 1981, the participants issued a statement that clearly describes the situation that women in the global South are facing:

> Poverty and oppression in the Third World are not just a situation of deprivation; they bring unjust and untimely death to millions of women, men, and children through hunger, disease, and repression. But death in the Third World is not only physical. Countless persons are degraded and have suffered the loss of their identity, dignity, and personhood. Not only individual persons are killed, but also entire cultures and religious traditions have been annihilated by colonialism and by more modern forms of repression. The poor and the oppressed are struggling not only for a better economic standard but for freedom and dignity, for life and full humanity. They risk their life for the sake of life, and undergo death to undo the powers of death.[18]

It is this massive and horrifying challenge that African women face every day. They, like their sisters in other countries of the global South, carry the burden of sacrifice.

Certain cultural practices undermine the dignity of women in various degrees in many parts of Africa. These humiliating and dehumanizing practices—genital mutilation, early betrothals, and widow practices—are passed on by the women themselves and embraced as cultural values and norms. There is no freedom to question or challenge such inhumane acts. A childless woman is treated with contempt in most African societies. In Nigeria, such a woman is both pitied because she is barren and feared because she may be thought of as a witch. She does not fit the expectations of those around her.[19] In most African societies, women have no rights. It is almost as though they lack feelings and, so, must be treated as such. So that, "the position of women in Africa today—both within the wider society and within Religion—is normally prescribed by what is deemed to be beneficial to the whole community of women and men."[20] But the African woman never gives up. She possesses a dense capacity to transform her own sorrow into joy, with great depth and character—an *Imago Dei*.

Women Imaging and Naming God:
The Contribution from Africa

Most African women express their understanding of God as both masculine and feminine, even though the main religions in Africa speak of God with masculine terminologies. Interestingly, "this maleness, however does not seem to be a cause for concern, as the language of talking about God uses no gender-specific pronoun."[21] In the African worldview, especially with the African woman, God is everything: "In God we live and move and have our being." This image of God is often reflected not in the name but in the experiences of her daily life. The African woman has many descriptive names and images of the one God—as many as her own daily personal experiences. Like other Africans, her "ideas of God can be grouped into four general categories. . . . what God does, human pictures of God, the nature of God, and people's relationship with God."[22] The African woman sees God as the sole creator of the universe. Her experience of giving life mirrors the attribute of God as giver of life. The African woman knows from experience that God creates and holds the world together, and no single word or symbol exhausts the concept of God. "For that reason there are many names which describe him as Creator, Creator of all things, Moulder, Begetter, Maker, Potter, Fashioner."[23] One cannot generalize about a single African concept of God.[24]

For an African woman, "God" simply means life, such that she is able to personify her every experience in the light of God's image. In some parts of Nigeria, "gender was not an organizing principle in Yoruba society prior to colonization by the West . . . [r]ather, the primary principle of social organization was seniority, defined by relative age."[25] The African woman perceives God not as male or female, though African women will speak of God as "father." The African woman speaks in a language that is purely religious and spiritual. If a Westerner would engage an African woman in a conversation of any sort, not only would she make constant reference to God as the all in all, present in all things, she might refer to God as "he" or "she." In most African languages, there are no gender specific terms. For example, among my ethnic community of Ishan (located in the midwestern part of Nigeria), we would often use the personal pronoun *uwe* (you) to refer to either male or female. The same applies to the Yoruba of western Nigeria (*iwo* = you). Most names which refer to the divine are used for both male and female. The dualistic gender problem presented by God-talk in the West does not exist in African cosmology in the same way.

The African woman "knows" God. She has an interior experience of the divine that is almost palpable. Her own life experiences constitute her primary revelatory texts. It is not a theory that she learns from a book. It is in her joy that she sings and prays to her father and mother, God who has blessed her with life. Her image of God is endless as much as the presence of the divine in all creation is infinite. The African woman's encounter with God is reflected in her God who is the light on her path when she is not sure of her journey, the provider-God who surprises her with some food for her family through the kindness of a neighbor, the protector-God who rescues her from the violence that she often encounters in society.

Oduyoye notes that "the way we experience God is portrayed in the language we use about God, especially the names by which God is known. . . . more names descriptive of people's experience of God are available in proverbs, songs, and prayers."[26] The inclusive language of God is often found in various expressions within African spirituality. In some African societies, it has been observed that God's image as father-mother appears very frequently in the prayers of the faithful. This was confirmed by Dr. Edward Sackey when he recorded parts of the Mass he attended at the Sunyani Christ the King Cathedral on May 8, 1994, as follows: "God our Father and our Mother, we thank you for bringing us together. We thank you for bringing Jesus to show us your love. Help us to extend this love to one another."[27] Unfortunately, "this inclusive image of God is rare at the English Masses in Ghana, because the *Missals* and *Lectionaries* used have been imported from Europe and America, with fixed prayers which present God as Father. But, the Father-Mother image of God still appears in the prayers of the faithful at these Masses because they are composed with a Ghanaian mentality."[28]

In contrast to Western tradition, Africans bestow names on their children that express the value of the life of the child, family, or the community, and experiences of God.[29] These naming traditions mirror the worldview of the African woman—she sees and names God in every experience. I would argue that this is where the African woman's experience differs from her Western counterparts. Although she has learned occasionally to address God as father, especially in Christian circles, she also knows that God is beyond and above any name or gender. And most African names with reference to God are unisex. In the Ibo culture of Eastern Nigeria, "some of the *Chi* names are gender-neutral, borne by both males and females."[30] This reflects God as present in both sexes equally. The African woman names God through her experience. God is her joy as well as her sorrow, her blessings as well as her challenge, her poverty as well as her wealth.

In her rituals, worship, and praise, the African woman expresses herself to her God who resembles the God that Moses encountered as "I am who I am" (Exod. 3:14). In naming her children, she encounters the God of that experience. For example, the birth of a child becomes an answered prayer, reflected in the child's name: *Osahon-Erhumwen* (God has answered my prayer). Here, her name for the divine is that of a God who cares and answers our prayers in times of need. The name of God here is synonymous with the name of the child. In this experience God is incarnate; in that child dwells the God who answers prayers. God might also be seen as a lover. For example, among the Yoruba, the name, *Oluwafemi* (God loves me) speaks of the experience of God's love. The child embodies that love and continues to be a reminder of God's loving presence in that family and community. Among the Ishan, the name *Eghonghon* (Joy) reflects God's abiding joy in the child and family: God is experienced as joy. For the Benin, the name *Itohan* (Compassion) reflects an experience of God's compassionate care.

In a very real sense, these names are expressions of who God is for the African woman. In fact, the words themselves will have little or no meaning if those involved in rituals do not touch the underlying reality and the underlying experience of who-God-is as expressed in the names used in worship and praise.[31] The expression of God for an African woman is not set aside for a particular experience called worship. Rather, it is like the air that she breathes. There is no experience outside of God. Her religious language is her breath and her body, soul, and spirit. The divine is present in all of creation and experiences: birthing, dying, eating, sleeping, dancing, loving, protecting, and so on.

The African woman sees God in figurative language: the One who is neither male nor female, as expressed in the lyrics of an Ishan song: *"We Ose, we Ose. We elolo ni re daghe. We isahan ni retu jo ode a. We ilolo ni mezele. Era no tuo oha tuamea. Bikue mhonle ni a rere o. Mhen digwe me roe aba. We Ose"* This is translated as "You are God, you are God. You are the eyes I use to see. You are the key that opens the door. You are the owner of my soul. The bush that burneth and is never consumed. What shall I render to you O God! I will bow down and worship your name. You are God."[32] She sees God as the light that guides her on her path through the dark, as the mother who knows her children's needs and is the rock of the family, as the father-protector of the family.

C. S. Song has observed that "the word that has become flesh has a great number of surprises in store for Christians and theologians confined to the traditional framework of understanding the ways of God . . . [t]here will be many, many questions and problems to upset us, give us headaches, and disturb our theological calm."[33] His thinking captures the contribution of African women to God-talk. The God who is objectified and perceived as one thing, male or female, does not exist in the African woman's worldview. Augustine's insight that "we are commanded to speak of God, and to do so not only in theological arguments but in acts of praise,"[34] embodies a call to the African woman's voice that has been so excluded and neglected from theological arguments.

> Racism within the women's movement is, in effect, double edged. On a more subtle and, therefore, perhaps more dangerous level than overt discrimination is the refusal to recognize the differences in the experiences of black and white women. 'Women's experience', which has been a key term in both theory and praxis, has been formulated purely from the privileged position of white women.[35]

Thus, a critical task of theology is to engage with the voices of African women who relate to a God of immanence on a daily basis and in whose experience of praise God is experienced as Spirit. In her soul, spirit, and body, the African woman praises God who is neither male nor female but life, presence, and mystery.

Conclusion

Women and men are called to share the dream of a renewed humanity in church and society and to commit to a liberating conversation—perhaps the most important ethical conversation that can be held in the church today—that recognizes, honors, and celebrates the indwelling of God in woman and man, in equality, justice, and mutuality. For "every human being bears the traces of the three divine Persons in his or her entire being and activity."[36] The experience of the African woman warrants a new language about God in order to "shatter the exclusivity of the male metaphor, subvert its dominance, and set free a greater sense of the mystery of God."[37] In this task of shattering of oppressive icons lies the challenge of developing new narratives, one that African women can tell with their voices. As Emmanuel Katangole notes,

> [I]t is a challenge to write theology in such a way that an ordinary African may be able to locate herself within it. It is an invitation for the theologian to be a story-teller—not in a naïve sense, but to develop a narrative theology of the ordinary Christian's struggles and aspirations in the face of such overpowering and totalizing stories as the African Renaissance.[38]

This task of building a narrative theology that engages ordinary women has within it the seeds of glory.[39] "Our stories are precious paths on which we have walked with God, and struggled for a passage to our full humanity. They are events through which we have received the blessings of life from the hands of God."[40]

For the African woman, God is also spirit. "The spirit-oriented nature of African Christianity builds on the indigenous religious traditions of Africa, which postulate the spirit world, with many inhabitants with whom direct communication is possible."[41] The African woman has learned to survive and find peace with her spirit and other prevailing spirits. The result is that she is the woman who knows the color, the shape, the height, the width, and the true nature of pain and suffering. The African woman is conceived and born in suffering and pain. The Christian symbol of the Cross is like the air she breathes. Her life is the exegesis of the suffering God. She finds herself constantly trying to claim and reclaim her humanity in a society that is set to dehumanize her in so many ways. She is treated differently because of her gender and will be regarded as second class all the days of her life.

The life of the African woman is that of servitude. She is very familiar with the suffering God. She knows the Jesus of the Cross and resurrection, and she knows the nurturing power of God in her being. She is a carrier of the divine. The African woman understands the Triune God in the light of community. For her, "communion becomes a profound source of energy for the healing of suffering. Knowing that we are not abandoned makes all the difference."[42] This is an experience of God that is purely Trinitarian. It affirms the fact that God is in relationship with humanity, bearing our pain and suffering with deep compassionate love. Our God lives among us, and we know our God. The songs of an African woman speak of a God that she will praise all her life, a God who is always present to her even in her darkest moments, a God who is kind and just and will always act justly against her oppressors. This God knows her suffering because suffering is not alien to God's nature.[43]

Christian theology over the years has portrayed a "macho" God who is controlling, powerful, strong, and demanding. Yet the images of God reflected in our scriptures reveal a God who is constantly pleading, nurturing, desiring, and bringing forth life in all creation. The African woman recognizes this "mothering God," because she considers herself a mother in every regard. The divine is fully exhibited in her nurturing being. She seems to affirm Rahner's assertion that "the Trinity itself is with us, it is not merely given to us because revelation offers us statements about it. Rather the statements are made to us because the reality of which they speak is bestowed upon *us*."[44] For the African woman, there is no mystery in the Trinity, because "Trinity is the last mystery of our own reality, and that it is experienced precisely in this reality."[45]

The femininity that we use to describe woman cannot ever equal the femininity of God. God is always more and exceedingly more in God's compassionate love. She takes on the role of the caring feminine in bringing each of us to birth and life. Our God is our mother, whom we experience as the womb that carries life in all its fullness. It is our dream to carry forth this life, so that the earth may be drenched in love and compassion through the pain and suffering carried by its children. And, yes, God is our father and our mother. But, in the words of Janet Gaden,

> [A]s I became aware of the alienating effect on me of all-male imagery of you, I learned to see other women, and indeed myself, as embodying you, and this in turn rounded out my sense of you. So I understand the desire of some women and men to correct the old imbalance of the father image by emphasizing the mother in you, though this is not what I want to call you.[46]

This, indeed, is the African woman's dream of her God, and her prayer to her father—the vast, ever-living, genderless Trinity of love!

Notes

1. Mercy Amba Oduyoye, *Hearing and Knowing* (Maryknoll, NY: Orbis Books, 1986), 9, 10.

2. Agbonkhianmeghe E. Orobator, *Theology Brewed in An African Pot* (Maryknoll, NY: Orbis Books, 2008), 28.

3. John Paul II, Pope. Holy Mass at the Airport of the "Army Air Wing" of Lilongwe, Malawi, May 6, 1989: #6.

4. Oduyoye, *Hearing and Knowing*, 9–10.

5. Rosemary Radford Ruether, "Prophetic Tradition and the Liberation of Women: Promise and Betrayal," *Journal of Theology for Southern Africa* 73 (1990): 24–33, at 25.

6. Elizabeth Johnson, *She Who Is: The Mystery of God in Feminist Theological Discourse* (New York: Crossroad Publishing, 1992), 45.

7. Molara Ogundipe-Leslie, *Re-Creating Ourselves: African Women & Critical Transformations* (Trenton: African World Press, 1994), 81.

8. Ibid., 10.

9. Ibid.

10. Ruether, "Prophetic Tradition and the Liberation of Women," 32.

11. Judith Plaskow, *Sex, Sin and Grace: Women's Experiences and the Theologies of Reinhold Niebuhr and Paul Tillich* (Lanham, MD: University Press of America, 1980), 29.

12. Johnson, *She Who Is*, 34.

13. Elisabeth Schussler Fiorenza, "For Women in Men's World: A Critical Feminist Theology of Liberation," in *The Power of Naming*, ed. Elisabeth Schussler Fiorenza (Eugene, OR: Wipf & Stock, 2006), 7.

14. William A. Brown, "Concepts of God in Africa," *Journal of Religious Thought* 39 no. 2 (Fall–Winter 1982–83): 5–16, at 8.

15. Mary Daly, *Beyond God the Father: Toward a Philosophy of Women's Liberation* (Boston: Beacon Press, 1973), 19.

16. Mercy Amba Oduyoye, "Jesus Christ," in *Hope Abundant: Third World and Indigenous Women's Theology*, ed. Kwok Pui-lan (Maryknoll, NY: Orbis Books, 2010), 168.

17. Ibid., 179.

18. "Final Statement of the Fifth EATWOT Conference, New Delhi, August 17–29, 1981" in *The Irruption of the Third World: Challenge to Theology* (Maryknoll, NY: Orbis Books, 1983), 203.

19. See Mercy Amba Oduyoye, "A Coming Home to Myself: The Childless Woman in the West African Space," in *Liberating Eschatology: Essays in Honor of Letty M. Russell*, ed. Margaret A. Farley and Serene Jones (Louisville, KY: Westminster John Knox Press, 1999), 103–20.

20. Mercy Amba Oduyoye and Musimbi R. A. Kanyoro, eds., *The Will to Arise: Women, Tradition, and the Church in Africa* (Eugene, OR: Wipf & Stock, 2005), 10.

21. Mercy Amba Oduyoye, *Daughters of Anowa* (Maryknoll, NY: Orbis Books, 2002), 110–11.

22. John S. Mbiti, *Introduction to African Religion,* 2nd ed. (London: Heinemann, 1991), 49.

23. Ibid. See also Aylward Shorter, *African Culture and the Christian Church* (London: Geoffrey Chapman, 1973), 54.

24. Shorter, *African Culture and the Christian Church*, 54.

25. Oyeronke Oyewumi, *The Invention of Women* (Minneapolis: University of Minnesota Press, 1997), 31.

26. Mercy Amba Oduyoye, "The African Experience of God Through the Eyes of an Akan Woman," *Cross Currents* 47, no. 4 (Winter 1997–98): 493–504, available at http://www.aril.org/african.htm.

27. George Kwame Kumi, "God's Image as Equivalently Father and Mother: An African Perspective," *African Ecclesiastical Review* 38, no. 4 (1996): 203–28, at 207.

28. Ibid.

29. E. Umoren, "African Names in Christian Initiation," *African Ecclesiastical Review* 14, no. 4 (1972): 350–52.

30. M. C. Onukawa, "The Chi Concept in Igbo Gender Making," *Africa* 70, no. 1 (Winter 2000): 107–17, at 113.

31. Sallie McFague, *Metaphorical Theology: Models of God in Religious Language* (Philadelphia: Fortress Press, 1982), 2.

32. Benita Okojie, "We Ose," http://www.youtube.com.

33. C. S. Song, *Tell Us Our Names: Story Theology from an Asian Perspective* (Maryknoll, NY: Orbis Books, 1984), 43.

34. Ibid., 42.

35. Linda Hogan, *From Women's Experience to Feminist Theology* (Sheffield, England: Sheffield Academic Press, 1995), 32.

36. Leonardo Boff, *Holy Trinity, Perfect Community* (Maryknoll, NY: Orbis Books, 2000), 39.

37. Johnson, *She Who Is*, 45.

38. Emmanuel Katangole "African Renaissance and the Challenge of Narrative Theology in Africa. Which story/whose renaissance?" in *African Theology Today*, ed. Emmanuel Katangole (Scranton: University Press, 2002), 211.

39. Mercy Amba Oduyoye, *Introducing African Women's Theology* (Cleveland: Pilgrim Press, 2001), 21.

40. Ibid.

41. Gerrie Ter Haar, *How God Became African: African Spirituality and Western Secular Thought* (Philadelphia: University of Pennsylvania Press, 2009), 23.

42. Ibid., 267.

43. Jurgen Moltmann, *The Trinity and the Kingdom: The Doctrine of God* (New York: Harper & Row, 1981), 4 and 24.

44. Karl Rahner, *The Trinity*, trans. Joseph Donceel (New York: Herder and Herder, 1970), 39.

45. Ibid., 47.

46. Janet Gaden, "Calling God Names," in *Changing Women Changing Church*, ed. Marie Louise Uhr (Newtown, Australia: Millennium Books, 1992), 38.

Women, Church, and Ethics: Deconstructing Marian Images with Catholic Women, *Nzanga*

Lilian Dube

Introduction

The image of my mother in a beige and brown uniform with the badge of the Catholic Association of St. Anne, the flame and the Cross, as she seemed peacefully rested after a vicious battle with pancreatic cancer, informs this reflection on Mary in postcolonial Africa and the grassroots feminist ecumenical movement. A sea of women dressed like her, now my mothers, surrounded her coffin with singing, dancing, and crying. One after another, they paused to give a testimony to her good works—to preach, teach, or admonish. Occasionally, they would be interrupted by a woman cracking a village tune that everybody joined, as traditional drummers beat all emotions out of the drums and people sang and danced vigorously, as if to drown the wails of the grieving family and friends. The uniformed women remained totally in charge at this stage of my mother's funeral. It was an evangelical moment! It was church. When the priest, *baba,* finally arrived, the uniformed women retained total control until the Catholic funeral procession began.

My mother was a full member of the Catholic Association of St. Anne, *Mbuya Anna,* and her mother had been a full member of the Wesleyan Methodist Mothers' Union, *Mai Ruwadzano.* Though I still wear no church uniform, and have been questioning the colonial politics of its origin, I'm fascinated by the spiritual and social movement that evolved from the interpretations, appropriation, and imaging of Mary in postcolonial Africa as sources of feminist theological reflection for the World Church.

While libraries fill with Marian sermons and literature, this essay captures the significance of Mary through the imaginations and experiences of African women. It explores various attributes accorded Mary by Catholic women in Zimbabwe through their creative struggles, aspirations, and spirituality. Their unique translations of Marian images at the Gokomere Hill Shrine, grottos at the nearby Gokomere Mission, and the Don Bosco churchyard in Masvingo inform a fuller understanding of Mary, the patron saint of Masvingo Diocese of Zimbabwe, and her influence in shaping Catholic women's self-imaging.

Uniformed Catholic women attending a Bible study at
Don Bosco Parish of Masvingo Diocese in Zimbabwe (July 17, 2010).

How do African Catholic women translate the "white" images and "white" apparitions of Mary in the remote, dusty hills, grottos, and postcolonial churches without being alienated or confused by them? Why do they relate to the old image of the White Virgin and Mother and accept nothing else? What chances do new images of Mary have of emerging through "a dialogue between past and present," as claimed by Marianne Merkx?[1] These questions guide my interrogation of African feminist theology from "white" Marian images and apparitions in this essay as ethical prerogatives of the World Church. The essay proposes socially engaged hybridity beyond the black and white images gracing the shrines, churches, and grottos.

Since the radical devotion to Mary within the Catholic tradition draws upon rituals, images, and apparitions, this essay focuses on Marian spirituality that draws from a general preference for the "White Mother and Child" over the "Black Virgin." This, in turn, calls for a feminist theological critique of racial politics in the postcolonial World Church. Thus, intrigued by Marian whiteness in Catholic sacred places particularly frequented by women, this work captures and examines the images of Mary through photography and critically analyzes the apparitions of Mary in these places. It weighs the dangers of reductionism in provincial black images of the local church against the illusions of universal images that are enshrined in the whiteness of the World Church. Thus, critical ethical prerogatives for the World Church include the deconstruction of dominant white and black images in Marian and other visual narratives.

Background

A study of Marian images in selected Catholic churches in Masvingo Diocese of Zimbabwe, where local artists have been sculpting icons with relevance in appearance and reality for their churches and grottos, forms the background of the study. The wood and stone icons and other decorative carvings of candlesticks, lecterns, and marquetry depicting biblical scenes abundant at Serima Mission Chapel[2] are a celebration of post–Vatican II inculturation. Yet, in the same diocese, at the shrine of "Our Lady of Peace," the Catholic women *Nzanga* (Catholic Women's Movement) opted for an old colonial image of Mary shrouded in whiteness and protested against the inculturated image carved in black granite intended to grace the shrine hills. This paradox leads to a search for alternative hybrid images that begins with the deconstruction of colonial images of Mary.

Masvingo Diocese is also significant for me due to my personal experiences growing up Catholic around the sacred spaces of churches and grottos in Masvingo during my spiritual formative years; at Bondolfi Mission, 1973–75; Berejena Mission, 1976–77; and Mukaro Mission, 1978–81. Revisiting the spaces of my cradle faith allows me to dialogue with the old and new Marian images as an African theologian engaged with the Virgin Mother's influence on women's vocation in the world and church. The Catholic Diocese of Masvingo stands out as a post–Vatican II beacon of inculturation, with African iconography at the famous Serima Chapel and a vernacular liturgical music satellite project for the entire Central African region spearheaded by Stephen Ponde,[3] lead composer and my headmaster at Bondolfi Mission. I was privileged to attend grade school there and learn to play the Catholic Mass drums and dance.

The Catholic Diocese of Masvingo houses the Shrine of Our Lady of Peace in rural Gokomere Mission Hills, reinforcing my justification for research on women, church, and ethics in the diocese, and exploring selected Marian spaces through photography. I capture the visual and literal merging of experience and theory for practical purposes and join feminists from the margins to "weave beads into strands" and reclaim a place of dignity in the World Church. It is indeed an effort to resurrect the prophetic aspects of Pope John Paul II's call for the recognition of the dignity and vocation of women.[4] Thus, the Marian spirit preached, danced, lived, and imagined by *Nzanga* Catholic women forms the background of a discussion of how the "daughters of the eternal Jerusalem" find their "supreme vocation" and messianic mission in the church facing the formidable challenge of AIDS in sub-Saharan Africa, where, as Michael Kelly argues, more women than men are becoming HIV infected.[5]

The Shrine

The history of the shrine of Mary in Masvingo Diocese,[6] as shared by Constance Ndoro,[7] is shrouded in deep spirituality punctuated by distinct visions of Mary appearing to Rosarian women praying in the hills near the shrine of Mary.[8] A black image of the Virgin Mary carved from local granite by local male sculptors was erected at the shrine with pomp and style. It was rejected by *Nzanga yaAnna*, who raised numerous objections. They questioned everything from the local black granite rock, to the features of the ordinary African women like themselves that spelled out powerlessness. Thus, the image of any black African woman was understood *not* to represent Mary at that most holy shrine, especially coming after several apparitions of Mary in White holiness. With the antiwhite campaigns of farm invasions by landless black people dominating the contemporary political climate of Zimbabwe, the image of a "White" Mother and "White" Child deep in the remote hills seemed contentious. The women defied the hierarchical powers of the church and successfully replaced the black Virgin with the white Mother and Child.[9]

Marian Apparition

Collective memory plays a major role in the women's encounter with Marian apparitions at the shrine. On various occasions, groups of devout Catholic women praying at the shrine have reported experiencing an apparition of Mary in her glory, grace, and "Whiteness."[10] Though these moments are described as electric and blessed, there are no known accounts of verbal interaction with Mary at Gokomere Shrine. It is more of a consummate experience of the purity and power of the divine Mother that brings a deeper understanding of the message in the apparition, even to those who claim no visual testimony. What all the women carry with them is a collective memory of the experience of the divine presence of Mary, which leaves them completely receptive to the interpretation of those blessed with the visual glory. The experience has been described as highly empowering to the witnesses of the apparition. Both feminist interpretations and phenomenological approaches were employed to interrogate and understand the mystical experiences and perspectives of these Marian devotees. This requires a suspension of judgment for the researcher and the reader.

Catholic Women's Associations, *Nzanga*

While the term *Ruwadzano* is commonly associated with Protestant churches, *Nzanga* is the Catholic equivalent for these grassroots Christian women's movements.

Mary in "glory, grace and whiteness" at Our Lady of Peace
Shrine in Gokomere Hills, Zimbabwe (July 17, 2010).

Research on the Catholic women *Nzanga* in Zimbabwe has not been fully under-taken. *Nzanga* are divided according to age-sets, *Nzanga yaMai Maria* for the younger unmarried girls and *Nzanga yaMbuya Anna* for the older married women. Both groups are heavily influenced by their allegiance to Mary the "Virgin," the "Great Mother," and "Our Lady of Peace." It can be argued that Mary has far-reaching influence in the church through these grassroots movements known as *Nzanga*. How Mary is imagined in this context is portrayed at sacred sites, the shrines, and grottos, as well as other public spaces explored in this essay.

Literature

My search for hybrid images reflecting the "great works of God" through Mary is informed by *Marialis Cultus'* focus on "the diversity of women in different societies and cultures which make it necessary also to make the picture of Mary more concrete,"[11] *Redemptoris Mater* to honor the Marian Year, 1987, and *Mulieris Dignitatem,* also written to honor the Marian Year and discuss the dignity and vocation of women modeled on Mary.[12] In an elaborate letter, Pope John Paul II thanks generations of women modeled against Marian images of the "Church in matters of faith, charity and perfect union with Christ."[13]

Carved in black granite, Mary was rejected by black Catholic women in favor of white "Mother and Child" images that now grace Gokomere Hills Shrine (July 17, 2010).

Therefore *the Church gives thanks for each and every woman:* for mothers, for sisters, for wives; for women consecrated to God in virginity; for women dedicated to the many human beings who await the gratuitous love of another person; for women who watch over the human persons in the family, which is the fundamental sign of the human community; for women who work professionally, and who at times are burdened by a great social responsibility; for *"perfect"* women and for "weak" women— for all women as they have come forth from the heart of God in all the beauty and richness of their femininity; as they have been embraced by his eternal love; as, together with men, they are pilgrims on this earth, which is the temporal "homeland" of all people and is transformed sometimes into a "valley of tears"; as they assume, together with men, *a common responsibility for the destiny of humanity* according to daily necessities and according to that definitive destiny which the human family has in God himself, in the bosom of the ineffable Trinity.[14]

Catharina Halkes critiques *Mulieris Dignitatem* for putting "too one-sided a stress on women as *par excellence* called to see Mary as their image and model and to follow her."[15] She argues that this is retrogression into the old traditional assumption that the picture of Mary applied to all women. Most convincing is her critique that "religious language is *par excellence* a pictorial, symbolic language. Images and symbols can give us greater space and so put us in touch with the infinite. However, if they are used to be imposed on people as values and norms, they are used wrongly and become harmful."[16] Of greater salience for this study is her suggestion to drop images when they no longer prompt recognition in all cultures. Her examples of symbolism of Mary as virgin, bride, and mother might be distasteful for feminist theology in the global North, but for most African women, these images uphold perceived essence.

Ethical Concerns

A study of sacred spaces shared by Catholic women devotees of Mary, such as grottos in Masvingo and the Marian shrine in Gokomere Hills close to Masvingo, reveals provocative revelations of black women's fixation with colonial symbols of power. For the church that made huge inculturation strides for nearly fifty years, contemporary preoccupation with white sacrality requires ethical responses from both feminists and ethicists in the World Church. The colonial distortion of vital sources of feminist thought in Africa cannot be shied away from in the name of personal revelations or subjective preferences of sacred tastes. Regardless of their religious freedoms, the invocation of Eurocentric white images for the African Church by Catholic African women remains highly provocative.

Why have African images failed to inspire the expression of spirituality for women at the popular Marian shrine in Masvingo Diocese of Zimbabwe? Why would the spiritual significance of local carvings be questionable among black women in rural and semirural settings—women whose contact with the outside world is minimal? Why would an image of Mary shrouded in whiteness not create obvious clashes for the African Marian devotees of Masvingo, even on the basis of self-identity?

The art of imagining Mary was developed within the larger context of Christian spirituality that has been monopolized by Western Christianity. Western Marian images, which foster the religious beliefs of the World Church, are predominantly white in color. Whether these works of art are displayed in cathedrals, school hallways, or in exclusive art galleries, such as the Getty Center in Los Angeles,[17] the dominant images of Mary are predictably white. These are also the images that continue to serve the devotional needs of the World Church and reflect everyday occurrences into the spiritual world. This symbolically monolithic manner of imagining Mary has influenced the African Church's imagination of divinity and, consequently, its own projections of Mary, Jesus, and God. It signifies unjust sociopolitical relations of a racially divided colonial church that linger in the

A dominant color for Mary in the Getty Center, Los Angeles (October 2010).

postcolonial African Church. In Africa, contemporary Marian images in Catholic gendered sacred spaces reveal residues of the canonization of white enshrinement. The enduring traits of Western symbols for Marian devotion still embroiled in colonial legacy are a result of careless image transplants of Mary during the nineteenth-century missionary project.

Deconstructing Images

The images of Mary in Africa are best understood through her social location and engagement. I argue that this couldn't be fully understood through the black or white abstract symbology of the Blessed Mother of Jesus Christ, and/or as the virgin daughter of Anna, especially for communities that are still recovering from the effects of colonial subordination that defined reality in black and white for hundreds of years. The world seen in multiple colors is more vibrant than in black and white. And the world in motion has far greater appeal to most African Christians, who would rather live out their faith in time than be fixated on monolithic statues. Hence, the women's movements are more appealing when they dislodge their bondage to both colonial and cultural negative self-images. Thus, the image of Mary as the power and spirit influencing the women's movement is much more appealing for people seeking liberating images of Mary beyond the shrines and dominant portraits of Mary, depicted as the socially and religiously subdued woman. The vibrant life-affirming spirit of Mary is most visible at funerals, at Bible reading sessions, and at occasions where women support the underprivileged, praying for the sick and delivering home-based care where AIDS is ravaging communities and wiping out entire families with no organized social support or doctors. The spirit of Mary is witnessed when women support one another in doing social justice. Therefore, exclusive preoccupation with fixed images of Mary nailed on the rocks in remote hills or gracing cathedrals and old grottos cannot fully yield an understanding of Mary in Africa. It takes a hybrid of fixed/static images and living images that capture the spirit of Mary to transform society and shape a more meaningful discourse of Mary in African Catholic circles and cross-denominationally.

The images of Mary from diverse cultures convince me that these works of art require feminist interrogation and critique grounded in the living realities that are theologically palatable to their communities. Thus Mary, the virtuous virgin, the loving, caring and committed mother, the teacher and admonisher, the prayerful intercessor, the trusted friend of the despised, and, most of all, the epitome of the simple and ordinary woman blessed and favored by God, can surely not be narrowly imagined through black and white dualism. Rather she is best portrayed through charitable works and lived out spirituality demonstrated through the churchwomen organizations, Nzanga's concerted effort to be church.

The dancing uniformed Catholic women who sang, cried, and comforted my grieving family by sharing the word of hope for eternity through Jesus Christ, and who assumed motherhood for the motherless, form the most appealing Marian image I can visualize. The image is colorful, dynamic, appealing, and practical. It is evangelical and deeply spiritual. It is most visible in the community and not hidden away in hills revealed only to the chosen few. Thus, the image of Mary in the movement of women inspired by Mary is the most appealing image this essay proposes.

The fascination with Mary as the virgin daughter of Anna does not supersede her motherhood in Africa. The daughter of Anna is invoked in the rites of passage

Capturing the hybrid spirit of Mary in community through African iconography at Serima Chapel, Masvingo Diocese (July 18, 2010).

that emphasize virginity and the subsequent rites of marriage and motherhood. The "uniformed" women's images of Mary are more fascinating than the art and sculpture, loaded with colonial insinuations and misunderstanding of inculturation discussed in this essay.

The mystery of motherhood revolves around bringing forth life, thus making the mother the sacred source of life. By aligning themselves with Anna, all the mothers are celebrating themselves in that light. It follows that Mary, too, becomes the epitome of the sacredness of motherhood when she becomes the God Mother, who also becomes a symbol of power and protection, an image most appealing to the women in economic, sociocultural, and religious instability. For this reason, the Virgin Mary's image is not rated the same as the Great Mother, "Mai Maria." Although virginity is celebrated in most African cultures for a variety of reasons that are neither defined by women nor favor them, girls are expected to move beyond this fixation and become fully women through fecundity. Therefore, Mary as mother of the church inspires the women who venerate and identify with her to create *Nzanga,* "church within the Church" and deal with the backlash of patriarchy.

Women, Church, and Power

The feminist theological quest for ecumenical dialogue leads to a search for powerful images of Mary for the larger Christian women's movement. It attempts to reframe Marian images for ecumenical purposes.

While distinguished women in African Independent Churches (AIC)[18] founded and led their own churches in southern Africa, most women in mission founded churches enjoyed considerable autonomy through all-women church organizations in their churches, *Manyanos/Ruwadzano/Nzanga.* Women in *Manyanos* (Xhosa word for women's prayer unions/Christian movements) or *Ruwadzano/Nzanga* (the Shona equivalent) explored leadership opportunities. These organizations provided distinctive outlets for Christian women's spirituality in southern Africa as they appropriated the gospel in their own contexts through feminist lenses. The focus of these social movements was emotional, and ecstatic prayers centered on the confession of problems and failings as well as community welfare. Ironically, these grassroots religious movements were not always celebrated in mainstream Christianity because they were sometimes "seen as threatening familial strength, community solidarity or government control."[19] Hastings, who equates the spirit of the *Manyano* in mainline churches with the spirit of the AIC, makes a similar observation. He argues that South African *Manyanos* are expressions of black women's reaction to male dominance, clerical dominance, as well as a reaction to white dominance.[20] Thus, their history is deeply located in the racial divisions of colonial Africa.

In Zimbabwe, *Ruwadzano,* which literally means women's fellowship, is vividly distinguished by denominational colors on different uniforms. Research on the African Christian women's movement of the colonial church in Zimbabwe has been structured along denominational lines.[21] My comparative research on the megaunification of interdenominational women's unions in Zimbabwe, *Mubatanidzwa Wemadzimai,* addresses details beyond the scope of this essay. Although there is not as much ritual and veneration of Mary outside the Catholic tradition, the images of Mary as "mother and spiritual guide" strike an interdenominational chord. The more recent works on women's movements in AIC provide a break from the study of *Ruwadzano* in western initiated churches, a rather forgotten wing of the women's movement in postcolonial Africa.[22]

By 1919, the *Ruwadzano* movement was established in Southern Rhodesia, where it was riddled with race and gender injustices.[23] Writing about the movement within the Methodist Church, Canaan Banana argues,

The problem of racism within the Methodist Church with its Double Mandate also affected the role and contribution of women to the mission of the Church. This concerned both the place of the *Ruwadzano/Manyano* movement in the Church and the space within which elevated African women could also take independent initiative.[24]

Although women were afforded the opportunity to display their capabilities and initiatives in church development, it was only as late as 1963 that black African women were officially accepted into influential leadership positions in the Methodist Church of Zimbabwe.[25] *Ruwadzano* was organized hierarchically, with the wife of the chairman of the mission district at the top as the district president, then the wives of the eleven circuit superintendents, all white, as the circuit presidents. Black women were less powerful in this female space, where their white counterparts regarded them as "unworthy" of leadership positions. Zimbabwe's political independence ushered in a significant power shift to black people in the church, and subsequently to black women in *Ruwadzano*.

Theological Reflection

Women, as baptized full members of the Catholic Church, emerge not solely as "helpers" of the hierarchy but as the church, with the power and gifts of the spirit of Mary. Their encounter with divinity, when the Blessed Virgin appears to them

Resilient and spirited Anglican women of Zimbabwe. Barred from Bernard Mzeki Shrine during the church's bitter leadership struggle, they pray at Marondera Show Grounds in defiance (June 27, 2010).

while praying, empowers them boldly to affirm their social location in the church. Thus, they confidently make decisions about crucial issues of doctrine regarding the diocese's shrine and acceptable images of Mary for that sacred space. In that regard, the Legions of Mary and Anna of Masvingo made a significant theological statement about their spirituality in defining Marian symbology against the dominant Catholic symbology on the same site. More interestingly, this is not simply the case of an individual woman with charismatic leadership qualities breaking through the ranks, but the collective work of an entire women's movement inspired by Mary, the "model of the Church in the matter of faith, charity and perfect union with Christ."[26] Pope John Paul II acknowledged the dignity and vocation of women:

> The Church gives thanks *for all the manifestations of the feminine "genius"* which have appeared in the course of history, in the midst of all peoples and nations; she gives thanks for all the charisms which the Holy Spirit distributes to women in the history of the People of God, for all the victories which she owes to their faith, hope and charity: she gives thanks for all *the fruits of feminine holiness.*[27]

Secondly, the apparition of white Mary to the praying women is shrouded in mystery and may represent a struggle to satiate some theological quest. Despite the fact that in my empirical research the phenomenological approach required suspension of personal judgment, the phenomenon still conjured up troubling colonial overtones. However, I celebrate the power of the laity to decide the color, size, and character of their object of veneration. This demonstrates the power of the collective, the power of rituals and symbols as tools to define women's intensive religious involvement in the Catholic Church. However, I found the preference of white over black, by those who are black, to be intriguing. Why would the Great Mother reveal herself only through one medium of whiteness to a predominantly rural black Christian women's group? This spells out troubling racial power dynamics that associate divinity with whiteness even in these remote African hills: possibly a hangover of colonization taking much longer to wane in remote rural places.

Thirdly, the image of Mary at the shrine in these rural African hills is not inconsistent with most postcolonial images of Mary in grottos around the country. How then could Mary appear in any other way to praying women? The white image is still the dominant image that women are spiritually and emotionally attached to.

Finally, while the church has made a lot of progress in the process of inculturation of African clergy, women's hierarchical positions in the church have remained static. For this reason, patriarchy in the Catholic Church is responsible for preventing Catholic women from seeing God in themselves. Thus, when Christian women are distanced from power, they are psychologically distanced from divinity in a ripple effect. By rejecting the remotest possibility of a venerable black

Mary (perceived to be misguided symbology), the Catholic women of Masvingo Diocese unconsciously distanced themselves from divinity and continued the vicious cycle of self-exclusion. The belief that Mary is not Mary unless she is white easily translates into the belief that God is, indeed, white. Not only is this theologically unsound, it typifies a classic example of internalization of oppression that the postcolonial church should consciously address.

Conclusion

When does the image of Mary stop being an image of Mary? This question is relevant with regard to the image in the Masvingo Shrine hills for two reasons. First, the research succeeded in upsetting my hypothesis and prompted me to think of alternative ways to discuss Marian symbology. Looking beyond fixed images to the vibrant movement of women doing justice in the spirit of Mary, hybrid images emerge. Second, through controversial images discussed in this essay, women have left their mark on the patriarchal rigidity of church tradition. It can, therefore, be concluded that though Mary is not depicted in African paintings and sculptures at Marian shrines, it is the "spirit" of Mary that has far reaching effect in making the church relevant in bringing the *missio Dei* to the brokenness of our world marked by AIDS. This challenges us to look beyond the shrines and to interrogate the fixed images that speak to us from hilltops, grottos, and cathedrals, often in tongues. Thus, though nineteenth-century Catholicism is associated with colonization and euro-centrism, the World Church is also applauded for subsequent particular instances of the rejection of domination. The post–Vatican II positive reimaging of the divine through inculturation set the stage for deeper social engagement processes in the church by women and laity. It can therefore be concluded that beyond inculturation lie hybrid images of women making "sincere gifts of self" to others and finding themselves in the process. This is my interpretation of the women, church, and ethics mirrored through Catholic women *Nzanga* where their dignity and vocation are intertwined.

Notes

1. Edward Schillebeeckx and Catharina Halkes, *Mary Yesterday, Today, Tomorrow* (New York: Crossroads, 1993), 1.

2. Serima Mission in Gutu District of Masvingo Province was built in 1948. It houses the unique Church of Our Lady with abundant carvings that spread the good word through local craftmanship.

3. Joseph Lenherr, "Advancing Indigenous Church Music," *African Music* 4, no. 2 (1968): 33–39.

4. John Paul II, Apostolic Letter *Mulieris Dignitatem, On the Dignity and Vocation of Women* (Boston: St. Paul Books, 1996).

5. Michael J. Kelly, *HIV and AIDS: A Social Justice Perspective* (Nairobi: Paulines Publications Africa, 2010).

6. The shrine of Our Lady of Peace, the patron of Masvingo diocese, was constructed in 1992 on the hills near Gokomere Mission.

7. Constance Ndoro, interview, July 17, 2010 (Shrine of Our Lady of Peace in Gokomere Hills of Masvingo Diocese).

8. Praying in the hills is generally associated with Wilderness Apostolic Churches, branches of African Independent Churches (AIC). It is a rare phenomenon among the most mainline churches. Rosarians are therefore a distinct group within the Catholic tradition whose deep spirituality and disciplined prayer lead them to remote places for prayer such as hills frequented by AIC prophets.

9. Constance Ndoro, interview, July 17, 2010.

10. Report by Constance Ndoro, the caretaker of the shrine of Our Lady of Peace in Masvingo, a job she shares with her husband Patrick Ndoro. Constance Ndoro, interview, July 17, 2010.

11. Edward Schillebeeckx and Catharina Halkes, *Mary Yesterday, Today, Tomorrow* (New York: Crossroads, 1993), 77.

12. Ibid., 76–77.

13. Cf. Second Vatican Ecumenical Council, Dogmatic Constitution on the Church *Lumen Gentium*, 63.

14. Ibid.; John Paul II, Apostolic Letter *Mulieris Dignitatem, On the Dignity and Vocation of Women*, 104.

15. Schillebeeckx and Halkes, *Mary Yesterday, Today, Tomorrow*, 77.

16. Ibid., 77

17. The J. Paul Getty Museum is located at the $1.3 billion Getty Center in Los Angeles that opened on December 16, 1997. It houses pre–twentieth century European paintings, drawings, sculpture, illuminated manuscripts, decorative arts, as well as nineteenth and twentieth century American photographs.

18. These are predominantly churches founded by black Africans primarily for black people in Africa. With the recent wave of migration of African converts, they are found everywhere in the African Diaspora.

19. Susan S. Sered, *Priestess, Mother, Sacred Sister: Religions Dominated by Women* (New York: Oxford University Press, 1996), 6–7.

20. Adrian Hastings, *A History of African Christianity 1950–1975* (Cambridge: Cambridge University Press, 1979), 115.

21. Ibid., 108–30; Chenjerai J. M. Zvobgo, *Wesleyan Methodist Missions in Zimbabwe 1891–1945* (Harare: University of Zimbabwe, 1991), 6–57; Canaan S. Banana, *The Church and the Struggle for Zimbabwe* (Gweru: Mambo Press, 1996); Lilian Dube, "Mai Chaza: An African Christian Story of Gender, Healing and Power," *Studia Historiae Eccelesiasticae* 34Suppl. (2008): 91–119.

22. Tumani Mutasa Nyajeka, *The Unwritten Text: The Indigenous African Christian Women's Movement in Zimbabwe* (Mutare: Africa University Press, 2006); Isabella Mukonyora, *Wandering a Gendered Wilderness: Suffering and Healing in an African Initiated Church* (New York: Peter Lang, 2007); Lilian Dube, Tabona Shoko, and Stephen Hayes, *African Initiatives in Healing Ministry* (Pretoria: University of South Africa Publications, 2011).

23. Zvobgo, *Wesleyan Methodist Missions in Zimbabwe 1891–1945*, 98.

24. Banana, *The Church and the Struggle for Zimbabwe*, 94.

25. Ibid.; Zvobgo, *Wesleyan Methodist Missions in Zimbabwe, 1891–1945*, 51.

26. Cf. Second Vatican Ecumenical Council, Dogmatic Constitution on the Church *Lumen Gentium,* 63.

27. Ibid., John Paul II, Apostolic Letter *Mulieris Dignitatem, On the Dignity and Vocation of Women,* 104.

GIVING A VOICE TO AFRICAN WOMEN THROUGH EDUCATION

Veronica Jamanyur Rop

Introduction

Many African countries have witnessed and continue to witness war. Nations once thought to be peaceful find themselves in the midst of the devastating effects of international conflict and internal strife. Sadly, women and children are hardhit by these conflicts. Their voices, like Rachel of old, weeping for her people, cry out to stop the violence. However, most African women lack a hearing and a public voice, and even fewer hold office to exercise authority. By virtue of their education, those few women who are public leaders bring constructive ideas and raise questions that challenge the church and their governments to do more. The church must move beyond providing material aid, welcome as it is, to empowering women in Africa. Scholarships for African women are one way to empower them to speak, and to speak with authority. Access to higher education for African girls and women, in practical subjects, but also in theology and ethics, is a first route of empowerment. Theology and ethics are important, given that the African people view almost everything, including the right way to interact with others, from a religious perspective. On this basis, theology equips women with a deeper understanding of Christian values, thus challenging their own cultural views with the hope of contributing toward much-needed justice and peace in Africa.

When I conducted peace education workshops for women working in primary and secondary schools (as a contribution toward reconciliation after the 2007–08 postelection violence in my native country of Kenya), I saw that African women have much to offer and wish to offer more in response to conflict of many kinds. Greater access to education, particularly in moral theology and ethics, might begin to meet their hunger and thirst for righteousness, while they become empowered to find their own voices of authority.

My essay has four parts. The first part explores the experience of African women in a culture of oppression, and highlights economic and political challenges, HIV/AIDS, and female genital mutilation (FGM), as critical issues. The second part focuses on the traditional and cultural formation of women and the misinterpretation of scripture as some of the causes that remain to be challenged in African societies. The third part promotes the ethical values of educating

African women and highlights the aims of education, African women in education, the moral dimension of education, and the importance of educating women
in theology. The last part examines the teaching of the church about women by
drawing examples from Jesus' attitude and behavior toward women; the section
concludes with some African theologians' views on the place of women in a
communitarian African society. I conclude by envisioning an inclusive African
community where a woman has a hearing and public voice.

The Experience of African Women
in an Oppressive Culture

There are many positive values that identify African heritage as deeply religious. African people are known to be hospitable, communally minded, and
religiously centered in their daily endeavors. But upon a closer look at the culture,
one realizes that many African communities neglect the role of women in social,
economic, and political development. In these communities, women find themselves excluded from open dialogue on matters pertinent to the religious, political,
and social activities of the community they belong to. In our contemporary, global-
izing world, this attitude contravenes the basic canons of moral action and human
rights.[1] At the international level, the UN Charter, the Universal Declaration of
Human Rights, and the Convention on Elimination of All Forms of Discrimination against Women (CEDAW) sought to guarantee better legal status for women.
Again while laying greater emphasis on the church's preferential option for the
poor and the outcast, John Paul II challenged all Christians to become the voice of
the poor of the world[2] and also challenged women to advance for the sake of our
dignity in the church and society.[3]

Economic Systems That Exploit Women

Looking at economic practices in Africa, one can observe that there is a need
to challenge economic activities at various levels that tend to exploit, exclude, and
deny women a voice, particularly in decision making. In Africa, the domestic labor
of women has economic value that is not acknowledged. In work in the field, she
accounts for the highest percentage of agricultural labor but does not have control
over what she produces. Education and cultural norms do not encourage women to
speak out in public. As a result, they are denied the right to participate in decisions
about the management of natural resources.[4]

African Women and Politics

Politics is the use of legitimate authority for the purpose of attaining the
common good of society. This common good, declares the Second Vatican Council,
embraces "the sum of those conditions of social life by which individuals, families

and groups can achieve complete and efficacious fulfilment."[5] Political situations in Africa point to the need to conscientize communities on various structures that discriminate against and subjugate women, relegating them to a second-class position in society. Arguably, a human person experiences her/his humanity to the extent that she/he is able to participate in the humanity of the other. One place that the human person defines herself/himself is in the area of politics. Politics is one field in which African women would be able to participate in leadership, education for coexistence, and active and responsible citizenship.[6]

But an African woman's experience is limited to the subordinate role designated for her by society, thus denying her this fundamental right as a human being. Women are discriminated against in the political arena, and justice is not rendered to them even when it is obvious that they have leadership qualities. They are excluded from executive posts and decision making. They are the majority when it comes to voter registration and actual voting, but the minority in parliaments and in cabinet posts.[7] While there is a growing civic consciousness in the sociopolitical sphere, little is being done to have equal gender representation in our parliaments. For those nations that claim to have passed laws relating to equal representation, those laws are yet to be implemented. Discrimination, therefore, in our systems, understood as inequality in representation, is a question of justice and human rights. Moreover, it undermines the dignity of African women. In his address at the *Jubilee of Government Leaders, Members of Parliament,* John Paul II stated that justice must be one of the fundamental concerns of political leaders. That is, political leaders must strive for justice that aims at creating conditions of equal opportunity among citizens and favors those who, for reasons of social status or education or health, risk being left behind or relegated to the lowest places in society, without possibility of deliverance.[8] Many of those who seem to be left behind are women.

African Women and the Challenge of HIV/AIDS

The AIDS pandemic in Africa is one of the alarming conditions still threatening the continent. This situation calls for the need to give a voice continually to women, as well as to educate women on preventive measures, and how to treat members of the community who are already infected or affected. The 2012 UNAIDS report shows that at the end of 2011, an estimated 34 million people were living with HIV globally, and about 23.5 million of these reside in Sub-Saharan Africa. Of the above population, adults aged fifteen to forty-five are estimated to make up about 0.8 percent of people living with HIV globally. Worldwide, the Sub-Saharan African region still remains the most heavily affected, with nearly one in every twenty adults (4.9 percent) living with HIV. The above number accounts for 69 percent of the people living with HIV worldwide.[9] On an encouraging note, UNAIDS reports a decline in new HIV infections and AIDS-related death in Sub-Saharan Africa. There were an estimated 1.8 million new HIV infections in 2011 compared to 2.8 million new infections in 2001. At the same time, about 1.2 million people died from AIDS-related causes every year, a decline from 1.8 million people. Sadly, 92 percent of pregnant women who are living with HIV and more than 90 percent of children who acquired HIV in 2011 reside in Sub-Saharan Africa. While UNAIDS's findings show that the AIDS situation has declined in Sub-Saharan Africa, one statistic still remains challenging. Women and girls continue to be disproportionally affected by the HIV epidemic in the region; women account for 58 percent of all people living with HIV in Sub-Saharan Africa in 2011. Worse still, 56 percent of the people living with HIV in Kenya report being verbally abused because of their HIV status. Most of those ill-treated are women.[10] In most cases, women are the primary caregivers for the sick and the dying. As caretakers, they are at greater risk than men when it comes to infection and death. In addition, most women are infected by their spouses. Their fears are confirmed by the UNAIDS report that heterosexual intercourse remains the pandemic's driving force and that sex workers continue to play a notable role in its spread.[11] In addition, in situations of armed conflicts or internal clashes, women and girls are targeted for sexual abuse. In all these circumstances, it is the women who bear a disproportionate share of the burden of this pandemic, and they need to be heard and educated.[12]

The Challenge of FGM

Another area in which women need their voices to be heard and acted upon is that of FGM, aka female circumcision. Female circumcision is a sensitive issue and touches directly on the dignity of a woman at both a personal and communal level. As such, women, as well as the community, deserve to be educated and informed on the complications and risks that come with FGM practice. Moreover, certain parts of the continent that do not practice FGM have a lot to offer in regard to safer ways to initiate women into adulthood.

Writing on female circumcision, Ephigenia Gachiri states that the practice of circumcising women has very deep roots that touch on all aspects of the African culture. Among African communities, female circumcision comprises different procedures such as clitoridectomy, excision, infibulation, and some unclassified procedures. These procedures not only entail physical pain, injury, and harm to the female genital organs and potential exposure to HIV/AIDS, but they can also lead to medical and gynecological complications as well as cause emotional and psychological sufferings. Undoubtedly, these procedures have serious implications for the life and the dignity of an African woman that outweigh the sociocultural values attached to them.[13] The African palaver culture could help here, since not all ethnic groups have the same methods/procedures of initiation. This means that, in the endeavour to preserve the value of African initiation, one must hold a palaver to discuss thoroughly the various initiation practices mentioned above, in order to discover the best method to safeguard the dignity of an African woman.[14] For this to succeed, a paradigm shift in the African thinking on the ethical dimensions of FGM is crucial. This shift also requires a reevaluation of the methods used in African initiation rites, procedures that put the lives of the initiates at risk and expose them to HIV infections, among other complications. At the Christian level, an appraisal of attitudes and practices toward the Christian values regarding human dignity and theology of the body is needed.

Why Oppression of Women Persists in Christian African Societies

Although many communities on the continent of Africa have embraced the gospel of Jesus Christ, oppression of women still persists. Some of the factors that have contributed to this situation include African traditional beliefs and practices that remain unchallenged and are in dire need of deeper evangelization. Discussing the importance of communal life in an African society, Bujo notes that as a result of placing the community above individual or group advancement, African people have ended up holding on to practices that do not necessarily promote the growth of their people.[15] This is mostly true of the experience of the African woman. However, it is equally true that the position she finds herself in in the community has not deterred her from self-emancipation or liberating her community from unethical customs, particularly those practices that seem not recognize the worth of a woman or give her a voice.[16]

Traditional and Cultural Formation of African Women

Defining the term "education," Paul Barry Clarke and Andrew Linzey point out that education involves imparting values and establishing institutions and other mechanisms that would enable these values to be implemented in a human society.[17] Traditional African education is believed to be a whole process of socialization that starts at birth and ends at death. The system is largely informal and basically learned subconsciously by observation, imitation, and by instruction or guidance. Older members of a community act as disseminators of knowledge to the young, indoctrinating them in the beliefs and values of the community. In some communities, this learning includes an aspect of formal learning when the youth undergo the circumcision ceremony, which is viewed as the climax of the learning process.[18]

Traditional education, which is provided during a period of seclusion following initiation or circumcision, includes forms of behavior and responsibilities that the community expects from an adult. Young men and women are taught how to be functioning and productive adult members of society. With regard to instruction of males, a greater emphasis is placed on gender difference. Boys are taught to regard all women, regardless of their age, as persons with low intelligence and as persons who, like children, are in constant need of adult or male supervision. Women, in turn, are instructed to obey and follow a male's instructions, and disobedience to any of his decisions violates communal norms. In some communities, girls are taught to kneel or bow before men as a sign of respect and are not supposed to speak to men until they have gone through the initiation ceremonies discussed above.

Moreover, while girls learn how to make household items, such as gourds and pots, and how to collect firewood and gather wild vegetables, boys are taught how to exercise authority in the family and society as well as to guard the territory. This role description gives a glimpse of how the genders are formed. While males are formed and encouraged from childhood to think of themselves as invulnerable, females are both subtly and overtly taught to think of themselves as entirely vulnerable and in need of the protection of a male figure.[19] This kind of education has been internalized, so that most women find it difficult to express their views publicly, especially before men, thus holding back potentially constructive ideas that might contribute to lasting peace on the continent. Since moral formation takes place in a community, and human persons construct their own social world, many African women have been taught and socialized into thinking of themselves as incapable of any serious decision. This attitude needs to be challenged.

Scriptural Pericopes that Encourage Oppression of Women

One major challenge facing contemporary African churches is the proper interpretation of scripture. Misinterpretation of scripture has contributed immensely to the oppression of and discrimination against women. For example, passages such as Ephesians 5:22–33,[20] about submission and subordination of various members of a household reveal how scripture can be used to oppress women. Readers who have interpreted these passages to mean submission and subordination of women have used them to justify the second-class position assigned to women. Consequently, women have been denied leadership roles in various fields and even in some churches. In societies that have been influenced by such misinterpretation, few women find themselves holding key positions either in political, societal, or religious institutions. In the family, it is assumed that an African woman/wife has to remain submissive and subordinate to her male counterpart. It is worth noting that the term "submission" as used in this context does not reflect the church's understanding of mutual submission. Rather it is a literal translation that denotes a woman's subordination and inferiority before her male counterpart. This understanding of submission is sought in what is termed a positive quality of a good wife.

Similarly, portraying the relationship between sexes in Christological-ecclesiological terms (man representing Christ and a woman humanity) seems to provide a religious legitimation for patriarchal structures.[21] MacDonald rightly points out that when the metaphorical nature of the language is forgotten, there is the possibility for abuse in which the texts can seem to justify male impunity in the face of female fallibility.[22] Although a few people have dared to challenge this position, some contemporary African societies still think that a wife, or a woman for that matter, has to remain submissive to her

male counterpart. Yet, like a man, a woman has an equal personal dignity that
has always been realized but is only possible through education that leads to
the proper interpretation of scripture.

Ethical Values of Education of African Women

UNESCO's data for 2009 shows that there are 793 million illiterate adults in
the world, and about 64 percent of these are women. Most of these women still
lack basic reading and writing skills. Sub-Saharan Africa is one of those regions
with the lowest literacy rates. In fact, the global distribution of adult and youth
literacy by region showed that Sub-Saharan Africa accounts for 21.4 percent of
all illiterate adults globally.[23] Arguably, the gender imbalances in African educa-
tional institutions are not as severe now as they were in the past two decades. It is
observed that there are more female students studying in African institutions at all
levels today than ever before, but more progress needs to be made.[24] Pius XI, when
talking about Christian Catholic education as a social activity, pointed out that
education is essentially a social phenomenon and not a mere individual activity.[25]
From this statement, we can see that education is very important to the social life
of every person, including African women. Again, in discussing the meaning of
the universal right to education, Vatican II declares that all persons of every race,
condition, and age, since they enjoy the dignity of a human being, have an inalienable right to an education that is in keeping with their ultimate goal, their ability,
their sex, and the culture and tradition of their country, and also in harmony with
their fraternal association with other peoples in the fostering of true unity and
peace on earth.[26] Education is both a normative system concerned with inculcating
values and morals and with transmitting appropriate knowledge and skills, and an
administrative system. As a normative system, traditional education is seen as a
whole process of socialization that starts at birth and ends at death.

Aims of Education

The idea of education from an African traditional perspective is holistic in
nature. It is aimed at forming a well-integrated personality with positive moral
dispositions and observance of the ethical norms and values of the society. In a way,
this perspective is in line with the teaching of Vatican II that true education aims
at the formation of the human person in the pursuit of her/his ultimate end and
of the good of the societies of which, as woman/man, she/he is a member, and in
whose obligations, as an adult, she/he will share.[27]

Therefore, education aims at enabling a person to become an agent and
instrument of peace in a wider society and leads that individual to make informed
decisions that are crucial in promoting human dignity. As such, educating a woman
empowers and equips her with skills that could translate into increased participation in production and policy making. This makes education a vital instrument in

the promotion of women's dignity. Indeed the statement of Pius XI that families have an obligation to give their children not only religious and moral education, but physical and civic education, is very relevant here.[28]

The Moral Dimension of Education

The objective of traditional education, particularly in moral formation, is to mold and equip young people for their place in the society as a group. The idea is to instill and perpetuate the community's cultural heritage as a means of holding the fabric of society together.[29] Moral formation implies an internalization of moral norms and values that motivate a person to conform personal behavior to those of the community.[30] For education to make a moral impact on the lives of African women, effective policies and measures to bridge the gender gap in education in every community are of vital importance. There is also the need to identify and challenge structures in the society that serve as avenues for gender discrimination. One way to do this is to conscientize and educate women in their true identity and in how God sees them as beloved and precious daughters, even though traditional education and cultural norms do not encourage them to speak out on what pertains to their dignity.[31] Ironically, one of the universal perspectives on women is that when a woman is educated, the livelihood of an entire community improves, and civic education and liberties are enhanced. This concept is depicted in an African saying: "educate a woman and you educate the whole village or nation." Education enables a woman to become an agent and instrument of peace in a wider society and helps her to make informed decisions. Educating a woman empowers and equips her with skills that would translate into increased participation in production and policy making.[32]

Educating Women in Theology

Traditional and civic education is not enough to correct the conditions in which an African woman finds herself. But educating her in theology would enable her to appreciate her position before God and fellow human beings, and contribute constructively to the wider theological conversation, as well as to get involved in transforming her community and institutions for gender justice. Becoming knowledgeable in moral theology and ethics may enlighten a woman about her rights and the church's social teaching, thus enabling her to contribute toward much needed reconciliation, justice, and peace in Africa. Furthermore, the condition of women in Africa calls for an understanding of what liberation theology offers. Since theology and praxis influence each other, ethics demands a theology that is in quest for genuine justice.[33] This is the cry of African women. Liberation theology would encourage an African woman to continue pressing for her emancipation and expose her to what others have done and are doing to make their voices heard.

Catholic Social Teaching about Women

It is an axiom of Catholic social teaching that both woman and man are created in the image and the likeness of God, and hence both have inherent and inalienable dignity.[34] This is evident in the life of Jesus and in church tradition.

Jesus' Attitude and Behavior toward Women

It can be argued that, in the eyes of his contemporaries, Jesus Christ became the promoter of women's true dignity and of the vocation corresponding to this dignity.[35] For example, in the story of the Samaritan woman, the disciples marveled that Jesus was talking with a woman (cf. John 4:27), a behavior different from that of his contemporaries.[36] Jesus' attitude clearly shows that Christ is the definitive confirmation of the woman's worth. Christ is the one who knows the dignity of woman, her worth before her creator and savior. Therefore, Jesus' attitude toward the women whom he meets in the course of his Messianic service reflects the eternal plan of God, who, in creating each one of them, chooses her and loves her in Christ (cf. Eph. 1:1–5). It is evident that in all of Jesus' teaching, as well as in his behavior, one can find nothing that reflects the discrimination against women prevalent in his day. An example of Jesus' love and respect for women is demonstrated in the following verses: Jesus not casting a stone at a woman caught in adultery (John 8:10–11), allowing a woman to anoint his feet with perfume (Luke 7:36–50), and above all, choosing women to be his disciples and the first witnesses of his resurrection (Luke 24:1–11). Admittedly, these scripture texts show that unlike his contemporaries, Jesus' words and conduct always express the respect and honor due women.[37]

Women in a Communitarian African Society

African culture has many sound traditions that are compatible with the teaching of the church. However, oppression, marginalization, and discrimination against women on the basis of gender calls for a deeper evangelization of the culture. In a communitarian society, the dignity of an African woman can be understood in her personality as a relational being. The truth of her existence in the image and likeness of the Triune God entails relationship, with the other "I." Hence, a woman exists in relationship with other persons, with God, and with the cosmos. She is not an isolated individual but a person; essentially a relational being.[38] Laurenti Magesa, an experienced African liberation and moral theologian, who approaches the ethics of African religion from African moral traditions, argues that in African thought, the main characteristic of the human person is not individuation; rather, it is relatedness.[39] While discussing the African specificity of human rights, viewed as a concept of human dignity, Richard N. Rwiza affirms that human dignity is foundational in providing proper relations with society. He further states that African ethics upholds individual identity and that a person's identity is not overshadowed by the community. Rather, her/his identity is respected. For this reason, while it is true that Africans value their group identity, it is also understood that an African woman does not lose her individual identity. Rather, she is defined by means of her relationality.[40] She cannot realize herself as a person all by herself. She becomes a person in relationship with others.

John S. Mbiti, a Christian religious philosopher, captures well African communitarianism, that is, African notions of interrelatedness and interdependence, in the following: "I am because we are and since we are I am."[41] This means that a woman is from the very beginning part of a network of relations that constitute her inalienable dignity, a dignity that is always to be respected.[42] Since she is part of the communion, she wishes to have a voice in what goes on in her community. Therefore, to make any impact in the lives of the general society, the church in Africa has also to model and bring out clearly this communitarian spirit by ensuring that no member is isolated, marginalized, ostracized, or discriminated against because of gender, through traditional practices and beliefs, or in political judgment. Constance Bansikiza identifies the dimensions of moral formation from an African perspective as human, religious, economic, and political. He points out that all members of the African community are expected to learn and internalize the rules and the expectations of their respective communities so as to think and act accordingly.[43] Education and having a voice in societal matters are avenues in which a woman can relate more effectively and constructively in building a more peaceful community.

Conclusion

In his critical observation of the challenges of inculturation, and in his discussion on "Mistaken Developments," Bujo states that a person who wishes to bestow life in fullness on African communities must find new paths in all those areas where tradition must be preserved. At the same time, the modern context must be taken into account. Bujo asserts that the church and theologians cannot be excused from this task. In fact, the Christian message must undoubtedly critique the culture in such matters, but this can succeed only if it acknowledges the tradition and points to a more promising alternative such as the centrality of the Cross in Christianity.[44]

From this perspective, one of Africa's big challenges is ensuring that women's voices are heard in various spheres and that those voices are educated and strong. Educating and empowering women gives them their own voice of authority and liberates them from all that they are not and makes them what they are meant to be: fully women, fully human. Since the church is keen to see that the conflict and violence in Africa come to an end, it is necessary for women's voices to be heard, given that they are the strength that keeps African families and communities together. This includes sustained focus on the issue of women's oppression until it is eradicated as well as offering more opportunities and encouraging African women to study theology at higher levels, particularly in moral theology and ethics. Although this is being made possible thanks to the Catholic Theological Ethics in the World Church (CTEWC)'s scholarship for African women, there is a need to promote these issues continuously and conscientiously, and to educate African society on the importance and value of educating women. Doing so would enable Africa women and the community as a whole to challenge oppressive and corrupt systems and structures, be they in church or in society. There is need for the African woman to reflect upon her African traditions, since this appraisal will enable her to assess the validity and relevance of African traditions to her social context today. Therefore, equipping African women with a holistic education is one way of envisioning a new and inclusive African community in which a woman has a hearing, a public voice, and actively participates in the process of reconciliation, justice, and peace.

Notes

1. Cletus N. Chukwu, *Introduction to Philosophy in an African Perspective* (Nairobi: Zapf Chancery Research Consultants and Publishers, 2002), 257.

2. John Paul II, *Tertio Millennio Adveniente*, no. 51.

3. John Paul II, *Christifideles Laici*, no. 49.

4. Anna Mary Mukamwezi Kayonga, "African Women and Morality," in J. N. K. Mugambi and Ann Nasimiyu-Wasike, eds., *Moral and Ethical Issues in African Christianity: A Challenge for African Christianity* (Nairobi: Acton Publishers, 2003), 137–51, 143–44.

5. Vatican Council II, *Gaudium et Spes*, no. 74.

6. Congregation for Catholic Education, *Consecrated Persons and Their Mission in Schools: Reflections and Guidelines* (Rome, 2002), no. 80.

7. Kayonga, "African Women and Morality," 143.

8. John Paul II, *Jubilee of Government Leaders, Members of Parliament and Politicians: Address of His Holiness Pope John Paul II*, no. 2.

9. UNAIDS, *UNAIDS Report on the Global AIDS Epidemic 2012: The Global Epidemic at a Glance*, http://www.unaids.org.

10. UNAIDS, *Regional Fact Sheet 2012: Sub-Sahara Africa*, http://www.unaids.org.

11. Ibid.

12. Mary Jo Iozzio, Mary M. Doyle Roche, and Elsie M. Miranda, eds., *Calling for Justice throughout the World: Catholic Women Theologians on the HIV/AIDS Pandemic* (New York: Continuum, 2008), 46–47.

13. Ephigenia W. Gachiri, *Female Circumcision* (Nairobi: Paulines Publications Africa, 2000), 29–34.

14. Bénézet Bujo, *Foundations of an African Ethics: Beyond the Universal Claims of Western Morality* (Nairobi: Paulines Publications Africa, 2003), 170–71.

15. Ibid., 163–65.

16. Bujo, *The Ethical Dimension of Community: The African Model and the Dialogue between North and South*, 1st Reprint (Nairobi: Paulines Publications Africa, 2010), 128.

17. Paul Barry Clarke and Andrew Linzey, eds., *Dictionary of Ethics, Theology and Society*, Reprint (New York: Routledge, 1997), 273.

18. Susan Chebet and Ton Dietz, *Climbing the Cliff: A History of the Keiyo* (Eldoret: Moi University Press, 2000), 60.

19. Kayonga, "African Women and Morality," 140.

20. Markus Barth, *The Anchor Bible. Ephesians: Translation and Commentary on Chapter 4–6* (New York: Doubleday, 1974), 609–11.

21. Annette Merz and Brian McNeil, "Why Did the Pure Bride of Christ (2 Cor. 11.2) Become a Wedded Wife (Eph. 5:22–33)? Theses about the Intertextual Transformation of an Ecclesiological Metaphor," *Journal for the Study of the New Testament* 79 (2000): 131–47, at 132.

22. Margaret Y. MacDonald and Daniel Harrington, eds., *Sacra Pagina: Colossians and Ephesians*, vol. 17 (Collegeville, MN: Liturgical Press, 2000), 341.

23. UNESCO, *Adult and Youth Literacy*, http://www.uis.unesco.org/.

24. Kayonga, "African Women and Morality," 144.

25. Pius XI, *Divini Illius Magistri*, no. 11.

26. *Gravissimum Educationis*, no. 1.

27. Ibid.

28. *Divini Illius Magistri*, no. 34.

29. Chebet and Dietz, *Climbing the Cliff*, 61.

30. Constance Bansikiza, *Restoring Moral Formation in Africa*, 1st Reprint (Eldoret: AMECEA Gaba Publications, 2003), 6.

31. Kayonga, "African Women and Morality," 144.

32. Chukwu, *Introduction to Philosophy in an African Perspective*, 257–59.

33. Christina L. H. Trina, *Feminist Ethics and Natural Law: The End of the Anathemas* (Washington, DC: Georgetown University Press, 1999), 116.

34. Pontifical Council for Justice and Peace: *Compendium of the Social Doctrine of the Church* (Nairobi: Paulines Publication Africa, 2008), nos. 109, 114.

35. John Paul II, *Mulieris Dignitatem*, no. 12.

36. Raymond Brown, "The Gospel According to John: 1–X11," in *The Anchor Bible* (New York: Doubleday, 1966), 180.

37. *Mulieris Dignitatem*, nos. 12–13.

38. *Compendium of the Social Doctrine of the Church*, no. 108.

39. Laurenti Magesa, *Anatomy of Inculturation* (Nairobi: Paulines Publication Africa, 2004), 93.

40. Richard N. Rwiza, *Ethics of Human Rights: The African Contribution* (Nairobi: CUEA Press, 2010), 158–59.

41. John S. Mbiti, *African Religions and Philosophy* (New York: Doubleday, 1970), 108.

42. Bujo, *Foundations of an African Ethics*, 116–20.

43. Bansikiza, *Restoring Moral Formation in Africa*, 15.

44. Bujo, *Foundations of an African Ethics*, 170–71.

THE CHURCH'S ANTIRETROVIRAL TREATMENT IN SOUTH AFRICA

Alison Munro

Introduction

Since 2004, the Catholic Church in South Africa has placed over 40,000 people diagnosed with AIDS on antiretroviral (ARV) treatment, with funding from the U.S. President's Emergency Plan for AIDS Relief (PEPFAR). The situation in South Africa, chronic though it still is in regard to ARV treatment needs, is no longer viewed as an emergency, and negotiations are under way between U.S. and South African authorities concerning future (decreased and different) support to South Africa, which has the unenviable record of being the country with the highest number of people with the HIV infection and the highest number of people on ARV treatment in the world.

The church is involved in its own negotiations with the South African Department of Health (DOH) concerning ongoing treatment for patients, once PEPFAR funding is no longer available, and with PEPFAR officials concerning decreasing budgets, drug supply, and new patient targets over the remaining years of the program. South Africa does need to take more responsibility for the health care needs of its citizens than it was willing and able to do in the past, but it still has insufficient infrastructure and human capacity across the country to provide treatment to everyone in need of it. There are concerns about transferring patients out of a functioning church-based program (and out of PEPFAR-funded programs generally), and about potentially losing the skills of many church (and other) personnel, highly trained through the PEPFAR program. These concerns have a bearing, direct and indirect, on the Southern African Catholic Bishops' Conference (SACBC) AIDS Office and the response of the Catholic Church to AIDS in South Africa.

The Beginnings of the PEPFAR-funded ARV Treatment Program

The South African Catholic Church's treatment program began in late 2003 with a grant from the Dutch Catholic funder Cordaid. It was rapidly scaled up as part of a nine-country award to Catholic Relief Services (CRS)[1] and implemented by the SACBC AIDS Office, from 2004, with PEPFAR Track 1 funding. Over the five years of the Track 1 program, the SACBC AIDS Office opened twenty-three treatment sites, most of them at home-based care (HBC) sites run under the auspices of the Catholic Church, many of which had received their initial home-based care funding through the SACBC AIDS Office from Catholic and other donor agencies.

The SACBC AIDS treatment program had the approval of the national DOH, but it battled, in some instances, to get the approval of the provincial DOH of the relevant provinces in which it was operational. Those were the days of denialism in South Africa, with the South African government not providing an all-out concerted effort to fight the pandemic. People were dying because treatment was not available in the public sector. There were tensions in some provinces between the church program and DOH facilities, which sometimes viewed the church program as a parallel structure. Much has changed in the intervening years, and the church is, by and large, viewed as a credible partner in the delivery of treatment services. There is, nonetheless, more work that needs to be done to build collaboration in public-private partnerships.

Expansion and Consolidation

As the DOH scaled up its treatment response and sites opened in health districts in different parts of the country over the next number of years, the SACBC AIDS Office was able to transfer a number of its patients from smaller centers with relatively few patients into the public health system. Withdrawing from them allowed the SACBC AIDS Office to add to patient numbers where the need for treatment was often greater because of the higher rates of infection in certain parts of the country. The biggest site, St Mary's Hospital, a major Catholic hospital in Mariannhill Diocese, KwaZulu Natal Province, owned by a religious congregation of sisters, serves as a public sector hospital and receives a subsidy from the DOH. It became a PEPFAR recipient in its own right when funding was transferred in "PEPFAR II" to local indigenous organizations. It, too, now faces the challenge of transferring patients into public health clinics in its catchment area.

The SACBC AIDS Office was able to withdraw, in all, from ten sites, and currently, in PEPFAR II, it is continuing to work with thirteen treatment sites, each of which has several satellite treatment centers situated close to where people live and often operating out of churches or church-owned buildings. In some instances, counseling of patients is done in the church, and treatment is provided in the sacristy. Elsewhere, shipping containers and "park homes" provide the setting for services if there is no clinic building—or none that is big enough. The SACBC AIDS Office PEPFAR-funded treatment program is in its final fifteen months and has intensified the phase of ensuring the sustainability of patient treatment for current patients beyond the PEPFAR grant period.

Ensuring Sustainability

CRS "transitioned" the PEPFAR award to the SACBC AIDS Office at the end of the first five years of the program. The expectation from PEPFAR was that U.S.-based organizations would hand over leadership of programs to indigenous organizations. This was intended as both a cost-cutting measure and a means to transfer skills. The SACBC AIDS Office was the first program to complete this transition; this accomplishment owed its success to the good working relations between CRS in South Africa and the SACBC AIDS Office. Now in phase two, the SACBC AIDS Office is in the process of transferring its program into various public-private partnerships to ensure long-term care and treatment for patients.

Negotiations are under way in all the provinces in which the SACBC AIDS Office program currently operates to ensure that the ARV drugs are received from the DOH so that patient treatment is not interrupted once PEPFAR funding is discontinued. Some of these negotiations are directly between the SACBC AIDS Office and the relevant DOH structures at the provincial and district or municipal level. In other instances, the deliberations involve the Centers for Disease Control (CDC),[2] the U.S. agency acting on behalf of PEPFAR, and the U.S. government, along with their South African counterparts. PEPFAR is looking at ways that will both allow South Africa to support the health care of its citizens and at the same time provide ongoing U.S. support for treatment in which it has invested millions of dollars over the past several years. PEPFAR's financial support for treatment[3] in South Africa is now less than what the DOH is spending, but the expertise built with PEPFAR support, directly and through nongovernmental organizations (NGOs) and faith-based organizations, needs to continue to help underpin the still struggling local programs in different ways.

Several Catholic facilities in the current program have recently begun receiving part of their drug supply from the DOH in their respective provinces. In other instances, the negotiating process is slow. Some provinces wish to supply the drugs and laboratory services directly to the church projects; this has to do both with their recognizing the quality care and service provided at church sites and the knowledge that sustainable provision of ARV treatment is the issue at stake. Many DOH facilities are not yet in a position to provide the services.

CDC is also slated to fund a centralized drug supply mechanism, and the purchase of ARV drugs on DOH tenders, for church and NGO projects currently providing treatment. This is a cost-cutting exercise but also part of the transfer of the PEPFAR program to DOH. It is known that PEPFAR-purchased drugs are more expensive than those purchased under the South African government tenders.

Public-Private Partnership Models Currently Unfolding

Two diocesan projects will close as church treatment programs by the end of the 2012 financial year, as they transfer all their patients to public sector clinics in places where there was previously no DOH-provided treatment when PEPFAR funding began in 2004. The church had its program in remote places before the DOH had even begun to provide treatment in the health subdistricts concerned. The DOH program is now better able to absorb the patients, and it makes sense that the church discontinues treatment services. This model, the transfer by the church of patients to DOH facilities, has been applied in most instances in which the church has, so far, withdrawn from providing services.

A second model looks at the provision of drugs and laboratory tests to the Catholic facilities by the DOH, with PEPFAR continuing for the moment to fund the personnel and administrative costs. Negotiations and discussions have often highlighted the fact that the DOH infrastructure on its own in the areas concerned is unable to handle additional patient numbers. The DOH is nonetheless committed to providing the drugs and laboratory services, with the church providing services to patients. This is the preferred model, with the church committed to continue serving patients, and with the support of DOH-funded drugs and laboratory services. It does assume that the church projects concerned will continue to be able to access the funding needed to support personnel and facility costs. It opens up whole new areas of collaboration between the church programs and the DOH. Not all who are involved understand all the dynamics and processes at play, and progress is often slow.

A third option involves the DOH requesting that the patients of some satellite centers of the main church site be transferred to their nearest government clinics, while the main treatment site itself receives DOH drugs and continues to initiate patients on treatment. Some of the challenges are different from those experienced in the other models, in particular around public-private partnerships, but as is the case in the second model above, what is called for is a commitment of partners to the patients who need to receive treatment services. Learning to work with DOH partners has not always been easy for church projects.

Sometimes, in models two and three, the church site is a referral center of public sector facilities, and in a few instances the church is supplying personnel to operate the DOH program. Given that funding dynamics will change and unfold in as-yet-unknown ways, one needs to appreciate the flexibility necessary to ensure quality patient care in evolving situations.

Drug and Laboratory Services

The most costly components of the SACBC AIDS Office program are the ARV drugs and the laboratory tests. Half of the SACBC AIDS Office's current treatment budget goes to pay for these costs, though with the provision of some DOH-supplied drugs, this fact is changing. Drugs that may be purchased under the PEPFAR grant have to have Food and Drug Administration (FDA) and Medicines Control Council (MCC) approval,[4] and while some drugs are generics, there still remains a high number of drugs that are patented and more costly than those the

South African DOH is using. Because of budget constraints, the SACBC AIDS Office program has also had to ensure that only specified laboratory tests are undertaken by doctors working with patients: the tests that are necessary, and not those that are "nice to have."

From the outset of the program, the SACBC AIDS Office undertook to adhere in its program to approved South African DOH drug regimens. This has facilitated the transfer of patients to DOH clinics and elsewhere. In a place where an overenthusiastic doctor had prescribed drugs that were not recognized as part of the DOH regimens, the SACBC AIDS Office had to ensure that these particular drugs were replaced by others before transfers of patients to other facilities could take place.

The results of a drug trial released in Washington and Johannesburg in late May 2011 gave some new hope to people with HIV. The results indicate that the earlier people go on treatment, the less likely they are to transmit HIV. Currently in South Africa, most people are put on treatment if they have a CD4 count of less than 200,[5] despite the new recommended guideline of a CD4 count of 350 and less for all patients, not just those who have tuberculosis (TB) and women who are pregnant. Already there are concerns about the cost implications related to the 350 CD4 count—clearly there are huge budget implications around this because more people, both in theory and in fact, will be on treatment.

Foreign Nationals and Treatment

The sociopolitical situation of Sub-Saharan Africa plays out in various scenarios in the arena of AIDS. South Africa is home to numerous refugees and asylum seekers from a number of countries in Africa. About 85 percent of the patients of one of the church-run treatment sites in Johannesburg is from elsewhere in Africa: the Democratic Republic of Congo, Malawi, Zambia, Zimbabwe, or Cameroon. There are patients who travel from Mozambique once a month to collect their drugs rather than deal with stigma in their own communities and countries. Some of these patients are, over time, being referred to treatment facilities in their countries of origin (particularly Zimbabweans), but some possibly fall through the cracks in the process. The Johannesburg church facility that serves mainly foreigners has done tremendous work in referring patients on treatment, who have the required documentation to be in South Africa, to local clinics. Good contact has been made with several clinics in Zimbabwe, from where most foreign nationals come for referrals. One obvious outcome of being able to refer stable patients elsewhere is that new patients can be initiated into treatment in an environment where they feel safe. Commendable though it is for the program to reach out to foreign nationals, one is also only too aware of the fragility of such an initiative in the grand scheme of events, when people are also likely to move on elsewhere, possibly even returning to their countries of origin, and possibly defaulting on treatment.

The Challenges to Provision of Treatment in South Africa

There are major challenges to the provision of treatment in South Africa, some of which are listed below, not in any special order of priority:

- The provision and procurement of drugs and laboratory tests, and the related costs, at current funding levels, is at some point unsustainable.
- Sometimes societal, cultural, and religious beliefs are obstacles to patients accessing treatment or remaining on treatment. Family members may insist that patients consult traditional healers rather than clinicians trained in ARV treatment management or that they desist from ARV treatment once it appears that their health is improving.
- Women access treatment more than men do. Roughly two-thirds of the country's patients are women, with people in general continuing to present themselves for treatment very late in the disease.
- Only small numbers of children are accessing treatment, often because of the difficulties around the consent of guardians or their lack of information, and the challenges that continue to be experienced, even by clinicians, around the treatment of children. More attention needs to be given to the needs of children and adolescents, and to the question of teenage pregnancies.
- Fear of the results also causes some people to avoid being tested and causes parents and relatives to refuse consent for the testing of their children. As a result, many people do not know their status and infect their partners.
- Stigma remains a huge barrier to access. There are well-documented case studies of people living with HIV, even educated people, who would rather die than present themselves for treatment.
- Lack of a culture of confidentiality in many small communities discourages people from disclosing their status and from seeking care from their local clinics.
- Dire social conditions faced by the poor, including unemployment, lack of adequate housing, poor delivery of basic services in underresourced townships and rural villages and in more than 2,000 informal shack settlements, a crumbling education system, and a vulnerable health care system are part of the reality facing the country and putting a strain on access to basic health services.
- South Africa has insufficient numbers of trained health personnel in the public sector to meet the country's health care needs beyond HIV. Newly trained nurses in Nurse Initiated Management of Antiretroviral Treatment (NIMART) often lack the confidence to make diagnoses for treatment in the absence of a mentor.
- There are still too many health workers who display a judgmental attitude toward people living with HIV. This is one factor causing people to

postpone care until they are very ill. Some still have the view that it is the patients' "fault" that they are infected and that they are not as deserving of care as are others.

- The country does not yet have a national patient data management system in place. New systems are in the development phase but are not yet in a position to manage data coming from the different provinces in a single national system.
- TB is not always accurately diagnosed and, consequently, not always treated. TB/HIV coinfection is an enormous challenge in South Africa.

Each of these points is a sober reminder of the enormity of the tasks and challenges to be addressed in an ongoing way, notwithstanding the huge gains and financial investments already made.

Some Current and Ongoing Questions for Ethical Reflection

Entering into an ARV treatment program was, from the beginning, an ethical question for the SACBC AIDS Office, notwithstanding the church's concern for the dignity of human life. Providing treatment was, in itself, deemed a good thing, with people being given a second chance and recovering rather than dying, regaining the ability to assume responsibilities for their own families and children in particular, and returning to work. There were, however, always the underlying questions around long-term commitment to patients and funding of the drugs, services, and personnel involved, given the donor component of the program. People who "expect" the church to provide treatment (or anything else for that matter) usually assume that the church has money and can afford to pay. Who could be supported on treatment and who not, given the limits of funding available? Who would pick up the costs, and what would happen to people once specific funding was no longer available? What if patients defaulted on treatment and drug resistance followed? These questions and others were indeed debated and the decision made that the saving and prolongation of human lives was the immediate good to be undertaken. Criteria for selection of patients had, nonetheless, to be developed given the limits to resources and infrastructure, and included, among others, that patients had to live in the geographic area, had to show commitment to adherence to the drugs provided even before ARV treatment proper began, and had to be willing to disclose their status to a family member or buddy. Adherence training includes a period of time in which patients take treatment for opportunistic infections before beginning ARV treatment itself. One result of the criterion related to geographic location was the consequence of including many foreign nationals in the program. Because of the specific circumstances around their being there, sometimes undocumented and keeping their options open for better jobs and living conditions, it became clearer over time that some of them would, in fact, return to countries of origin or settle elsewhere in South Africa. Doctors and nurses determining who qualified for treatment clinically could not be expected to recognize various scenarios that could, and did, play out in the socioeconomic and political arena.

The questions remain, but some are now differently nuanced, and there are additional ones. For patients being transferred to DOH facilities, concerns now are about patient follow-up and the quality of care in a system that is not always perceived to put patients' needs first and that does not have the personnel and infrastructure to assume the total burden of care. Can the church continue to provide care to patients it had initiated on treatment and who are now being treated in the DOH system? Will these services be offered in a voluntary capacity? What does this collaboration for the good of patients actually look like in practice? Also, what happens to some/all of the people trained under PEPFAR to provide treatment services who are possibly/actually no longer employed in church projects? Some personnel trained in church programs will be absorbed by the DOH and will provide much-needed additions to the cadre of health personnel in the country. This may not be true of some less-qualified caregivers and counselors. Are church personnel able to work with the DOH in providing patient support and follow-up services, knowing that once patients leave church treatment facilities, there is a greater chance that some of them will default on treatment, given that strict adherence monitoring and tracing of those not turning up for treatment is not always part of the DOH protocols?

Patients themselves do not want to move away from church treatment facilities because of the care they have received. It is often difficult for them to understand that they need to move elsewhere as funding realities change. A patient delegation at a facility I visited, for instance, had their arguments ready, providing me with every reason they could why the church should not even consider transferring them elsewhere for treatment. They are beneficiaries of clinical services but also of the church's social teaching in action. They named its effects as they saw them, which included staff opening the clinic after hours to accommodate someone who couldn't be there during clinic hours for fear of losing her job, taking time with individual patients and their families, praying with them, assisting them in accessing income-generating activities, employing some of them in the program, and recognizing their rights as human beings. Both locals and foreign nationals who are asked to move experience fears of being discriminated against: for having AIDS-related illnesses, for having been started on treatment in church projects in the first place. Anxiety in foreigners is often compounded by their circumstances.

Condom use remains a perpetual dilemma. Our SACBC AIDS Office position over many years has been that people need to be informed of the church's teachings on sexual behavior before and within marriage; equally, they need to be given the correct information about the efficacy of condoms when properly used. After that they need to make their own informed decisions and follow their consciences. The facts in practice are often clouded by statements by church officials and by the public's willingness (often through the media) to castigate the church as a kind of scapegoat for the ongoing transmission of HIV. Every time we negotiate with DOH officials, we have to find some way of constructively addressing the issue. Many (though not all) DOH personnel are of the opinion that the church's position (or perceived position in some cases) is a major obstacle in the fight against AIDS and certainly something that has to be dealt with if the DOH and church are to work together. The added complication at present in ongoing negotiations around the future and continued provision of treatment is the fact that the DOH expects facilities it supports, for example, with ARV drugs, to also provide condoms. On the face of it, and certainly for ill-informed DOH officials, it could look like "No condoms from the Church, no drugs from the DOH." The SACBC AIDS Office has maintained its position, with knowledge of the fact that nurses and counselors working at the grassroots in our facilities are often those who have to work in sometimes very difficult circumstances related to the issue.

Prevention of HIV infection remains a deeply challenging issue. Even if the rate of infection is coming down in certain areas, and among certain sectors of the population, the fact remains that too many people continue to be infected on a daily basis in the country. If people were to take more responsibility for their personal behaviors, some of these infections could be avoided. This is indeed a difficult area for moral theology. People bear the consequences of bad personal choices, and these have repercussions on others as new infections spread among different people. Clearly, there are also people who bear the consequence of structural injustices and social realities over which they, as individuals, have little control: women and girls who are raped, women and children who see prostitution or commercial sex work as a means of holding families together when there is no employment, communities where there is no social cohesion because of breakdown in societal norms and cultural values, migrant labor and resulting second families, and so on. It is all too easy to blame individuals in these circumstances, and all too often we do so from the comfort of a position where we don't personally have to deal with a breakdown in family life, unemployment, poor education, and lack of formal employment.

Some Concluding Remarks

It has been said that AIDS hit South Africa at a very bad time: when apartheid was being dismantled and a new democratic South Africa was being created. Put differently, priority was given in the 1990s and beyond to building a new country (a difficult enough endeavor even without the unfolding devastation caused by AIDS across the subcontinent). Poor training and capacity among AIDS workers was both a legacy of the apartheid system and a direct result of the AIDS pandemic that devastated communities and demanded that people with little background and skills in the areas concerned deliver services to patients, including children, made vulnerable to and by AIDS. Eighteen years into democracy, the socioeconomic and political challenges facing South Africa remain enormous. Urban informal settlement dwellers are often at the forefront of so-called service delivery protests, clamoring for houses, municipal services, employment, and improved infrastructure. Family life remains under siege; oftentimes children grow up in one-parent families, sometimes never knowing their fathers. Crime and corruption are often perceived to be the order of the day, even when crime statistics are said to be down on those of previous years. The new middle class is at times mercenary in its approach to making money, often at the expense of the poor.

Despite the efforts of the DOH, which has committed major resources to fighting AIDS, one can sometimes be forgiven for thinking that other problems the country is facing take precedence over the problems related to AIDS: hence, our recognition that there are no easy solutions to what the country faces.

Notes

1. Catholic Relief Services in Baltimore, USA, received a PEPFAR grant to implement treatment in nine countries, mostly in Africa.

2. CDC, headquartered in Atlanta, which manages several PEPFAR treatment grants in South Africa, has offices in Pretoria.

3. Now estimated at 10 percent of overall output, down considerably from what it was previously.

4. The FDA is the U.S. drug approval body, MCC the South African one.

5. This has to do with the very late presentation of people for treatment rather than with their being denied treatment at the higher CD4 count level.

THE ECCLESIA OF WOMEN IN ASIA: LIBERATING THEOLOGY

Sharon A. Bong

Introduction

In this essay, I foreground the theology and praxis of the Ecclesia of Women in Asia (EWA), a forum of feminist Catholic women doing theology in Asia. What does it mean for EWA, conceived and instituted in 2002, to do theology as "feminists," "Catholics," "Asians," and "women" in Asia in the twenty-first century?[1] I frame this assessment of EWA's decade of Asian feminist theologizing through the rubric of feminist standpoint epistemologies, to better show how its theology functions both as "successor knowledges" and as "subjugated knowledges"[2] within the pluralism of ethnicities, cultures, and religions in Asia.

EWA's mission, theologizing from the mind, heart, and bowels of Asia, lies in its commitment to "the formation of inclusive and just ecclesial communities and societies by theologizing from Asian women's perspectives and recognizing Asian Catholic women as equal partners in the life of the Church."[3] It aims to

1. gather the voices of Asian Catholic women theologians and make them heard;
2. give visibility to the contribution of Asian women in shaping and transforming the church and world;
3. express the desire of women to be respected as fully responsible ecclesial partners and leaders in the life of the church;
4. recognize and actualize woman as image of God; and
5. endeavor to build communities that are inclusive, equitable, sustainable, and just at local, regional, and global levels.

EWA's objective is to encourage and assist Catholic women in Asia to engage in research, reflection, and writing toward doing theology that "is inculturated and contextualized in Asian realities; builds on the spiritual experience and praxis of the socially excluded; promotes mutuality and the integrity of creation; and dialogues with other disciplines, Christian denominations and faiths."[4] To meet these aims and objectives, it organizes a biennial conference that serves as a platform where Asian Catholic women's theologizing is not only heard and reflected on but also published. Through the five biennial conferences held to date, conversations have been initiated and sustained among religious and laywomen, academic, pastoral, and grassroots women, as well as women from other faiths and beyond Asia, including partnerships with, among others, the global network of Catholic Theological Ethics in the World Church. In addition, in the two-year interim between each conference, conversations flourish in cyberspace.

As a body of feminist Catholic women theologizing in Asia, EWA's theology and praxis, articulated in the publication of its four edited volumes, offers a groundbreaking collection of knowledge: unique and impactful, particularly given its genesis and its narrative of becoming. Evelyn Monteiro (a founding member of EWA), in her keynote address delivered at the inaugural conference that witnessed the birthing of EWA, attributes the difficulty in identifying Catholic women theologians to "the near invisibility of women . . . [that] reveals a reality that Asian Catholic women theologians are either not known or they are small in number."[5] EWA's genesis, wrought from this invisibility and concomitant silence (hence the significance of the first conference theme—"Gathering the voices of the silenced"), through the mobilization of Catholic women theologians in Asia into a movement in the twenty-first century and the formalization of EWA through the adoption of its constitution and bylaws, are the bases upon which I draw the parallel between EWA's theologizing and feminist standpoint epistemologies. EWA's four edited volumes (the fifth is forthcoming) are titled after its respective conference themes: *Ecclesia of Women: Gathering the Voices of the Silenced* (edited by Evelyn Monteiro and Antoinette Gutzler); *Body and Sexuality: Theological-Pastoral Perspectives of Women in Asia* (edited by Agnes M. Brazal and Andrea Lizares Si); *Re-imagining Marriage and Family in Asia: Asian Christian Women's Perspectives* (edited by Sharon A. Bong and Pushpa Joseph); and *Feminist Theology of Liberation Asian Perspectives: Practicing Peace* (edited by Judette A. Gallares and Astrid Lobo-Gajiwala).[6]

Let us count the ways in which EWA's theologizing constitutes a feminist standpoint epistemology.[7] First, the nature of its theologizing is grounded in lived realities and the Asian context. Second, its foundational "biases" imbibe a feminist ethos and an inclusive praxis. Third, these give rise to its truth-claims in starting thought and theology from the embodied narratives of Asia's poor in general, and poor women in particular, which in turn authenticates its theologizing. The sum worth of EWA's theologizing, as feminist, Catholic, and Asian, constitutes a feminist standpoint epistemology. A standpoint is defined as a "morally and scientifically preferable grounding for our interpretations and explanations of nature and social life."[8] It is therefore not disembodied from the material, temporal, and spatial conditions of both social researcher and subjects of knowledge (that is, those studied) who inhabit the social order.

In the first section of this essay, I show how EWA's theologizing as a feminist standpoint epistemology is, in the first instance, successor knowledge. In the second section of the essay, I show how EWA's theologizing is also a subjugated knowledge. It engenders an "oppositional consciousness"[9] in forging its own voice and identity from preceding knowledge. It validates knowledge that is contextualized and situated in insisting upon the agency of social actors or those studied and engendering a transformative and emancipatory methodology.

Successor Knowledge

EWA's theologizing is successor knowledge to two centuries of thought and theology that had preceded it and more, when one considers the ideologies of ancient civilizations borne from the wellsprings of Asia. What follows in this section are selected threads of thoughts and theologies that inform the theologizing of EWA.

From the beginning—the genesis of EWA—inspiration was drawn from Pope John XXIII's "bold reference to the rights of women" as articulated in his encyclical of 1963, *Pacem in Terris*, where he states that "Since women are becoming more conscious of their human dignity, they will not tolerate being treated as inanimate objects or mere instruments, but claim...the rights and duties that befit a human person."[10] Reference was also made to the Asian Synod of 1999, *Ecclesia in Asia*, that voiced a "special concern for women, whose situation remains a serious problem in Asia."[11]

In envisioning an Asian women's ecclesiology, critical departures ensue. Monteiro is cognizant of not "creating a reverse order of hegemony" but rather "entrusts the women-Church to birth an alternate model of being Church in Asia, namely, an ecclesia of partnership-discipleship in Asia."[12] This model of becoming church is enshrined in EWA's mission statement and aims as stated above. Antoinette Gutzler reimagines the *ekklesia*, the "magisterium of women," which is integrated with the "*magisterium* of the poor" in heralding the third epoch of Christianity, post–Vatican II, in Asia.[13] She draws on Karl Rahner's analyses of the "three epochs of the church's history"—the transitioning from a Jewish Christianity to a Gentile Christianity in the first epoch, to the movement of Christianity into Hellenism and European culture and civilization in the second epoch, to the "defining moment" that is Vatican II.[14] She extends Rahner's reflection on the "self-actualization" of the church as a "world Church" that, in the context of Asia, needs to evolve from a "local church *in* Asia" (as a literal offshoot of the colonial heritage of Christianity in most parts of Asia) to a "local church *of* Asia" (transplanting and hybridizing Christianity in Asia given the complexity of Asian Christians as a religious minority in Asia, the Philippines excepted).[15] She further adopts Aloysius Pieris's affirmation of the "magisterium of the poor," albeit with a gendered lens, by insisting on a magisterium of the poor women of Asia, which offers "transforming grace" in realizing the vision of a "world church" in Asia.[16] This, in turn, authenticates the church in Asia—"from whence comes this authority [to speak]"—actualized by the *Ekklesia* of Women in Asia through its ethos of inclusivity.

The women theologians of Asia are not all poor, by virtue of their capacity to access the body of feminist theorizing and theologizing. Pushpa Joseph demystifies the cult of ideal Indian womanhood—the "epic-heroine type" and the "mother-goddess"[17] by drawing on Elisabeth Schüssler Fiorenza's critique of "alleged 'voluntarism'" of women who internalize feminine values such as "submission, self-sacrifice, and self-denying love";[18] employing the work of Uma Narayan, a feminist-postcolonial theorist who argues against seeing feminism as a "western" construct, a ploy used by some to discredit feminism as a resource for women's empowerment;[19] and offering a comparative textual analysis of Sojourner Truth's poem "Ain't I a Woman?" Truth was an African American slave and subsequently hailed as a womanist (black feminist).[20] Gemma Cruz draws on Fiorenza's identification of "religious-cultural kyriarchal politics of 'femininity'" that serves as a barrier to the emancipation of survivors of domestic violence,[21] Elsa Tamez's demystification of "machismo" culture that naturalizes male violence against female submission, and Mary John Mananzan's attribution of the problematic biblical exhortation to wives to "submit" to their husbands as justification for domestic violence.[22] Jeane Peracullo, in arguing for the need to transcend the impasse of pro-life/pro-choice labels and embrace instead a holistic sense of the "body-self," draws from Simone de Beauvoir, the existentialist feminist who, in deconstructing biologism (biology-is-destiny), advocates a "flight from the body" or materiality as a source of women's oppression;[23] eco-feminists, such as Mary Daly, who valorize the alignment of women and nature;[24] and a "feminist ethic of care" proposed by Carol Gilligan.[25] In particular, she draws from feminist theologian Agnes M. Brazal and feminist theorist Marilen Danguilan, the former on "doing a phenomenology of *pakikipagkapwa*" that potentially facilitates mutuality and reciprocity and the latter on having compassion that leads us to "respect a woman's right and freedom to be in control of her own life."[26]

The women theologians of Asia are rich by virtue of their access to the deep reserves of culture and spiritualities of Asia. Pushpa Joseph reclaims *eros* by tracing its genealogy in Greek philosophy to the Platonic ideal of the human premised on the dualism of mind/body and suggesting a return to *eros* as *sakti* in Tantric philosophy, "the creative energy" that emanates from God.[27] She does this to celebrate women's "bodiliness."[28] Nozomi Miura reclaims the "Asian sense of body" that eschews a mind/body split in its experience of a "psychic and somatic unity [of] body and soul" and uses the analogy of a *stupa*, which can be correlated in Buddhist traditions to a human body, to show the sacredness of the human body.[29] Julia Ong looks to the Muslim tradition of invoking "ninety-nine names of God . . . [where] the one hundredth name is SILENCE" in proliferating meaningful images of God.[30] This is notable, given the impetus behind the conceptualization of EWA—the "gathering of the voices of the silenced."

Subjugated Knowledge

EWA's theologizing is a subjugated knowledge in its deconstructive capacity:
the ways that it departs from masculinist theorizing and theologizing, and challenges institutionally driven sexism and systemic gender-based violence perpetrated
within the family, faith community, the church, the state, and globally. It is also a
subjugated knowledge in its reconstructivist capacity in engendering a transformative and emancipatory theologizing for men, women, and creation. It does so by
starting thought and theology from the lived realities of Asia's poor, in general, and
Asia's poor women, in particular. Epistemic privilege is thus accorded to the disenfranchised who "know" because poverty, suffering, and marginalization are written
on their bodies. In "gathering the voices of the silenced," EWA invests agency onto
them. These include Filipina domestic helpers in Hong Kong who "number more
than 150,000 and are subjected to gendered violence economically, physically and
sexually and unjust working conditions that are body-negating experiences;"[31]
Taiwanese sex workers who amid the feminist debates of either viewing sex work
as work or as a degradation, show how one should refrain from the platitude of
saying to them "'Do something else,' without first walking in their shoes to see how
many options they really have;"[32] aging Korean women who are struggling to come
to terms with their body-image of "torn-to-pieces-hood" within a "spirituality of
imperfection;"[33] and survivors of clergy sexual misconduct in the Philippines who
make visible the complicity of "religio-cultural roots of violence against women."[34]

Theologizing from the lived realities of the disenfranchised is sound theology,
since a theology that matters is one that is embodied. Gemma Cruz proposes an
"embodied theology" that more deeply explores the incarnation—God, out of love
for humankind, "[takes] on human flesh in the person of the historical Jesus"—in
reclaiming the bodily integrity of Filipina domestic helpers. She articulates also
a "theology of daily reality" to recuperate the routinized activities pertaining to
housework and caregiving, to reinvest dignity in the work performed by Filipina
domestic helpers.[35] Agnes M. Brazal posits an "intercultural hermeneutics"[36] as a
"Christian feminist peace praxis"[37] in foregrounding women as having the greater
propensity toward cultural sensitivity and inclusiveness in mediating between
cultures, particularly ones that are gender discriminating. Brazal's theologizing
draws on the Filipino concept of "*pakikipagkapwa* (having regard for or relating
to another)"[38] that she connects with the Trinitarian God to show how interculturality is intrinsic to both as they are "characterized by relationality, equality in
diversity, creativity, and fecundity."[39] Sophie Lizares-Bodegon and Andrea Lizares
Si posit an "eco-feminist theology" that bears the hallmarks of embracing the earth
and matter as "immanent" and "bio-centric," rather than "anthropocentric" and
being "missiological," in that it seeks to build "Communities of the Covenant" in
caring for all creation.[40]

The hallmark of EWA's maturation in its narrative of becoming as Asian,
feminist, and Catholic is its inclusiveness of not only diverse viewpoints but

also of oppositional standpoints. As a successor knowledge, EWA's theologizing foregrounds the "Asian woman"—which is vital as an effect of identity politics that insists upon differences that matter: Asian women are oppressed differently and disproportionately. In doing so, a predominantly heterosexualized discourse, evident from the inexhaustible work involved in de-naturalizing the dualisms of man/woman, mind/body, violence/passivity, culture/nature, is offered. The discursive limits of employing such essentialism, however strategic—the identification as Asian women in advancing Asian feminist theologizing—becomes apparent with the turn to Asian queer theologizing. EWA's subjugated knowledge includes Judette Gallares' reconstructionist approach in rereading the silencing of the apostle Junia through her "sex change," where her masculinization masks her prominence, stature, and authority as a "woman in leadership;"[41] and Sharon A. Bong's "epistemology of the sacred body" that emerges from the "faith experience" of gay, lesbian, bisexual, transgender, intersex, queer, and questioning persons whose ways of knowing integrate a queering of hermeneutics (the "view from above") and the everyday tension of self-identifying as Christian and gay (the "view from below").[42]

Conclusion

EWA's Asian feminist theologizing, seen as both successor and subjugated knowledge, questions underlying assumptions and grounds of knowledge production, posing questions such as the following: Whose knowledge? Who knows? How does one know (by seeing from above and below)?[43] Are we having it both ways—with universalized *and* contextualized truth claims?[44] In having it "both ways"—affirming love and the ethos of social justice as universal Christian values, and also starting theology from the particularized or situated realities of women and other marginalized people—EWA's Asian feminist theologizing liberates theology.

Notes

1. Members of EWA also comprise religious and laywomen who are based in Asia.
2. Knowledges are in the plural form to mark the diversity and oppositional voices.
3. On EWA's mission statement, aims, objectives, programs, and activities, see its website http://ecclesiaofwomen.ning.com/.
4. Ibid.
5. Evelyn Monteiro, "Keynote Address," in *Ecclesia of Women in Asia: Gathering the Voices of the Silenced*, ed. Evelyn Monteiro, SC and Antoinnette Gutzler, MM (Delhi: ISPCK, 2005), xvi.
6. EWA's fifth biennial conference held in 2011 was themed "Wired Asia: Towards an Asian Feminist Theology of Human Connectivity." Selected conference papers will be published in 2014 as *Feminist Cyberethics in Asia: Religious Discourses on Human Connectivity*, eds. Agnes Brazal & Kochurani Abraham (Palgrave Macmillan).
7. Donna Haraway, "Situated Knowledges: The Science Question in Feminism and the Privilege of Partial Perspective," in *Simians, Cyborgs and Women: The Reinvention of*

Nature, ed. Donna Haraway (London: Free Association Books, 1991), 183–201; Sandra Harding, *The Science Question in Feminism* (Milton Keynes, United Kingdom: Open University Press, 1986); Sandra Harding, *Whose Science? Whose Knowledge? Thinking from Women's Lives* (Milton Keynes, United Kingdom: Open University Press, 1991); and Nancy Hartsock, *The Feminist Standpoint Revisited and Other Essays* (Boulder, CO: Westview Press, 1998).

8. Harding, *The Science Question,* 26.

9. Haraway cited in Harding, *The Science Question,* 192.

10. Monteiro, in Monteiro and Gutzler, *Ecclesia of Women,* xvii.

11. Ibid., xvii.

12. Ibid., xviii.

13. Antoinette Gutzler, MM, "From Whence Comes This Authority? The Ekklesia of Women in Asia: A New *Magisterium* For The Church," in Monteiro and Gutzler, *Ecclesia of Women,* 160.

14. Ibid., 152–53.

15. Ibid., 152, 151.

16. Ibid., 156, 160.

17. Pushpa Joseph, FMM, "An Indian Critique of the Cult of Ideal Womanhood," in Monteiro and Gutzler, *Ecclesia of Women,* 25.

18. Ibid., 23.

19. Ibid., 27.

20. Ibid., 29.

21. Gemma Cruz, "Battered Women's Experience as a Critical Feminist Strategy for a Transformative Theology," in Monteiro and Gutzler, *Ecclesia of Women,* 54.

22. Ibid., 61.

23. Jeane C. Peracullo, "A Feminist Reclaiming of the Mother's Womb: Beyond Pro-Life/Pro-Choice Rhetoric on the Body, Subjectivity and Reproduction Control," in *Re-Imagining Marriage And Family In Asia: Asian Christian Women's Perspectives,* ed. Sharon A. Bong and Pushpa Joseph, FMM (Kuala Lumpur, Malaysia: SIRD, 2008), 114–15.

24. Ibid., 128.

25. Ibid., 129.

26. Ibid., 127.

27. Pushpa Joseph, "Re-Visioning Eros for Asian Feminist Theologizing: Some Pointers from Tantric Philosophy," in *Body And Sexuality: Theological-Pastoral Perspectives of Women in Asia,* ed. Agnes M. Brazal and Andrea Lizares Si (Manila: Ateneo De Manila University Press, 2007), 34–57.

28. Ibid., 52.

29. Nozomi Miura, RSCJ, "Pauline Body in 1 Corinthians: A Metaphor of Whole Human Being and of Christian Community," in Brazal and Lizares Si, 131–32.

30. Julia Ong Siu Yin, IJS, "Gender Identity And Ezekiel 16," in Brazal and Lizares Si, *Body and Sexuality,*116.

31. Gemma Tulud Cruz, "Em-Body-Ing Theology: Theological Reflections on the Experience of Filipina Domestic Workers in Hong Kong," in Brazal and Lizares Si, *Body and Sexuality,* 60, 64, 67.

32. Theresa Yih-Lan Tsou, "Theological Reflection on Sex Work," in Brazal and Lizares Si, *Body and Sexuality,* 77.

33. Han Soon Hee, RSCJ, "Reflections on the Spirituality of Ageing Korean Women: The Empowerment of the Sacred in Their Body-Image and Inner Life," in Brazal and Lizares Si, *Body and Sexuality*, 207.

34. Leonila V. Bermisa, MM, "Facing the Reality of Clergy Sexual Misconduct in the Church: A Step toward Justice and Healing," in Brazal and Andrea Lizares Si, *Body and Sexuality*, 221.

35. Cruz, in Brazal and Lizares Si, *Body and Sexuality*, 68–69.

36. Agnes M. Brazal, "Cooking/Stitching Cultures: Interculturality as a Christian Feminist Peace Praxis," in *Feminist Theology of Liberation Asian Perspectives: Practicing Peace*, ed. Judette A. Gallares, RC and Astrid Lobo-Gajiwala (Quezon City, Philippines: Claretian Publications, 2011), 68–69.

37. Ibid., 66–67.

38. Ibid., 69–71.

39. Ibid., 76.

40. Sophie Lizares-Bodegon and Andrea Lizares Si, "No Mother Is for Sale: Practice Towards an Ecofeminist Theology," in Gallares and Lobo-Gajiwala, *Feminist Theology of Asian Perspectives*, 257–58.

41. Judette Gallares, RC, "And She Will Speak: Junia, the Voice of a Silenced Woman Apostle," in Monteiro and Gutzler, *Ecclesia of Women*, 97–99.

42. Sharon A. Bong, "The Narratives of GLBTIQ Persons: Towards an Epistemology of the Body," in Gallares and Lobo-Gajiwala, *Feminist Theology of Asian Persepctives*, 95–97.

43. Sandra Harding, "Rethinking Standpoint Epistemology: What Is 'Strong Objectivity'?" in *Feminist Epistemologies,* ed. Linda Alcoff and Elizabeth Potter (New York: Routledge, 1993), 49–82.

44. Ibid., 74.

Power-Beauty Feminism and Postcolonial Leadership

Agnes M. Brazal

Introduction

A popular Philippine creation myth narrates the simultaneous emergence of man and woman from bamboo, a powerful symbolic expression of the relatively egalitarian relations of women and men in the Philippine islands in precolonial times.[1] It is conjectured that it is the Spaniards, who colonized the Philippines in the sixteenth century, who named the first man as *Malakas* (strong; powerful) and the first woman *Maganda* (beautiful).[2] While the Spanish representation of the man as powerful and the woman as beautiful may had been intended to impose a complementary and dualistic gender ideology, we find traces of how this power-beauty discourse has been ingeniously subverted to represent a more fluid gender relation between women and men.

In a number of contemporary and traditional Philippine discourses, strength is not just identified with men, and beauty with women; the powerful person (woman) is the one who exhibits both strength and beauty (whether physical or moral).[3] This essay explores the power-beauty dialectic in Philippine culture, its manifestation in popular Christian discourses and theological reflections, and uses it as lens to examine postcolonial female leadership. Employing a postcolonial theoretical framework, we shall examine how colonial interests are represented or reinforced in cultural texts, and how these are subverted. We shall also foreground particularities in gender perspectives as they have evolved in the Philippines particularly in relation to power-beauty.

Until recently, feminist discourses in the West have been characterized largely by what has been referred to as *kalliphobia* (hostility to beauty). Many Western feminists view beauty practices as contributing to the production and regulation of femininity and maintaining the unequal power relations between the sexes and among women.[4] Beauty in fact has not generally been considered a worthy subject for feminist interrogation,[5] and instead feminists opt to speak about the body. Some changes have been noted, however, by Rita Felski, who reviewed some contemporary writings on beauty. She claims that "[t]he trajectory of feminist work on beauty has shown a distinct (though far from unanimous) shift from the

rhetoric of victimization and oppression to an alternative language of empowerment and resistance."[6] This essay hopes to contribute to this debate in its focus on
the Philippine's more fluid "power-beauty" articulation.

Power-Beauty Dialectic

The Philippine female image of power is always linked to beauty, either
physical or moral. Mina Roces, a historian who studied kinship politics in the
Philippines, calls for the contextualization of feminism within this cultural narrative instead of simply appropriating radical feminist arguments that, valuing female
beauty, objectifies women, and suggests subjugation to men.[7] In her analysis of
gender and power in the post–WW II Philippines, Roces shows how regardless of
physical features and so long as she conforms to the expected decorum, a woman
associated with political power—either via kinship[8] or by virtue of being elected
into a political office—is regarded as beautiful.[9] In turn, physical beauty can also
translate into female power, as can be seen from the number of Filipina beauty
queen title holders who have become powerful via their marriage to prominent
men, or election or appointment into political positions.[10]

Moral Beauty

Roces further identifies the emergence of two new symbols of female power
during the period of the Marcos dictatorship (1972–86), the militant nun and
political activist.[11] These women draw their power not in being related to a
powerful man. They exert moral power-beauty as they speak with or on behalf of
the victims of martial rule.[12]

In many Philippine languages, the ethically good is referred to as "beautiful"
while moral evil is called "ugly."[13] *Kagandahang-loob* (literally translated as "beautiful inner self," or roughly equivalent to "gracious goodness" or shared nobility)
designates an "act of generosity displayed spontaneously on account of the goodness of the heart."[14] Gracious goodness is done out of free will, neither expecting a
payment nor a reward, and arising from a genuine concern for the good of the other
or the common good.[15] Philippine discourse makes a further nuance in distin-
guishing between the good inner self (*kabutihang-loob*; KBL) and the beautiful
inner self (*kagandahang-loob*; KGL). While in ordinary language, KGL (beautiful
loob) and KBL (good *loob*) are used interchangeably, gracious (beautiful) goodness
is superior from the perspective of many Filipinos, according to the moral theologian Dionisio Miranda, because "it designates a *loob* (an inner self) that is not
only good but nice, not only pleasant but beautiful, not only correct but gracious.
Were the subject that of social graces, the difference would be one between basic
etiquette and courtly refinement."[16] Gracious goodness thus surpasses the good
because it is also beautiful. Miranda refers to gracious goodness as the "queen of
virtues," the "virtue of virtues" in the Philippine context. He argues, "In the context

of scholasticism's debate over which of the virtues constitutes the form of all the other virtues, KGL [beautiful inner self] may claim to have that 'touch of class.' That 'cut above the rest' to be considered 'the best of the best.'"[17]

Strength Plus Beauty Is Power

In oppressive situations, gracious goodness alone is not enough. It has to be accompanied both by *lakas ng loob* (literally strong inner self or courage) as well as the strength of collective unity. Filipino psychologist Virgilio Enriquez refers to *lakas ng loob* as an "inner resource for change," which enables Filipinos to overcome hardships and engage in cooperative resistance against unjust situations.[18]

The 1986 People Power revolution that toppled the Marcos dictatorship highlighted the power of beauty combined with strength. Hearts of military men and passive citizens were touched by nonviolent action combined with "attractive" goodness (KGL)—women giving roses and sandwiches to military men, citizens volunteering their cars or themselves to block the tanks that were arriving. As the Filipino theologian José de Mesa notes, "What we have here is one collective memory in national consciousness which will continue to remind people of what is possible through generous self-giving and unity, i.e. graciousness toward others. It was undoubtedly a moment when graciousness reigned supreme."[19] The strength (*lakas*) of unity by a critical mass of Filipinos demonstrated in the People Power and the events leading to it was equally necessary to exert a powerful pressure on the military and the passive citizens to cross alliances as well as for the U.S. government to withdraw its support to Marcos.

Roces claims, though, that the late Corazon "Cory" Aquino, who assumed the presidency after the 1986 People Power revolt, had not been reinvented as beautiful because even with her official power, she was perceived to be powerless.[20] It seemed though that Cory also tried to be the opposite of what the previous regime signified. As Imelda Marcos, the partner of the late dictator Ferdinand Marcos in the "conjugal dictatorship," had often been described as "beautiful,"[21] Cory would not have wanted to be represented in the same way. But her funeral procession, where tens of thousands of people amassed in the streets wherever the procession passed, with some even wiping their handkerchiefs on the truck carrying her casket—in the same manner that folks wipe venerated saints—shows popular perception of Cory as a source of power because of her moral beauty, despite some flaws in her leadership.

The precolonial *babaylan* (shamans who are mostly female, and a few crossdressers), however, is the iconic symbol of female power and leadership in the Philippines. While male leaders who stood to gain from the new patriarchal religion seem to have more readily capitulated to the Spanish colonizers, it is the *babaylanes* who persisted longer in the resistance.[22] A famous painting by Fernando Amorsolo, *The Burning of the Idols*, depicts the command of Ferdinand Magellan[23] for all idols to be burned. The *babaylanes* were represented as young beautiful women voluntarily surrendering the idols to be burned in the flames that are in the shape of a devil's mask. On the contrary, early texts show that it is not young women but young Christianized boys who collaborated with the missionaries in destroying the idols. Furthermore, the status of the *babaylan* depends more on her age than on her physical beauty, in contrast to what other scholars claim.[24] The power and prestige of the *babaylan* resides in her command of traditional knowledge and capacity to mediate with the spirits to heal, ensure a bountiful harvest or good catch, or intercede individually or collectively for the good of the community. In one place, the *babaylanes* were even called *Daitan*, meaning friendship and peace, suggesting that they are friends of the spirits and bringers of peace to the community.[25]

Power-Beauty in Folk Catholicism

Power-beauty articulations can also be found in Philippine folk Catholic beliefs and practices, particularly in the Santacruzan religious procession and the nineteenth-century Christ image of the revolutionaries.

The Santacruzan

The Santacruzan, which dates back to the Spanish colonial period, is the most widely celebrated folk religious procession in the Philippines. It commemorates the legend of the finding of the Cross of Jesus by Queen Helena and Emperor Constantine.[26] The procession features literally beautiful women representing strong personages in the Bible and in Christian history who have made special contributions to the growth of the faith.

The biblical characters in the procession include women in the Old Testament, such as Judith, who beheaded Holofernes to save the Israelites, and Esther, the Jewish Queen of Persia, who protected from persecution the exiled Jews in Babylon. Behind the Old Testament personages are the women who followed Jesus in his passion and death, like Mary Magdalene. It is interesting to note that a century before feminist scriptural hermeneutics reached the country's shores, the Philippine popular imagination had already given recognition to the important role of biblical women like Esther, Judith, and Mary Magdalene in the Santacruzan. The highlight of the procession, however, is Queen Helena, with the young Constantine at her side.[27]

The symbols are a mixture of colonial (e.g., Queen Helena and Emperor Constantine) as well as anticolonial figures (including the presence of an anonymous queen of justice, queen of the convicted innocent, and queen lawyer-defender of the poor).

In a way, the Santacruzan is truly a people's procession. Since it is not strictly controlled by the church, communities are able to add new muses to the entourage to adapt to the changing historical and cultural context. For example, the muse representing the Philippine flag was probably not in the original procession, considering that the country won its independence from Spain only in 1896. Additional muses were transmitted from place to place and from one generation to the next until they assumed the status of "tradition."[28] Today, cross-dressers/transvestites, as well as feminist activists, have started staging reinterpreted versions of the Santacruzan. The central figure, however, always remains Queen Helena.

The celebration on many occasions has degenerated into a pompous show of material wealth, a fashion show, a fund-raising event, and a tourist spectacle. Rachel Bundang notes how, in their Filipino-American Santacruzan processions, "all the juicy character parts are doled out to the daughters and sons of 'the beautiful people' (i.e., the professionals, the wannabes, and the social climbers)."[29] This should not, however, prevent us from appreciating and reappropriating the liberating insights in the people's religious practice, as, for example, the celebration of women power in the history of salvation, and the conviction that women of faith and courage (*lakas ng loob*: strong inner self) are beautiful.

Nineteenth-Century Revolutionaries' Beliefs

The link between power and beauty is also exemplified in the image of Christ of the nineteenth-century revolutionaries against imperial Spain. In the folk Filipino concept of power (which we share with the Javanese), a leader or a group's success is proportionate to its inner concentration of power[30] as determined by the state of its *loob* (inner being). While verging on idealism, this belief points to the importance the natives give to the nature of one's *loob*, or inner self. An amulet, for example, can be effective only to the extent that the one possessing it has undergone renewal and purification through ascetic practices, prayer and rituals, and self-discipline.[31]

In the singing of the Phillipine *Pasyon* during Holy Week,[32] the nineteenth-century revolutionaries fighting the Spanish colonizers began to link more the powers of Christ to his beautiful *loob*, which is not only pure and controlled but attracts others in its graciousness. As powerful talismans are believed to emit light and make their possessors radiant,[33] Christ himself has been described in the *Pasyon* as radiating with light.[34] Only a person with a beautiful *loob* that attracts others can be a light to others. A beautiful *loob* includes following the straight path and exhibiting compassion.[35] Again we see here a link between *lakas* (power) and *ganda* (beauty) of the inner self (*loob*). Gracious goodness (*ganda ng loob*), or what is attractively humane, is powerful.

Power Accumulation or Erotic Power?

From an indigenous Philippine perspective, as in the rest of Southeast Asia, power is believed to permeate everything in the universe, including stones, trees, clouds, and fire. This power, which is limited, can be concentrated in certain objects (talismans) or individuals referred to as the "men of prowess." In the transference of power, the gain of one means the loss of another. This traditional concept of power, however, tends to reinforce hierarchical structures. For example, the notion that the amount of power in the universe is limited, and only a few (e.g., the wealthy, the priests) can accumulate power, can justify patron-client relationships both in the church and society at large.[36]

Classic Western juridical theory held a similar view regarding power as a right (a commodity) that one possesses, which can then be transferred to another via a legal act or contract.[37] Some contemporary theorists have moved away from this view of power as a "substance" that can be fixed in an individual. Rather, as Michel Foucault notes, power is a "relation of force": it circulates in the form of a chain and is never possessed as a commodity.[38] Power is continuously flowing depending on the negotiations, relations, and competition between groups, institutions, and discourse, even if some people may have greater capacities to influence the forces of power.

Sacred power, as social power, can also be regarded as a relation of force. Sacred power is present whenever power is utilized to attain mutuality or right relations, or to generate greater "power with" so that we can live more just and compassionate lives.[39] This sacred power lies in the interconnectedness of all things. In Jesus' life, we see erotic power at work (see below) as he himself was nurtured and formed by his family and friends. What we see in Jesus' ministry is not a unilateral transfer of power from the powerful to the powerless but of power in mutual relation at work. His interaction with women, non-Jews, and sinners helped form his vision of the *basileia* of God. One of the first things he did was to call others to join him in a union of men and women to help generate more "power with" to realize the *basileia* of God.

Rita Nakashima Brock speaks of this sacred power as erotic power. Erotic power is relational power or the life-giving energy in relationships that "creates and connects hearts."[40] She prefers to use the term "erotic" to stress the mutuality that characterizes the relationship this power brings about as well as the attraction to beauty that this involves. It is, in fact, erotic power that we also witnessed at play during the 1986 People Power revolution as goodness attracted others to act in solidarity in dismantling the dictatorship.

Faith as Embodiment of God's Power-Beauty

In the New Testament, *energeia* is one of the Greek terms for power; it means effective action. God's Reign or rule is divine power itself in its gracious saving activity within our history. It is power guided by gracious beauty. In his earlier works, de Mesa rearticulated God's revelation in Philippine categories as the experience, primarily through "feeling" of God's *kagandahang-loob* (beautiful self). This is experienced in God's concern for our total well-being, as incarnated in the life of Jesus.[41] Faith, on the other hand, is the interiorization (*pagsasaloob)* of God's gracious goodness in the deepest core of one's self. While de Mesa's articulation strikes a chord among Filipinos, for some, especially Christian, social activists, it lacks a "bite," sounding too soft in capturing prophetic discipleship and leadership, especially in the context of military repression. We posit that what it lacks is *lakas* or strength—the missing element in the power-beauty articulation—which de Mesa recognized later as important too in our culture. While gracious goodness in itself is a source of power, it is necessary to underline separately the value of inner strength (*lakas ng loob*) and the strength of collective unity. God's revelation, understood as the experience of God's *lakas-ganda* (power-beauty),[42] and faith as the embodiment of God's gracious goodness and power, possess the potential better to capture socially engaged Christians' understanding of who God is in terms of what God does for humanity through us. In fact, *lakas ng loob* (courage; strong inner self) has been identified in a nationwide psychometric study of Filipino personality as among the seven highly prized values of Filipinos.[43] This inner trait is important both for female and male Christian leaders. The harmonious balance of courage and gracious goodness is the key in Philippine power-beauty feminism.

We have also noted that many Filipinos have a cultural predisposition to give greater value to gracious goodness over simple moral goodness. This may partly explain some of the negative association of feminism with "angry women." Power guided by gracious goodness (shared nobility and not just charm) does not, however, exclude the expression of anger. Jesus himself got angry at the money changers in the temple. The revolutionaries who were attracted to Christ's beautiful *loob* engaged in a revolution against imperial Spain. We do have our own share of courageous women who fought with various colonizing/neocolonizing forces.

Judith and Esther: Models of
Postcolonial Feminist Leadership?

Power-beauty feminism regards moral beauty as a central dimension of right action and highlights the need for feminist leaders to combine the use of power with gracious goodness in the task of decolonizing both the church and society. Power-beauty feminism also recognizes the role of physical beauty as capital but, unlike postfeminism, does not assume that equality between women and men has already been achieved.[44] There is nothing in the scriptures that precludes a woman from using her beauty to gain power if this is used to "decolonize" or create spaces for the minority or subjugated voices in society. Esther and Judith, two of the biblical women featured in the Santacruzan, are both physically attractive women who deployed their physical and moral beauty as well as strength to resist domination and save their nation.

The narrative or fictional story of Judith begins with the Assyrian imperial campaign to expand its territories and take revenge against nations like Israel, which initially resisted surrender.[45] Judith models prophetic resistance to imperial forces, symbolizing the weak who through a combination of gracious goodness (Jth. 8:7–8;

29) and courage inspire unity and solidarity and defeat the mighty. There is an ambivalence, though, to what extent she is an exemplar today against other forms of domination such as patriarchy[46] and ethnocentrism. On the one hand, she has indeed shown herself to be a strong woman who spoke with wisdom and authority and was not afraid to criticize the male elders or leaders (Jth. 8:11, 32, 14:1).[47] She herself conceived the plan to cross the enemy's territory, mislead them and decapitate Holofernes, the head of the Assyrian conquering army. Her "goodness" is erotic, inspiring solidarity and prophetic resistance (Jth. 15:11–12). She also recognizes that her woman slave deserves freedom and releases her (Jth. 16:23).[48]

On the other hand, Judith returned back to the "private" space of the home after the victory was won. There is the absence of any indication in the text of her questioning the all-male leadership structure in her time.[49] She saw the captivity of the Shechemite women and their daughters as booty and the killing of their slaves as part of God's plan (Jth. 9:4). She did not raise a voice of protest when the rest of the people of Bethulia plundered the Assyrian camp and seized a large amount of booty. Unlike them, though, she did not keep the booty from Holofernes' property to enrich herself, but rather offered them back to God (Jth. 15:6–7, 11).

Similarly, Esther is endowed with physical beauty, which she capitalized on to become queen of the Persian Empire and to save the Jews in diaspora from annihilation.[50] As a young lady, she manifests goodness in her obedience or prudence by heeding the wise advice of her elder cousin/adoptive father Mordecai[51] and in her solidarity with the Jewish people when she decided to help save them from extinction by genocide. She showed courage or inner strength when she risked her life not just once but twice in an attempt to convince the king not to pursue the policy of genocide against the Jews (Esther 4:16, 8:3–4). She acted shrewdly and boldly;[52] she is an exemplar in the use of charm and self-effacement against imperial powers. The narrative about Esther, however, subsumes the gender struggle to the exiled Jews' nationalist and survival agenda. The text also implicitly condemns Queen Vashti's antipatriarchal revolt, when she refuses to be displayed by the king as his trophy "beautiful" wife in his banquet (Esther 1:11–12). Queen Vashti herself is a woman of beauty and strength of character. She is punished for publicly disobeying the king, paving the way for Esther's entry and eventual integration into the patriarchal feudal structure. Like Judith, Esther retreats into the background after saving the Jews from annihilation, while the king and Mordecai run the empire (Esther 10:2–3).[53] Her leadership remains informal or unofficial. Her resistance is a form of "subversive submission,"[54] which leads to some gains but leaves the patriarchal structure intact.

Conclusion

Our postcolonial discourse analysis has shown links between beauty and Philippine female image of power. Proximity to power makes a woman beautiful, while beauty, whether moral or physical, is a source of power. We examined Filipino women leaders in the light of this power-beauty dialectic. We reread, too, aspects of our faith tradition, using as a lens this power-beauty connection. The Santacruzan celebrates the power-beauty of women in the history of salvation. The image of Christ of nineteenth-century revolutionaries highlights the power of Christ's gracious goodness and how that sacred power is guided by moral beauty. For women's use of power to be truly liberating, however, there is a need to shift from the indigenous understanding of power, as accumulated by and concentrated in a few individuals, to the notion of power as erotic, attracting others to goodness. Faith in the Philippine context can also be further explored as the embodiment of God's power and beauty. Lastly we looked at Judith and Esther, two figures in the Santacruzan, as embodiments of power-beauty but also ambivalent models of postcolonial feminist leadership. Our exploration has shown the potential of the power-beauty discourse as a category for feminist theologizing in the Philippine context and for examining postcolonial feminist leadership.

Notes

1. Some of women's rights in precolonial times that the Spanish civil law eradicated were "the right to divorce, to have children regardless of marital status, property rights, freedom to contract business arrangements independently of the husband, retention of maiden name, and a central role in religious practices." Teresita Infante, *The Woman in Early Philippines and Among the Cultural Minorities* (Manila: UST Press, 1975).

2. In the Visayan region's version of the myth, the man and woman are simply referred to as Sicalac and Sicauay, respectively. Damiana Eugenio, *The Myths*, vol. 2, *Philippine Folk Literature* (Quezon City: University of the Philippines Press, 1993), 293–96.

3. Mina Roces, *Women, Power and Kinship Politics: Female Power in Post-War Philippines* (Pasay City: Anvil Publishing, 2000). By power, we mean the capacity to influence others to act in a certain direction.

4. See Kathy Davis, "Beauty (the Feminine Beauty System)," in *Encyclopedia of Feminist Theories*, ed. Lorraine Code (Abingdon, Oxon, United Kingdom: Routledge, 2000), 39; Sheila Jeffreys, *Beauty and Misogyny: Harmful Cultural Practices in the West: Women and Psychology* (East Sussex, United Kingdom: Routledge, 2005).

5. Reacting to the Western patriarchal dichotomy associating, on the one hand, beauty with women or the ideal body of the mother, and, on the other hand, the sublime with the creativity of males, very few feminists write on female or maternal beauty. Maggie Hume, "Beauty and Woolf," *Feminist Theory* 7 (2006): 237–54.

6. Rita Felski, "'Because It Is Beautiful': New Feminist Perspectives on Beauty," *Feminist Theory* 7 (2006): 280. Among the few women theologians who have written on beauty from a feminist perspective are Susan Ross, *For the Beauty of the Earth: Women, Sacramentality, and Justice* (New York: Paulist Press, 2006); Susan Ross, "Women, Beauty and Justice: Moving Beyond von Balthasar," *Journal of the Society of Christian Ethics* 25, no. 1 (Spring/Summer 2005): 79–98; and Michelle A. González, *Sor Juana: Beauty and Justice in the Americas* (Maryknoll, NY: Orbis, 2003). Susan Ross relates African women's ecological advocacy to the preservation of the earth's beauty and their art and craft (basket weaving) to reconciliation and sacramentality.

7. Roces, *Women, Power, and Kinship Politics*, 127.

8. Ibid., 162.

9. Ibid., 17.

10. Ibid., 172. This is possible in the bilateral kinship politics in the Philippines where "power is perceived to be held by the kinship alliance group and not just the persons in office." Ibid., 2.

11. Ibid., 18. Roces distinguished the militant nun and unarmed activist from the women rebels who took up arms. The latter continued to be subordinated to the Communist Party of the Philippines, which was led mainly by the men.

12. Ibid., 182. While most women politicians do not want to be identified as feminists, this has not been the case among some nuns and political activists who embraced feminism and integrated feminist theories in their analysis of political and social oppression in the Philippines. Ibid., 107, 133.

13. Leonardo Mercado, *The Filipino Mind: Philippine Philosophical Studies II* (Washington DC: Council for Research in Values and Philosophy, 1994), 88–89.

14. Isabel S. Panopio, *Society and Culture: Introduction to Sociology and Anthropology*, 3rd rev. ed. Realidad Santico Rolda (Manila: Katha Publishing, 2007), 90.

15. Leonardo de Castro, "Kagandahang-Loob: Love in Philippine Bioethics," *Eubios Journal of Asian and International Bioethics* 9 (1999), 39–40.

16. Dionisio Miranda, SVD, *ButingPinoy: Probe Essays on Value as Filipino* (Manila: Divine Word Publications, n.d.), 177.

17. Ibid., 177–78.

18. Virgilio Enriquez, *From Colonial to Liberation Psychology: The Philippine Experience* (Manila: De la Salle University, 1994).

19. José de Mesa, "Providence as Power and Graciousness," in *Toward a Theology of People Power: Reflection on the Philippine February Phenomenon,* ed. Douglas Elwood (Quezon City: New Day, 1988), 38. For Roces, the beauty-power dialectic does not operate in men but this can be contested. See Agnes Brazal, "Harmonizing Power-Beauty: Gender Fluidity in the Migration Context," *Asian Christian Review* 4, no. 2 (Winter 2010): 32–46.

20. Roces, *Women, Power, and Kinship Politics,* 170. Aquino survived seven coup d'etats during her term.

21. Tapping on the power of the Malakas-Maganda creation myth, the conjugal dictator Ferdinand and Imelda Marcos had themselves represented in palace portraits as Malakas and Maganda to designate themselves as the ideal First Couple in the governance of the nation as family.

22. Carolyn Brewer, *Holy Confrontation: Religion, Gender and Sexuality in the Philippines, 1521–1685* (Manila: Institute of Women's Studies, St. Scholastica's College, 2001), 309–50.

23. The world-renowned Ferdinand Magellan was the captain of the first European ship to land in the Philippines.

24. "The little idols that they had kept hidden . . . were handed over to the Christian boys to drag about through the whole village, and at last they were burned. By this means and by the punishment of a few old women who acted as priestesses and who were called *catalonans* [babaylans], the idolatry of the whole region was brought to an end." Diego Aduarte Historia de la Provincia del Sancto Rosario de la Orden de Predicadores en Philipinas, Japon, y China, Tomo I, En el Colegio de Santo Tomas, por Luis Beltran impressor de Libros, Manila, 1640, 174, cited by Brewer, *Holy Confrontation*,199. Brewer castigates

scholars who represent the babaylanes as young, beautiful women, citing for instance, Jaime Veneracion who claims, without citing his sources, that "being beautiful was considered an advantage" and that "the beauty of the babaylan was important . . . in [the] drama, song, dance ritual that she performed." Jaime Veneracion, "From Babaylan to Beata: A Study on the Religiosity of Filipino Women," unpublished paper, University of the Philippines, n.d., at 3, cited by Brewer, *Holy Confrontation*, 201.

25. Francisco Ignacio Alzina, Historia de las islas e indios de Bisayas (1668), cited by Alicia P. Magos, *The Enduring Ma-aram Tradition: An Ethnography of a Kinaray-a Village in Antique* (Quezon City: New Day Publications, 1992), 9.

26. The historical origin of the Santacruzan is not clear though it is generally accepted that it began during the Spanish regime. The story of the Cross seems popular as well in Mexico where we hear of the well-known Auto cuando Santa Elena hallo la Cruz de NuestroSeñor in 1539. Nicanor G. Tiongson, "Byzantine Happenings," in *Filipino Heritage: The Making of a Nation*, vol. 7, *The Spanish Colonial Period (Late 19th Century) The Awakening* (Manila: Lahing Pilipino Publishing, 1978), 1864. See also Teodora T. Battad et al., *Various Religious Beliefs and Practices in the Philippines*, vol. 1 (Manila: Rex Book Store, 2008), 18.

27. For a general idea of the lineup in the Santacruzan, see Jboy M. Gonzales, SJ, "The Santa Cruz de Manila: Does It Have a Future?"http://www.thepoc.net.

28. Carmen Guerrero Nakpil, "The Meaning of the Santacruzan," in *Woman Enough and Other Essays* (Quezon City: Ateneo de Manila University Press, 1999), 79–80; and Martin F. Manalansan, IV, *Global Divas: Filipino Gay Men in the Diaspora* (Quezon City: Ateneo de Manila University Press, 2006), 129.

29. Rachel A. R. Bundang, "'This Is Not Your Mother's Catholic Church': When Filipino Catholic Spirituality Meets American Culture," *in Pinay Power: Peminist Critical Theory*, ed. Melinda L. de Jesús (New York: Routledge, 2005), 69.

30. Benedict R. O'G. Anderson, "The Idea of Power in Javanese Culture," in *Culture and Politics in Indonesia*, ed. Claire Holt, Benedict R. O'G. Anderson and James Siegel (Ithaca, NY: Cornell University Press, 1972), 1–70.

31. Reynaldo Clemeña Ileto, *Pasyon and Revolution: Popular Movements in the Philippines, 1840–1910* (Quezon City: Ateneo de Manila University Press, 1979), 25, 41.

32. The Pasyon is a narration of the history of salvation from creation to the second coming of Christ, with particular focus on the passion, death, and resurrection.

33. Ibid., 41.

34. Ibid., 45.

35. Ibid., 86, 180.

36. That power can be concentrated in certain things (e.g., saints, hosts), which its possessor may absorb, also reinforces superstitious beliefs and overreliance on amulets and talismans.

37. Michel Foucault, *Power/Knowledge: Selected Interviews and Other Writings 1972–1977* (New York: Pantheon Books, 1980), 88.

38. Ibid., 98.

39. Carter Heyward, *Saving Jesus from Those Who Are Right: Rethinking What It Means to Be Christian* (Minneapolis: Fortress Press, 1999), 55.

40. Rita Nakashima Brock, *Journeys by Heart: A Christology of Erotic Power* (New York: Crossroads, 1991), 26.

41. José de Mesa, *Kapag Namayani ang Kagandahang-Loob ng Diyos* [When God's

Gracious Goodness Reigns] (Quezon City: Claretian Publications, 1990), 37–82. In John 10:11, the Greek term *kalos* (beautiful) was used to refer to Jesus as the "good" shepherd. Jesus is the shepherd with a beautiful *loob*. Rebecca Cacho and Estella Padilla, "Kapag Ganda ang Pinag-usapan: Isang Mungkahing Dulog sa Pagteteolohiya," [Speaking about Beauty: A Proposal for Theologizing], *Hapag* 9, no. 1 (2012): 63.

42. This understanding of revelation contrasts with that of Han Urs von Balthasar's, which rejects an understanding of revelation that has as its starting point human experience. See Ross, "Women, Beauty and Justice," 83. For further elaboration on the power-beauty of God, see Brazal, "Harmonizing Power-Beauty," 43–44.

43. Virgilio Enriquez and Ma. Angeles Guanzon, *Manwal ng Panukat ng Ugali at Pagkatao* (Quezon City: Philippine Psychology Research and Training House, 1983), cited by Virgilio G. Enriquez, *From Colonial to Liberation Psychology: The Philippine Experience* (Manila: De la Salle University Press, 1994), 74.

44. Angela Mc Robbie, "Top Girls? Young Women and the Post-feminist Sexual Contract," *Cultural Studies* 21, nos. 4–5 (July–September, 2007): 718–37.

45. The book of Judith was probably written during the Hasmonean dynasty in the second century BCE or early first century BCE (165–37 BCE). Denise Dombkowski Hopkins, "Judith," *Women's Bible Commentary*, ed. Carol A. Newsom and Sharon H. Ringe (Louisville, KY: Westminster John Knox Press, expanded ed. 1998), 279–85.

46. See also Amy-Jill Levine, "Sacrifice and Salvation: Otherness and Domestication in the Book of Judith," in *"No One Spoke Ill of Her": Essays on Judith* (Atlanta: Scholars Press, 1992),17–30.

47. That this was threatening to the first-century patriarchal society is suggested in St. Clement's Letter to the Corinthians, chapter 55:3–5, when contrary to what the scripture text says, he wrote: "Many women who were empowered by the grace of God accomplished many manly deeds. Judith the blessed asked from the elders of the city permission to go to the camp of the foreigners when the city was besieged." The biblical text narrates that Judith did not even inform the leaders her plan and just told them that she will leave to do her mission (Jth. 8:32–34; 10:9–10). Jan Willem Van Henten, "Judith as Alternative Leader: A Reading of Judith 7–13," in *A Feminist Companion to Esther, Judith and Susanna*, ed. Athalya Brenner (London: T&T Clark International, 1995; reprint ed. 2004), 246–47.

48. Though we do not hear the voice of the nameless maid in the text, Judith's concern for her might indicate that she asked of her willingness to assist her in her mission and that she voluntarily consented. See Robin Gallher Branchi, "Judith: A Remarkable Heroine, Part 2," http://www.biblicalarchaeology.org.

49. Musa Dube, "Rahab Says Hello to Judith: A Decolonizing Feminist Reading," in Fernando Segovia, *Toward a New Heaven and a New Earth* (Maryknoll, NY: Orbis Books, 2003), 54–72.

50. The Book of Esther in the Hebrew Bible was probably written in the early period of the Hellenistic empire (late fourth to third century BCE). "Esther: Introduction," *The Bible New Revised Standard Version*, http://www.rosings.com.

51. See Madipoane Masenya, "Esther and Northern Sotho Stories," in *Other Ways of Reading: African Women and the Bible*, ed. Musa W. Dube (Geneva: Society of Biblical Literature, 2001), 38.

52. Read about Esther's guile in Alexander Green, "Power, Deception and Comedy: The Politics of Exile in the Book of Esther," http://jcpa.org; "Esther: A New Interpretation of the Joseph Story," in *Ruth and Esther: A Feminist Companion to the Bible* (2nd

series), ed. Athalya Brenner (Sheffield, United Kingdom: Sheffield Academic Press, 1999), 5–6.

53. Itumeleng J. Mosala, "The Implications of the Text of Esther for African Women's Struggle for Liberation in South Africa," *Semeia* 59 (1992): 129–37; Timothy S. Lank, *Shame and Honor in the Book of Esther* (Atlanta: Scholars' Press, 1998), 165; Bea Wyler, "Esther: The Incomplete Emancipation of a Queen," in *A Feminist Companion to Esther, Judith and Susanna*, 111–35. As in the story of Judith, the Jews destroyed those who attacked them (Esther 8:11) but in contrast, three times it was expressed that "they laid no hand on the plunder" (Esther 9:10, 15, 16) signifying that this was for them a war of defense.

54. M. Herzfeld, "Silence, Submission, and Subversion: Toward a Poetics of Womanhood," in *Contested Identities: Gender and Kinship in Modern Greece*, ed. P. Loizos and E. Paptaxiarchis (Princeton, NJ: Princeton University, 1991), 79–97.

Provoking the "Resident Evil": Feminist and Gender Provocations to Clericalism in the Philippine Context

Aloysius Lopez Cartagenas

Feminist discourse in Asia, particularly in the Philippines, is no longer confined to the unmasking of androcentric assumptions in church and society. Many Filipino feminist scholars "have already passed the stage of polarizing, oppositional, and dualist discourses on 'women as victim, men as problem.'"[1] There has been instead a shift to focus on transformations in gender identities and relations brought about by dramatic cultural, social, political, and economic changes in the contemporary world. Asian women theologians, in particular, are reconstructing theologies of the body and sexuality, building on their respective rich indigenous cultural and religious heritages. More importantly, they are appreciating current evidence drawn from what can be rightly called "gender fluidity"[2] in light of the Christian faith and tradition.

The official church is aware of the unmistakeable shift. In more recent years, observes the Congregation for the Doctrine of the Faith (CDF), one can find an approach where "physical difference, termed sex, is minimized, while the purely cultural element, termed gender, is emphasized to the maximum and held to be primary."[3] Unlike feminist theological discourse, the official church considers the current approach to be ideological, being no less than the mere "human attempt to be freed from one's biological conditioning."[4] As a "theory of the human person," it is contrary to official church teaching and has serious consequences for our understanding human nature, the data in scripture, and the relevance of the fact that the Son of God assumed human nature in its male form.

The dominant impulse in the Roman Catholic tradition that the claim on gender fluidity provokes is clericalism. By that we mean the dominant ethos in the church's ordained priesthood: the discourse that constructs and legitimizes its all-male structure, the unswerving loyalty it exacts from male priests for its preservation, and the duty of acquiescence of the people of God for its reproduction. While a full-fledged inquiry on clericalism would likely be enlightening, it remains beyond the scope of this essay; I shall nonetheless explore how feminist-gender provocations can expose it, in a more searing light, as the church's "resident evil."

The Reproduction of the Masculine in Clericalism

How is male/manhood/masculinity constructed in the ethos of clericalism? In the predominantly Roman Catholic Philippines, the priest is a father, and the parish is his small family. The people on whom he exercises his fatherhood are his children, and they are to call him *Padre*. To be a "father" or "fatherhood" is not only descriptive of his role but, more importantly, a prescriptive ideal of masculinity that priests are held up to.

Archetypes and Stratification

It is interesting to note that, unlike their male counterparts in Philippine society, Filipino priests as "fathers," and their notions of fatherhood, have rarely been studied. Nonetheless, a typology of fathers and fatherhood by a Filipino sociologist[5] can help us sort out the varieties and classify "church fathers" into at least four archetypes. They are as follows:

1. the generative priest, who sees himself as guide and finds personal fulfilment in getting involved in the lives and activities of his parishioners;
2. the determinate priest, who has a fixed view of fatherhood and thus tends to control the direction of the parish and the destinies of his parishioners;
3. the dilettante pastor, who may be weak or dysfunctional but nonetheless seeks relief from stress in warm relationships with people;
4. the procreator priest, who sees himself mainly as provider to the spiritual and/or temporal needs of the parish.

Masculinities within the clerical fatherhood are not only a variety, they are also stratified. From the vantage point of power relations between these four types, one can see that there are those who belong to the hegemonic, subordinate, and marginalized strata.[6] This is very evident, for instance, in parish assignments. In dioceses where economic disparity among parishes is wide, the aggressive and ambitious would compete for high-income parishes, the less assertive and competitive usually settle for communities at the margins, while the rest, being subordinate or dependent, wait for whoever holds the final decision. This power arrangement has been almost always a cause of organizational dysfunction, a source of masculine frustration, and for some a reason to leave active ministry.[7]

As to how these archetypes and stratification of fatherhoods/masculinities interface, the report of a national survey of the Filipino clergy can shed light.[8] When asked about the three most indecent lifestyles of priests, respondents rank "material attachment and extravagance" the worst, followed by illicit affairs with adult women/men and the "habitual recourse to worldly good time/drinking and other similar vices."[9] When they were asked to identify the top three factors that are weakening the Philippine church, they listed the clergy's "lack of transparency and honesty in the management of church resources ... clerical intrigues and politics ... [and] arrogance and abuse of power."[10] One cannot underestimate the relevance of this data. For one, it is drawn from a rare but honest self-appraisal of an all-male leadership in a local church. But, more importantly, the data suggests the pervasive and problematic character of priests belonging to the provider-procreator and determinate archetypes of masculinity and fatherhood. It also implies that character traits associated with generative or dilettante types do not pose a problem to the clerical order, except that those who embody such types of masculinity and fatherhood are likely subordinated or marginalized within its ranks.

Socialization and Construction

There are different facets of Philippine social and ecclesial life that nurture the masculine identities of every future priest and, consequently, socialize him into the clerical ethos. The construction of the masculine starts in the family and parish and is continued in society and the seminary. In the family, for instance, tasks assigned to sons are predominantly those that do not require socioemotional skills, but rather physical strength and endurance. Boys grow up relating with their fathers in terms of authority, restriction, obedience, and control. They are initiated into community events with more freedom, tolerance, and understanding than girls. In most parishes, only boys are allowed to be altar servers and, like the girls, prepare themselves for eventual membership in church organizations strongly characterized by sex segregation (such as Knights of Columbus for males and the Catholic Women's League for females).

This gender socialization through early segregation is later reinforced by homo-social activities and homo-sexual interactions in homogeneous settings. I will mention only two settings here: the *barkada* and the seminary. As a cultural phenomenon and a social institution in Filipino life, the *barkada* "designates a strong social bond reinforced by peer pressure that unites especially younger males together, whether for bad, for good, or for indifferent purposes."[11] Its most striking purpose is to provide to its members "a reassuringly institutional framework for their initiation to sex, drinking and gambling."[12] It may be a type of solidarity but one that is certainly conducive to some exploratory behaviour, which may not be socially and culturally acceptable, without incurring the embarrassment of any public frown or even judgment. Members are ever solicitous with one another, ready and willing to tolerate and chide on an acceptably reciprocal basis. In such an environment, masculine identity is cemented by male solidarity and masculine proclivities are nurtured by male acceptability.

For every young male who desires the priesthood, the reproduction of his masculinity is extended and strengthened in the seminary. Being a homogeneous place of residence, the seminary is easily a hub of homo-social activities and homo-sexual interactions. Instances where males compete fairly against females or collaborate with them are very minimal if not wanting. Therein the male body is constituted as a site of discipline and restraint vis-à-vis the female body. This gendering caters to what the church and Filipino society fears the most. According to studies, what is feared—hated, even—most of all is (for a man) to be mistaken for a woman. "The male body ought to be strong, invulnerable—impenetrable, even—and it is revealed as an anomalous body precisely at the moment where it appropriates to itself a social . . . role associated with vulnerability."[13]

Clericalism, in this light, can be rightly seen as an institutionalized extension of the male *barkada* phenomenon. In the Philippines, it is not uncommon for parishioners to have to contend or accommodate the *barkada* of the priest and their masculine proclivities and all-male social activities. Such "habitual recourse to worldly good time, drinking and other vices"[14] is quite pervasive, so much so that in a national survey mentioned above, priests themselves rank it their third most disturbing lifestyle. There are less harmful forms of behavioral homogeneity, but they seem only to nurture loyalty to the clerical caste. It does not take long for any male initiated into the clerical fraternity to gradually learn virtually to identify the needs of the church with his own and the caste to which he belongs. The identification goads the cleric to conceal the dysfunctions and/or abuses relative to the exploratory behavior of their own kind. It is striking that in the Philippines, priests who sexually abuse women and minors are seen as less than clerics who are priest-fathers (i.e., priests who have procreated with one or several women) or priests in heterosexual or homosexual relationships with consenting adults. In fact, the priests themselves rank the latter the second most disturbing lifestyle within their ranks.[15] An internal protocol has been formulated to address these cases;[16] but, while the clergy is prone to publicly investigate reports of abuse of women and children, the clerical brotherhood prefers to settle cases of priest-fathers in secret. Of the five most appropriate qualities of an ideal priest, the clergy ranks second the "pastoral charity" toward brothers in the priesthood, next only to "openness and sensitivity to God." The "humility and courage to reach out," "love for truth and truthfulness," and "openness to be helped from outside" constitute the remaining three. That order of priority appears disturbing because such fraternal charity may likely extend to concealment of the crimes or criminal accomplices of their own kind.

It must also be said that the clerical *barkada* is not a homogeneous body. As sketched earlier, diversity and stratification of masculinities do exist among the clergy and set the parameters for the negotiation of power and contestation of privilege. As the saying goes, "some are more equal than others." What clericalism ultimately offers to its members is only an apparent haven, if not an illusion of social harmony and masculine equality. Perhaps to compensate for that void, male bodies docile to the clerical order have to be constantly reproduced and, where necessary and useful, stratified. For every young man who expresses desire for the priesthood, this homo-social breeding prepares him for membership in the clerical club and is a privileged access to power in manifold forms.

Transitions and Constants

There have been transitions in the masculine gender nonetheless. Over three decades, Filipino men have to deal with the migration of "their women" to work abroad and the demands of gender equality. The feminization of the Filipino diaspora has, for instance, brought about the phenomenon of husbands increasingly acquiring and doing traditionally ascribed female characteristics and roles.[17] As women's empowerment in the workplace and in the public sphere widens, Filipino men gradually support women's activities, not excluding those that envision a more egalitarian gendered possibility.

Similar transitions in the representation of masculine identities are also evident in priestly training. A 2004 nationwide survey of major seminaries shows future priests are not only moving against the cultural current of Filipino machismo but also strongly disagreeing with the fixation of traditional identity and roles of women as normative.[18] This seems to suggest that the phenomenon of hegemonic fathers and priests is on the exit, as what have been traditionally labelled as feminine characteristics are integrated in their persona and roles and insisted on as a norm for a more fulfilling "fatherhood."[19] At any rate, these gender role reversals strongly suggest that while maleness as sex is biologically given, maleness as gender is not at all fixed. Masculinities are constantly negotiated and reconstructed with regard to changing femininity.

Some things, however, remain constant. Drawing from personal experience within the clergy, I note the current reluctance of some bishops to image the priest as leader of a community. The image of "father of God's family" is still very much preferred over the more inclusive and gender-sensitive root metaphor of leader. Moreover, while the Base Ecclesial Communities (BEC) movement is indeed very alive, as Philippine bishops call it a new way of being church, in reality the movement, with its calls for a more egalitarian and empowering church, is fragmented and forced to survive by coexisting with the old yet still dominant way, which is built on the shoulders of church organizations constituted by the segregation of the sexes. These constants show that official calls for the renewal of the clergy merely represent "a sometimes vigorous, sometimes timid, but always doomed and always renewed effort, if not at counterbalancing, at least at softening,"[20] never at dismantling, the array of gendered hierarchies that pervade the entire texture of relations in the church.

The Reproduction of the Feminine in Clericalism

How is woman/womanhood/femininity constructed by an all-male clergy? How is this construct reproduced and on what grounds? The question is relevant if we seek to understand power asymmetry in the church and the construction of self or identity. As an all-male clergy constructs the self of woman, it simultaneously constructs the notion that the clergy member is her master by virtue of his maleness.

The Logic of Male Succession

The Catholic Church teaches that "priestly ordination, which hands on the office entrusted by Christ to his Apostles of teaching, sanctifying and governing the faithful, has . . . from the beginning always been reserved to men alone."[21] If the role of Christ in exercising his ministry of salvation were not taken by a man, there would not be the "natural resemblance," which must exist between him and his minister. "That is why," the CDF explains, "we can never ignore the fact that Christ is a man."[22]

The teaching has a subtle but resilient appropriation in the Philippine context. Women may be primarily destined to be mothers, but the ideal one bears a son and nurtures his vocation to the ordained priesthood. Every female body may have the biological capacity for a male progeny, but not all have the kind of feminine genius to provide the earliest stirrings on male bodies for service in the Body of Christ. Hers alone is the female body and the special type of genius that are irreplaceable to ensure the male succession.

The logic sets mothers of priests apart from other mothers and women. Motherhood of priests may not always offer economic or political power in Filipino society but, unlike other forms of motherhood or even womanhood, it alone enjoys the most in symbolic capital. The idealization of mother and son-priest relations runs disturbingly deep. When, for instance, he leaves or gets into trouble, the mother, quite instinctively, as if by moral necessity, suffers if not bears part or much of the shame and atones for her son. Needless to say, the female object of a priest's affection or exploratory behavior is culturally constructed as a temptress, not unlike Eve who tempted Adam in the creation story, and must therefore bear the stigma for the rest of her life. Meanwhile the priest has to abandon the woman or else face the canonical consequences. The female offspring of the affair suffers her mother's fate, while the male progeny does not. In fact, should he seek to pursue priestly vocation, he can be admitted for training to the male succession.

The Logic of Domesticating the Feminine Genius

Motherhood may be the primary vocation of women,[23] but their presence and role "in the life and mission of the Church, although not linked to the ministerial priesthood, remain absolutely necessary and irreplaceable."[24] Women, not unlike Mary, have the feminine "dispositions of listening, welcoming, humility, faithfulness, praise and waiting." While femininity is a "fundamental human capacity to live for the other," which every baptized person should have, women are more attuned to it and live it "with particular intensity and naturalness."[25] This is, according to church teaching, the "genius of women," which men, even those in the clerical order, do not naturally have because they are biologically male.

Dioceses all over the Philippines have seen in varying degrees, diverse modes and at different levels, a participation of women never witnessed half a century ago. But, while Filipino women are showing professionalism and competence on a par with male clerics, their participation in church life and ministry is highly circumscribed. Theirs is only a role complementary if not subservient to a male cleric's running the affairs of God's family (a base community, parish, diocese) and/ or merely a function useful to the clergy's management of God's household (the church, rectory, or school). Other than that, including the service of an ordained ministry of leadership that a male cleric exercises, the woman is portrayed as having nothing of such genius at all.

The logic disciplines the clergy to believe that, because their bodies are male, they do not have the genius of women and must therefore construct an identity that can supply for such natural lack. The feminine is, in turn, imagined as a genius that is irreplaceable in all respects save that of exercising the priestly ministry with men. Women in the church seek to achieve normative ideas of holiness, participation, and service, but clericalism simply predicates the use and domestication of their bodies, and paradoxically they end up being the most dependent on the resources and/or decisions of an all-male clergy.

Socialization and Construction

Some features in Filipino society provide fertile ground for the domestication of the genius of women in the church. Although the Philippines is no longer ranked among the lowest countries in gender inequality, there is an overwhelming agreement among studies that women are essentially perceived of and valued as wives, mothers, and homemakers.[26] Filipino society continues to be stratified according to "roles with high versus low status attached to them," and "those in roles of low status are expected to defer to the opinions of those above them."[27] That is why a wife, for instance, may have significant influence in families where joint decision making is practiced, but "she still holds a less powerful position compared to her husband."[28] In cases of serious disagreement, the wife is almost always expected to give in for the sake of family harmony.

From the perspective of male-female relations, Filipino men are hardly socialized into mutuality with women. There has been a significant decline in gender segregation in matters of work and occupation, but it is the wife, not the husband, who mainly carries the burden of household management, domestic chores, and child care.[29] Women, more than men, have to live up to a stricter moral code of being faithful, modest, and chaste; they are also likely to feel more guilt about their sexuality than men. In a poor country, such as the Philippines, family resources are spread too thinly among members, and it is the daughter, not the son, who must make a choice to seek economic relief: marry early, preferably to a foreigner, or marry late to work, preferably abroad, to support siblings. Women now account for 65 percent of the total number of Filipino workers abroad, a much more dramatic ratio than the global figure of 48.6 percent for global migration.[30]

Transitions and Constants

Transitions are, nonetheless, at hand. Most significant, at least in the church, is the increasing feminization of the hitherto male domain of knowledge production.[31] In most, if not all, major seminaries and/or schools of theology in the Philippines, women religious and laywomen in increasing numbers study together with men. In a few institutes of higher learning, feminist concerns have been counted as integral to contextualized, inculturated, and interdisciplinary theologizing and, consequently, they have revised the formulation of their vision, mission, and goals. Studies on gender issues are now part of many academic curricula, interest in degree programs and research exclusively devoted to feminist theology is evident, and scholarly publications of women theologians are in ever-increasing abundance and widening scope. These practices depart from merely reproducing the norm; they rupture the structural constraints, thereby opening the door for a more truthful and inclusive production of knowledge in the church.

Yet some features remain well entrenched in the face of contestation and negotiation. The academic curriculum of most arch/diocesan seminaries still follows the classical taxonomy, albeit with a few adjustments, which includes no input from recent feminist scholarship. Women teachers in religious education and catechists are plentiful, but only a few are qualified to teach in schools of theology run by the diocesan clergy. Priests do engage and consult women in the formation of future priests, but, except for one major seminary, they are excluded from the decision-making process leading to ordination. Future priests are keen on empowering women in the church, yet a significant number are ambivalent toward women holding leadership positions; they even rank women and gender issues the least of social concerns that should be part of their training.[32]

Nevertheless, what we observe in the Philippines is an emerging disposition among women to create spaces where gender conventions are challenged and reconstructed rather than maintained and reproduced. Women, both lay and religious, are not only resisting patriarchal construction and demands of their bishops and priests, they are, most importantly, reclaiming their human originality. This transformative practice shows the untruthfulness of the account that women "will deform and lose what constitutes their essential riches" if they "appropriate to themselves male characteristics contrary to their own feminine originality."[33]

Provoking the Evil-in-Residence

Human beings, although biologically sexed as male or female, negotiate, partially comply with, compromise with, clarify, resist, or even transgress the formation of their identities or selves according to socially constructed roles and expectations as they confront the dramatic transformations of their life-world. Gender is a malleable construct rather than a fixed inscription of one's body or a predetermined outcome of one's biological sex. The body does not seem to be "the source that influences the formation of self-identity, or even sexual identity" but more "the slate upon which one expresses one's self of the moment."[34] It is the locus upon which the self is inscribed and expressed.

The fluidity of gender constitutes perhaps the most serious feminist provocation to clericalism to date. Firstly, clericalism's insistence on the "natural resemblance" of male priests with the maleness of Christ is misplaced. There is no question that Jesus of Nazareth was biologically male. But while he had a male body, he negotiated, partially complied with, transgressed, or reconstructed the social, cultural, and religious codes of manhood/masculinity and womanhood/femininity expedient to every man and woman of his times.

For this reason, what takes on light in the ministry of Jesus is not the mystery of man nor of woman but of the human person. He who is "the image of the invisible God" (Col. 1:15) "is himself the perfect human being . . . he who worked with human hands, thought with a human mind, acted by human choice and loved with a human heart."[35] The *humanum* in Jesus, rather than his male sex or gender, is revelatory of God's salvific intentions in and through the divine economy of signs. The evidence of gender fluidity allows us to see that it is the humanity of the one who exercises the priesthood, not his maleness or her femaleness, that bears the "natural resemblance" of Christ. In the priestly ministry of a male or a female, the ministry of Jesus can take on full light.

Bishops and priests refusing to acquiesce to the logic of male succession are no longer wanting. For now it would suffice to say that their refusal is a provocation to the claim of absolute certainty that the church, in fidelity to the example of the Lord, does not consider herself authorized to admit women to priestly ordination. This transformation from within the clerical ranks deserves a more sustained and rigorous theological-ethical inquiry. As something crucial to the credibility of the church as a sacrament in Christ, it is an important sign of the times that should not be ignored but read by the whole people of God and an increasing consensus of faith that should not be disdained but interpreted in the light of the gospel.

The fluidity of gender is also a provocation to the theology of complementarity. It is premised on a claim that a woman born is naturally female and desirous of femininity, whereas a man born is naturally male and desirous of masculinity.[36] Current evidence is increasingly proving this claim to be contentious. In fact, there is now a seeming official openness to a fluid construction of gender.[37] That "which is called 'femininity' is more than simply an attribute of the female sex" says Benedict XVI; it rather "designates . . . the fundamental human capacity to live for the other and because of the other." It is just that "women are more immediately attuned" to such capacity.[38]

This may not be a full-blown transgression of complementarity, but, for now, it may help the church's teaching authority to appreciate why there are "varieties of men and varieties of masculinities which are not necessarily problematic."[39] It is just that these varieties are "often destabilizing, contradictory, and unsettling, and sometimes disempowering"[40] to gender constructs premised on a "biology-is-destiny" formula. The church magisterium's fear of the fluidity of gender is not well founded. The church would do well rather to fear clericalism's essentialist gender construct because it is the evil that deforms what constitutes the essential human richness—*the imago Dei*—in every male and female.

Complementarity does not seem to be a truthful account of the human. For this reason, clericalism, the ethos in which complementarity moves and has its being, represents a lie, and to transgress it is a moral obligation. An increasing number of Filipino priests, as well as even aspirants to the priesthood, transgress clerical constructs of masculinity and/or fatherhood even as they unmask the androcentric assumptions of the official discourse on the feminine genius. This provocation by males to the current male form of Christ's ministerial priesthood is yet another sign of the times, provoking a more truthful account of men and masculinities in the church.

Conclusion

With the help of recent data and fresh feminist discourse on gender fluidity, I have tried to expose clericalism as the church's evil-in-residence. Its exclusion of women from the ordained ministry based on a misplaced resemblance of the biologically male priest with the maleness of Jesus Christ is a false theological narrative. Premised on an essentialist gender construct, clericalism is a dehumanizing ethos because it domesticates the feminine genius into extremely circumscribed participation in the church. As a system of institutional organization, it is dysfunctional because it reproduces itself by rewarding fidelity or acquiescence of God's people, particularly women, to the preservation of the all-male clerical caste. Although the grip of clericalism can only be aided and sustained by some cultural proclivities, recent developments in Philippine social and ecclesial life are contesting if not transgressing those cultural barriers. It is a positive sign of the times that in my country critical discourses are formulated, new narratives are emerging, and fresh hermeneutics of gender and ministry are gaining ascendancy in church and society. Clericalism may well be the "terrifying beast" that many of us, like the prophet Daniel, are so frightened of that we turn pale and rather keep everything to ourselves (Dan. 7:19–28). But thanks to feminist and gender provocations its centuries of "crushing its victims with its bronze claws and iron teeth and then trampling on them" are already numbered. To weed it out completely we need more than a "gentle debunking."[41]

Notes

1. See, for instance, Leonora Angeles, "The Filipino Male as 'Macho-Machunurin': Bringing Male and Masculinities in Gender and Development Studies," *Philippine Journal of Third World Studies* 16 no. 1 (2001): 9–30; and Niceta Vargas, "The Impact of Feminist Theologizing on Five Catholic Schools of Theology in the Philippines" (a paper presented

at the initial meeting of the Circle of Feminist Theologians of the Philippines on 28 May 2011 at the Villa Consuelo Retreat House, Novaliches in Quezon City, Philippines).

2. Agnes Brazal, "Harmonizing Power-Beauty: Gender Fluidity in the Migration Context," *Asian Christian Review*, 4, no. 2 (2011): 32–46.

3. Congregation for the Doctrine of the Faith, "Letter to the Bishops of the Catholic Church on the Collaboration of Men and Women in the Church and in the World" (CMW).

4. CMW, 3.

5. Allen Tan, "Four Meanings of Fatherhood," *Philippine Sociological Review* 22, nos. 1–4 (1994): 27–39; also see Angeles, "The Filipino Male," 18–19.

6. Robert W. Connell and James Messerschmidt, "Hegemonic Masculinity: Rethinking the Concept," *Gender and Society* 19, no. 6 (December 2005): 829–59; for an in-depth work on the nature and construction of masculine identity, see Robert Connell, *Masculinities* (Berkeley: University of California Press, 2005).

7. Emmanuel Fernandez, *Leaving the Priesthood: A Close Reading of Priestly Departures* (Quezon City: Ateneo de Manila University Press, 2001).

8. See the report in *History and Grace: A Renewed Clergy, a Renewed Church, a Renewed Country* (Manila: UST Publishing House, 2005). The data are results of a workshop by more than a thousand priests during the National Congress of the Clergy held in Manila on July 5–9, 2004. Data interpretation was done by the Social and Research Center of the Pontifical University of Sto. Tomas in Manila.

9. Ibid., 239, tbl. II-D.

10. Ibid., 246, tbl. II-I.

11. The term defies a coherent description and its ethnography is multilayered. Nonetheless, our discussion on the theme is indebted to Jean-Paul Dumont, "The Visayan Male Barkada: Manly Behavior and Male Identity on a Philippine Island," *Philippine Studies* 41, no. 4 (1993): 401–36, at 432.

12. Ibid., 428.

13. Paul-Francois Tremlett, *Power, Invulnerability, Beauty: Producing and Transforming Male Bodies in Lowland Christianized Philippines* (London: Occasional Papers, School of Oriental and African Studies, 2006), 21.

14. *History and Grace*, 239, tbl. II-D.

15. Ibid.

16. Catholic Bishops Conference of the Philippines, *Pastoral Guidelines on Sexual Abuses and Misconduct by the Clergy* (Manila: CBCP, 2004). For studies on the issue, see Leonila Bermisa, "Facing the Reality of Clergy Sexual Misconduct in the Church," in *Body and Sexuality*, ed. Agnes M Brazal and Andrea Lizares Si (Quezon City: Ateneo de Manila University Press, 2007), 216–33; and Aloysius Cartagenas, "The Terror of the Sexual Abuse by the Roman Catholic Clergy and the Philippine Context," *Asian Horizons* 5, no. 2 (June 2011): 348–71.

17. Alicia Tadeo Pingol, *Remaking Masculinities: Identity, Power, and Gender Dynamics in Families with Migrant Wives and Househusbands* (Quezon City: University of the Philippines Center for Women's Studies, 2001).

18. See the *Benchmark Survey of Philippine Seminaries 2004, Profiles of Theology Seminarians: Values and Relationships vis-à-vis Women Perspectives and Ecclesial Concerns,* published by the Episcopal Commission on Seminary Formation and the Office on Women of the Catholic Bishops Conference of the Philippines (CBCP). The survey covered ten

major seminaries run by the diocesan clergy and two run by religious men, and three schools of theology administered by religious. See Table 12, nos. 1, 8–10, 12, and 18 for perceptions of manhood while Table 12, nos. 2–6, 11a, and 14 may indicate their reception of the feminization of the ideal man.

19. On the insistence of priestly training that integrates the masculine (*animus*) with the feminine (*anima*) in the humanity of the candidate, see, for instance, the *Updated Program of Priestly Formation* (2004) by the Episcopal Commission on Seminaries of the CBCP.

20. Dumont, "The Visayan Male Barkada," 431.

21. John Paul II, *Ordinatio Sacerdotalis* (OS).

22. Congregation for the Doctrine of the Faith, *Inter Insigniores* (II).

23. John Paul II, *Mulieris Dignitatem* (MD).

24. OS, 3.

25. CMW, 16, 14.

26. Consult the findings of a review of 131 studies on this theme sponsored by the UNICEF and Ateneo de Manila University in Ma. Concepcion Liwag et al., *How We Raise Our Daughters and Sons: Child-Rearing and Gender Socialization in the Philippines* (Quezon City: Ateneo Wellness Center, 1999), esp. 16. In the 2011 Gender Inequality Index (GII) of the United Nations Development Program, the Philippines ranked 75 among 146 countries while Thailand and Indonesia are ranked at 69 and 100, respectively. See hdrstats.undp.org/images/explanations/PHL.pdf.

27. Fernando Zialcita, "Bridges and Barriers to a Democratic Culture," in Maria Serena Diokno, ed., *Philippine Democracy Agenda: Democracy and Citizenship in Filipino Political Culture, Vol. 1* (Quezon City: Third World Studies Center, 1997), 39–48, at 44.

28. Belen Medina, *The Filipino Family* (Quezon City: University of the Philippines Press, 2001), 173; see also ibid., 163–64.

29. Ibid., 280–81.

30. Rhacel Salazar Parrenas, *Children of Global Migration: Transnational Families and Gendered Woes* (Quezon City: Ateneo de Manila University Press, 2006).

31. Vargas, "The Impact of Feminist Theologizing," esp. 7–9, 9–11, 14–15, 16–17.

32. *Benchmark Survey*, tbls. 30 and 15.

33. MD, 10.

34. Christine Gudorf, "Body, Self and Sexual Identity: Reflections on Current Evidence," in *Body and Sexuality*, 1–33, at 18–19.

35. Second Vatican Council, *Gaudium et Spes*, 22.

36. Sharon Bong, "Queer Revisions of Christianity," in *Body and Sexuality*, 234–49.

37. Agnes Brazal, "Sexuality from a Post-Colonial-Intercultural Feminist Perspective" in *Roots and Routes: Catholic Feminism in the Philippines* (publication forthcoming).

38. CMW, 14.

39. Angeles, "The Filipino Male," 11.

40. Ibid.

41. John Allen, "Benedict's Gentle Debunk of Clericalism," *National Catholic Reporter* (March 30, 2012), http://www.ncronline.org.

RESISTANCE:
A LIBERATIVE KEY IN FEMINIST ETHICS

Kochurani Abraham

Freedom is acquired by conquest, not by gift. It must be pursued constantly and responsibly.

—Paolo Freire (*Pedagogy of the Oppressed*)

Symbols in hand, a *veena* upon my shoulder, I go about; who dares to stop me?
The *pallav* of my *saree* falls away (A scandal!)
Yet, I will enter the crowded market place without a thought.
Jani says, My Lord, I have become a slut to reach Your home.

—Janabai ("Cast Off All Shame")

The emphatic assertion of freedom by Paolo Friere, twentieth-century Brazilian pedagogue, was already realized in the life of Janabai, a fourteenth-century poet, mystic, and *bhakta*[1] of India. At a time when women's mobility was absolutely controlled, she conquered her space and freedom, resisting the way of acquiescence of the women of her times, and overcoming the many socioreligious impediments in her path.

Even though Janabais are few in history, at present we see resistance becoming a weapon of the "weak"—as James Scott would argue—but the weak who are paradoxically becoming "strong." Only those with strong aspirations, passions, and convictions have the courage to defy established systems of suppression and oppressive control. It is striking to find women choosing the path of resistance, even in a provocative manner. On July 15, 2004, at Imphal, the capital of the northeastern Indian state of Manipur, around forty women took to the streets, stripped naked, and staged an angry demonstration outside the Assam Rifles paramilitary forces building to protest the death in custody of a thirty-two-year-old young woman,

Manorama, who was raped, tortured, and murdered by the paramilitary soldiers. Defying the passive and modest imagery of traditional Indian women, the Manipuri women created history by storming the streets of Imphal with placards that challenged "Indian Army rape us," "Indian Army take our flesh!"

Janabai could not have imagined that the "slut" she chose to become in the fourteenth century would turn into a weapon of justice for women in the twenty-first century. Similarly, the SlutWalk phenomenon, begun in Toronto, is becoming global. This was reenacted in Indonesia, a Muslim country, in September 2011, when around fifty women donned miniskirts and marched the streets of Jakarta expressing their anger at the local governor's remark about how women ought to dress in order to avoid rape. It is remarkable that in cultures where modesty and submission are glorified as the feminine virtues, women are daring to resist the norms that crush their integrity and curtail their moral/spiritual agency, deploying means that are counterhegemonic. Thanks to the political underpinnings of the feminist movement, women are finding ways and means to give vent to their anger at whatever is distorting their human dignity.

Expressions like SlutWalk, apparently scandalous to established foundations of conventional ethical norms, call for a rethinking of ethical questions, taking into consideration women's subjectivity, their critical voice, and their agency. It is within this framework that I wish to engage critically with the defined norms of feminist ethics. In the light of Indian women's experience of gendered oppression, I will examine the appropriateness of care ethics as a gender-neutral, universal norm. In relation to the ambiguities that surround the traditional ethical questions concerning women, I will discuss the notion of resistance as liberative ethics from a feminist theological standpoint.

The Contextual Exigency for a Liberative Feminist Ethics

The starting point of feminist ethical reflection ought to be women's experience of gendered oppression, as it should be in the larger feminist theological discourse. To me, the urgency of evolving a liberative feminist ethics stems primarily from the agonizing increase of violence against women. The silenced cries of Nirmala, a recent victim of domestic violence, speak for her and for other women in similar life-threatening situations. Nirmala, aged fifty-six, was a senior officer at the Government Secretariat in Kerala, a southwestern state of India. On March 18, 2012, her alcoholic husband of twenty-five years hit her brutally on the head in a fit of rage and left her lifeless, with her skull ripped open. On realizing that his wife was dead, he called his two sons—both students of engineering in a city college—in the late hours of the night and unscrupulously said to them, "I have finished your mother off. Take her away if you wish!"[2]

Nirmala's neighbors testify that violence was a regular feature in her marriage, primarily due to her husband's inability to accept her economic independence, which was augmented further due to his alcoholism. Nirmala, socialized to be a "good" Indian wife, accepted this aggression as simply part of her life, and covered up much of her suffering from her family and colleagues, until the violence that she tolerated for years resulted in her death.

Nirmala's case is not an isolated one, the experience of violence, to different degrees, being a daily feature for many women. The obvious question is: why do women tolerate such violence or continue to remain in abusive marriages to the end? In my recent doctoral research on Catholic Syrian Christian women who are high on human development indices, a figure as high as 62.5 percent of the respondents acknowledged that, for the sake of children and the family, they put up with violence.[3] The tolerance quotient of Indian women seems to be high, thanks to their gendered socialization in the so-called feminine virtues of submission, self-sacrifice, and passivity, and to their indoctrination into the idea that conserving family is primarily a woman's responsibility.

When women take an uncritical stance toward abusive and exploitative situations under the mask of "virtue," they collude with oppressive situations without searching for alternatives. Virtue is benevolent in the Aristotelian view of "ideal character traits," but the question is, who defines what is "ideal," and for whom? In ordinary parlance, virtue is just "behavior or attitudes that show high moral standards."[4] This notion of virtue becomes a burden on women because, in a culture informed by patriarchy, it is the woman who is idealized as the epitome of virtue and expected to be the transmitter of the traditional socioreligious norms.

The price that many Indian women pay for being "virtuous" comes in different measures. While for some it is utter helplessness before violence, for others it is an increasing vulnerability to exploitation, especially within the "feminine space" of the household. Giving a hearing to some women whom I encountered in my field research will explain this fact. Sheeba (name changed), a working woman in her thirties, is on her feet throughout a sixteen- to eighteen-hour day. The first to wake up and the last to see bed in a family of five—herself, her husband, and three children—she shoulders the full responsibility for housekeeping and the children's care besides her eight to nine hours' employment in a bank. In her words,

> I like being active, but often I am so exhausted with the constant preoccupation to keep everything going well. I feel guilty if I am not spending myself for my family because I know this is expected of me and I feel torn apart by the many demands made on me. Of late I find myself becoming like a machine and that frightens me. What will happen when the machine cannot run anymore? And I ask myself: Is this what a woman's life is all about?

The case of Beena (name changed) is not much different, although she is not employed outside the home. Being a housewife in a traditional lower–middle-class joint family in India, with ageing parents and five children to care for, and the constant visits of extended family members, she too finds herself stretched to the limits:

Marriage has become a trap for me. When I put rice to cook on the fire
every morning, I see the pot becoming a symbol of my own life, filled to
the brim and made to withstand the scorching heat of the fire in order to
provide food to others and this process continues day after day. I am angry
at the unending work when my bones ache to the core and I think of my
younger days with nostalgia. I wanted so much to study more and get an
office job, but now it's nothing but the endless drudgery from which there
is no escape!

Both Sheeba and Beena fit into the mold of the "ideal woman" according
Indian cultural and religious standards, the one who spends herself for others in
unconditional self-giving, particularly for the family. The greater the internalized
notion of the "ideal woman," the less freedom women have to resist their own
exploitation in the family.

Subscript to the "Virtuous Feminine"

The Indian woman's identity is constructed by her position at the intersection
of class, caste, and religion with gender. The moral and ethical norms that control
her life differ according to the place she occupies on the caste hierarchy. The higher
she is on the caste ladder, the greater will be the obligation to fit into the "virtuous"
mold, since virtue is defined by the brahminically inscribed patriarchal ideology.

Scholars observe that, as per the brahminical legal texts, a woman's essential
nature was identified with her sexuality (*strisvabhava*), which was to be channelized
only into legitimate motherhood within a tightly controlled structure of reproduction that ensured caste purity and patrilineal succession. A woman's duty (*stridharma*)
was defined as fidelity to the husband. While a woman's sexuality, or *strisvabhava,*
was represented at the general level as sinful and considered a threat, the ideal notion
of womanhood constructed by the patriarchal ideologues was represented as the
"*Pativrata*"—the woman submissive and devoted to her husband.[5]

The notion of submission became ingrained in the Indian female psyche
through the dependency prescriptions of *Manusmriti*—the law code by presented
by Manu, the most prominent ideologue of the brahminical system. Manu insisted
that women remain dependent on their fathers in their childhood, husbands in
their youth and adulthood, and sons in old age.[6] Even though this was a code of
conduct for the twice-born *varnas,* or those on the higher rungs of the caste ladder,
these norms have had a strong molding influence on the Indian mind as a cultural
paradigm that stretched beyond the boundaries of religion.

It is ironic that, while female behavior was regulated within the *strisvabhava-
stridharma* framework, and the consequent dialectic between the promiscuous and
the chaste woman, the good/bad woman dichotomy was written into the notions
of upper-caste/lower-caste women. As Indian feminist V. Geetha observes, laboring
lower-caste women were not expected to adhere to *stridharma,* as they were treated

as the sexual property of the men for whom they worked. Their socially subordinate status marked them as "low" women, who are sexually deviant but paradoxically, despite the fact that they were not expected to be chaste, they were yet enjoined to remain "pure," as sexual purity preceded and anticipated caste purity and, by implication, honor.[7]

It is within this caste-inscribed ideological framework that the subordination of women assumed a particularly severe form in India through the powerful instrumentality of religious traditions that have shaped social practices.[8] All the mainstream religions have contributed to the legitimization of sociocultural norms that keep women subordinate and dependent on male protection, Christianity being no exception. The hegemonic effects of religious indoctrination become all the more marked in cultures like India, where women are usually faithful adherents of religious practices. This was brought out strikingly in my study, where 52.9 percent of the respondents consider that God has given men the right to rule over women, and 78 percent find that the teaching "wives be submissive to your husbands," repeated at the Catholic Syrian Christian marriage, is relevant.

The religious *prescriptions*[9] about the "ideal woman" being the most self-giving mother have also marked Indian women's involvement with the development question. Scholars observe that in contemporary India, two images of women coexist in dialectical tension: woman as the self-sacrificing wife and mother—who is an emblem of national culture and tradition—and the woman as an "abstract worker." The assumption that women are (or should be) primarily housewives and mothers, and secondarily workers permeates development discourses, where traditions colored by religion still overshadow the advances of modernity. Women's identity is polarized along a "mother-worker" continuum. The notion of mother is associated with one who is traditional, domestic, and economically dependent, while the identity of the worker is associated with the modern, the public, and the economically independent.[10] In this setting, where women are increasingly exploited under the label of feminine virtues upheld by conventional religious doctrines and ethical norms, a rethinking on care ethics becomes necessary.

A Feminist Appraisal of Care Ethics

While virtue ethics has gained currency for its accent on building character rather than mere fulfillment of one's duty, ethics of care has found almost universal appeal for its attention to relationality. As K. P. Addelson observes, in contrast to an atomistic view of human nature, the ethics of care posits the image of a "relational self," a moral agent who is embedded in concrete relationships with others and who acquires a moral identity through interactive patterns of behavior, perceptions, and interpretations.[11] Within the framework of care ethics, it is also assumed that relationships are bound by mutual interdependence, and its practice involves the values of attentiveness, responsiveness, competence, responsibility, negotiation, and mutual recognition.[12]

Care ethics is alluring because care is the foundation for sustaining life in all its dimensions, and everyone, irrespective of age, sex, class, or creed, likes to be cared for. However, it poses a problem when the question of caregiving is not a free choice, but rather becomes an imposition on the female sex due to gender. In cultures and religious traditions marked by patriarchy, caregiving is strongly a feminine task, and there is no mutuality in caregiving. Consequently, an emphasis on care ethics as a universal norm may foster gender stereotypes, and block women's growth in rationality, career ambitions, self-assertion, and autonomy.

In this context, the significance of viewing ethics from a feminist perspective becomes pertinent. Feminism, as a worldview with a political stance geared at affirming the full humanity of women, challenges the thinking patterns that are colored by gendered polarization of the sexes. It is "about understanding the ways in which 'men' and 'women' are produced and inserted into patriarchies that differ according to time and place."[13]

Indian patriarchy "rests on defined notions of masculine and feminine."[14] This privileges the man, as the "head" of the family, to hold the reins of control over the family's ideological and material resources, with decision making as his prime responsibility. The woman is assigned the role of being the "heart" who is expected to safeguard the "sanctity" of the family in love and care. In this context, if ethics is to be qualified as feminist, it entails dealing with the patriarchally informed ideologies and ethical norms that deny women the full flowering of their human potential and capabilities. In this task, feminist ethics needs to engage in conversation with social and critical theories that address women's experience of subordination.

Enabling Women's Critical Voice and Agency: An Ethical Imperative

When women internalize the patriarchal assumptions of their subordinate status that condition their identity construction, they tend to become "politically unconscious," which is a state of dialectical amnesia where social actors collude with their own oppression even when it exposes them to self-contradiction.[15] This state reflects what Paolo Freire describes as the "culture of silence" of the dispossessed, which creates in the oppressed ignorance and lethargy that are the direct products of a whole situation of economic, social, and political domination, as well as of paternalism, of which they are victims.[16] In this context, only a critical consciousness can enable individuals or social groups to challenge the premises and practices of their culture, and in doing so confront the premises of self, their own lives and feelings, and rethink the social order, and even rethink themselves, challenging dominant concepts of reality.[17]

The poverty of a life lies not merely in the impoverished state in which the person actually lives but also in the lack of real opportunity—due to social constraints as well as personal circumstances—to choose other ways of living.[18] Only when women, in their situation of marginalization, perceive critically the social, religious, political, and economic contradictions in which they are submerged do they begin to see alternatives. A critical consciousness would enable women to perceive the reality of oppression, not as a closed world from which there is no exit but as a limiting situation that they can transform. They can overcome the contradictions in which they are caught only when this perception enlists them in the struggle to free themselves.[19]

Amartya Sen relates the necessity of evolving critical thinking in women with regard to the question of agency. As Giddens explains, agency is the "capacity to make a difference,"[20] and this can find realization in the socioeconomic, political, cultural, spiritual, or any other dimension of life. Discovering their agency is crucial for women because, as feminist theorist Naila Kabeer observes, it gives them "the ability to define their goals and act upon them."[21] In Sen's opinion, agency is "an antidote to victimization."[22] When women refuse to be victims of the situations in which they find themselves, they are enabled to discover possibilities, have choices, and enter the path of development.

However, Sen argues that the agency of women can never be adequately free if traditionally discriminatory values remain unexamined and unscrutinized. While values may be culturally influenced, it is possible to overcome the barriers of inequality imposed by tradition through greater freedom to question, doubt, and reject if unconvinced. An adequate realization of women's agency relates not only to the freedom to act but also to the freedom to question and reassess the prevailing norms and values. The pivotal issue is critical agency.[23]

The question is, how free are women to question and reassess the theological indoctrinations that legitimize and reinforce sociocultural experiences of oppression? The problem is grave where women, having internalized this theology, accept their subordinate role as the normal order of things. Worse still is when the disciplinary power exercised through religious indoctrination is interiorized to the point that women police their own behavior to conform to patriarchally inscribed religious and ethical norms. This internalization of the "feminine ideal" by women in the socioreligious system of surveillance perpetrated by the patriarchal ideology is reminiscent of Foucaldian "panopticism."[24]

In such situations where power is most insidious, and it becomes normalized, generating compliant subjects who actively reproduce hegemonic power relations, Sen's proposition of "critical voice" becomes pertinent. Critical voice is constitutive and instrumental to the well-being of a person, and Sen asserts that only the person with critical voice is truly free. The category of "women's voice" denotes the subjective, experiential viewpoint of women.[25] If critical voice is an essential ingredient of becoming free, women need to be tutored in the art of having a voice and making it critical. This is where resistance has its role to play in liberative feminist ethics.

Resistance as a Key to Liberative Politics

Even though passivity has overshadowed the traditional imagery of the Indian woman, the increase in expressions of voiced struggle and dissent is indicative of an emerging consciousness that is liberative. Narratives of "subterranean resistance" offered by ordinary women in their daily lives, and "stories of silent but staunch resistance to dominating regimes," are all signs of the subversive powers at work in feminist politics.[26]

Through resistance, women can reclaim their subjectivity and agency, and can cast away the robe of victimhood, refusing to remain "inert and passive objects of defining discourses as people without any control over their lives."[27] Resistance becomes a means for contesting power relations that are marked by domination and oppression, and a tool in the hands of women in their everyday negotiation of power. The narration of Lissie (name changed), an assistant professor in her mid-forties, illustrates this point:

> The boldness I have today is not something I got from my childhood. I grew up in a very controlled environment where my mother wanted us girls to be "good girls," which meant very obedient girls. It is only after my marriage I realized that I have a personality and that I can have choices in life. My mother-in-law, who was a strong woman, was my mentor and she taught me to resist and overcome my earlier conditioning of passivity. She encouraged me to stand on my own feet and so, at the age of thirty-nine, once my kids were well into school, I did my post-graduate studies and I am employed today.
>
> Initially my confidence was a threat to my lawyer husband, maybe because his friends' wives were all submissive types. But I became conscious of the fact that the more I restrained myself, the more he would dominate. My husband has a short temper, but I learnt to negotiate his outbursts without being trapped by them. To give an example, once my husband flung a file with papers as he got angry with someone. I was there in the room, but I refused to bend down and pick up the papers that were scattered on the floor. When I did not do it, he picked them up himself, and I am sure he got the message that he will not get me to dance to his tunes.
>
> Another area that marked my growth is that of sexuality. I would say that it is important for women to own their sexuality. As a young wife I was more constrained, maybe from my family background of "good woman" training. But when I grew into a healthier consciousness of myself as a woman, I learnt to become sexually assertive. For this I had to say a conscious "No" to the imagery of the wife as a passive partner in sex and this has had a very positive effect on my marriage in terms of building an adult to adult relationship with my husband.

Over these years I have also grown into a healthier understanding of spirituality. I find much of our religion and ritual practices blocking women's growth instead of helping them. I do not believe that only women need to be submissive as taught by the church because in any healthy relationship submission has to be mutual. I also wonder, if Christ is the head, why can't we women be like Christ? As a woman I am realizing that we find our strength and power only if we discover a freeing and integrating spirituality.

Social theorists define resistance as "those behaviors and cultural practices by subordinate groups that contest hegemonic social formations, that threaten to unravel the strategies of domination,"[28] and Lissie's story exemplifies this. By contesting hegemonic social formations, women reclaim their subjectivity. To be a subject is to know and act,[29] or, as feminist theorists argue, subjectivity is a site for the interaction of multiple contending forces, offering a spectrum of possibilities ranging from total subjugation to extreme self-assertion.[30] Resistance against ideologies, belief systems, and behavior patterns that are oppressive become possible through the assertion of one's subjectivity, and this facilitates the construction of the self-hood of women.

When women come to a new awareness of self, they can look critically at the premises on which their lives are founded, and this helps them to reclaim their agency, as clearly elucidated by Lissie in the reclaiming of her economic, sexual, and spiritual agency. In questioning and reassessing the prevailing norms of women's behavior in these areas, Lissie exercised critical agency, and that has made a difference in her life.

Resistance becomes an essential ingredient of feminist ethics because feminist ethics is a political ethic. As Metz argues, a political ethic is required, not merely as an ethics for order but an ethic for change.[31] Feminist ethics is political in the sense that it sets the platform for change in women's lives, addressing the different dimensions of gendered oppression and violence that distort women's growth as human persons. It is political also in the sense that it can no longer remain just an issue of personal well-being but has wider sociocultural implications. Seen from this perspective of effecting change in the lives of women, particularly the women "bent" by the socioreligious condition of their particular contexts, the personal and collective dimension of resistance becomes significant in feminist ethics.

In the politics of the Reign of God initiated by Jesus Christ, resistance against oppressive beliefs and practices—however "sacred" they were meant to be—is a regular feature, as testified by the gospels. The liberative dimension of resistance as a political ethic finds a powerful echo in Mary's revolutionary cry, the *Magnificat*! As history has proved over and over again, the established structures of domination are dismantled when the "lowly" learn to resist tyrannical power relations personally and collectively. From this standpoint, resistance can also be termed a "feminist virtue," in line with the redefinition of virtue as "justice, fidelity, and self-care"[32]—where *justice* implies setting right gender relations in an egalitarian way;

fidelity means being faithful to the truth of who a woman is as a human person; and *self-care* entails women becoming responsible to care for their own health and growth in all dimensions, resisting the "feminine virtue" of being only for others. This cannot be universalized once and for all, but needs to evolve corresponding to the particularities of women in the different contexts.

Finally, feminist ethics requires a feminist gaze. As Nivedita Menon argues, to see like a feminist is not to stabilize, it is to destabilize. It is a gesture of subversion toward power; it disorganizes and disorders the settled field, resists homogenization, and opens up multiple possibilities rather than closing them off.[33] Given that feminist ethics is oriented toward the liberation of women, and weighs the value of acts and policy in those terms,[34] the primary focus of feminist ethical theologizing is the affirmation of women's human dignity and of egalitarian gender relations. It is from this standpoint that resistance becomes a liberative key in feminist ethics.

Notes

1. *Bhakta* signifies devotee, and Janabai (1298–1350) is one of the best loved *bhaktas* of Maharashtra, India. The *bhaktas* resisted socioreligious norms of their times to give expression to their intense mystic experience of personal devotion. This piece is a selection from Janabai's poem " Cast Off All Shame," cited in Susie Tharu and K. Lalita, *Women Writing in India,* vol I, (New Delhi: Oxford University Press, 1991), 83.

2. *Malayala Manorama*, March 20, 2012, 3.

3. Kochurani Abraham, " Between Patriarchy and Development: Power Negotiations by Catholic Syrian Christian Women in Kerala," an unpublished doctoral thesis done under the guidance of Prof. Felix Wilfred, Dept. of Christian Studies, University of Madras, May 2011.

4. Sally Wehmier, ed. *The New Oxford Advanced Learner's Dictionary* (New Delhi: Oxford University Press, 2005), 1705.

5. Uma Chakravorti, "Conceptualizing Brahminical Patriarchy in Early India: Gender, Caste, Class and State," in Manoranjan Mohanty, ed., *Class, Caste, Gender* (New Delhi: Sage Publications, 2004), 271–95.

6. *Manusmriti* IX:3.

7. For a detailed analysis of the interplay of caste, sexuality, and gender, see V. Geetha, *Patriarchy* (Calcutta: Stree Publications, 200), 133–44.

8. See Uma Chakravorti, *Gendering Caste through a Feminist Lens* (Calcutta: Stree Publications, 2003).

9. Paolo Friere uses the term *prescription* to mean the imposition of one's choice upon another. The behavior of the oppressed is prescribed behavior, following, as it does, the guidelines of the oppressor. See Paolo Freire, *Pedagogy of the Oppressed* (New York: Seabury Press, 1970), 23.

10. Cf. Rachel Simon Kumar, "Claiming the State: Women's Reproductive Identity and Indian Development," in *Feminist Future: Reimagining Women, Culture and Development*, ed. Kum Kum Bhavani, John Foran, and Priya Kurien (New Delhi: Zubaan 2006), 74–88.

11. K. P. Addelson, *Impure Thoughts: Essays on Philosophy, Feminism and Ethics* (Philadelphia: Temple University Press, 1991).

12. F. Williams, "Good-Enough Principles for Welfare," *Journal of Social Polic.* 28 no.4 (1999): 667–87.

13. Nivedita Menon, "Feminism and the Family—Thoughts on International Women's Day," in *Seeing Like a Feminist* (New Dehli: Zubaan Books, 2012).

14. V. Geetha, *Patriarchy*, 8.

15. Steven Parish, "Hierarchy and Its Discontents: Culture and the Politics of Consciousness" in *Caste Society* (Delhi: Oxford University Press, 1997), 135–36.

16. Richard Schaull, "Forward," in Freire, *The Pedagogy of the Oppressed*, 10.

17. Steven Parish terms this as "politics of consciousness." See Parish, "Hierarchy and Its Discontents," 7–10.

18. Jean Drèze and Amartya Sen, *India: Economic Development and Social Opportunity* (New Delhi: Oxford, 1995), 11.

19. Paolo Freire's analysis of the contradictions in the lives of the oppressed is totally applicable to women. See his *The Pedagogy of the Oppressed*, 25–26.

20. A. Giddens, *The Constitution of Society* (Cambridge: Polity Press, 1984), 14.

21. Naila Kabeer, "Resources, Agency, Achievements: Reflections on the Measurement of Women's Empowerment," *Development and Change* 30 (1999): 435–64.

22. Drèze and Sen, *India: Economic Development and Social Opportunity*, 178.

23. Amartya Sen and Jean Drèze, *India: Development and Participation* (Oxford: Oxford University Press, 2002), 258.

24. The "panopticon" the central control tower in prisons suggested by Jeremy Bentham in the eighteenth century, reinterpreted by Foucault to show the effect of disciplinary power. See Michel Foucault, *Discipline and Punish: The Birth of the Prison*, trans. A. Sheridan (New York: Pantheon), 1977.

25. Sally J. Sutherland Goldman, "Speaking Gender: Vāc and the Vedic Construction of the Feminine," in *Invented Identities*, ed. Julia Leslee and Mary McGee (New Delhi: Oxford University Press, 2000),70.

26. Feminist scholars are increasingly unearthing stories of resistance by unassuming Indian women, giving expression to the liberative dynamics of gender discourses. See Anindita Ghosh, ed., *Behind the Veil: Resistance, Women and the Everyday in Colonial South Asia* (Ranikhet, India: Permanent Black, 2007).

27. Ibid., 2.

28. Haynes Douglas and Gyan Prakash, eds., *Contesting Power: Resistance and Everyday Social Relations in South Asia* (Berkeley: University of California Press, 1992), 3.

29. Freire, *Pedagogy of the Oppressed*, 16.

30. Cf. Radha Chakaravarty, *Feminism and Contemporary Women Writers: Rethinking Subjectivity* (New Delhi: Routledge 2008), 189.

31. J. B. Metz, "Theology in the New Paradigm: Political Theology," in *Paradigm Change in Theology: A Symposium for the Future*, ed. David Tracy and Hans Kung (Edinburgh: T&T Clark, 1989), 355–66.

32. James Keenan, "From Padova to Manila," in *Transformative Theological Ethics: East Asian Contexts*, ed. Agnes Brazal et al. (Manila: Ateneo de Manila University Press, 2010), x.

33. Menon, "Feminism and the Family."

34. Carol S. Robb, "A Framework for Feminist Ethics," in *Feminist Theological Ethics: A Reader*, ed. Lois K. Daly (Louisville, KY: Westminster John Knox Press, 1994), 13–32.

Dowry as a Social-Structural Sin

Shaji George Kochuthara

Introduction

Case 1: I have come here to share the story of my daughter Bismayati Patro. She was a graduate, twenty-two years old, and had completed a Post Graduate Diploma in Computer Application. She was also a National and State awardee in Kabbadi, swimming and football. The man who became her father-in-law (Ramachandra Rout) saw her once on the way back home from her college and sent the proposal of her marriage with his son. As we were not ready for it, we refused. But he came frequently to our home and requested us to give him our daughter. He told us that they didn't need anything.... Finally we did her marriage at a temple on April 25, 2008, with Amiya. Though there was no demand from their side, we had given some jewellery to both of them and had told them we would give Rupees 50,000 for buying some assets for Bismayati.... Barely two days after the marriage, our daughter, her husband, and her father-in-law left for Delhi, where her husband was working. We gave again Rupees 20,000 for purchasing some required assets at Delhi.... After four months they came back. Two days after their arrival, my husband visited our daughter ... but Ramachandra Rout did not allow her to talk to him. This worried us and made us begin to suspect that she was being tortured by her in-laws. Then we came to know that her mother-in-law had committed suicide because of dowry torture. We then went to her family to bring back our daughter if she was in trouble.... She stayed with us for two months after which the father and son came and begged our apology.... Bismayati went back, believing that she could manage the situation by herself.... After returning to her husband's home she was again tortured by them physically and mentally. Again after two weeks we brought her back, and again Bismayati's husband took her back.... Again father and son put more pressure on us from time to time for money.... On December 3, Amiya came with Bismayati for money, but it was not possible for us to arrange money at that time. We promised to give it within a week. In spite of our request that they stay at our house, they went back to their village the same day. After two days of their return, on December

108

5, Amiya contacted us over phone to enquire whether we had arranged the money or not and threatened that if we did not arrange the money to be given to them, we would have to forget our daughter. On December 6 at 4:15 in the morning we got a phone call from Amiya, the husband of Bismayati, that our daughter had committed suicide. . . . After seeing the truth we were shocked. It was not a suicide, it was a murder. . . . It was very much clear that they had poured kerosene and set fire on the dead body.[1]

Case 2: A woman training for the Indian Revenue Service (IRS) has complained to the city police that her husband, who is also an IRS trainee, filmed their sexual acts including some unnatural acts. The man was threatening to make the videos public if she did not pay him more dowry. The couple, both from affluent families, had married just seven months ago after meeting at the IRS entrance exam. The cops have booked the husband, his mother and sister under various laws.[2]

Case 3: Mysore: Police registered a complaint against a judge attached to the Chitradurga district court on charges of dowry harassment. DCP (crime) Rajendra Prasad told that Vidya, a legal adviser, has accused her husband Shivashankar, her in-laws, and the judge, Shashikala, of harassing her for dowry. Shashikala is Shivashankar's sister.[3]

Horrific! Barbaric! Shocking! Isn't it? But those in India may not feel these stories as strange, because almost every day, such incidents are reported in the newspapers. Such stories do not have much news value. Often they would be given as an insignificant news item, and many more incidents are not reported at all.

In India, the dowry system,[4] the practice of paying an amount of money to the bridegroom's family by the bride's family, has been the leading cause of the continuing degradation of women and discrimination against them. Consequently, the girl child/woman is considered to be a burden and curse to the family. In practice, dowry is not merely a one-time payment at the time of the marriage. Often, demands for money/property/gifts continue even years after marriage. The estimated number of dowry-related deaths in India is above 25,000 a year.[5] But the evil of dowry is not limited to killings and suicides related to it. The lives of millions of women are made unbearable due to dowry. Many other social evils have their roots in the dowry system. Dowry has become a powerful and oppressive structure that continues to degrade women and promote a number of evils like female foeticide, malnutrition of the girl child, prostitution, sex trafficking, divorce, and constant tensions and conflicts in family life.

Religions, including Christianity, consider marriage a sacred rite of the union of man and woman. Invariably, the essence of marriage is considered to be love and mutual affection, based on equal dignity (though different religions may interpret this equality differently). The practice of dowry, however, makes marriage an unequal and exploitative union from the very beginning, contradicting the meaning of marriage. Religions have not taken the issue of dowry with adequate seriousness, and Christianity does not seem to be an exception to this.

The Dowry System in India

According to the Dowry Prohibition Act (originally passed in 1961 and amended three times in 1980s) of the Indian Civil Law, dowry is defined as "any property or valuable security given or agreed to be given either directly or indirectly by one party to a marriage to the other party to the marriage or by any other person, to either party to the marriage or to any other person at or before (or any other time after the marriage) in connection with the marriage of the said parties."[6] Dowry is punishable by law. In spite of that, it continues to be widely practiced in Indian society. No religion/caste/region/socioeconomic group is free from the practice of dowry.[7] "Eradication of dowry from the Indian society has always been a losing battle for social reformers."[8]

Even today, most of the marriages in India are arranged by the families. Issues of status, caste, and religion may come into the decision, but dowry is, nevertheless, central to the transactions between the families of the bride and groom. By custom, Indian marriage is patrilocal: the wife goes to live in the house of her husband's family following the wedding. The wife is often seen as a servant, or if she is employed, a source of income, but has no special relationship with the members of her new household and therefore no base of support. Some 40 percent of women are married before the legal age of eighteen. Illiteracy among women is high. In some rural areas, the illiteracy rate rises to 63 percent. As a result, they are isolated and often in no position to assert themselves. All these factors make the condition of married women precarious. "Love marriages" (that is, love affairs that lead to marriage) are on the increase, but even these have not succeeded in evading the menace of dowry. Even if a love marriage takes place with the agreement or collaboration of the families, dowry becomes a decisive element. The man's family demands dowry as a legitimate claim; the woman's family may offer the dowry even if it is not demanded (exceptionally!), thinking that their daughter would be humiliated and harassed otherwise. It is not rare that many such love affairs end up tragically, due to disagreements over the amount of dowry. Even the boys who are courageous enough to break the tradition of arranged marriages often become timid at the end over the issue of dowry.

Dowry can take different forms. Usually it consists of an amount of money and jewelry and/or property offered to the bridegroom or his family by the bride's family when the marriage is fixed. In most cases, it includes a demand from the bridegroom's family. Even a middle-class family may demand millions of rupees from the bride's family. In recent years, it may also include the expenses of further studies (often in a foreign country) for the bridegroom or money that he needs to begin a new business. The demands differ depending on the family's socioeconomic status. For example, "A high-flying south Delhi family may demand a Mercedes, while one in a rural area of northwest Delhi may settle for a motorcycle."[9] Thus, the difference is not in the demand but only in the amount of money or the type of gift demanded. Besides such expenses at the time of marriage, which are properly classified as dowry, the demands on the part of the bridegroom or his family can continue for years. For example, jewelry and gifts are expected when the wife becomes pregnant, to cover hospital expenses related to pregnancy and childbirth; when the child is born; when the husband needs a new vehicle; when there is a celebration in the family of the husband; and at important religious festivals. On every such occasion, the wife's family is expected to give the husband or his family money, jewelry, or other gifts or properties. The demand may be explicit or implicit. If the demands are not met, the wife/bride will have to face humiliation, mental and physical harassment, and torture. These demands are considered as the legitimate "right" of the husband or his family. Often when one demand is met, another demand surfaces on the very next occasion. In the worst cases, wives are simply killed to make way for a new financial transaction—that is, another marriage. Shocking as it may sound, even men (husbands) who are convicted and imprisoned for killing their wives find another bride soon after the completion of their term in prison.

Dowry is sometimes justified as the right of the bride to have her share of the family property, just as the bridegroom has his share of the property of his family. Undoubtedly, the woman has a legitimate right to own her share of the family property. What happens in the dowry system as it is practiced today, however, is that an amount of money often much higher than the woman's actual share is demanded by the bridegroom and his family. Significantly, the dowry is not usually kept as a property of the bride, but it becomes the property of the bridegroom's family. Moreover, no transferring of the property to the bridegroom takes place at the time of marriage. Another argument used is that, since the parents of the bridegroom have spent a lot of money for his upbringing and education, it is legitimate that his family demands a payment from the bride's family at the time of marriage. Here it is easily forgotten that the bride's family also has spent for her upbringing and education. Even if the bride is well educated and earning a good salary from work, such things do not count. On the contrary, in such circumstances, her parents have to pay a greater amount as dowry to find a suitable match. It is also argued that, since the bridegroom's family has to spend a lot of money for the wedding celebrations, they have a right to ask for the dowry. However, it is easily ignored that the dowry demanded is many times more than the actual expense of the wedding; moreover, the bride's family also spends a lot of money for the celebrations. Many think that since the bride is going to the bridegroom's family, dowry is necessary to obtain a decent status for her in the new family. Here, the ethical issue is considering her worth in terms of the material property she brings, and not in terms of her worth as a person.

The Dowry System in India: A Historical Overview

The custom of dowry started with the giving of presents to the young woman entering into marriage by her parents and relatives as an expression of love and affection. Gradually, it became a monstrously corrupt practice involving questions of family prestige and social status.[10] In the traditional dowry system, dowry was said to connote female property, or female right to property, transferred at a woman's marriage as a sort of premortem inheritance. Dowry was associated with caste and status. It was a way of demonstrating and sometimes obtaining status. A father received no material gain when he properly gave a dowry for his daughter, but he achieved status and honor. The practice of dowry in this way was restricted to high castes, especially Brahmins. The dowry consisted of *stridhan* (woman's wealth) and *dakshina* (a gift destined for the groom and his family). *Dakshina*, which was a free gift, had a religious significance, in that it was supposed to raise the status of the giver.[11] Other castes had the "inferior" tradition of bride-price; that is, the family of the bride received gifts from the family of the bridegroom as a compensation for giving away their daughter.

But changing socioeconomic structures have altered the shape and meaning of dowry. It has become a modern monstrosity that people try to legitimize by linking it to the ancient custom that, in fact, was totally different. Dowry has deteriorated into a bargaining system in which bridegrooms look for the highest bidder. The main reason for this deviation is said to be the cash-based economy that has commercialized the dowry system.[12] As Shiv Visvanathan points out, "In fact the irony of dowry is that the same word describes two systems. The first is the idea of dowry in a *gift economy*, where it was a token, a presentation from a father to a daughter, or guarantee of security and dignity in times to come. But dowry is no longer a gift but a *demand*. Today dowry is capital, which pump primes a parasitic economy of males living off ransom or surplus generated from the girl."[13] Today, dowry is not limited to any social group or caste.

Dowry and "Unnatural Deaths"

Rather new developments associated with the dowry system are the widespread violence and extreme forms of violence associated with it. As indicated above, there are thousands of women "tortured, killed and driven to suicide by the menace of dowry and other demands associated with marriage, which is one of the new manifestations of India in transition."[14] Bride-price, dowry, and economic transactions associated with marriage were known in the past, but not murders and tortures for dowry as we find today. In 1997, Vimochana, a Bangalore-based nongovernmental organization (NGO) that deals with women's issues, initiated a study campaign on "Dowry Violence and the Unnatural Deaths of Women in Marriage." It was found that 1,133 cases of unnatural deaths of women in Bangalore were reported in 1997. The vast majority of these cases were categorized as "suicides" or "kitchen/cooking accidents," but the reality was different. In 2009, in the Victoria Hospital (Bangalore), Burns Ward, 438 women were admitted, of which 292 died. The majority of women killed or driven to suicide were between the ages of eighteen and twenty-five, married for a period of three months to one year. From one woman dying in every three days in the 1980s and mid-1990s, today the deaths of at least three women are reported in a single day just in the city of Bangalore.[15] "We come across three dowry deaths every day, that builds into a monthly total of 100. However, we suspect hundreds more go unreported," says Donna Fernandes, head of Vimochana. "Very few women survive the tragedy. Shockingly, almost all cases are booked as accident cases," Fernandes adds.[16] This does not mean that other parts of the country are free from this evil. According to the Crime Clock 2005 of the National Crime Records Bureau, India reported one dowry death every seventy-seven minutes.

Many of the victims are burned to death—they are doused in kerosene and set alight. Routinely the in-laws claim that what happened was simply an accident. When evidence of foul play is too obvious to ignore, they change the story to suicide. In the wake of a growing amount of violence and evidence of death associated with dowry, the Indian Penal Code has defined dowry death as follows: "If a woman dies due to burns or bodily injury and in suspicious circumstances within seven years of her marriage and if it is shown that just before her death she was subjected to cruelty or harassment by her husband or his relatives in connection with demands for dowry, such death will be known as 'dowry death.' In this case her husband or his relatives will be considered to cause her death."[17] This shows a greater sensitivity in the legal system toward the suffering and pain of women due to dowry. Even today, however, many such cases are not reported to the police; the family of the woman who is tortured or killed generally considers a court case as causing more shame to the family. Naturally, the husband's family would make use of all means, including bribery, to present the death of the woman as natural. Moreover, patriarchal prejudices of the investigating officers and judges often turn such cases in favor of the husband or his family.

"If the figures of deaths and violence against women related to dowry and domestic violence are systematically collated and projected onto a national level, it should shock an apathetic and complacent polity to wake up to the fact that what we are living with and enduring is the incredible genocide of women that is not being addressed in any systemic way either by civil society or the State."[18] Moreover, this systemic evil cannot be seen just as an individual case of violence, but it promotes a series of evils and violence. As Visvanathan says, "A dowry death is not one act or one event. It does not begin with torture or end with burning. It is a charm of *unbeing* we must comprehend because it cannibalises the idea of women and spreads it over an assembly line of violence."[19] He lists female feticide, malnutrition of female children, forced prostitution, sexual trafficking, and more as connected to dowry, and he argues that "dowry is no longer a domestic problem."[20]

Social-Structural Sin

In recent decades, moral theologians have pointed out that "[o]ne of the greatest failures of Catholic moral theology in the past was the failure to consider the structural problems."[21] While engaging in a minute analysis of the individual person rejecting God or undergoing conversion, moral theology did not give much attention to the institutional and structural nature of sin, grace, and conversion.[22] Thanks to the renewal of Vatican II, the Latin American liberation theologies of the 1970s, and the studies of other human sciences, such as sociology and anthropology, today there is generally a greater awareness of social sins within the church.[23] As S. Arokiasamy stresses, a "theology of sin should clearly include a challenge to, and conscientization about the societal dimensions of sin, virtue, conversion and reconciliation. The 'hardness of heart' spoken of in the Bible is not a matter of the heart of individuals alone, but also of the compulsions and oppressions which get embodied in laws, customs and structures of society."[24] In the New Testament, sin is seen not merely as a personal failure of the person in his/her relationship with God but also as something preventing the Kingdom of God becoming a reality.[25] That is, sin does not just appear in the heart of humans but is also incarnated in social structures and situations that contradict the Kingdom of God.[26] A greater understanding of the call to conversion to the Kingdom of God and the relationship between the person and the society "reveals forces and structures that work to the detriment of justice and of the freedom and dignity of the people."[27] Though human persons are the agents of sin, sin is often mediated through social institutions and structures. Gradually these structures attain a kind of autonomy and cause evil without conscious participation of the individuals. As Hormis Mynatty points out,

> Even though human persons are the agents of sin, sin often is mediated through social institutions and structures. The evil effects of sin often get embodied in social structures both ideological and operational. In the long run, these structures and institutions attain quasi-autonomy and produce evil without conscious participation of the individuals. Individuals and society as a whole internalize such unjust structures and institutions without much critical consciousness and thus reproduce them, and perpetuate evil in the society out of proportion.[28]

On the one hand, individuals can be determined by these unjust structures, but on the other hand, they maintain and perpetuate them. The habits of thinking, attitudes of mind, customs, traditions, cultural practices, laws, and institutions of society that embody the structural dimension of human behavior influence human behavior like a kind of social unconscious. Social sin is the conscious and willful participation of a group or a society in cooperating with sinful social structures and thus maintaining and perpetuating them and failing to do anything to change them when it is possible.[29] "Consciously or unconsciously people perpetuate evil through unjust social structures, where some values other than the human person have become the organizing and dominating value of a system or the society."[30] When the social sins continue to be perpetuated, they become powerful sources of evil and thus become oppressive, determining to a large extent the self-realization of the person and the development of the society in the long run.[31]

Does it mean that persons are not responsible for the structural evil and its evil effects? We can say that, though such evil is mediated through the structure, moral responsibility for sinful structures rests on concrete persons. Moral commitment to the transformation of society and the creation of a new humanity demands taking a stand against sinful structures.[32] Regarding social-structural sins, one difficulty is that many may not consider themselves personally responsible for them. They may say that they are helpless to change them or are just following the tradition or are compelled to act in that way. Becoming morally responsible, however, means becoming aware of our own lives—our "fundamental option," our attitudes, values, and actions. Christian moral formation has focused more on personal choices, actions, and sins, and hence we are more consciously aware of our personal sins. It seems that Christian moral formation has not given an equal importance to the social dimensions of our choices, actions, and sins, and hence we are often ignorant of our responsibility for social sins. Growing to moral maturity demands also becoming aware of, and taking responsibility for, the social dimensions of our lives. Again, people participate in social-structural sin either by conscious participation with, and perpetuation of, sinful structures, or simply by the omission of possible action to change them. There is a dialectical relationship between the sinful social structures—social and personal sin.[33] Pope John Paul II has pointed out that social structures function through human agency. Persons are responsible for social-structural sins. Therefore, one cannot speak about social sin as a different category from personal sin.[34]

Dowry: A Social-Structural Sin

Dowry is a typical case of social-structural sin. "Dowry has become a social menace in modern India leading to the oppression on women, physical violence on the bride, causing a financial and emotional stress on the parents of the bride, marital conflict and so on. This menace exists even today in the society even though it is a criminal offence to take Dowry during marriage."[35] It is being practiced with the justification that it is an ancient custom, although as we have seen above, the practice of dowry was different in the past. We have also seen that other arguments to defend dowry are not reasonable. As in the case of other social-structural sins, no one takes up the responsibility for this evil. Everyone seems to be happy to pretend helplessness and evade responsibility. Strangely, people who are otherwise nonviolent and peaceful, who may not resort to any kind of aggression, may adopt any kind of violent measures, including killing, for dowry. This is an indication that a kind of unconscious and uncritical following of a system that is characteristic of social-structural evil is at work in the practice of dowry and dowry-related violence. Any social-structural evil causes a number of other evils. This is true with regard to dowry. Some of the evils resulting from dowry include the following.

Dowry is the leading cause of the continuing belief that a woman is inferior and a burden to the family. This belief influences the treatment that a woman receives at every phase of her life. "There is no doubt that dowry demands and sharp escalation in the amounts of money being spent by families in putting together dowries has contributed to viewing daughters as a burden and consequent devaluation of women's status."[36] Since girls are considered to be a continuing burden, millions of female fetuses are aborted. There are places where girl children are killed immediately after birth or even later. According to the 2011 census of India, the sex ratio is 914 females per 1,000 males, the lowest since India's independence. The main reason for this is selective female feticide. According to some studies, selective abortion of female fetuses accounts for up to 12 million missing girls in India over the last three decades. Some studies say that up to 35 to 40 million female feticides have taken place in India.[37]

The belief that the woman is inferior and a burden also results in the malnutrition of girl children. Parents naturally prefer to feed the boys better, who will be "assets" for the family, while ignoring the girls who will be only a "burden" for the family. In addition, dowry results in the denial of education/higher education for girls. The better qualified she is, the more burdensome a girl becomes for the family, because to find a boy of equal status means paying more dowry.

Many girls are compelled to remain unmarried, remaining an unwelcome presence in their own families. Their dignity and rights are denied, and their lives become ones of suffering. In fact, the impossibility of paying dowry, and therefore remaining unmarried, is one of the factors that push many women into prostitution.

There are cases where families have to sell their property or incur huge amounts of debt to pay the dowry of their daughters. Often they never manage to pay the debt, and many such families end up as mass suicides.

It can be argued that dowry makes marriage an unequal relationship from the beginning. Many realize that the real motive for marriage was not love but economic gain. This spreads dissatisfaction and unhappiness from the beginning of the couple's family life. Moreover, ongoing demands on the part of the husband and his family leave the wife to suffer silently, caught between the unjust demands of the husband and his family and the agony of her parents. Thus, dowry denies the possibility of a marital life built on love, mutuality, and reciprocity. This denial of love and support on the part of the husband and the family context where the woman has to live always as a subordinate and a source of income for the husband's family is one of the leading causes of female suicides.[38]

It has been shown that the dowry system encourages domestic violence. Women are harassed, tortured, and even killed by the husband or his family in the pursuit of continuing economic benefits. There is no doubt that "violence in the private sphere is as serious and heinous as violence in the public."[39] But the husband and his family feel a sense of legitimacy in doing so, since it has become an essential part of the present-day dowry system. Since girl children are considered a burden mainly due to dowry, a woman can be ill-treated, tortured, and even killed if she gives birth to a girl child. This is another form of violence resulting from the dowry system. It is no wonder that relationships between the families of the husband and wife are often tense due to the dowry system.

I argue that the present dowry system, and the concept of woman as a burden, denies her the possibility of becoming independent. In general, whatever she brings as the dowry or whatever she earns even after marriage is considered the property of the husband and his family, a "payment" due for taking care of her who is only a "burden." She has to live forever as a "bonded laborer" or a slave. Dowry, therefore, violates basic human dignity, in that the worth of a person is calculated by the material benefit from that person. Dowry commodifies and degrades women.[40]

Dowry and the Christian Community

Dowry is widely practiced among Christians, although there may be some regional differences. However, the Christian community, including its leadership, is rather silent about it. Moreover, dowry-related violence becomes part of the lives of many Christian families. Evidently, the church leadership does not accept it as legal but takes no practical, committed action to resist this practice or to present it as against the Christian vision of the man-woman relationship and family. Only passing comments are made in the documents dealing with women or the family. Only rarely do church leaders speak out against dowry. The catechetical program of the church does not include, in general, any teaching against dowry. Marriage preparation courses are usually silent about the practice and about dowry-related violence. Even when it is clear that dowry is given and received, no attempt is made to show that it contradicts the Christian concept of marriage. Similarly, youth movements or women's groups in the church hardly ever take up this issue with seriousness and sincerity. Everyone seems to accept it passively. On the contrary, implicit acceptance of the system can be seen in practice. For example, many parishes ask for a contribution to the church on the occasion of marriage. A bigger amount is demanded from the bridegroom on the ground that he and his family receives dowry. Instead of fighting against the evil of dowry, it seems that the church is satisfied if it gets a share of it! Funds to help poor families to pay dowry are collected without ever raising awareness among the faithful of the evil and sinfulness of the practice.

The Plenary Assembly of the Catholic Bishops' Conference of India (CBCI) does acknowledge that the reality of women of all sections reveals instances of domestic and societal violence on women. It invites us to follow the model of Christ, in liberating women from oppressive structures: "In a culture where women were seen only in relation to men, Christ not only liberated them from their oppressive traditions but upheld their dignity."[41] The Plenary Assembly acknowledges the continuing violence against women violates their dignity: "Depending on the regions, female feticide, infanticide, rape, molestation, kidnapping, abduction, battering, dowry deaths, murdering, trafficking for sex and slavery exist even today."[42] This stance against dowry is indeed commendable. Though dowry is not the only factor that damages the dignity of women, when we understand that it is the most powerful patriarchal custom that denies the dignity and equality of women and promotes violence against women, we may feel that a stronger condemnation and rejection of the dowry system is required.

The Roman Catholic Church considers marriage as one of the sacraments. In Catholic sacramental theology, the highest meaning of marriage is love.[43] Bernard Häring says,

> The one vocation of all the faithful in Christ is to become ever more a visible image of God's love and to guide others towards the same goal. Marriage as sacrament has to be seen in this light, where the two persons become one flesh, one in a community of life and love, helping each other in their complementarity and reciprocity. Together they come to a true image of God's fatherly-motherly love and an image at the same time of the covenant of love and fidelity between Christ and the Church.[44]

The love union of the partners is associated with the sacramentality of marriage, and mutually pleasurable sex and children are expressive of this union.[45] That is why Walter Kasper says that "The love that exists between man and wife is . . . an epiphany of the love and faithfulness of God that was given once and for all time in Jesus Christ and is made present in the Church."[46] Marriage is a life of love. The "vocation and fundamental option of couples is to love each other in the most complete and most profound way."[47] This conjugal love, which is the reflection of God's love, is the essence of marriage. The self-giving that the conjugal love demands involves the whole, total person, including the affections and emotions, the mind and the will, and personal freedom.[48] In addition to their acknowledgement of mutual love and self-giving, they are proclaiming to each other, in effect, "I love you as myself, as God loves his people and as Christ loves his Church."[49]

Dowry makes all these discourses on the sacramental meaning of marriage and love meaningless. Dowry reduces marriage to an economic transaction. In practice, dowry can become the only criterion for marriage. Even when everything else is perfect, the proposed bridegroom and his family abandon the plan of marriage if the amount demanded is not paid as dowry; or, even when there is no motivation of love, marriage may be decided upon if a higher amount is offered as dowry. Thus, the dowry system completely contradicts the Christian meaning of marriage. Sadly, considering marriage as a source of financial income continues even years after marriage. That Christians are a minority and, hence, they cannot challenge and change the traditional customs is not a convincing argument. Often when there is legislation regarding homosexuality, premarital sex, euthanasia, artificial reproduction, contraception, and abortion, which are not in agreement with the Christian understanding, we challenge them and organize even public protests against them. Why, then, can't we take the lead in changing the dowry system that violates the Christian conviction of the dignity of women and totally contradicts the Christian understanding of marriage? The Christian community is called to be the salt of the earth and the light of the world (Mt. 5:13–14).

The Christian community should make a critical analysis of the dowry system in which it participates, in light of Jesus' call for integral liberation. The dowry system demands a reconsideration of our understanding of sin that focuses only on personal sin. Sin is a negative and destructive relationship with the society, resulting either in the breaking of positive relationships or refusal to develop them, hindering both personal development and that of the society.[50] "Our Christian vocation requires that we become aware of the structures of sin around us and within us, and of our responsibility for their removal."[51] A deeper understanding of sin includes its expressions, not only in intrapersonal and interpersonal relationships, but also in the socioeconomic, political, and cultural life. Call to conversion includes this whole fabric of the reality of sin. S. Arokiasamy says that, "social sin creates an environment in which personal sin becomes easy and acceptable, and virtue is made socially—we could also add culturally—difficult."[52] He considers the dowry system as a sinful expression in culture, a structural sin that is rooted in the image of woman as inferior and that reinforces further that image.[53] Dowry violates the basic human dignity of women. Denying the dignity of any human person, whether man or woman, is against the Kingdom values, and "Undoubtedly, a structure that violates human dignity is a sinful structure."[54]

One dimension to be specially attended to is the fact that, in the case of social-structural sin, persons do not feel their own responsibility. Any catechetical formation should include steps to make the faithful aware of the social-structural dimension of sin and the responsibility that each one has in fighting against it. Participating, sustaining, and perpetuating social-structural sin should not be presented as nobody's sinfulness, but rather as the sinfulness of each person involved. Moreover, the Christian community also should make a critical analysis of its structures that discriminate against women and deny them equal dignity. Social-structural evils are often interrelated. Any system, structure, or tradition that discriminates against women will only facilitate discrimination against them in other forms and practices.

Conclusion

In Indian society, dowry is the strongest agent that perpetuates patriarchy, and the Christian community is an active participant in it. Theologians, including feminist theologians, have not made serious attempts to challenge and change the practice of dowry and to show it as a crime and sin. Dowry continues to be practiced in the Christian community without being questioned, further destroying the dignity of women, denying them equality, and inflicting injustice upon them. Moreover, it contradicts the very meaning of marriage. A clear stance against the dowry system and concrete action plans to prevent it should be integral to the Christian commitment to Kingdom values. That would be a great witness that the Christian community could give in the multireligious, multicultural context of India.

Notes

1. Binapani Patro, "Mother of Bismayati," in Vimochana Editorial Collective, *Daughters of Fire. Speaking Pain, Seeking Justice, Sustaining Resistance. Voices and Visions from the Court of Women on Dowry and Related Forms of Violence against Women*, Bangalore: Streelekha Publications, 2011, 48–50. The book contains anecdotes, papers, poems, etc., presented at the "Daughters of Fire, the India Court of Women on Dowry and Related Forms of Violence," held from July 26–29, 2009 in Bangalore, India (hereafter referred to as *Daughters of Fire*). The India Court of Women on Dowry was organized by Vimochana, an NGO that has been working for the empowerment of women and especially fighting against dowry and violence related to dowry. The court was organized in collaboration with a number of organizations both in India and abroad and was conducted at Christ University (Bangalore) and Dharmaram Vidya Kshetram (Bangalore).

2. "IRS Trainee Booked for Filming Wife, Threatening to Release Videos," http://articles.timesofindia.indiatimes.com.

3. "Chitradurga Judge Faces Dowry Case," http://articles.timesofindia.indiatimes.com.

4. Although the dowry system exists in different forms in many countries, we are addressing here only the practice of dowry in India. For a detailed analysis of the dowry system in South Asia, see Werner Menski, *South Asians and the Dowry Problems* (New Delhi: Vistaar Publications, 1998).

5. According to official records, more than 2,500 bride-burning deaths are recorded every year. Unofficial sources estimate more than 25,000 cases of bride-burning every year. Many more are left maimed and scarred as a result of attempts on their lives. In spite of the prohibition of dowry by law, in recent decades there has been a steady increase of dowry-related violence—10 to 15 percent every year.

6. "Know Your Law. Law Relating to Dowry Offences (The Dowry Prohibition Act, 1961)," *Legal News and Views* 22, No. 6 (June 2008): 29.

7. Abraham M. George, *India Untouched. The Forgotten Face of Rural Poverty* (Chennai: East West Books, 2004), 207.

8. Alka Kurian, "Feminism and the Developing World," in *The Routledge Companion to Feminism and Postfeminism*, ed. Sarah Gamble (London: Routledge, 2001), 74.

9. Maneesh Pandey, "Dowry Deaths on the Rise in City," http://articles.timesofindia.indiatimes.com.

10. P. D. Mathew, *Law Relating to Dowry Offences*, Legal Education series no. 27 (New Delhi: Indian Social Institute, revised edition 1998).

11. Neena Joseph, "Stridhanavum Charitra Paschathalavum" (in Malayalam, "The Dowry and the Historical Background"), *Stridhanathinetire Streesakthi* (The Power of

Women against Dowry) (Neyyattinkara: Neyyattinkara Integral Development Society, 2002), 4–6.

12. Jane Rudd, "Dowry-murder: An Example of Violence against Women," in *Women's Lives and Public Policy: The International Experience*, ed. Meredith Turshen and Briavel Holcomb (Westport, CT: Greenwood Press, 1993), 92–94.

13. Shiv Visvanathan, "Dowry: Beyond the Sociology of Despair," in *Daughters of Fire*, 39.

14. Rita Noronha, "Empowerment of Women in the Church and Society," *Vidyajyoti Journal of Theological Reflection* 72, no.6 (2008): 410.

15. Vimochana Editorial Collective, "A Web of Violence," in *Daughters of Fire*, 3; See also Vimochana, "When Homes are Torture Chambers: Vimochana's Work with Victims of Domestic Violence," in *Urban Women in Contemporary India*, ed. Rehana Ghadially (Los Angeles: Sage Publications, 2007), 100–08.

16. "IT City Plagued by Dowry Deaths," http://articles.timesofindia.indiatimes.com.

17. "Know Your Law," 30.

18. Vimochana Editorial Collective, "A Web of Violence," in *Daughters of Fire*, 3.

19. Shiv Visvanathan, "Dowry," in *Daughters of Fire*, 39.

20. Ibid.

21. Hormis Mynatty, *Proposals for a Comprehensive Moral Methodology* (Bangalore: Asian Trading Corporation, 2008), 149.

22. Vimal Tirimanna, "The Sinful Talk of Sin," *Asian Horizons* 4, no.2 (2010): 444.

23. Ibid.

24. S. Arokiasamy, "Sinful Structures in the Theology of Sin, Conversion and Reconciliation," in *Social Sin: Its Challenges to Christian Life*, ed. S. Arokiasamy and F. Podimattam (Bangalore: Claretian Publications, 1991), 111.

25. Jon Sobrino, "Jesus' Relationship with the Poor and Outcasts: Its Importance for Fundamental Moral Theology," *Concilium* 130 (1979): 16.

26. Mynatty, *Proposals for a Comprehensive Moral Methodology*, 147.

27. Arokiasamy, "Sinful Structures," 90.

28. Mynatty, *Proposals for a Comprehensive Moral Methodology*, 146.

29. Hormis Mynatty, "Concept of Social Sin," *Louvain Studies* 16, no.1 (1991): 17.

30. Mynatty, *Proposals for a Comprehensive Moral Methodology*, 149.

31. Mynatty, "Concept of Social Sin," 9.

32. Arokiasamy, "Sinful Structures," 107.

33. Mynatty, *Proposals for a Comprehensive Moral Methodology,* 172.

34. John Paul II, *Reconciliatio et Paenitentia*, no.16.

35. Gurudeve, "The Origin of Dowry System—British Policies Convert Gifts to Bride into an Instrument of Oppression against Women," http://www.hitxp.com/

36. Madhu Purnima Kishwar, "Strategies for Combating the Culture of Dowry and Domestic Violence in India," in *Daughters of Fire*, 89.

37. Shaji George Kochuthara, "Millions of Missing Girls! Female Foeticide and Ethical Concerns," *Catholic Theological Ethics in the World Church Newsletter Forum* (2012), http://www.catholicethics.com/july2012.

38. Kurian, "Feminism and the Developing World," in *The Routledge Companion to Feminism and Postfeminism*, 75.

39. Donna Fernandes, "Investigating Kitchen Accidents," in *Daughters of Fire*, 45.

40. Kurian, "Feminism and the Developing World," in *The Routledge Companion to Feminism and Postfeminism*, 74; Veena Oldenburg, "Dowry Murders in India: A Preliminary Examination of the Historical Evidence," in *Women's Lives and Public Policy: The International Experience*, Meredith Turshen and Briavel Holcomb (Westport, CT: Greenwood Press, 1993), 145–57.

41. "Empowerment of Women in the Church and Society": Statement of CBCI in the 28th Plenary Assembly of the CBCI, Jamshedpur, February13–20, 2008, *Vidyajyoti Journal of Theological Reflection* 72, no. 4 (2008): 303.

42. Ibid., 301.

43. The acceptance of marriage as a sacrament was not an easy process. Often there were doubts whether marriage could be considered a sacrament. It may be interesting to note here that one of the greatest difficulties raised by canonists and medieval theologians regarding the full sacramentality of marriage was the frequent economic clauses tied to marriages. It was argued that considering marriage as a sacrament created the risk of simony. Cf. Angelo Scola, *The Nuptial Mystery* (Cambridge: Cambridge University Press, 2005), 194–97.

44. Bernard Häring, *Free and Faithful in Christ*, vol. 2 (Middlegreen, United Kingdom: St. Paul Publication, 1979), 534–35.

45. Cf. L. S. Cahill, *Sex, Gender, and Christian Ethics* (New York: Cambridge University Press, 1996), 193.

46. W. Kasper, *Theology of Christian Marriage* (New York: Crossroad, 1981), 30.

47. M. Attard, "Can Marriage Make You a Saint?" *Carmel in the World* 16 (1977): 211.

48. Ibid., 217.

49. M. G. Lawler, *Secular Marriage* (Mystic, CT: Twenty-Third, 1985), 70.

50. Mynatty, *Proposals for a Comprehensive Moral Methodology*, 149.

51. Arokiasamy, "Sinful Structures," 90.

52. Ibid., 93.

53. Ibid., 103–04.

54. Felix Podimattam, "Theology of Social Sin," in *Social Sin: Its Challenges to Christian Life*, ed. S. Arokiasamy and F. Podimattam (Bangalore: Claretian Publications, 1991), 70.

Promoting Women's Dignity in the Church and Society in Hong Kong— Inspirations from Church Leaders and Women Christians as Leaders

Mee-Yin Mary Yuen

Does the Asian Church Need Feminism and Feminist Theology?

Throughout history, women have been excluded, neglected, discriminated against, and suppressed, both in society and the Catholic Church: this is evidence of the destruction of the good and right relationship of God's creation. Since the 1960s, as the secular feminist movement in Europe and North America became stronger, the church has become more alert to the issue of gender equality, reflecting this in its theology and practices.

In the Catholic Church, however, especially Chinese church communities, many people still have reservations about feminism and feminist theology, regarding it as too radical and as ignoring the church's tradition. There are many schools of thought on feminism,[1] which, despite their differences, share a common goal to improve the status of women and to liberate them from oppression, so that women can live up to their true selves and share equal opportunities with men. They aim at reforming social structures, cultural values, and popular mind-sets. Women are not only the target of concern but also moral subjects and moral agents who contribute their opinions, perspectives, and experiences to social change.

Feminist theology, like other feminist critiques, arises out of women's consciousness. It participates in social reform through reconstructing theology and religion. Moreover, feminist theology emphasizes both theory and practice. It can be considered as moral theology, standing on the side of the oppressed to bring individual conversion and social change. Realizing that women's experiences of oppression cannot be fully reflected in mainstream theology, Christian feminists suggest that a more holistic and inclusive theology should be developed, through reinterpreting the Bible, Christian doctrines, and church history, in order to rediscover women's experiences and unveil the patriarchal ideology inherent in theology.[2] Therefore, with the goal of bringing justice and humanity on earth, feminist theology and ethics should not be ignored or rejected in the church.

Some people contend that feminism and feminist theology emanate from the West and may not be suitable for other places such as the Asian region or Chinese society. While it is true that feminism started in the West, feminist theology, which is considered as a branch of liberation theologies, developed rapidly in developing countries and marginalized communities, including Asia, Latin America, and African American communities. These theologies developed into diversified forms according to different contexts.[3] Feminism is not now unique to the West.

Moreover, some people argue that the status of women nowadays is much higher than before. In particular, they argue that because, in many places, including Hong Kong and other countries of Asia, gender equality has been achieved, there is no need to talk about feminism anymore. It is true that women's status has been greatly improved in the past few decades, but this is not the whole picture. In reality, many women still suffer from oppression and repression, unfair treatment, different kinds of abuse and violence, and are unable to develop their potentialities and talents. There is a need, therefore, to uncover and address the issue of gender inequality in society and the church. More important is to find an ethic that can sustain gender equality and the dignity of women.

Although there are many commonalities among the feminist thought of different places, many feminist theologians in the developing countries realize that their experiences are not totally the same as those in the West. The various feminist theologies that arose from their contexts challenge sexism in their own cultures and societies. Meanwhile, feminist theologians in non-Western and the nonwhite world also challenge racism, classism, colonialism, and neocolonialism. I will now turn to the context and features of doing theology and feminist ethics in Asia.

Doing Feminist Theology in Asia

Asia is a continent of diversity and plurality in terms of its cultural and religious traditions, as well as its socioeconomic and political situations. One can say that Asian cultures, religions, and societies are interdependent, interacting, and mutually transforming. But Christians represent only 3 percent of the Asian population. Thus, doing theology, including feminist theology, in Asia is very different from doing theology in many Western countries, where Christianity is nominally the main religion. There are also stark differences in the economic situation of various Asian countries. While in recent years there has been rapid economic progress in some East Asian countries, poverty and economic disparity still feature prominently in other Asian countries, even within the rapidly developed areas such as Hong Kong and China. The life of the underprivileged and marginalized is a reality that Asian theologians cannot neglect. Doing feminist theology in Asia focuses particularly on women and injustice.

Moreover, Asian women have diverse experiences based on their different ethnicities, castes, and sexual orientations. Some Asian feminist theologians have begun to call for more attention to the diversity of women's experiences, and to address the real contradictory experiences and the multiple agencies of women from all walks of life and across cultures, that is, the hybridity of women's existence.[4] Some also introduce postcolonial theory into Asian feminist biblical interpretation and theological discourse, to demonstrate the multiple identities of women and the numerous ways to analyze marginalization. There is always an Other within the Other. Therefore, there is no simple dualistic caricature of the power dynamics behind the pairings of domination/submission, insider/outsider, powerful/powerless and colonizer/colonized.[5] Most Asian women and men (except those from Japan and Thailand) share a common history of colonial domination, neocolonialism, and westernization, albeit to varying degrees.[6]

In these Asian contexts, as Sharon Bong demonstrates in her essay in this volume, Asian women have recently gathered to discuss ways of doing Asian feminist liberation theologies. Their consensus is that the starting point of theology should always be women's experiences, letting women tell their own stories, especially neglected and marginalized women. Apart from Christian texts, feminist theologians also employ local resources such as myths, folk stories, and religious, cultural, and philosophical traditions. Moreover, they try to reinterpret those biblical texts that result in discrimination and oppression to women. In finding the true values of women, they use an integral spirituality. In linking theory to practice, Asian feminist theologies shift from an academic-centered to a liberative action-orientation in order to create solidarity among sisters and promote social transformation.[7]

As a Hong Kong–Chinese woman who is interested in social ethics, I would like in the following sections to examine how the church leaders in the Catholic Church, from the West and Asia, exercise their leadership in upholding the vision of gender equality and protecting the dignity of women and men. In particular, I will analyze their social teachings and pastoral guidance to religious and laypeople, from the perspective of Asian feminist liberation theology. The question I raise is, is their practice of leadership adequate to the task of gender equality and gender justice? Taking Hong Kong as an example, I would also like to demonstrate how Christians in the church were inspired by church teachings and other religious leaders' guidance to bring liberation to women in society and church through various ministries. First, in order to put theological ethics in context, I would like to describe briefly the impact of globalization on women in Hong Kong through two women's narratives.

Women under Globalization
in the Hong Kong Context

Globalization has as many critics as champions.[8] Hong Kong has experienced both the positive and negative effects of globalization. As an open economic entity, Hong Kong has experienced rapid development in international trade, capital mobility, and the transfer of communication and technological information since the 1980s and 1990s. However, many low-income workers cannot benefit from this and have suffered greatly. In order to do social ethics in the Hong Kong–Chinese context, I am especially concerned with the adverse effect of globalization on underprivileged women and men. Low-income women workers, migrant workers, and ethnic minorities are considered to be the most vulnerable ones in this context. I will use two narratives to illustrate the lives of local and migrant women in real-life contexts.

The first woman, Mei Fong (not her real name), is a low-income worker in Hong Kong. She migrated from mainland China with her parents when she was young. She has been a textile factory worker since the 1970s and earned an income that could support a decent living. However, since the late 1980s and early 1990s, most of the factories closed down and moved to other developing countries with lower labor costs. The factory in which Mei Fong worked faced a similar fate. She was forced to work as a cleaning worker in a government department, but under a subcontractor company, with much lower salary and poor working conditions. After complaining against the employer of the subcontractor company for the practice of deducting monthly holidays, she was laid off.

The phenomenon of subcontracting work to another company is not uncommon in an age of globalization. Workers at such companies do not have basic benefits and protection. Many workers earn an extremely low hourly based income without holidays. Mei Fong's experience reflects the reality that under economic globalization the economic gains of the transnational corporations or large enterprises may not benefit the majority of the labor force, particularly women workers. Globalization of trade does not necessarily reduce inequalities, but rather brings about the polarization of wealth both between and within nations.[9]

Another story is about Dolores (not her real name), a migrant worker from the Philippines working as a domestic helper in a Hong Kong family. She graduated from university in 1990s but could not find a job in the Philippines that could support her family. Without other choices, she came to Hong Kong and started working as a domestic helper. She benefited by being able to earn money to support her family, but she had to leave her family and do the kind of work that she did not intend to do. She took one whole year to adjust to her new job and to overcome the psychological obstacles. Finally, she survived with support from her friends and a Filipino migrant workers' group—The United Filipinos in Hong Kong. This group was set up in 1985 to support striking migrant workers' rights and provide various kinds of support to Filipino workers. Because of her active involvement, Dolores became the chairperson. She well understood the difficulties that many other migrant workers face in having unreasonable employers and unfair treatment. Quite a number of them face rampant abuse and are subjected every day to deception, extortion, poor working conditions, psychological and physical violence, and even deportation. They dare not complain because they may be dismissed and unable to pay their debt to the company that arranged for them to work in Hong Kong.[10]

From these two narratives, we can see that each woman has her own unique story, relating to her family, work, and daily life. Sometimes there may be conflict of interest among women. Yet both local and migrant women workers experience similar negative impacts of migration and economic recession under globalization, and a lack of support from the government. Nevertheless, they are not just passive victims waiting to be saved. They try to change their fate through solidarity with other women, as Dolores shows in her leadership role.

I will now turn to the church's teachings, and examine how they can or cannot uphold the moral lives and agency of women.

Papal Social Teachings and the Dignity and Rights of Women in Society

Many governments in the world, including the Hong Kong government, place the overall economic development and prosperity of their ruling territory over the human flourishing of each and every person in society. The Hong Kong government has adopted an oversimplified logic of the "trickle-down" theory from neoclassical economics—or the belief that overall economic growth will trickle down to each person and every group in society. However, this metanarrative of economic development does not reflect the reality of people's lives. Social and economic policies of the government privilege the business sector and neglect the welfare of the common people. To understand the situation of women, we must look into the particular context of each of these women and respect each of them as an individual. In view of this, I will first examine some principles of papal social teachings that can uphold women's dignity and moral agency in bringing change and then its inadequacies.

The principle that all human persons have the same human dignity regardless of one's status, background, gender, race, and class is the foundation of Catholic social teaching. Being created in the image of God, all women and men enjoy equal inalienable dignity. People are ends in themselves and have their own worth. All people have to respect that dignity and help each other to flourish.[11] Relevant to this is the Catholic theory of human rights. Human rights, realized in community, give specific meanings to human dignity, offering a coherent integration of political and economic rights and a balanced appreciation of both rights and duties. With this emphasis on human dignity, the principle that "the dignity of people must come before profit" becomes a central tenet in Catholic social teaching with regard to human work and workers' rights.[12]

In the encyclical *Laborem Exercens* (On Human Work) in 1981, John Paul II gives priority to the subjective dimension of work. The value of human work is not primarily the kind of work being done but the fact that the one doing it is a person (nos. 6, 7). John Paul II also elaborates on the rights of the workers in the broad context of human rights that establishes the minimum conditions for a just society (nos. 16–23). Bearing these principles in mind, when we look at the example of the

two women in Hong Kong, we affirm that they should have equal rights as men to
have work, and to work in a conducive and healthy environment.

Apart from these general principles, in the 1963 social encyclical *Pacem
in Terris*, John XXIII, in seeing the sign of the times, states that, based on the
ever-increasing awareness of women on human dignity, women cannot be looked
upon as an object or a tool (no. 15). In *Gaudium et Spes*, bishops from all over the
world agreed that they should not neglect those problems that result in women
being treated unjustly, including the trafficking of women, the lack of freedom
to choose a husband, or the inability to embrace a state of life or to acquire an
education or cultural benefits equal to those recognized for men. Women, said
Gaudium et Spes, should also enjoy equal rights to higher education and cultural
benefits (nos. 27, 29, 60). In other church documents, John Paul II called for
real equality in every area: equal pay for equal work, protection for working
mothers, fairness in career advancements, and equality of spouses with regard
to family rights.[13]

It is true that the above-mentioned church teachings show the concern of
church leaders for women's social rights and status. However, when speaking
on the roles of women and men, based on the biblical vision of the sexually
differentiated human person and women's physical capacity to give life, church
documents emphasize "the difference and reciprocity between the sexes," the
complementarity between men and women, and women's special contribution in
human relationships and caring for others.[14] While acknowledging the attention
that church leaders give to work and family, and the appreciation for women's
special gifts, a number of Catholic feminist theologians are critical of these
teachings on the essential difference between sexes, pointing out that too much
emphasis on women's special genius of nurturing excludes women as leaders of
the church. They also argue that the church neglects the issue of domestic abuse
and sexual violence.[15] I agree that the church's recognition of the value of housework is a counterbalance to the failure to recognize it as work. However, the
crucial issue is whether women have freedom to choose their roles and not be
restricted by traditional values as they try to develop their potential. Moreover,
the papal teachings do not discuss how to nurture the capabilities of women,
which are important factors for women to exercise their agency. There is also a
lack of women's voice in the social teaching.

The Asian church leaders' teachings can provide another viewpoint for
reference.

The Asian Church's Teaching and
Concerns on Women in Society

At the Asian church level, members of the Federation of Asian Bishops'
Conferences (FABC) have discussed the situation of women and their roles in
a number of meetings, leading to the organizing of the Bishops' Institute for the

Lay Apostolate (BILA) on Women.[16] In 1995, the BILA on Women held the first meeting, "Role of Women in Church and Society Towards 2000." The meeting started with narratives of the lived experience of women. Through listening to the cries and pain of women, the Asian bishops and other participants tried to understand the living environment of sex workers, exploited women workers, low-income women, and women suffering from violence, as well as the experiences of church workers who serve these women. After this, the guest speakers conducted an analysis, synthesis, and theological reflection, in order to help participants to integrate the personal experiences of immersion, social analysis, and theological reflection. Daily liturgy and prayers became part of theological reflection. As a participant in one the BILAs on Women, I felt this process could help us to compare and contrast the experiences of women in various places, to find out the causes of problems, and to make recommendations.[17]

The whole process of the meeting allowed participants to have direct contact with women who faced various kinds of problems and to hear their voices directly. We could see the effects of economic development under capitalist, patriarchal ideology. However, these difficulties did not just bring despair to women but to the church as well. In solidarity with women, the Asian church showed a willingness to uphold the dignity of women, to face the injustices in the church and in society that discriminate against women and the poor, to denounce all the cultural customs and practices that bring injustice to women, and to join other groups and religions to eliminate all forms of violence against women.[18]

We can see the common concern about the role and status of women in society between the papal teachings and the FABC teachings as mentioned above. However, the ways of producing these documents or teachings were very different. The papal teachings were characterized by general analysis, statements, and principles about the situations of women, whereas the FABC approach was a bottom-up one in which the process of reaching a consensus among the representatives of various local churches was highlighted. It also emphasized the importance of listening to women's voices before doing any analysis or making any conclusion or suggestion. This approach shares many commonalities with the methods of other Asian theologians, both women and men, in the way they do theology.[19]

Although the documents of the FABC have no binding authority like papal social teachings, they give recognition and encouragement to those who devote their time and effort in women's work. They also inspire many people who advocate for gender equality and social justice in a variety of ways. In different parts of Asia, many religious groups, diocesan commissions, and laypeople are involved in various kinds of ministries that show concern for women, working with groups such as new immigrants, abused women, women workers, migrant domestic workers, ethnic minorities, and sex workers. This is a reflection of the important interaction between various church groups and church teachings about upholding women's dignity and gender equality.

Social Teaching on Women in the Church

While feminist theology shares with feminism the goal of examining and improving the role and status of women in society, the uniqueness of feminist theology can be found in its emphasis on investigating the role and status of women in the church as well as the theology that affects the church's attitudes toward gender issues and women's roles.

Using the basic principle that all are equal before God, the Catholic Church has gradually changed its own self-image from one that was exclusive and hierarchal to one that is moving toward equality and communion in Christ.[20] In Vatican II's *Gaudium et Spes*, leaders of the universal church proposed some common wishes, including the hope that "many of the laity will receive a sufficient formation in theology and that some will dedicate themselves professionally to these studies" (no. 62). In *Ecclesia in Asia*, Pope John Paul II states that women should participate in the life and ministries of the Asian church. In order to strengthen the quality of service, "women should have more opportunities to learn theology and other disciplines" and "women should be allowed to participate more in pastoral work, diocesan and parish work, and the diocesan synod" (no. 45).

Moreover, the BILA on Women of the FABC also made some recommendations to strengthen women's roles: encouraging more women to participate in church organizations and councils, introducing women's theology in seminaries and formation centers, and providing support and opportunities for women to receive theological education.

These messages that affirm the possibility of receiving theological education and serving in various ministries for laywomen are very encouraging. However, some scholars and laywomen think that there is still a big gap between these statements and reality. The law, rules, system, and theology of the church cannot fully match these suggestions, especially on issues such as women's participation in decision making, their role as leaders, women's ordination, the specialization of work between women and men, the nature of ministry, and so on. These issues are still very controversial and sensitive. Some church leaders even prohibit believers from discussing these issues. There is a pressing need for church leaders to be more open to, and listen to, women's voices in order to discern the signs of the times that are compatible with the core teachings of the church and the message of the gospel.

Promotion of Women's Dignity in Hong Kong by Women Christians

Despite the limitations of the church's teachings, some religious women and laypeople in Hong Kong are able to make use of the church's social teachings, particularly the principle of the inherent dignity of all people, to work in ministries to uphold dignity of women and men. Others are encouraged and inspired by leaders of their religious communities to start new ministries. These women who are involved in various ministries can also be considered as leaders with a vision to create a culture of mutual respect, caring especially for the most vulnerable women. Below are some examples in the Hong Kong church.

Ministry for Women Sex Workers

Sister Ann Gray, a Scottish missionary sister of St. Columba who had worked in Hong Kong for over ten years, was one of the founders of a ministry serving women sex workers. In 1991, she was invited by her superior general to reflect on the needs of women in her mission area and to envision a collaborative project that would in some way respond to their real needs and give witness to Christian community in practice. After doing some research, analysis, and observation, Sister Ann realized that women sex workers were the group of women who were most neglected and abandoned by society. She and her colleagues started doing outreach work, visiting women on the streets, night clubs, pubs, and massage centers. Some of these women were locals; some were from mainland China, Thailand, and the Philippines. "Action for Reach Out" was set up in 1993, with the aim of serving women sex workers as human persons.[21]

Since these women lived on the margins of society, the aim of this ministry was to accompany them in their struggle, treating them with respect, accepting them just as they were, and in this way sharing with them a sense of the presence of God among them, so that they could nurture the sense of love, care, and value of a person. Sister Ann and her colleagues set up a drop-in center where women could come and chat. Workers and volunteers also do outreach work to get in touch with the sex workers. They provide health care education, legal consultation, counseling services, and social activities. A peer education program was set up so that these women who once worked on the streets as sex workers could share their experiences with other women.

At the beginning of the ministry, Sister Ann and her colleagues were unable to gain support from people in the society and the church. Gradually, more and more Christians accepted her vision. She was invited to share the ministry and her mission in parishes and Christian communities. She also received donations from individual Christians and groups. There were also volunteers from the church, including myself, who worked with Sister Ann in doing outreach work. In 2005, Action for Reach Out was handed over to the local people who had given several years of service in this group when Sr. Ann Gray's services were needed in Scotland.

Organizing Self-employed Support Groups
for Ethnic Minority Women

With the aim of serving all socially marginalized workers in Hong Kong, regardless of their age, religion, and sex, the Catholic Labour Centre (Kowloon) of the Hong Kong Catholic Diocese was set up in 1991. Based on the social teachings of the church, particularly on the dignity of workers and the right to decent employment, the center has organized outreach programs to educate grassroots workers about their rights at work in Hong Kong. The Centre has also formed mutual support groups for self-employed ethnic minority women, mostly immigrants from Pakistan.

Around 2005, the Labour Centre, with its lay director, Dorothy Lee, started organizing the Pakistani women who attended the female Cantonese class as a self-employed support group. Realizing that many Pakistani women were competent in sewing and embroidery work, with an artistic sense and rich cultural background, the Centre encouraged these women to make embroidered clothes for sale to local Chinese. In this way, the Pakistani women could earn an income to support their families, as many of them were from low-income families. With this background, the Hidden Women Art Craft Studio was set up. The members of this studio made embroidered clothes adapted to the local taste, artistic home decoration, stationery products, and hand painting. Most of the Pakistani women claim that this was the first time for them to earn money. During this process, their confidence was built up by receiving appreciation from customers; and, through their contact with the rest of society, the self-employed group provided support and connection among group members, as well as information about newly introduced social policies aimed at ethnic minorities in Hong Kong.[22]

Apart from serving the ethnic minority women, in order to recruit volunteers from parishes, the Centre has invited parishioners to join a project called "Who is your neighbor?" Most of the volunteers teach the Pakistani women and children the Chinese language and distribute labor law leaflets on the street. In the orientation session, mutual respect for each other's religion was emphasized, as most Pakistanis were Muslims. During the course of providing services, the volunteers experienced inner change because they had never encountered South Asian residents before. They had a media-inspired stereotypical impression, and had never thought of their South Asian neighbors as friendly and kind hearted. After joining the service, their reflections transformed their attitudes.

Other Ministries

The above-mentioned ministries are just two examples that demonstrate what Catholic religious and laywomen in the Hong Kong church have done in upholding women's dignity and rights, enabling other people to follow their examples in serving the marginalized and neglected women in Hong Kong society. There are other women who work to affirm the dignity of women and men and to highlight women's voices, including those ministering to people living with AIDS,[23] offering pastoral care to women migrant workers, and those helping women parishioners to discover the potential and value of women. Moreover, some laywomen and men of the Diocesan Justice and Peace Commission and Labor Affairs Commission, through their appointment or employment by the bishop of Hong Kong as members or staff, have advocated for the rights of workers and the poor, and for a just and fair political structure. They also conduct formation in parishes to spread the message of Catholic social teaching.[24] Apart from these social ministries, there are also women leaders who have contributed in education and formation, enabling both women and men in developing their potentialities and abilities as more humane, knowledgeable, rational, and compassionate people.[25]

Furthermore, some religious leaders in the Catholic seminary, including priests and nuns, are pioneers in developing a four-year evening theology degree program for laywomen and men, so that laywomen like me can share an equal chance of receiving theological education as those trained to be priests, in order to be equipped to serve in various ministries of the church. Since 1989, the Holy Spirit Seminary of Theology and Philosophy has trained more than 150 graduates, with more than 70 percent of them laywomen. The seminary has also employed women religious and laywomen in teaching various kinds of courses. Some of the graduates, both women and men, are encouraged to undertake further studies so that they can teach in the seminary in the future. It should be noted, however, that the perspective of Asian feminist theology has not yet been fully introduced and recognized in the theological courses there.

Conclusion

Thinking theologically is important in a religious tradition because the concrete expression of church life is based on the understanding of Christian faith. Therefore, in seeking to find justice in the church and society for women, Christian theology and the church's teaching must do justice to women who have hitherto being neglected. In this essay, I have shown that church leaders from the Vatican and Asia have provided encouragement and guidance in upholding the vision of gender equality and protection of the dignity of women and men, through their teachings, vision, and pastoral guidance to religious and laypeople. Taking Hong Kong as an example, I have demonstrated that some religious and laywomen and men in the church have made significant efforts in bringing liberation to women in society and the church through various ministries. Leadership is not confined to those at the top level of the hierarchal church; other religious and laypeople in ministries are also leaders who inspire other believers to follow their footsteps.

However, there are shortcomings in the social teachings and the actual practice of the church. These include the emphasis on complementarity between women and men in the church's social teaching; the lack of women's voices in formulating teachings and making decisions in the church; and the gap between these official teachings and the law, policies, and practices of the Vatican and local churches. More effort should be put into formulating a feminist ethic that does justice to women and putting the recommendations of the FABC into practice.

Nevertheless, more and more church leaders realize the importance of promoting gender equality in church and society. Many religious and laypeople are able to appropriate various principles and notions in the social teaching to support their works. These teachings are indeed inspiration and encouragement to people with the vision of building a society and a church of inclusiveness and equality.

Notes

1. The diversified forms of feminism include liberal, socialist, existentialist, fundamentalist, postmodern, eco-feminism, etc. For more details, see to Gu Yan Ling, ed. *Nuxing zhuyi: lilun yu liupai* [Feminism: Theories and Forms] (Taipei: Nushu wenhua, 1996), ix–xvii.

2. Lisa Sowle Cahill, "Feminism and Christian Ethics: Moral Theology," in *Freeing Theology: The Essentials of Theology in Feminist Perspective*, ed. Catherine Mowry LaCugna (San Francisco: HarperSanFrancisco, 1993), 212–13; Kao Tianxiang, "He wei nuxing shenxue?" [What Is Feminist Theology?], in *Huidao shengming yuandian* [Go Back to the Original Point of Life], ed. and trans. Liao Jinchang (Taipei: Tianzhujiao jiaowu xiejinhui chubanshe, 1995), 11–17.

3. There is no simplified classification of feminist theology. The term "feminist" is regarded as associated mainly with white, middle-class, well-educated women. In the United States, African American women use the word "womanist," whereas Hispanic women employ the term "mujerista," along with the insights of Asian American women. See Susan A. Ross, "Feminist Theology: A Review of Literature," in *Feminist Ethics and Catholic Moral Tradition: Readings in Moral Theology No. 9*, ed. Charles E. Curran, Margaret A. Farley, Richard A. McCormick (New York: Paulist Press, 1994), 12.

4. Wong Wai-Ching, "Negotiating for a Postcolonial Identity: Theology of the Poor Woman in Asia," *Journal of Feminist Studies in Religion* 16, no. 1 (2000): 22–23; Kang Nam-Soon, "Creating Dangerous Memory: Challenge for Asian and Korean Feminist Theology," *Ecumenical Review* 47, no. 1 (1995): 21–31.

5. Kwok Pui-lan, *Introducing Asian Feminist Theology* (Cleveland: Pilgrim Press, 2000), 61–62.

6. Chung Hyun-Kyung, *Struggle to Be the Sun Again: Introducing Asian Women's Theology* (Maryknoll, NY: Orbis Books, 1990), 22–23.

7. Mary John Mananzan, "Feminist Theology in Asia: A Ten-year Overview," in *Challenges to the Inner Room*, ed. Mary John Mananzan (Manila: The Institute of Women's Studies, St. Scholastica's College, 1998), 112–13.

8. See J. A. Scholte, "Beyond the Buzzword: Towards a Critical Theory of Globalization," in *Globalization: Theory and Practice*, ed. E. Kofman and G. Youngs (London: Pinter, 1996), 53.

9. John C. Dwyer, "Dignity of Persons," in *The New Dictionary of Catholic Social Thought*, ed. Judith A. Dwyer (Collegeville, MN: Liturgical Press, 1994), 724–37; Marvin L. Krier Mich, "Human Dignity: Respect for Every Life," in *The Challenge and Spirituality of Catholic Social Teaching*, rev. ed. (Maryknoll, NY: Orbis Books, 2011), 67–68.

10. Michael J. Himes and Kenneth R. Himes, "The Trinity and Human Rights," in *Fullness of Faith: The Public Significance of Theology* (New York: Paulist Press, 1993), 59.

11. Working Group of Globalization and Hong Kong Church, *Quanqiuhua yu laogong* [Globalization and Labour], in *Globalization and Responses of the Hong Kong Church*, ed. Too Kin Wai (Hong Kong: Hong Kong Christian Institute, 2006).

12. Civic Party, *Yanjiubaogao: lingting waiyong de shengyin, cong waiyong jiaodu kan xianggang zuidi gongzi de lifa* [Research Report: Listening to the Voices of Foreign Domestic Helpers, Minimum Wage Law from the Perspective of Foreign Domestic Helpers] (Hong Kong, 2009), 8–10.

13. John Paul II, *Familiaris Consortio*, nos. 23–25; John Paul II, "Letter of Pope John Paul II to Women," July 1995; John Paul II, *Mulieris Dignitatem*.

14. Pontifical Council for Justice and Peace, *Compendium of the Social Doctrine of the Church* (Vatican: Libreria Editrice Vaticana, 2004), no. 147.

15. Christine E. Gudorf, "Encountering the Other: The Modern Papacy on Women," in *Readings in Moral Theology No. 9: Feminist Ethics and the Catholic Moral Tradition*, 66–89. Also see Michael P. Hornsby-Smith, "Family," in *An Introduction to Catholic Social Thought* (Cambridge: Cambridge University Press, 2006), 160–63.

16. For details of these meetings, please refer to the final statements: "Role of Women in Church and Society Toward 2000." Final Statement of BILA on Women, Thailand, November 19, 1995, in *For All the Peoples of Asia: Federation of Asian Bishops' Conferences Documents from 1992 to 1996 Vol. 2*, ed. Franz-Josef Eilers (Quezon City: Claretian Publication, 1997), 91–96; "BILA on Women II Final Statement, Pattaya, Thailand, 12–17 Oct. 1998"; and "BILA on Women III Final Statement, Hua Hin, Thailand, 15–21 Oct. 2001," in *For All the Peoples of Asia: Federation of Asian Bishops' Conferences Documents from 1997 to 2001*, vol. 3, ed. Franz-Josef Eilers (Quezon City: Claretian Publication, 2002), 73–77, 79–87.

17. "Role of Women in Church and Society toward 2000," no. 2.

18. "Role of Women in Church and Society toward 2000," nos. 3 & 4.

19. Peter C. Phan, "A Common Journey, Different Paths, the Same Destination: Method in Liberation Theologies," in *Christianity with an Asian Face: Asian American Theology in the Making* (Maryknoll, NY: Orbis Books, 2003), 45. Also see Michael Amaladoss, *Life in Freedom: Liberation Theologies from Asia* (Maryknoll, NY: Orbis Books, 1997); Virginia Fabella and Sun Ai Lee Park, ed., *We Dare to Dream: Doing Theology as Asian Women* (Hong Kong: Asian Women's Resource Centre for Culture and Theology, 1989).

20. *Lumen Gentium*, no. 32. See also Eph. 4:5, Gal. 3:28.

21. Mary Yuen and Missionary Sister of St. Columban, "History of the Missionary Sisters of St. Columban in Hong Kong: Serving the Most Needy and the Underprivileged," in *History of Catholic Religious Orders and Missionary Congregations in Hong Kong Volume Two: Research Papers,* ed. Louis Ha and Patrick Taveirne (Hong Kong: Centre for Catholic Studies, the Chinese University of Hong Kong, 2010); Tsui Chung-Man, *"Shen de Shizhe, Xinggongzhuozhe—fang Jiaien xiunu"* [Messenger of God and Sex Workers—An Interview with Sr. Ann Gray], in *Wanquan guanshe shouce* [Handbook of Social Concern], ed. Li Yee-Ching et al. (Hong Kong: Justice and Peace Commission, 2004), 43–46.

22. Dorothy Lee, "Culturally and Religiously Sensitive Service to local Pakistani"; Mary Yuen, "Migrants as Neighbours or Strangers?—Faith Reflection on Solidarity with Pakistani Women in Hong Kong," in *Who Is Your Neighbour? Stages of Life of Pakistani Women in Hong Kong* (Hong Kong: Hong Kong Diocesan Pastoral Centre for Workers Kowloon, 2010).

23. Mary Yuen and Missionary Sisters of St. Columban, "History of the Missionary Sisters of St. Columban in Hong Kong: Serving the Most Needy and the Underprivileged"; Mary Yuen, *"Quanhuan aizi bingren—fang Maijieni xiunu"* [Caring for AIDS Patients—

An Interview with Sister McGinley], in *Wanquan guanshe shouce* [Handbook of Social Concern], 47–50.

24. For details of the work of these two commissions, see their websites: http://www.hkjp.org/index_en.php and http://www.hkccla.org.hk/.

25. For example, Pauline Cheng, Hilda Kwan, and Paula Leung are Catholic women leading the ministries of forming catechetical teachers, setting up the library system of Caritas Hong Kong, and leading the Catholic primary and secondary schools for three decades since the 1970s. See Wong Wai-Ching and Choi Po-King, eds., *Huaren funu yu xianggang judujiao koushu lishi* [Oral History on Chinese Women and Hong Kong Christianity] (Hong Kong: Oxford University Press, 2010).

Theology, Women, and Rights of the Poor (A Reading of the Latin-American Itinerary)

Maria Clara Lucchetti Bingemer

The winds of change for women's emancipation in the Christian West, and in Latin America in particular, did not blow initially from inside the churches. It came from within the lay process of secularization through very concrete and profane struggles (vote, salary, workday, sexuality, rights of the body), as women began to extricate themselves from the domestic private space where they had been confined into the public space as political and economic actors engaged in changing social structures and in economic and cultural production.

The public voices of women in the Christian world in Latin America do not date back more than five decades. After the great event of the Second Vatican Council, the female voice began to be heard more and more, occupying spaces inside the church and doing so effectively. Women coordinated communities at different levels, questioned the denial of women's access to priestly ministry, and produced theoretical reflections about religious experience and the doctrinal contents of Christian faith. The fact is that today it is not possible to do theology in our continent without taking into account the contributions of women.

This essay intends to recover the main steps of this itinerary, demonstrating that at each step of theological growth it was, at one and the same time, both a feminist struggle and a struggle for wider human rights. Initially, we will see how, in the initial phase of its existence, theology constructed by women in Latin America was very close to liberation theology, connected to the question of the poor and to the struggle to help them to assume a place as subjects of history. I will show how, in a second stage, women theologians in our continent started to do the work of rereading Christian theology more widely, not just from their experience as women, but vindicating, through their right to be different, the authority to pronounce an "other" theological word. In a third moment of my reflection, I will show how advances in feminist theology and in gender reflection altered the direction of Latin-American theology. I will also show how the question of feminism and the rights of women in feminist theology are intertwined with the question of land and ecology, thus generating "ecofeminism." Finally, I will reflect on the question of women's empowerment, which entails many delicate but inescapable themes such as corporeality, reproductive rights, and the question of ordained ministries.

Illumination:
The Poor as the Cradle of Theological Work

Theology constructed by women in Latin America finds its date of birth around 1968, when the Medellin bishop's conference undertook the reception of Vatican II within the continent. The key to this reading was the inseparability between the announcement of the gospel and the struggle for justice.[1] Medellin's three steps were evangelization together with the struggle against oppression and injustice, theology together with critical analysis of socioeconomic and political reality, and agglutination and strengthening of base communities enlightened by the reading of the Bible in order to transform unjust social conditions. These steps opened new pathways so that theological reflection might find a new subject as the starting point: the poor and marginalized of the continent.

Building on this during the 1970s, Latin American women started to explore theology within Latin American churches from the point of view of the close interdependence of the poor and the option for the poor. Their vision and their listening turned toward their sisters in the north, who were opening up discussions about the possibility of thinking and speaking "beyond God the Father," and the patriarchalism that was dominant in theology.[2] They saw as a strong and beautiful challenge the possibility to jump-start a theology in which they participated as producers and not only consumers. Nevertheless, Latin American theology done by women is not completely similar to feminist theology done in the northern hemisphere. It is inseparable from the option for the poor, since that is constitutive of its configuration.[3]

The women who in those years entered theology courses, and went on the adventure of the elaboration of their own thinking about the mystery of God and His/Her revelation, did not do it moved only by their personal desire, although it is clear that at the roots of the act of doing theology there was and is always a desire. For those pioneers, however, a desire bigger than themselves allowed them to dare the impossible: to venture into a world that had been dominated by men and, almost entirely, by celibate clergy. This was a world where feminine thinking and presence had only an "indirect" entry. This was the world where the "crazy" ones of that first moment started to articulate their reflections and dared to take their first theological steps.[4]

However, there was also the challenge of reality. Women who intended to do theology in this initial moment had their eyes turned to the reality of the poor and perceived that theology should be done in close dialogue with social sciences. They also perceived a phenomenon that later on was called the "feminization of poverty."[5] A poor person who is also a woman is doubly poor, since her female condition adds to her poor and marginalized condition, making it more complex and more difficult. It was then that a new solidarity emerged in Latin America, one that linked women theologians with poor women who were at the communitarian grassroots. The former understood themselves as spokespersons for the latter and responsible for recovering their rights. The encounters of female theologians and those working in pastoral settings, through a fertile and revealing progression, demonstrated a collective face of passion and a commitment to struggle for justice that was inseparable from the building of the Kingdom of God.[6]

The encounters, colloquia, and congresses among women theologians were repeated at national, continental, and intercontinental levels. The movement realized by them started to call attention, to raise curiosity and reactions—both favorable and unfavorable—at times full of joy and hope, at others, aggressive, ironic or sarcastic, and rejecting this uncomfortable novelty. Ecumenical since their beginning, those encounters helped Latin American female theologians to live out—beyond the covenant with grassroots women—a fertile interaction between Catholics and Protestants, which brought a mutual enrichment and built a solid basis for the future.

Women theologians' struggle in Latin America acquired a new status; different from desire or dream, it started to become a very concrete reality. Besides their presence in the pastoral grassroots, women worked to develop an opening within faculties and institutes of theology, in a long and laborious effort in order to obtain academic degrees that would allow them equal voice vis-à-vis their male companions. This represented a whole journey, a search for recognition, presence, and visibility in spaces that had been predominantly masculine. It was an attempt to attain citizenship and legitimacy through different and alternative ways of doing theology: a way where head, heart, and bodies are united in a fertile and harmonic dance whose product is a different reflection about faith.

During the 1990s, Latin American female theologians felt the impact of the fall of utopias, and the crisis of liberation theology, their cradle. Socioeconomic and political questions dominated their agendas. Similar to almost all intellectuals at that historical moment, they had to confront reality and try to search for new directions in their method of doing theology. They did so, faithful to the first intuition that faith and justice go together and are inseparable, but sufficiently creative to understand that times were changing. It became necessary to pay attention to other fields of learning and science, such as anthropology, philosophy, and natural sciences, in order to find appropriate partners for their reflection about revelation and faith.

Rethinking Theological Concepts from Women's Perspective

The result of all this was the desire to rethink all the great theological issues from the perspective of women. Ivone Gebara identifies it as a second stage of the trajectory of Latin American feminist theology, in what she calls the "feminization of theological concepts."[7] Despite, however, the increasing presence of women in academic reflection spaces, theological concepts remained patriarchal. Women sought a theology with a face, with soul, with a feminine configuration, with a female perspective, stressing the importance of rediscovering the feminine expressions of God. Here began a more fruitful and solid moment of publications, with women theologians trying to revisit and rethink the great treatises of dogmatic theology and the Bible itself, while not departing from their experience and feminine feeling.[8]

On one hand, Latin American women's theology perceived itself to be indebted to American feminist theology, without which there would not be a way to legitimate their itinerary. However, it also identified an important distinction in form and content with regards to the northern sisters. The fight for equality and struggle against sexism did not primarily drive them. Instead, they struggled to build an inclusive discourse, where the difference of being a woman was a constitutive and comprehensive datum from the beginning.

That way of thinking and building a theological discourse, which starts from the fact of being a woman, finds a legitimate and positive acceptance in the theological community. Magazines, newspapers, and publishing companies opened their doors, and women began to be read, received, and discussed in the theological community as a whole.[9]

In naming that stage of the process, many authors avoided the word "feminism" or "feminist," as there was a desire to keep a distance from the vindictive and antagonistic tone of theology done elsewhere. Preference was given to expressions like "theology from the perspective of women" or "theology made by women" or "theology from women."[10]

In the same vein, scholars produced doctoral dissertations and academic papers of all kinds. In the area of systematic theology, many works reflected on Jesus' relationship with women, or the maternal face of God the Father, or even the thought of an inclusive church that would see women as subject, the producer of symbolic goods, and not only a passive consumer of them—a joyful and participatory church.[11]

This way of doing theology remains. In addition, it is not isolated from female theological work worldwide. It finds conceptual affinities with some European theologians of the same generation and moves among the key concepts of reciprocity, uni-duality, and relationality, always seeking dialogue with male theologians and the theological community as a whole.[12]

The claims of this kind of theology no longer aligned with early feminism, whose main struggle was for equality, but for another right: the right to be different and the affirmation of women as different, and as wanting to be different. In this way, theology in dialogue even with women works through other areas of knowledge,[13] emphasizing the identity of the woman as "other," "different" from men. Women who want to be so—other, different—even in the way they feel and think about God, producing a theology other than feminism that includes more self-reliance than theology built on the paradigm of equality.

A stream of Latin American theologians felt the need to take a step beyond the discourse of difference and reciprocity. They felt the absence of a more fundamental critique and a radical change in the concept of God: an absence that reinforces the stereotype of women as maternal, sensitive, weak, created. Therefore, inside that movement, in discussions on the issue of female identity, two possible directions emerged: the first insisted on the affirmation of difference, and the second sought to resist the idealization or essentialization of those differences, understanding them to be part the culture and history in which they arose, from which they operate, and in which they are still maintained. These issues remain present and are expressed and worked more incisively in the stage that follows, in which gender category and mainly gender perspective play a leading role.

Taking Gender Perspective Seriously

From the second half of the 1990s, Latin American feminist theology had to face some major challenges of history and culture, which forced it to review some of its presuppositions. First was the realization that it should overcome the mismatch between the accelerated progress of feminist theology made elsewhere, or even feminist reflection made here, and in other areas of knowledge.[14] Second was the belief that feminism, gender theory, and feminist theology could no longer be ignored, since "knowing their roots in proper context, capturing its various meanings, following its historical process and understanding their various forms of expression" was an unavoidable imperative.[15]

At this stage then, theologians were challenged to rethink the issues of female identity, anthropology, cosmology, and theology holding patriarchal discourse. Feminist theology is a radical change not only in the way we think the data of revelation and the text of scripture but in the way of thinking about the world, about relations between people, about nature and divinity.

It became clear to the new generations of theologians that it was not possible to build a theology recycled out of old patches without triggering the birth of a new one that longed to see the light. In feminist theology (now that we are no longer afraid to take that name), the intention is to bring fundamental questions that challenge the very structure of theological thought developed up until now. It was not a theology from the point of view or the perspective of women, presented as an addition or as a separate section of the official theology made so far by men theologians, but a substantive challenge to all dominant theology, patriarchal and sexist.[16] Thus, Latin American women theologians have been willing to talk with female colleagues who had introduced new methods of working with the Bible, with revelation, and dogma. Above all, they have followed those steps that their primary belonging, namely, liberation theology, has given them.[17]

As liberation theology widened, so, too, the range of interest broadened, to include other issues that were not only strictly socioeconomic and political:

ecology, culture, the crisis of modernity, gender, race, and ethnicity. Latin American feminist theology found, through the perspective of gender, a most appropriate angle from which to build its reflection and discourse. The aim to include those on the margins of society and economic progress was not lost. Instead, the problem was, perhaps more than ever, to challenge and question theology. The "poor" as object of reflection and investigation, who had been the quintessential theological subject in Latin American theology of the 1970s and 1980s, were now joined by those identified as "excluded" from any benefits brought by social progress and welfare. These now have more diversified faces than before, and form a rich mosaic of much larger and complex challenges to theology in multiple directions. Ivone Gebara, a major voice of this new phase, will say that "Liberation Theology, offering a collective vision of God and emphasizing the social nature of sin, did not change the patriarchal anthropology and cosmology on which Christianity is based."[18]

What became necessary was a qualitative leap in a new direction in order to achieve the liberation of half of humanity. This is how Gebara defined that leap in feminist theology: "To speak of God and of the gender issue is to make a double claim: first it is to say that what we say about God is connected to our historical experience, our life experience; then, that our same idea of God, and our relationship with him/her or his/her mystery, is marked by what we call . . . social and cultural construction of gender."[19]

That is how other feminist struggles, those present in first world theologies and in Latin America, in social and human sciences,[20] became interesting also to theologians. Topics such as corporeality, sexuality, morality, with all its hot and sensitive issues in reproductive rights, and all that pertains to Christian morality; the mystery of the human body, its functions, its vocation, its mystery created by God: all became part of the agenda of Latin American feminist theology. In that field, we must recognize that the Protestant theologians took larger steps than Catholic ones, because the church structures, in evangelical communities, are very different from those in the Catholic communities.[21]

That is also how ecofeminist theology emerged and developed at a continental level.[22] Presently in Latin America, only a few theologians have written extensively about ecofeminism.[23] Openness and attention to this new interdisciplinary field of reflection has enabled Latin American feminist theology to dialogue with all areas of environmental reflection: philosophy, social sciences, environmental law, and more. It is an area that promises tremendous growth for the future. Any reflection on ecology in relation to land rights and nature is spliced with reflection on the rights of women. Since ecofeminism means the end of all forms of domination, theology cannot avoid the concomitant debates. Nor can feminist theology, which is becoming the key to freedom from all forms of oppression and of the struggle for nonrespected rights.[24]

Women and the Rights of the Body[25]

Theological reflections on woman's sexualized body and questions of gender are always important themes of theological work in Latin America. In a universe where the body is so visible and mainly male, women enter as a troubling factor. It is this "trouble," through their body being "other" from the one of man, that expresses and marks the experience of God, the thinking and talking about God, in another and peculiar way. The feminine body becomes the condition of possibility through which women turn into an important agent when we talk about spirituality, mysticism, and theology. This body, however, has been on many occasions a source of discrimination and suffering.

Theological reflection on this theme demonstrates that major discrimination against women within the church says something more profound and serious than simple physical might, intellectual formation, or ability to work. The church is still molded by the patriarchal identity so prevalent in the Judeo-Christian tradition. Patriarchal identity underlines male superiority, not only by an intellectual bias, but by what we may call an ontological bias. Put another way, women are oppressed by their own bodies, and feminist theology tries to overcome this discrimination through its discourse.[26]

This discrimination is associated strongly—in the theological field—with the fact that the woman is considered responsible for the entrance of sin into the world, and, consequently, for death. This was officially denounced by Pope John Paul II in his encyclical *Mulieris Dignitatem*, though it remains among the rationales through which women are discriminated against.[27] This also explains why mystical experiences of women are regarded with mistrust and suspicion, with a strict surveillance by men to control and exorcize them. Many very rich mystical experiences of women, touched by God's grace with very intimate messages, remain in the hands of a few. Cases like that of Teresa de Ávila become exceptions that confirm the rule.

In church history, women were kept at a prudent distance from the sacred and everything that surrounded it, such as liturgy and ritual objects, and away from direct mediation of God. All this requires a "pure" body, and there was a strong doubt that women could aspire to purity. Despite all the progress made, with the participation of the woman in several levels of ecclesial life, there remains the stigma of woman as the seductive source of fear, of sin, and a threat to male chastity and clergy celibacy. Mystery or "high" mysticism was rarely recognized in women who were relegated to the field of minor devotions of lesser importance.

This is a terrible reality that demands a very serious reflection within the church, since, if it is possible to fight against intellectual discrimination (by access to studies and formation), and against professional injustice (searching for specialization and showing capabilities), what can we do with our female bodies? More than that, should women deny and ignore their own bodies, their own special bodies created by God, so as to become honorable and enter in profound communication with the Creator and occupy their space in the church? This is a field still raw in theological terms in Latin America, but it should call the attention of theological women in the not-too-distant future.

Theology, turning toward this concern, enters into dialogue with the thinking about gender produced by society. Feminist thinking has been posing questions connected with the woman's body for a long time, not only the classical themes of violence against women, which enabled several initiatives in terms of human rights and public policy, but in questions of reproductive rights and autonomy in terms of the body.[28] It is, in fact, a very difficult and delicate field, but a most important one. Feminist theology is being asked more and more to act decisively, especially in the field of moral theology, with contributions of women moral theologians opening the way.[29] Nevertheless, it has to be said that it is a field in which much advancement still has to be made, with creative fidelity and, above all, boldness.

Feminist Theology, Power, and Service: Time for Empowerment?

Although the word "empowerment" only recently entered the vocabulary of feminist Latin-American theology, it looks like it will remain important.[30] When we talk about delegating power, or training people to act with more authority, or decentralization, we cannot think about other than women. The empowerment of women is a reality in society; human sciences provide evidence.[31] Feminist theology in all latitudes, including Latin America, returns to this category, incorporating it in its thinking and discourse.[32] Talking theologically about power, empowering, giving power, implies, of necessity, the question of women and church ministries.

The question of ministries is a crucial one for Christians today. Among them, particularly the woman—and always and necessarily lay, as she has no access to ordained ministries—feels questioned and in the center of a conflict that confines her only to a certain number of services in the church. The fact that the Roman Catholic Church does not ordain women and does not intend to, either in the short term or middle term, and has, moreover, officially barred the debate, feels like a sting in the flesh for women who embrace, in a radical way, the passion of the construction of the Kingdom of God and who are dedicated to ecclesial service. The fact of this impediment, on the one hand, and the enormous needs to which these women are dedicated, on the other, are passionately felt and suffered by them. At the same time, the Spirit shows these women how urgent it is to continue the call for reflection on this subject.[33]

The new ecclesial paradigm, which replaces a church centered on the dualism of clergy/laity with a constantly renewed community and with new dimensions for charisma and ministry abundantly born by the Spirit, will allow contemporary women to find a space in which to be pilgrims in their desire for, and the realization of, an effective and greater service to the people of God.

In the 1980s, when the fruits of Vatican II began to mature, and the church in Latin America assimilated more deeply the conferences of Medellin and Puebla, women dared to challenge an ecclesial situation in which injustice and oppression were a constant presence. Many women, both lay and religious, began to take over ministries in their communities. From the coordination of communities to liturgical celebrations, countless services were rendered by women leading their communities as they lived out a church model in which power is freely shared, and decisions are made more collectively.

The occupation of such an open space began to outline a new paradigm for the church, one that was highly positive and very much welcomed by the people. In the 1990s, these routes were deepened, following new and difficult paths through which the Christian woman could find her place in the ecclesial space. The services women rendered testify to the leap that has taken place in their ecclesial consciousness and to the renewal that is being processed in these women and from them, as the strength of the Spirit moves them to serve.

The Brazilian Conference of Bishops recognized explicitly the contribution of women in its contribution to the conference of Aparecida.[34] The same document of Aparecida mentions the importance of women in different ecclesial services, stating, for the first time, that women should accede to the levels of decision making in the church.[35]

Maybe there is a rich vein for reflection on the future direction of women's ministries. In the wake of reflection about empowerment, feminist theology may find new ways to enable women to live powerfully in service to God and people. For this, it may help to follow another track that has begun to be evident in feminist theology in Latin America: the retrieval of women's historical testimonies, and the research on their lives, experiences, and thoughts. More and more theologians, both male and female, are choosing to reflect on the writings and biographies of great mystics of today and yesterday.[36]

It is certainly a way to empower women, to reflect on well-known personal stories that speak of a profound and radical experience of the divine, as it makes visible the power of God and God's sovereign freedom that creates, without ceasing, the world and humankind. A theology of testimonies, rather than a theology of texts, can become a rich challenge for a feminist Latin American theology in its attempt to rescue the rights of the women who have been invisible and have been muted by the oppression of society and all institutions.[37]

Conclusion

As a theology between ecclesiality and citizenship, feminist theology in Latin America finds itself today in a rich and promising moment, with many projects that help and stimulate it.[38] In addition to these projects, there is a proliferation of graduate programs, with many female students following feminist lines of investigation. This shows that this theological stream is alive and is a powerful sign in the world and the church.

One thing, at any rate, is clear. The theological reflection of Latin American women has a long road ahead. Even as it is called to communion with sisters from other latitudes, and to learning and reciprocal and fertile friendships, it will always have its original seal.

Consistent with its first moments, Latin American feminist theology will remain, as before, the reflection on faith and the identity and being of women: their conditions, their bodies, their configurations, their feelings, their thinking, and their speeches. But as all of that happens in a context marked by conflict and injustice, it is also a reflection on ecclesial belonging that is inseparable from citizenship: a tireless effort to connect faith with theology, understanding theology as a human word illuminated by the Word of God. This is the way that feminist theology might contribute to a more humane world, where human rights are more respected and more practiced.

Notes

1. I disagree here with the periodization of M. C. de Freitas, who in her introduction to the book *Genero e teologia. Interpelações e perspectivas* (São Paulo: Loyola, 2003), 24–25, places the birth of Latin American feminist theology in the 1980s. I find that the more distant embryos for theology in Latin America are beyond that, in the 1970s. However, the author would agree with that statement if it is only in the 1980s that theology made by women in Latin America reaches a degree of systematization that can be considered rigorous and academic but remains inextricably militant.

2. Cf. M. Daly, *Beyond God the Father, Toward a Philosophy of Woman's Liberation* (New York: Beacon Press, 1973).

3. Cf. S. Suaiden, "Questões contemporâneas para a teologia—Provocações sob a ótica de gênero," in de Freitas, *Genero e teologia*, 147.

4. "Crazy" means *locas*. I allude here clearly to the mothers of the Plaza de Mayo, in Argentina, called "las locas" by the dictatorship they challenged.

5. The introduction of this concept is given by the American Diane Pearce, in an article published in 1978. For her, the feminization of poverty is a process that developed from the time when women with children, who had no husband or partner living in the same household, took responsibility for the maintenance of the family. In this perspective, the feminization of poverty is when women, home alone, have to take care of their children and provide for their well-being.

6. The topics of the meetings, which took place at the national level and Latin American level attest to this agglutination and organization done by the female pastoral theological community as an active subject in the ecclesial community: "Woman: That He Learned to Instead Ignore"(1984), "Women: In Search of Its Identity" (1985), "The Woman Broke the Silence" (1986), "Doing Theology in the Feminine Plural" (1987), followed by others who maintained key points of these first steps: the occupation of a different place not assigned to women before; the encounter of a new identity, given by the other; the breaking of the silence and the access to visibility and audibility in ecclesial space; configuring a theological community, which, in solidarity and plurality, assumes and accomplices in the knowledge and in the theological task.

7. Cf. I. Gebara, "III Semana Teológica—Construyendo nuestras teologías feministas," *Tópicos 90—Cuadernos de estudios* (Santiago de Chile, Ediciones Ruhue, 1993), 71–124, quoted by S. R. Lima e Silva, http://ejesus.com.br/lista/8/conteudo/6250/.

8. The publications are too numerous to cite at that stage. It would occupy too much space in this essay and would run the risk of forgetting names and major works. I refer, therefore, to the doctoral thesis of M. P. Aquino, "Our Cry for Life. Latin American Theology from the Perspective of Women" (San José, Costa Rica: Ecumenical Research Department, 1992), that offers an exhaustive bibliography. Refer also to the extraordinary work of E. Tamez, the great Mexican biblical scholar resident in Costa Rica, who has not only thought about the Bible in a new way but organized several publications to make known the work of her fellow Latin American theologians. Worth noting is also the work for several years of the program Teologanda, Argentina (cf. http://www.teologanda.com.ar) which includes not only the period of the history of theology in Latin America but seeks to make a more complete mapping of the same.

9. See the publication of articles and books of theologians such as M. C. Correia Pinto, A. M. Tependino, T. Cavalcanti, M. T. Porcile, and more. Prominent Latin American journals such as *REB* and others opened their doors to women and began publishing their theological work.

10. See, for instance, the publication organized by M. Brandao, *Teologia na ótica da mulher* (Rio de Janeiro: Editora PUC-Rio, 1990).

11. Cf. A. M. Tependino, *As discípulas de Jesus,* Petrópolis, Brazil, Vozes, 1990); M. C. Bingemer, "A perspective da Trindade na ótica da mulher," *REB* 46 (1986): 73–99; D. Brunelli, *Libertação da mulher: Um desafio para a vida religiosa na igreja Latino Americana* (Rio de Janeiro, Publicações CRB, 1988).

12. I identify among European theologians influential names such as Guilia Paolo Di Nicola, Georgette Blaquierre, and Kari Elisabeth Børrensen.

13. I think, for instance, of R. Darcy De Oliviera, *Elogio de la diferencia. O feminino emergente* (São Paulo, Brasiliense, 1991).

14. Cf. M.C. de Freitas, "Gênero/Teologia Feminista: Interpelações e perspectivas para a teologia-Relevância do tema," in SOTER (org), *Gênero e Teologia. Interpelações e perspectivas,* 2003, 23.

15. Cf. ibid., 27. Cf. also the works of M. J. Rosado Nunes on gender and religion in her publication at *Revista de Estudos Feministas* Vol. 13, no. 2 (2005): Dossiê Gênero e Religião.

16. Cf. S. R. de Lima Silva, "Teologia feminista latinoamericana," in http://ejesus.com.br/lista/8/conteudo/6250/. Cf. also the text of I. Gebara, "Entre os limites da filosofia e da teologia feminista," in SOTER (org), *Genero e teologia,* 153–70.

17. I risk this interpretation, making it clear that this is our reading of the facts, without necessarily implying a broad consensus across the theological community about the process of feminist theology.

18. Cf. I. Gebara, "Teologia cósmica: Ecofeminismo e panenteísmo," *Folha mulher, projeto Sofia: Mulher, teologia e cidadania,* Rio de Janeiro, ISER, n. 8, Ano IV, 1994, PP 70–75.

19. I. Gebara, *Rompendo o silencio: Uma fenomenologia feminista do mal* (Petrópolis, Brazil: Vozes, 2000), 218.

20. Cf. the works of M. I. *Matos, Melodia e sintonia: O masculino, o feminino e suas relações em Lupicínio Rodrigues,* 2nd ed (Rio de Janeiro: Bertrand Brasil, 1999); M. I. Matos,

Gênero e terceiro setor, 1st ed. (São Paulo: Cultura Acadêmica, 2005), ; M. J. Rosado-Nunes and M. P. Aquino, *Teología feminista intercultural* (Mexico City: Dabar, 2008); M. J. Rosado-Nunes, *A mulher, a igreja e os processos de libertação* (São Paulo: Departamento de Teologia, 1984); M. C. Bruschini and S. G. Unbehaum, *Gênero, democracia e sociedade brasileira,* 1st ed. (São Paulo, Editora34, 2002).; M. C. Pinto, *Tempos e lugares de gênero,* 1st ed. (São Paulo: Editora34, 2001).

21. Cf. W. Deifelt, "Derechos reproductivos en América Latina. Un análisis crítico y teológico a partir de la realidad del Brasil," in *Población y salud reproductiva,* ed. Manuel Quintero (Quito: Ediciones CLAI 1999), 31–49; W. Deifelt, "Temas e metodologias da teologia feminista," in *Gênero e teologia,* 171–86; Marga Ströher, Wanda Deifelt, and André Musskopf, *À flor da pele: Ensaios sobre gênero e corporeidade* (São Leopoldo: Sinodal/ CEBI, 2004). Cf. also the more ecumenical work *Corporeidade e teologia* (São Paulo: Soter/ Paulinas, 2007) and many issues of *Revista de Estúdios Feministas* from Universidade de Santa Catarina, Brazil.

22. *Ecofeminism* is a term originally "created" by F. d'Eaubonne, a French feminist, in 1974, and symbolizes the synthesis of environmentalism (or ecology) and feminism. It was later applied to the root of the Chipko Movement in India and to the Women's Pentagon Action in the United States. It is the theory that seeks the end of all forms of oppression. It relates connections between the domination of race, gender, social class, and domination of nature.

23. Cf. mostly I. Gebara, *Teologia ecofeminista* (São Paulo: Olho d'água, 1988).

24. In the United States, see the reflections of Rosemary Radford Ruether, ed., *Women Healing Earth: Third World Women on Ecology, Feminism, and Religion (Ecology and Justice)* (Maryknoll, NY: Orbis Books, 1990), 135–42; Rosemary Radford Ruether, ed., *Gaia and God: A Feminist Theology of Earth Healing* (Maryknoll, NY: Orbis Books, 1994), which had considerable influence on Latin American feminist theologians. Also see the magazine *Mandrake* 6 (2000), all of it on ecofeminism—articles, debates, and various interviews.

25. A substantial part of this section was presented at the World Catholicism Week of the Center for World Catholicism and Intercultural Theology, at De Paul University, Chicago, in April 2010.

26. Cf. the book of Soter Assembly 2004, *Corporeidade e teologia* (São Paulo: SOTER-Ed Paulinas, 2007), which deals with this aspect of theology. Worth mentioning is M. I. Millen, W. Deifelt, and L. Ribeiro, among others. Cf. M. C. Bingemer, *Experiencia de Dios en cuerpo de mujer* (Buenos Aires: San Benito, 2007).

27. Cf. *Mulieris Dignitatem,* http://www.vatican.va.

28. See, for example, Catholics for a Free Choice, which describes itself as a feminist organization, interreligious in nature, seeking social justice and change in existing cultural and religious qualities in our society, respecting diversity as necessary to the attainment of freedom and justice. http://catolicasonline.org.br/QuemSomos.aspx.

29. Cf. the works of M. I. Millen, *Os acordes de uma sinfonia. A Moral do diálogo na teologia de Bernhard Häring* (Juiz de Fora, Brazil: Editar, 2005); M. I. Millen, M. I. C. O corpo na perspectiva do gênero, *Horizonte Teológico* 3, no. 5 (2004): 35–56; Maria Joaquina Fernandes Pinto, *Alteridade e bioética: Um novo olhar sobre o outro e sobre a vida.* Repensar, Rio de Janeiro, vol. 1, no. 1, 49–65, 2005. ; Maria Joaquina Fernandes Pinto, "Jesus Cristo e a vivência da afetividade: implicações para vivermos a nossa," in *A pessoa e a mensagem de Jesus,* 1st ed., ed. Mário de França Miranda (São Paulo: Loyola, 2002), 76–83; N. Falcon,

Recuperación de lo femenino (Buenos Aires, San Benito, 2008).

30. Empowerment is an approach to project work that looks at the delegation of decision-making power, autonomy, and participation. It involves division of power, sharing, and decentralization.

31. Cf. M. C. Pinto, "Empowerment: uma prática de serviço social,", in *Política social*—(Lisbon, ISCSP, 1998), 247–64.

32. Cf., for instance, the thesis of L. Etsuko Tomita, *Corpo e cotidiano: A experiência das mulheres de movimentos populares desafia a teologia feminista da libertação na América Latina* (São Paulo, PUCSP, 2004).

33. The Apostolic Letter *Ordinatio Sacerdotalis*, reaffirms, through the words of Pope John Paul II himself, that the church has no authority to ordain women to the priesthood. It further states that this doctrine is based on the continuous tradition of the church. On November 18, 1995, the Congregation for the Doctrine of the Faith published a response to the question raised in many quarters about whether this issue in the church belongs to the deposit of faith. The response of the commission does not give the pope's statement the status of an *ex cathedra* statement but says it is doctrine "founded on the written Word of God" and was "from the beginning constantly preserved and put into practice in the tradition of the Church," besides being "presented infallibly by the ordinary and universal Magisterium."

34. Note that if "the Church makes the Eucharist and the Eucharist makes the Church," as it is explicitly affirmed in the Encyclical of John Paul II, n. 26, according to the whole tradition of the Church, ("If, as I have said, the Eucharist builds the Church and the Church makes the Eucharist, it follows that there is a profound relationship between the two, so much so that we can apply to the Eucharistic mystery the very words with which, in the Nicene-Constantinopolitan Creed, we profess the Church to be 'one, holy, catholic and apostolic.' The Eucharist too is one and catholic. It is also holy, indeed, the Most Holy Sacrament . . .") the fact that 80 percent of Brazilian Catholics are prevented from celebrating the Eucharist on Sunday means they are deprived of an important dimension of ecclesiology.

35. Cf. *Documento de aparecida*, 458.

36. See the works of V. Azcuy, *La figura de Teresa de Lisieux. Ensayo de fenomenología teológica según Hans Urs von Balthasar* (Buenos Aires: Ediciones de la Facultad de Teología, 1997, 2 vols.); L. Pedrosa De Padua, *Santa Teresa. Mística para o nosso tempo* (Rio de Janeiro: PUC-Rio e Reflexão, 1st ed. 2011); C. B. Mariani, *Marguerite Porete, Teóloga do século XIII. Experiência mística e teologia dogmática em O Espelho das Almas Simples de Marguerite Porete.* (Brasil: Pontifícia Universidade Católica de São Paulo, 2008) (doctoral thesis); W. Tomassi, *Etty Hillesum. La inteligência del corazón* (Madrid: Narcea, 2003). See also M.C, L. Bingemer, *Simone Weil. A força e a fraqueza do amor* (Rio de Janeiro: Rocco, 2007) (Italian edition, Torino, Zona, 2007; Spanish edition, Estella, Verbo Divino, 2009); *Simone Weil: uma mística em los límites* (Buenos Aires: Ciudad Nueva, 2011 (Brazilian edition Bauru, EDUSC, 2014).

37. Cf. Jon Sobrino on the need for a "theology of texts rather than a theology of witnesses" in his writings on Monsignor Romero and on the martyrs of the University of Central America.

38. For instance, see the project of *Teologanda in Argentina* (http://www.teologanda.com.ar) or the position of Chair of Feminist Theology at the Universidad Iberoamericana, in Mexico City.

MISSING IS THE WOMAN/ *HACE FALTA LA MUJER*

Emilce Cuda

Introduction

The beginning of a political discourse for the recognition of human dignity is the point at which the fate of the people becomes meaningful history. Since the beginning of history, representation of all voices has remained less than universal. It is missing the public political word of the woman. Theology, the word where the Other is manifested, articulates two insights: it recognizes all human beings as children of God, and, consequently, it recognizes equality amidst differences. These theological principles provide not only an eschatological sense of history but also the ethical basis of politics. But this representation remains on the level of *not yet*. It is missing the public theological word of the woman.

However, the feminine word has, at times, become manifest. The South American economic and financial crises of the early 2000s produced a political void wherein the public word of the woman finally appeared in a legal and legitimate way, when three women were recognized as victors in South American presidential elections. Theological practice consists of making audible the ineffable, the voice of the Other. When South American female theologians take responsibility for making the woman audible (in their political context) as the Other of society, they are doing theology; when they work to convert the plight of women into verbal claims for social rights, they are doing theological ethics. In the present day of the twenty-first century, female theologians break into the destinies of their people, continuing the struggle for recognition. The theological resource of South American women—in the face of a negativity that has *defined* peoples to the margins of humanity—is the *yes* of Marian spirituality. Her ethical practice is the word that articulates two traditions: catholic equality and popular culture. In the context of recent elections, where different peoples have placed their vote of confidence in women, the theological female voice finds sufficient legitimacy to announce that no social and political model is ethically legitimate if it does not incorporate all voices in the global debate.

In this essay, I will approach the practice of women doing theology in Latin America from an interdisciplinary perspective, through the presentation of some particular cases, putting theology in dialogue with politics and psychoanalysis.

Women's Events

Context

In order for ethics not to be suspended in the political realm, it should be constructed on the basis of a concrete reality. A theological ethics would not be effective if it were built from a reflective judgment that, taking into account a revealed truth, did not also stem from social experience. A theological ethics should not be purely abstract, but should account for a concrete particularity; in this case, that of the twenty-first century South American woman, represented as the Other of a society that—even with democratic and egalitarian pretensions—does not recognize her word as voice, but rather as noise. I will begin by referencing some women's events, political, on the one hand, theological, on the other, that, because they are now present in the public sphere, are representative of many Others beyond simply feminist demands. This representation seems to have been made possible by the discursive articulation around the category of woman as an empty signifier of the Other that now surfaces and says the ineffable.

The categorization of woman as receiver and mediator is no stranger to South American Marian Catholicism nor to an indigenous identity constructed around the figure of the *Pachamama*: Mother Earth. Devotion to Mary is not only a sign that distinguishes the Catholic mode of the region but is also a signifier on which the culture is structured. This is shown by the devotions to the *Virgen de Luján* in Argentina, the *Virgen del Carmen* in Chile, and *Nuestra Señora Aparecida* in Brazil, to cite a few cases.

Interestingly, from these countries where the majority of the population is Catholic—76 percent in Argentina, 74 percent in Brazil, and 69 percent in Chile—come the first cases of women elected president in the region. More significant still is that these women have gained a historic level of popular acceptance: 84 percent in 2010 for Michelle Bachelet in Chile, 56 percent for Dilma Rousseff in Brazil in 2010, and 54 percent for Cristina Kirchner in Argentina in 2011. While the public voice of the woman was formerly silenced in South America (being the excluded Other of a democratic society that could not manage to include her), it is now manifest. The financial and economic crisis of 2000 produced the political vacuum that allowed the word of the Other to be recognized. In several countries, that Other is now represented through the public word of woman as a legitimate political subject, articulating numerous assertions through the mode of representative democracy that was not attentive to one of its two founding principles: equality in inequality.

Women and Politics

The ineffable becomes audible in the twenty-first century. Three women from popular parties were recognized through presidential appointments for being able to articulate the social demands of various sectors, appearing in their person as a signifier of the Other that is now manifest through legitimate word. Michelle Bachelet, a pediatrician and member of the Socialist Party who was born in Chile in 1951, assumed the presidency of Chile in March 2006 as a candidate for the Coalition of Parties for Democracy, having been named in 2002 as minister of defense in the government of Ricardo Lagos. Cristina Fernández de Kirchner, a lawyer and member of Peronism, born in Argentina on February 19, 1953, had her first post as deputy in 1989, was a senator in 1995, and was elected to the presidency for two consecutive terms in 2007 and 2011. Dilma Rousseff, an economist and member of the Workers Party, born in Brazil in 1947, became president in 2011 after being named chief of staff in 2005 by Lula da Silva. The three are the first women elected president in their respective countries in continuity with the projects of the presidents that preceded them. These women share some characteristics: they fought for the public voice of the Other from their youth; they have promoted the marginalized in their public policy; they have successfully confronted the global economic crisis without transferring the cost to less-favored social sectors; and they have allocated legal, institutional, and economic resources to solve social problems. Cristina Fernández de Kirchner, for example, has provided for the Universal Child Allowance, a monthly sum of money for anyone who is in poverty and destitution with children under age eighteen. In the case of Chile, Bachelet, who was prominent among the list of the world's most powerful women in *Forbes* (twenty-fifth place) because of her social policy, was elected at the end of her term in November 2010 to assume leadership of the new UN Women committee, reaching the highest office at that institution below that of the secretary general.

Politics and Religion: South American Presidents

Is it possible in political discourse to articulate a theological ethics without falling into political theology? Although the people of South America are mostly Catholic, their states are historically liberal. This means that in the case of the three women cited here, even with their ethical sensibility and political action in relation to social problems, such as poverty or violations of universal human rights, their relationship with the Catholic Church is tense. Bachelet's link with religion was a political one, rather than one based on religious practice. Herself an agnostic, she opened the Office of Religious Affairs in Chile, inviting a distinct form of dialogue with different faiths in order to ensure that all religions could express themselves and communicate with the government. While Michelle Bachelet is not baptized, she promoted religious freedom, and though her roots—from her father—were Masonic, her government included the following: practicing Jews in her cabinet, Catholic chaplains as advisors in the government house, Protestant pastors in their diplomatic missions, and Jesuit priests as social counselors. Thus, she promoted an ecumenical and interfaith position that included ethical contributions from all religious sectors. By contrast, Cristina Kirchner became separated from one sector of the Catholic Church and found herself in tension with its hierarchy due to a number of factors: human rights policy in relation to what happened in Argentina during the military dictatorship in 1976–83, allegations that implicated Catholic sectors in that era's disappearances and deaths, the Equal Marriage Act law, and the potential submission to Congress of a law on abortion. In Brazil, a long controversy over abortion accompanied Dilma Rousseff's presidency, resulting in tension between the Catholic Church and the state. However, when the new woman president sent a letter to Pope Benedict XVI asking for his blessing on the government and expressing the desire for extensive dialogue, relations were smoothed over.

Theology and Politics from the Word of the Woman

Political and theological practice involve making audible the ineffable, that is, reorganizing public space (understood as a discursive vacuum) so that the voice of the Other is revealed as the word of the ineffable. In the twenty-first century, South American women seem to be taking responsibility for this task. The woman, as representative of the Other of society—a society that by its practices of exclusion prevents the realization of human dignity that each one deserves as child of God—is making possible the hearing of the claims of the Others in politics and theology. The woman, a word that says nothing (in the Lacanian sense), acts as mediator of the Other, as recipient of the demands of the Other, and as theological and political subject that embodies and expresses the Other. The claim for basic necessities becomes through her discourse for social rights. The nonword of women bursts into the twenty-first century, inaugurating a new history for the peoples of South America, while continuing the old struggle for recognition.

Faced with the political negativity that relegates entire peoples to the margins of what is properly human, the theological resource of the Latin American woman is the *yes* of Marian spirituality, that is, a nonword that from silence offers the empty space of her body so that the word of the Other becomes incarnate. The ethical practice of woman as a public subject (political and theological) is the articulation of two traditions: catholic equality and the struggle for popular emancipation. In the context of recent elections, when different peoples have given women their vote of confidence, the public recognition of the female theological voice announces that no social and political model is ethically legitimate if it does not incorporate all voices to global debate (as expressed by Metz[1]). Meanwhile, representation will not be complete until the voice of woman is heard at all institutional levels.

The cases cited in the political field present us with material for analyzing the appearance of the public word of women in South America, as the articulation of a new political stage for the Other, revealed in novel representations. This has the potential to be an interesting exercise for Catholic theological ethics. The presence of the word of the woman in state affairs, especially in its highest office, the presidency, coincides with the advancement of the woman in all social structures, so that she ceases to be perceived as the Other, tremendous and fascinating at the same time,[2] inspiring fear and love simultaneously, and instead becomes perceived as part of a pair, as equal in difference. In recent years many women have benefited in political, academic, economic, industrial, and commercial arenas. The voice of women is now, little by little, a word of authority in the public sphere, taking on relevant roles on decision making for the distribution of common goods. However, this is not so evident in the field of theology in South America, where the voice of the woman is still tenuous. Nevertheless, as part of the historical-political process that is now recognizing women as the legitimate representation of the public word, the female theologian is also beginning to break through the ecclesial space, albeit partially. In the twenty-first century, female theologians in the region are assuring that their voice is no longer represented as mere noise by an ecclesiastical structure somewhat out of step with the chorus of voices in American and European Catholicism, but, rather, as word. What follows is a sampling of women who, beginning in 2000 onward, have managed to embody in their word and within theological/social discourse the representation of the Other.

Female Theologians and Politics

In 2002, María Pilar Aquino published a collaborative work that allow the voice of the female theologian to be heard.[3] The authors, a group of Latin American female theologians based in the United States, promoted the female theologian as a legitimate voice for political reflection and reflected on the relationship between religion and justice in their own sociocultural context. They reported and analyzed the inequalities of which women are victims, including the categories of gender, race, citizenship, and ideology, and showed how these inequalities affect the entire community in the region. This group of women, through the recovery of popular religious practice, promoted the voice of woman as a practice of inclusion of nonbeing, that is, of the outcast political being. In Argentina in 2001, Virginia Azcuy published the first book devoted to theology done by women.[4] The work examines women as a theological locus in relation to the changing ecclesiastical models of the last two decades. In 2004, the same author published the first of a series of books devoted to women doing theology. The work has an ecumenical focus on Christian theology done by Latin American and German women. This gender partnership culminated in a congress of women theologians, gathered in San Miguel and attended by theologians from Latin America and the Caribbean, Europe, and the United States. From Brazil came the voice of the Other represented by María Clara Bingemer, who in 2002 wrote of the struggles women face to be recognized in the discipline of theology.[5] The same author wrote on ethics and theology in 2004, raising the question of the responsibility of the Catholic intellectual in facing social problems.[6] Ivone Gebara in 2000 wrote of the silencing of women's voices, a voice silenced in the treatment of the issue of social evil.[7]

These examples of South American women theologians attempt to show how the woman's voice is making itself heard in public word, albeit confined to the discursive spaces of Christian theology, and not in the political arena where the male word continues to represent the voice of the Catholic Church. Women managed to be heard in the state, as demonstrated by the aforementioned three examples of South American presidents who achieved large electoral majorities, but still need their voice to be heard in the field of theology as heard in the public arena. This voice is not yet heard as breaking into public social space. On the contrary, it continues to be listened to as if that of a woman talking about women, rather than that of women as legitimate political and theological subjects in the public and universal word that speaks of justice through the particular case of women.[8] However, there are women theologians who have made a place in the public space, making their voices heard as word in Catholic ethics with regard to social conflicts. In 2004, Virginia Azcuy addressed the issue of politics by asking, in the context of globalization of exclusion, about the relevance of new thinking about the *option for the poor* as a way to do theology in Latin America. Following Gustavo Gutiérrez, her concluding points—picking up on a statement of the Episcopal Conference of Argentina in 2003—is to see the option for the poor as a path to holiness.[9]

In a 2002 text on Simone Weil, María Clara Bingemer presents significant thoughts on the public word of women. For the author, Weil is an example of a *woman of the word*, who has managed to speak simultaneously in philosophical, political, and mystical spaces. She writes that the woman opens public space to the Other so that the Other appears and speaks with a word: "that proclaims in the square, denouncing injustices and shouting at the struggle against oppression." But too, she speaks "a word experienced and savored in the bridal chamber of the heart, suffered in the silence of compassion and the solidary pain with the crucified Christ in the smallest of others." In sum, she speaks "a word active and efficient, transformative and critical."[10]

According to Bingemer, the word in Simone Weil is made flesh by being proclaimed in terms of action and passion—paired categories, which, as Bingemer and Weil noted, was first highlighted by Meister Eckhart. One might wonder whether the effectiveness of the public word of women would be any different from that of men, if it is not articulated differently. Finally, Ivone Gebara, in a 2000 text, asks "How does one re-read the religious tradition in a way that is liberating, to become alive and to help to build relationships of equality, respect, justice and solidarity?"[11] For Gebara, unlocking the issue of inequality toward women does not require that women want to be like men, but rather that one address all modes of inequality from this particular inequality. It is a method of deconstruction— and a method of theology—for the author working in the fields of politics and theological ethics. To put it another way, one must deconstruct the categories that generate inequality and function to oppress, that is, economic oppression masked as social inequality, as noted by Charles Tilly.[12] To deconstruct the category of woman as the ineffable Other—tremendous and fascinating—is a way of starting to make audible that which was previously construed as mute, putting difference in the place of sameness maintaining its difference.

The Universal Recognition of the Word of Women as Public Word in Representation of the Other

Political Word

Woman—as with the Aristotelian notion that "man is a political animal"—is always a woman in the *polis*, through the word, in speaking with others, in public. The struggle for the recognition of human dignity stretches through the history of humankind, but only when there is awareness of this need is there history; when this need is not recognized, there is only the illusion of being an innocent victim of fate. As Aristotle said—once again—man (and woman) is word, and outside of that reality is an animal or a god, but not man. From the first paragraphs of the *Politics,* he says that the social realm is one shared by all animals, but politics is only shared by men, because animals have a voice to complain, but only men have the word necessary to proclaim what is just.[13] Therefore, whoever is out of the *polis*, of the *logos*, out of the public discourse, will be an animal or God, but not man; they will be the Other. Therefore, whatever stands in the way of woman's public word also prevents her from achieving access to what makes her human. The notion of the public word as a universal right is the point at which the fate of peoples becomes a meaningful story, but if that story does not provide for the voice of women as publicly audible, their representation is not possible within the social sphere. The present remains *not yet* if it is missing the word of the woman in public spaces, that is to say, in politics. Any democracy that does not recognize the word of the woman as a legitimate representative of social and political demands is merely, an *already-but-not-yet*.

The logic of politics, Ranciére argues,[14] exists precisely to intervene—from the origins of the social realm—in the construction of the visceral hatred of the Other, and turn it into word *between* equals, as Hannah Arendt said.[15] When men and women talk to each other as beings in conversation, they forge an effective way to make the inaudible audible, giving a name to the anonymous, and making it possible to hear a word instead of the noise from voices or complaints. The logic of politics is, then, an argument that drives society to recognize the inequality of bodies that exists above and beyond the mythical equality of a restricted democracy. To recognize real inequality is to recognize that not all voices are acknowledged as word; outside of this act there can be no ethical pretense to universality, as was stated by Metz in his critique of Habermas.[16] The public word is a political word if it transforms the polemical space of "common sense" into an apparently consensual space, to uncover the deception of equality under the rule of law, which aims to unify the crowd under the One, hiding and silencing difference, in this case, the woman.

The Other of Politics

If we accept for a moment the theory of Neoplatonism (taken up by the Greek patristic fathers and the *via negativa* at the beginnings of modernity),[17] for whom the Other, despite attempts at defining it as outside the One, is nevertheless part of the One because the One contains the Other as part of its equality in difference, then women cannot be left out of public discourse as the Other of the political community. In other words, there is no *polis* without the word of the woman; it is always contained within it, whether audibly or ineffably. Having been placed for so long in the place of nonword—that is, word not recognized as public word—the woman, when she appears, necessarily produces both aversion and fascination, as in Otto's definition of the Other.[18] This argument enables us to think about politics and theology (both disciplines of discourse analysis, the first with the public, the second with the divine) as practices that are destined to produce a discursive emptiness, so that the word of the Other can appear and be spoken. Thus, the task will be to challenge the mythical equality of modern societies with the reality of equality in difference, and to challenge the mythical equality of South American democracies that still resist, in many cases, women's public discourse. To think of the One as Triune is a task proper to Christian theology; that should not take contemporary political theory lightly when thinking about a solution to the exclusion of the different, in this case, women.

On the outskirts of orthodox Christian theology, the Neoplatonists and the entire current of apophatic theology—from the ancient Greco-Roman world through the medieval era up until it emerges, in some sense, in modern political thought—attempted to show that there can be no liberation in the One without a denial of the alienated being, of the nonbeing, of the Other. And that liberation was brought about by the *logos*, insofar as it is a word that interrupts the real by denying all previous negations.[19]

One characteristic that these theological-political subjects have in common is having inhabited a historical moment of social conflict, and attempting a conciliatory solution in the *logos*, in discourse as a locus of negation and affirmation of being. From that point on, the word has gone on to possess—not only theologically but also politically—a liberating function, inasmuch as it is the negation of all negation of the word as an expression of being. In other words, there cannot be social unity without the incorporation of the Other; without the Other expressing difference, there is only the illusion of unity, a false One. Eriugena also tried to show how the liberation of being must entail first overcoming the non-being, and that any difference only moves toward likeness, but never toward an identical equality.[20] This difference was taken up and expressed by Nicholas of Cusa—philosopher, theologian and diplomat—as the One in the many, trying to address how it is possible to reconcile the contraries between differences while saving the particularities of both.[21] Hegel and Marx, for their part, also tried to show the possibility for overcoming alienation in a collective being that contains difference. Both philosophy and theology have struggled to reconcile unity with diversity by exploring the possibility of doing this by way of the dialogical as real.

It stands, then, if being is revealed in discourse, in the incarnate word as a denial of any determination that places being in the location of the Other, then there cannot be woman without word: to deny her silence is a theological and political operation. Here one is invited to think that any denial of public discourse is at the same time a negation of being, preventing the possibility of its becoming being in relationship with others. Any liberation of the self beyond the determination in which it is trapped, is a word that appears in the public space and says *no* to its status as the Other to which it has been determined.

In South America, both political theorists and theological ethicists, if they wish—from a performative discourse—to act socially in terms of acceptance of the Other as part of the One (with respect to gender issues in this case), should be aware they are moving, as in any society, into an antagonistic space. However, this antagonism, typical of all social relationships, may be addressed if they can articulate both discourses, allowing an open totality grounded in difference, where the woman can also act as an articulating subject. It is possible, from the universal public word, to arrive at a social unity that contains difference, if one takes the logic of the empty space as nexus between the One and the Other, where the Other appears, makes itself manifest, and says *no* to the determination of the false One.

The Word as the Claim for the Political

For Christianity, the *logos*—as Incarnate Word—is the answer to the question of man preoccupied by totality as the truth of being; however, that *logos* is not a word that determines, but rather demands. Pilate's question about being attempts to identify Jesus as king of the Jews. But Jesus sets a limit by positioning himself not as king, but as Incarnate Word, as an act of word, as testimony. Even so, Pilate keeps wondering: "What is truth?" (John 18:37–38). According to these verses in the gospel, the answer to the question of being seems not to be a teleological determination, but rather an eschatological practice, a practice in history, which occurs in the very act of speaking of the word as both witness and a practice. Word is not complete truth without being acknowledged as response. The truth about being seems to be in the word as a performative, discursive practice and therefore creating, generating, and liberating (John 1:1). The word becomes part of history, and from history rises out of its nonbeing to its higher self, to recapitulation. In the gospel, being is the Word Incarnate. Being, as much as it is God, is command; being, as much as it is man, is a response. It is demand of the Creator Being and response of the created being. It is not a word that determines, but rather one that invites a response—that is, a practice, a witness.

When teleology (inasmuch as it is the study of revealed divine discourse about the truth about God and about humanity) acts as public word in defense of the political role of woman, it becomes eschatological practice, liberating practice in search of reconciliation in difference. Therefore, all theological ethics that intervenes as public word in rejection of any discourse that determines the woman to be the Other becomes political practice. Overcoming antagonism takes place in unity in diversity, without invalidating difference. Therefore poverty—which engenders

inequality—is solved with the acceptance of difference, that is, with the emancipation of all those who are denied for being the Other. The emancipation of the
woman as word can be understood as the practice of her public word, aiming to
deny any particular determination, overcoming its nonbeing to enable the promotion of equality (understood as sameness). This is the labor of a practice—not from
a political theology or epistemology in line with immanent or transcendent teleological ends—but according to the specific conditions of each community in the
same movement of the word in history as answer to a transcendent call that elicits
a response without determining it.

Mysticism and Populism: Woman's Word

The Woman as Signifier of the Political

Just as the word is the common denominator between politics and theology,
the word of the woman in South America today seems to be the common denominator between theology as mystical practice and politics as populist practice. Both
practices seek the representation of the Other through the word of the woman;
both use a method through which the word of the Other appears in discursive
articulation. Mysticism and populism say the ineffable as Ernesto Laclau notes
in his article "On the Names of God."[22] He notes that the Other is appointed
by a chain of negative equivalences that transcends the terms by destroying the
specific meaning of each, thus exceeding their ineffable content. This structure of
the destruction of the signifier/signified relationship in the realm of mysticism has
a parallel in populist discourse, where such rhetorical movements are the ones that
produce political action itself. Another sense of the Other appears in a discursive
chain of negative terms, in the equivalence of the terms or between the new relationships they establish with each other. Thus, the Other, ineffable, appears in the
discourse without being named. By destroying the signifier of the term that names
it, the Other appears in the empty signifier: "A mystic like Eckhart tried to think
in terms of 'unity in diversity,' and that is why the analogue of equivalence was
critical to his discourse. The universe of differences had to be driven to its unity,
without the resulting loss of the differencing moment."[23] In mystical discourse as
well as in populist discourse, the word of the Other appears when its difference
can be articulated in the empty signifier. Populism—as the One—occurs when a
particular social demand takes on the representation of the Other and names the
unnameable, making it universal and morally valid.

The political method of populist discourse is rhetoric—according to Laclau—
and, as in mystical theology, frames the vacuum to make the ineffable, the Other,
appear, cataloguing the differences and thus making sense of the undifferentiated.
Following this populist logic of discursive equivalence, social demands articulated
by women who are theologians and presidents in South America serve the function
of recovering the dialectical negation of the Other when social tension is resolved

(according to Laclau) the moment a particular demand assumes the *hegemonic representation* of all differences excluded from the system; this is called populism. This has occurred in the twenty-first century in South America through the word of the woman as one who articulates social demands. In three countries—Brazil, Argentina, and Chile—representation (with more than 54 percent) of the Other was in the woman's word, as one that manages to be the voice of all the ineffable Other. Cristina Fernández de Kirchner, for example, articulates the demand of the Others with Work Plans, the Universal Child Allowance, the Equality in Marriage Law, and the repeal of the "Full Stop Law" (which left out any sentencing of the perpetrators of genocide of the last military dictatorship).

The Nonword and Apophatic Democracy

By way of comparison, let us see the method of mystical theology practiced by women. Eckhart, who had been sent by the Catholic Church to try to bring Germany back into the realm of the word Beguines and Beghards (women and men who excluded themselves from public discourse), was condemned by his discovery: woman acting through her nonword becomes a political subject, a denier of social determination. These women, in an attempt to avoid being named as the Other, excluded themselves from the public by imprisonment; they did not allow themselves to be put in the place of the Other through the discourse of the master. Thus, the word of the woman appears as nonword: the woman who, in the void produced by her absence from public space, says the word of the Other. In this way the master concludes that being appears when the word of the Other is made manifest in a vacuum. Thus, the creature does not contain being except by participation; as it is directed by the Other, as it is emptied so that the word of the Other appears within. Two Bible verses are key to understanding this Eckhartian position: "those who work in me shall not sin" (Sir 24:30) and "those who reveal me will have eternal life" (Eccles. 24:31). These quotations, chosen by Eckhart, show the negative dialectic of the discursive vacuum, as the silence of the woman allows the word to appear and speak, not as possession—because the intent of the act of emptiness marks the freedom of the creature in its intentional awe before the Other—of space for the Other, as a word representative of the nonword, even of the Other.[24]

The apophatic theology of fourteenth-century Europe, just like the twenty-first century's apophatic democracy in South America (both represented in the word of women), shows the method by which the absolutely Other and the Other, respectively, appear. Now the woman's body speaks—as the void where the word becomes flesh, as a body that can exile itself of any determination to be the Other, which can be ecstatic, which can annihilate, which can liberate every negated word of being-there, of every positive word that named it, so that the nonword, the word of the Other, will be revealed as a public word. This idea is reflected in the Middle Ages, says Alain de Liberá,[25] as "white souls in joyful bodies." According to him, Rhenish mysticism (to which Eckhart had been dedicated) symbolized in man the law, thought, word, and desire, and in women the overflow, affection, condition, the nonword, the action/passion—as seen in the reference above to Simone Weil made by María Clara Bingemer. In this way mysticism and politics become articulating and meaning making. The nonword of the Other, the word of the woman who does not know what she says—according to Lacan [26]—represents the Other. To Alain de Liberá, the one sensing loses his word before them, and the sanction disappears because he has been mesmerized by the Other. In the fourteenth century, the debate moves from the ontological determination of Neoplatonism to the social plane. Women do not want to be identified by their fathers or by the pope. They say no, without a word. They talk with their bodies. The body appears and speaks. The body is the word. The subject's body becomes the void where the word of the Other appears. The body is an empty signifier where the Other appears and says *no* to all determination.

Now, if all we had in the political discourse of women was a succession of negative terms, the possibility of representing the Other as enunciating the ineffable would be impossible. To say that the Other is neither A nor B nor C does not exclude the possibility that it could be either D or F. That is, if it focuses on the *no* of the denial, there would be no way to build a coherent opening dimension of the enunciation of the word of women, on the basis of which rests the possibility of expressing the ineffable in politics. What is being sought is to make visible through language the ineffable presence of the Other that has been excluded from democratic societies. Therefore, we do not want to say what the Other is not, but rather what the Other is. But what is beyond the expressible transcends the specific meaning of positive terms. However, the female enumeration of denials establishes an equivalence between negative terms, and it is in this equivalence where the Other appears. The "equivalential enumeration" (as Laclau called it), on the one hand, destroys the sense of the term, which is affirmed through a practice of exclusion, oppression, and exploitation; on the other hand, it generates a new sense, not from the term itself, but through the equivalence that is established between all these terms. Put another way, the political sense of this appears when a woman, with her public word, articulates these denials, so that the Other appears. What we are saying is that the Other is unlike any particular attribute.

Equality as Likeness

In mystical theology, the road to bliss is given by likeness, not by equality of identity. This is relevant in the field of politics if one is to understand the new democratic styles practiced by the women presidents in South America. Democracy is now seeking to establish equality while maintaining difference. Those things that are different still resemble each other, and the One follows a path that goes through several stages, as in Plotinus,[27] until the One is made manifest in likeness. In political discourse, social similarity or equivalence exists between unrelated demands—those of people who are gay, the poor, the disappeared, or children.

In South America's new democratic forms, the word of the people, the Other, the "*okhlos,*" is made manifest in women's public word, political and theological, not in the manner of the presidentialism of the twentieth century with its decisive male word, but rather as an empty signifier, as a body where the word of the Other is embodied as discursive representation. The people are not just a part of this, they are all that appears currently in the southern region of the Americas, in the articulation of denial by the word of woman.

Now, the populist democratic milieu—that is, the discursive equivalence, the equality—just as in mysticism, sees its moment. On October 24, 2011, the day of the presidential elections in Argentina, the presidential candidate, Cristina Fernández de Kirchner, happened to have 54 percent of the vote. A week before that her percentage was lower; it was the next week as well. It can be seen in this discursive practice that the before and after do not matter, but rather it is in the *already and not yet* that the Other is manifested. At that moment, a set of articulated demands and negations made likeness possible. Fifty-four percent of voters were able to express themselves around a signifier, a representation of the word of the people incarnate in a woman's body. When such an operation is successful, it not only manages to construct a universal chain of equivalency, but also manages to destroy preexisting relationships of equivalency on which existing social inequality was operative. Unity, in politics as in mysticism, is achieved in the difference; the event of the manifestation of the One does not dissolve it, but instead assumes it through unity in difference.

Michel de Certeau, in *The Mythical Fable*, says that mystical literature is "a subtraction (an ecstatic one) operating through the seduction of the Other, and a (technical) virtuosity to force words to confess what they cannot say. [It is] a technical freedom capable of manipulating words that are no longer anchored in being."[28] The word appears to be impossible; it cannot speak itself; it says nothing. For him, the field of social discourse is divided into two poles. A top pole is inhabited by a parent named as the One; a lower pole is inhabited by an unnamed woman as the Other. Between these two poles a crowd moves, capable of reversing the poles. In the mystical realm, a woman can take the place of the father, the lower can take the place of the upper—if she is able to not allow herself to be determined by the word of the one doing the naming. It is the word that can cross that border, what is said must authorize action in order to take place, just as in diplomacy or war. The word unites opposites, saying what will occur, repeating the words of the Other, as noted by de Certeau. Theological political work in the multitude of modern society seems to consist of denoting otherness within institutions and the symbolic. The role of woman as political and theological subject is to reveal difference, so that she may speak what cannot be said because there is no word, only a laugh or a groan.[29] Michel de Certeau, referring to Teresa of Avila, mentions that she introduces the right to name when she changes the names by which things have been determined.[30] Thus, "mysticism is the anti-babel; it is the quest for a common speech after its split, the invention of a language of God or angels that resumes the dissemination of human languages."³¹ Cristina Kirchner named herself *presidenta*, which in Castilian means making *president*—present participle of *presidir*—in the feminine.

By Way of Conclusion: The One and the Other

In Lacan, the One appears in the *logos*: "if the unconscious is really what I say, being structured like a language, the level at which we have to question this One is at the level of language." The One manifests itself in a multiplicity of discourses, as in theophany in which the *logos* is written: should politics and theology, then, be matters of theophantic capacity? Nevertheless, "mysticism is not everything that is not politics. It is a serious thing, and we know this from certain people, mostly women, or capable people like Saint John of the Cross, because to be macho does not require to position oneself on the side of the phallus." The political is a public word used to express disagreement about what is just, and the mystical is a nonword where what is needed/missing is made manifest, and the Other appears *tout juste*—right there—in the multitude. The mean in Aristotle is the nonword in Lacan.³² Politics is a discourse about justice; mysticism is precisely what is missing and appears and does not appear. The nonword of the Other, the woman says "it is clear that the essential testimony of the mystics is just to say that they feel, but do not know, anything." The word appears in the *polis*, that which is beyond has no words, but, rather holds mystical ejaculations, which are "neither talk nor verbiage; ultimately, they are the best thing to read."³³

Notes

1. Johannes Baptist Metz, *Dios y tiempo* (Madrid: Trotta, 2001), 106.

2. Rudolf Otto, *Lo sagrado* (Buenos Aires: Claridad, 2008).

3. María Pilar Aquino, *A Reader in Latina Feminist Theology. Religion and justice* (Austin: University of Texas Press, 2002).

4. Virginia Azcuy, *El lugar teológico de las mujeres, un punto de partida* (Buenos Aires: Proyecto 39, 2001).

5. María Clara Bingemer, *Experiencia de Deus em corpo da mulher* (Sao Paulo: Loyola, 2002).

6. María Clara Bingemer, *A Argila E O Espírito. Ensaios sobre ética, mística e poética* (Río de Janeiro: Garamond, 2004).

7. Ivone Gebara, *El rostro oculto del mal. Una teología desde la experiencia de mujeres* (Madrid: Trotta, 2002).

8. Virginia Azcuy, *Mujeres haciendo teología* (Buenos Aires: San Pablo, 2007).

9. Virginia Azcuy, "Opción por los pobres. Desafío de santidad social,", in *De la justicia a la solidaridad. VII Jornada de reflexión ético-teológica*, ed. Humberto Miguel Yañez (Buenos Aires: San Benito, 2004), 159–82.

10. María Clara Bingemer, "Simone Weil: cuando la palabra es acción y pasión,"in *Mujeres de palabra*, ed. Liliana Yunes and M. C. Bingemer (México: Obra Nacional de la Buena prensa, 2004).

11. Ivone Gevara, "Théologie dela libération au féminim et théologie féminist de la libération," *Alternatives Sud* 7 (2000): 225–40.

12. Charles Tilly, *La desigualdad persistente* (Buenos Aires: Manantial, 2000).

13. Aristóteles, *Política* (Orbis, Madrid, 1985), 27, 1253ᵃ.

14. J. Ranciére, *El desacuerdo. Política y filosofía* (Buenos Aires: Nueva visión, 2007), 7–8, 20–45.

15. Hannah Arendt, *La Condición humana* (Buenos Aires: Paidós, 1998), 38.

16. M. Ruz, *Nueva teología política* (Córdoba: Educc, 2010), 190; Metz, *Dios y tiempo*, 40, 165, 177.

17. For concepts statements about the One and the Other, see the following works: Plotinus, *Enneads*, First Ennead; Eriugena, *De natura deorum*, Book I; St. Augustine, *On the Trinity*; Nicolas of Cusa, *De Docta ignoracia*.

18. Otto, *Lo sagrado*, 17.

19. Plotino, *Enéadas*, Enéada I, 1–9; VI, 9.

20. Eriugena, *The Peiphyson*, libro I.

21. Nicolas de Cusa, *La docta ignorancia*.

22. Ernesto Laclau, *Misticismo, retórica y política* (Buenos Aires: Fondo de Cultura, 2006).

23. Ibid., 116.

24. Andrés Quero Sánchez, *Maestro Eckhart. Sermones y lecciones* (Pamplona: EUNSA, 2010), 24, 23–31.

25. Alain De Liberá, *Pensar en la edad media* (Barcelona: Anthropos, 2000).

26. Jacques Lacan, *Aun. Seminario 20* (Buenos Aires: Paidós, 1991).

27. Plotino, *Enéadas* VI, 9.

28. De Certeau, *La fábula mística* (México: Universidad Iberoamericana, 2004), 43.

29. Ibid., 57.

30. Ibid., 162.

31. Ibid., 189.

32. Lacan, *Aun*, 79.

33. Ibid., 92.

Of (Befriending) Dragons and Escaping the Underworld: Two Voices in Caribbean Catholic Feminist Ethics

Anna Perkins

Undoubtedly, women theologians are a special gift to the Church, especially the Caribbean Church as we struggle to shape our lives as a people.
Our specific contribution, as I see it, is to help carve a space within the
Church so that true and inclusive participation can enable the Church
as Communion to become an effective place of encounter for liberation,
progress and salvation.[1]

Caribbean Catholic feminist ethics is a little-known creature in the field of
Catholic feminist ethics. This is perhaps unsurprising, because while the Anglophone Caribbean in particular has a burgeoning tradition of secular feminist
scholarship, it has been argued this tradition silences or ignores the voice of religious women. Jamaican gender theorist Judith Soares maintains that feminism in
the Caribbean is, in certain respects, exclusive, as it relates specifically to women
of faith who "have been upheld for a long time by feminists (not only in the
Caribbean) as 'reactionary' and unable to contribute to the women's struggle for
change."[2] Treating Christian feminists in this manner, Soares concludes, has led to
the stunting of the Caribbean feminist movement. This is certainly troubling in a
region where spirituality and faith form the bedrock of the identity of the people.
Not engaging with the theological and ethical reflections of religiously committed
women, as, for example, the "Nannyish T'ealagy" of Jamaican Marjorie Lewis, a
United Church minister, or the liberationist postcolonial reflections of Catholics
like Jamaican Theresa Lowe Ching and Trinidadian Diane Jagdeo, may well have
weakened the feminist discourse in the region.[3] Clearly, religious feminist reflection should have a place in the discourse about women's lives in the region, and this
space must be created as a matter of urgency.

Introducing Caribbean Catholic Feminist Ethics

This essay introduces Anglophone Caribbean Catholic feminist ethics through
a reflection on selected works of two women theologians, both religious sisters,

Diane Jagdeo, OP (RIP), and Theresa Lowe Ching, RSM. They are perhaps the best-known women theologians in the area pastored by the bishops of the Antilles Episcopal Conference (AEC), which includes the Anglo-, Netherlander- and Fran-cophone (except Haiti) countries of the region. Both have been responsible for the training and formation of generations of priests, theologians, religious, and layper-sons (myself included) through their work at St. Michael's Seminary/St. Michael's Theological College, Jamaica (Lowe Ching) and the Regional Seminary of St. John Vianney and the Uganda Martyrs, Trinidad (Jagdeo). Both are trained systematic theologians, and their work demonstrates that theology and ethics/spirituality are not distinct enterprises that operate separate from and in competition with each other; rather, they overlap, illuminate, and enrich the other to the benefit of humanity. Their feminist ethics is deeply rooted in a theology and spirituality that becomes evident in an examination of their work. Like other Catholic femi-nist theologians, Lowe Ching and Jagdeo "have long been at the leading edges of creative and life-giving thought in Catholic theology [in the Caribbean], coura-geously blazing new understandings of being catholic and of being in community with Church and world."[4] While beginning from different points of origin and having differing themes, there are some important points of contact between the thought of these two theologians; much of their reflections, for example, dwell on women in church and society.[5] They critique all ecclesial or secular structures that do not promote the full flourishing of all human beings. The images—dragon, cave, underworld, enchantment—used by both theologians are rooted in their Caribbean reality while having potential to speak to others from different national, ethnic, and cultural experiences. Jagdeo confesses that, in the Caribbean context within which she and Lowe Ching do their theology, she

> [M]ust "read" the scripts of the daily lives of people in local communities which force me to see the relevance and irrelevancies of many theological positions, even of my own. There is definitely an integral connection between doing theology and participation in community, in fact, there is no such thing as doing theology outside of a shared faith community.[6]

Befriending the Dragon

Lowe Ching, a Jamaican of Chinese descent, makes a constant and recurring call for the inclusion of women's experiences and the involvement of women in doing theology. (She acts on this call in her dedication to including laywomen in theological studies.) This call for inclusion is a constant theme in her theological reflection but does not seem to be taken sufficiently seriously in decade after decade, as her recurring call indicates. In capturing this unwillingness to give women's issues a serious space in the theological enterprise in the region, Lowe Ching tells and retells a poignant story from "back when the world was new"[7] of a powerful she-dragon, the mother of all, whose dominion spread from shore to shore.[8]

In her passion, [the dragon's] awesome power shaped and sculpted the land; a cliff of granite destroyed, a dazzling white beach created. Islands and lagoons, sand bars and channels emerged in response to her restless movement. But with her smile, the seas rippled in delight. Dancing sunbeams made diamonds in the waves, and gentle swells, resonating to her pleasure, caressed the shores of a thousand islands, sending warm tides surging through quiet wetlands, the swampy nursery of all living things.[9]

Then one day, "for reasons that seemed good at the time," the dragon is lured from the sea and confined in a cave by the powers that be. They feared the restless destruction and creation she caused. The beloved St. George stood guard with sharpened sword and stout spear to keep her "encaved." Yet, the seas continued to be rolled by the children of the dragon, while she continued confined to the "Stygian gloom." (It is not possible to keep the dragon's effects totally at bay.) On one occasion, she broke loose, and her violent passion, which had been compressed in the cave, rolled over the land until she was again corralled and confined by St. George and a crew of hastily assembled knights. All was well again with the land. Or was it? Then one day out of nowhere the heretical question was asked, "What would it be like to make friends with the dragon?" What if the dragon were not really the terrible beast described in song and fable? Perhaps she was only angry for having been locked in a dark cave for millennia? What would friendship with such a force entail?

Of Dragons

The use of a story is not unusual for Lowe Ching, as she makes clear that women's spirituality is rooted in women's experiences and is therefore more fully captured in images, stories, and symbols.[10] This story is particularly apt, as the geological formations resulting from the dragon's creativity and destruction immediately bring to mind the islands of the Caribbean with their white sand beaches, dancing sunbeams, and rippling waters. It is perhaps also unsurprising that Lowe Ching is attracted to the image of the dragon, which is one of the signs in the Chinese Zodiac calendar.[11] Like the dragon in Lowe Ching's narrative, the dragon in the Chinese Zodiac is magnificent. It is flamboyant, attractive, and full of vitality and strength; the symbol of power and wealth. The year of the dragon promises "new life, creativity and adventure and this 50th Anniversary of Vatican II also calls for a new springtime of renewal and rebirth in Church and society."[12] Unlike the restless dragon, however, in China, the dragon is the imperial symbol, the sign of the emperor, or the male element Yang. (The female energy, or Yin, to the dragon is the tiger.) There is no hint of destructiveness in the Chinese dragon. Interestingly, the dragon of Lowe Ching's story encapsulates the creation *and* destruction that leads to the balance of energies that the Chinese Yin-Yang dualism aims for. Evil is said to result from an imbalance in Yin and Yang, and good comes from the two being in harmonic balance. Yet it was the fear of the destructive power of the dragon that led to her corralling and the loss of her full power to the world. Embedded in such action, there is an inherent misunderstanding of the nature of the world in that life and death, happiness and sorrow, creativity and destruction are fundamental.

A Trapped Space

Lowe Ching represents a decidedly postcolonial liberationist approach to feminist theology and ethics in the Caribbean. The story of the dragon captures the experience of marginalization, oppression, curtailment of creativity, anger and frustration and, some would add, suffering, that have marked women's lives in the region and globally. This common experience has initiated the struggle for liberation that informs the feminist movement and feminist theology, and continues to develop in various parts of the world. Lowe Ching is especially tried by the fact that, in almost two hundred years of social teaching in the Catholic Church, "addressing issues of injustice and oppressive situations in the society, has for the most part neglected to mention any special concern regarding women."[13] She laments that the church has not kept pace with the changes in society to ensure the fuller empowerment of women.

Diane Jagdeo, a Trinidadian of "mixed" (African/Indian) heritage, would describe the corralling of the dragon as violence: a distortion of power (*dynamis*) or lifeforce. The Caribbean can be described as a space characterised by violence, especially against women:

> In many instances throughout the Caribbean today, we are witnessing this kind of context and thus the sufferings and victimization of women have becoming more radical, traumatic and life-debilitating. I would like to examine women's power from the point of view of our history of suffering, since it is a history that constantly blurs hope, impedes the dreams of a better world and snuffs out personhood for women of the Caribbean.[14]

In Jagdeo's perspective, the Caribbean is not simply a "forced context," as fellow Trinidadian theologian Gerald Boodoo describes it.[15] Rather, from the perspective of Caribbean women, it has become a "trapped space: one within which women's freedom is curtailed but in which they seek for loopholes, transgress boundaries, and become creative. In such a space, women are not the only ones that are trapped. Jagdeo is clearly arguing that all people are in "a trapped space" when one group is denied their freedom and full flourishing (perhaps confined to the Stygian darkness). Her description of the responses of people (men) in a trapped space echo those of the powers-that-be who confine the dragon of the deep using violence and threat of force:

Whenever people experience their situation as forced or their space diminished, threatened or challenged, the other is not automatically a friend or loving neighbour. The other is readily perceived as a threat, a potential enemy, a usurper of space and authority. In the face of a potential power that the other seemingly has, one does not easily and readily empty one's self so that the common good may be established. It is truer to say that the power that "lords it over" others is more likely to be evoked. In any forced context in which some person or group feels that the other may have the upper hand all thoughts of goodly "kenosis" runs foul and "dynamis" or "exousia" quickly turns into rage and domination—kyriarchal. The attacker uses brute strength that is dominated by a narrow egotistical vision of the other. The other is the enemy, (in reality this person may be your wife or a loved one or one whom you deeply admire). The end result is violence, abuse, and when that rage is vented upon a woman, she may be also raped and killed.[16]

Such is the painful experience of women in the Caribbean; the self-emptying of the Savior takes on a singular meaning in such a context, as Jagdeo outlines. Befriending in such a space is clearly a difficult, nigh impossible, prospect.

This question of befriending has a further importance for Jagdeo; she, however, speaks of befriending the poor, among whom are found women. Befriending the poor requires that they be known by name, become our friends and neighbors with real names, faces, and needs that are also our needs. Jagdeo claims that befriending the poor causes that very label to drop away, and caring and sharing among friends becoming the driving force for lobbying for social justice. Befriending clearly needs to be at play in the very ways in which Caribbean people live and encounter the other.

The Underworld

The trapped space is also captured in the image of the underworld, which Jagdeo also uses to describe the experience of women in the Caribbean. Jagdeo hearkens back to Greco-Roman mythology, even as she recognizes local Caribbean folklore's way of enchanting, that is, "providing a powerful way of teaching life values whilst maintaining respect for the other."[17] Showing her classical training, Jagdeo calls upon the story of Aeneas, the Trojan hero, who wanted to go to the underworld to visit his dead father (elsewhere she describes her own theological journey as an Odyssean voyage that has brought her back to the shores of contemplation).[18] The Sibyl, whose help Aeneas implores, warns him that it is easy to go down into the underworld, but difficult to recall the steps and reenter the upper air. Jagdeo, therefore, likens the task and toil ahead of Aeneas to that of women in the church, who experience life in the underworld of oppression and are struggling to escape/emerge from it. She charges that women continue to be challenged by a one-sided *ecclesia* in which participation does not take mutuality seriously and denigrates women through the use of "words without wisdom." This is the very struggle that Lowe Ching highlights over and over again, to little avail. Yet to "recall our steps and pass out to the upper air is the greatest task and toil for Caribbean women today."[19] A boundary must be crossed, and a frontier transgressed, for women to come to their fullness in the ecclesial and social spaces of the Caribbean.

The notion of boundaries and frontiers is strong in Jagdeo's ethical reflection. In a response to (Sri Lankan-born former general secretary of the Council for World Mission, London) Preman Niles' 1999 presentation on intradisciplinary/religious dialogue, she outlines the complexity of the new frontiers that are present in such dialogue (which she feels Niles did not sufficiently spell out). She rejects the warrior model that assumes that boundaries are clear and that crossing them is a deliberate initiative on the part of those who cross (a militaristic way of approaching boundaries that can/does not lead to self-understanding, but rather to a new tribalism). She favors what she calls the "Anansi"[20] model, which sees boundaries as much more fluid, where one is as much "crossed over" as crossing over. In this model boundaries are crossed unnoticed, unannounced. The person engaged by this model does not behave as if she alone has "a monopoly on understanding or articulating the fullness of reality."[21] This is the process that engages dialogue as fundamental and does not stop at articulating a common vision or vantage point. The Anansi model "challenges us to a new reading of reality and thus our perception of our place in it."[22]

Space is constructed and reconstructed; boundaries/frontiers are complex, and new challenges in the form of new forms of consciousness present themselves. Jagdeo calls for intradisciplinary dialogue in order for a new sense of consciousness and identity to form (both individual and communal). She calls for a dialogue with "poets and artists who struggle to articulate our Caribbean reality in inclusive and innovative ways thus reaping the benefits of a new and integrated vision of life for the peoples and nations of the Caribbean."[23] Hers, like Lowe Ching's, is clearly a very inclusive vision that takes account of the cultural context of the Caribbean.

A Vision of Woman

Both women draw from the values, characteristics, and experiences of women that might assist in transforming church and world. Indeed, both are adamant that much in the experience of women is essential to the transformation of both *ecclesia* and *civitas*. Jagdeo, for example, speaks of women having learned what oppressed people experience through their time in the underworld. But being in the underworld has taught women to trust their deep instinctual spirit and to trust their kinship with the divine. Importantly, as she describes women, particularly Caribbean women, she employs a methodology that transforms words of abuse and ridicule directed at women; among such words, which she transforms, are "homemaker" and "enchantress"; homemaker is no longer a term that domesticates and confines women, but rather invites into a sacred space. Similarly, enchantress lures us into the mystery of the divine being, evoking presence and enhancing relationships. Jagdeo draws the image of the Caribbean woman, who is "hidden" among other women, captured in statistics but not a person:

> You encounter her in the streets, and yards, in the market and sometimes she pops up on our television screens. She lives in my neighbourhood. But more, she appears at your side when your flesh is broken and your bones fall apart empty of sinew and your wounds are sore and your soul is languishing in darkness and desolation. You meet her in the eyes of women weeping for their children and looking for shelter and food for their families and then you meet her again laughing and dancing as she points your spirit to a new time, and a new space. To a space through the fence that holds you bound and gagged.[24]

For Jagdeo, the Caribbean woman is both ordinary and extraordinary, fully immersed in her Caribbean reality while pointing toward new possibilities in a cultural and ecclesial space that holds women "bound and gagged." Addressing the ordinary Jamaican woman (and man), Lowe Ching wrote a well-received series of reflections on spirituality and women's spirituality in the *Jamaica Observer* newspaper's "All Woman" supplement during the 1990s. In those weekly reflections, she, too, seeks after words to describe the spirituality of this hidden woman, who is like all women: "[W]oman is kin to nature and experiences nature's rhythms in her very being."[25] She repeated this idea of women being closer to nature but ties it even more closely to religious experience: "Is it any wonder that images of nature predominate in women's religious experience, given their affinity to nature and their being in tune with nature's rhythm of birth and rebirth?"[26] She further described women as having a natural passion for life: "In the face of all of this woman is challenged to release her natural 'passion for life' confident that the life-giving Spirit is her guide and model."[27] "Inherent in woman's way of living in the Spirit is then a natural 'passion for life,' which she needs to grasp and set free as a counter-force against all that threatens human life."[28] (Jagdeo similarly echoes this belief in women's passion for life, claiming that "enchantment is a native gift of women."[29]) Woman's vocation in Lowe Ching's ethical framework is to act against all that threatens life and living.

Furthermore, in describing the Trinitarian God, Lowe Ching speaks of inclusiveness, mutuality, and communion as divine characteristics that are present in a special way in women's spirituality: "The same characteristics of inclusiveness, mutuality and communion are likewise attributed in a special way to women's manner of being and acting; hence women's spirituality can be considered as being basically Trinitarian, or patterned after the Trinity."[30] The natural Trinitarian spirituality that Lowe Ching identifies as being present in the way women live allows them to give due worship and acknowledgment to the One True God, who as Creator includes, sustains and nourishes all of creation; as Redeemer justifies sinful humanity and brings healing and forgiveness, drawing all human beings into a discipleship of mutual love and service; and as sanctifying Spirit leads all into wholeness, integrity and Truth, into the very life of a Holy and loving God.[31]

At first blush, this seems like an exclusivist, essentialist reading of the nature of women and women's experience and spirituality. Indeed, Jagdeo's and Lowe Ching's discussions of women's experience, vocation, and spirituality/ethics would appear to fall into the trap of essentializing the feminine and arrogating to that group certain characteristics that the "Other" (men) lack. However, that is certainly not the case, as both women are clear that the call is to a more inclusive and mutual space that is no longer the Stygian deep, the underworld, or the trapped space.

Lowe Ching is not unaware of the impact of assigned gender roles in the ways of defining women: "Woman alive in the Spirit knows the interconnectedness of all creation. Beyond the dualism of assigned gender roles, she strives for integration, interdependence and fruitful collaboration. She has, indeed, experienced the mutual enrichment of giving and receiving."[32] Lowe Ching embraces an alternative vision of inclusivity, unity in diversity, community, creativity, traditionally associated with women, as will be detailed below. However, she does not deny the values of industrial modernity, which includes rationality, order, thoroughness, sobriety, achievement, and efficiency.[33]

Both women attempt, therefore, to positively revalue women and women's experiences in a space that has denigrated, belittled, and rejected them. Only then can the process of true inclusiveness and mutuality begin. That is the important task of a Caribbean theology/spirituality/ethics. Nonetheless, both positions can be enhanced by a nuancing that treats of women who do not actually live the mutuality and inclusiveness that is claimed as a natural part of the experience of women. At the same time, they need to be aware that there are women who may be repulsed by the physicality inherent in the "natural" claims being made of women. How can these women also be engaged in the conversation around women's experiences?

A Task for Caribbean Theology/Spirituality/Ethics?

The space within which a Catholic Caribbean feminist ethics unfolds is a changed world context, a new historical moment that calls not for repeated responses from the past but for new solutions built on

A self-critical analysis both locally and globally [which] is necessary to uncover the advances that have been made in the quest for greater freedom and integral development of persons in the Caribbean as well as the degree to which certain problems have persisted or even worsened and now demand more adequate solutions in the light of new questions that have arisen in the context. It is here, in particular, that women's experience and input could greatly advance this task.[34]

This quest for freedom from oppression positions the Caribbean in a postcolonial space that confronts a postmodern world.[35] Lowe Ching sees this space as impacted increasingly by feminist discourse and liberationist movements concerning the consciousness and agenda of contemporary society.[36] It is into this space that the woman theologian enters with a particular vocation. As woman, she brings a special perspective, and, as Jagdeo professes in her lyrical fashion

> The voice and wisdom of women must sound like a trumpet heralding a time of new birth of a Church that has been too clerical, too distant, to "other," too dry! Caribbean women must bring to the Church their life's flavour of creativity and boldness, daring and enchantment, so that the Church is seen and experienced as a celebratory inclusive community, that life itself in spite of all its darkness and suffering is seen as celebratory . . . It must radiate joy while taking seriously the suffering, pain and trauma which mark our lives both individually and as a people.[37]

Doing Theology as Woman

Jagdeo was the first woman to teach in the regional seminary. Rooted in feminist traditions and aware of the debt owed to foremothers, she is clear about her Caribbean experience shaping her theological reflection. Jagdeo describes doing theology as searching after the truth like the woman in the gospel who, having lost her drachma, searches earnestly until she finds it. "Doing theology is like embarking on an odyssey, and this adventure is taking me into the spaces and places of and within my own Caribbean people."[38] Among the spaces within the Caribbean that Jagdeo, echoing *Gaudium et spes*, explores, are the hopes, fears, and anguish of the people who suffer, especially from the widespread destruction resulting from frequent hurricanes. "Healing land and healing lives (ecology and human well-being) seem to me to be the theological agenda for us in the Caribbean."[39]

Theological Method

In Jagdeo's hands, the Caribbean woman (and woman theologian) emerges as a wisdom figure, the Divine Sophia who is luring and is alluring, who lures you to follow your deeper instincts and to find your true self. Thus, in an attempt to speak of wisdom's power, Jagdeo calls for walking the path of wisdom and "letting wisdom be our guide" to wisdom.[40] Jagdeo declares, "Wisdom is a fire. And theology keeps it ablaze. The theologian is the stoker of the fire."[41] As a method of doing theology, wisdom requires attentive listening, asking the right questions, creative use of the imagination, and truthful action.

> [Importantly,] having drunk from the streams of wisdom, it leads us to commitment to truthful action. Because wisdom does not seek to establish life in self-centered, egotistical pursuits, it frees us to "set up spaces in daily life in which well-being, true joy, humanizing emotions, liberating understanding and celebration can be experienced by all." Wisdom establishes justice as the foundation to a peaceful society. Wisdom desires to foster a humanity that is compassionate and merciful, loving and hopeful.[42]

This wisdom method contrasts with yet sits well with Lowe Ching's liberationist methodology, which is captured succinctly in Segundo's hermeneutical circle. The liberationist method begins with concrete reflection on faith, and

> raises concrete existential questions in search for meaning and articulates them in specific contexts; uses social analyses to probe beneath appearances and get at underlying causes; reflects upon the Christian message in order to throw new light on these questions; and finally, engenders a praxis that is more adequate in the living of the Christian faith."[43]

Both methods lead to ethical living, living that encompasses justice and is marked by "think[ing] about the consequences of your actions for seven generations."[44]

Toward a Conclusion

Theresa Lowe Ching and Diane Jagdeo, Caribbean Catholic feminists, are theologians and ethicists who seek after spirituality and engage in criticism, recovery, and reconstruction. They identify structures that have historically been damaging to the full flourishing of women (and others) both inside the church and society. They explore the religious, cultural, and social traditions of their communities in order to identify and recover elements such as experiences, words, symbols, and metaphors that might be beneficial to women and the oppressed. They then proceed to reconstruct a narrative that is more inclusive, equal, mutual, and diverse. Lowe Ching's narrative leads us to conclude that the freeing of women's potential has been the missing link that has prevented a real transformation of our ecclesial and societal structures.[45] Likewise, Jagdeo calls for a release of women from the "underworld" of church and society in order to establish mutual relations/relationality, radical equality, and community in diversity. This is a task that should be supported.

Notes

1. Diane Jagdeo, "To All My Dominican Sisters and Brothers," in *Building Bridges: Dominicans Doing Theology Together*, ed. Dominican Sisters International (Dublin: Dominican Publications, 2005), 85.

2. Judith Soares, "Addressing the Tensions: Reflections on Feminism in the Caribbean," *Caribbean Quarterly* 52, nos. 1 and 2 (June–September 2006): 187–88.

3. The breadth of the contribution of religiously committed women was recently captured in *Righting Her-Story: Caribbean Women Encounter the Bible Story*, ed. Patricia Sheerattan-Bisnauth (Geneva: World Communion of Reformed Churches, Office for Justice and Partnership, 2011). This creative compilation of bible studies, poetry, song, and stories of outstanding Caribbean women covered a range of issues impacting women's lives in the region.

4. Susan Abrahams and Elena Procario-Foley, "Preface," in *Frontiers in Catholic Feminist Theology: Shoulder to Shoulder*, ed. Susan Abrahams and Elena Procario-Foley (Minneapolis: Fortress Press, 2009), 1.

5. All the writings from both theologians analyzed in this chapter include Theresa Lowe Ching, "Women Doing Theology: Towards a Transformative Vision and Praxis," in *Theologising Women,* ed. Judith Soares (St. Michaels, Barbados: Women and Development Unit, UWI, 2007); Theresa Lowe Ching, "The Role of Women in the Society and in the Church," Sedos Residential Seminar, May 8–12, 2012 (unpublished paper); Theresa Lowe Ching, "The Role of Women in Church and Society: Befriending the Dragon," *Groundings: Catholic Theological Reflections on Issues facing Caribbean People in the 21st Century* 8 (May 2002): 16–30; Diane Jagdeo, "The Power of Woman in Caribbean Life: Implications for Ecclesiology," Paper presented at the 10th Annual Theology in the Caribbean Today Conference, January 6–10, 2003, Trinidad and Tobago, http://caribbeantheology.com/sr__diane.htm; Diane Jagdeo, "Women's Contribution in Transforming the Caribbean Church," *Groundings: Catholic Theological Reflections on Issues facing Caribbean People in the 21st Century* 9 (September 2002): 27–39; Diane Jagdeo, "Fostering Intra-Disciplinary Dialogue: Facing the Challenges, Reaping the Benefits," *CJRS* 20, no. 1 (April 1999): 60–62; Diane Jagdeo, "To All My Dominican Sisters and Brothers," in *Building Bridges*, 85–90.

6. Jagdeo, "To All My Dominican Sisters and Brothers," 86.

7. The fable is drawn originally from Donna Markham, "Befriending the Dragon," a lecture delivered at LCWR Conference, Spokane, Washington, 1990.

8. Echoes the title of William Watty's brief treatise on Caribbean theology, *From Shore to Shore: Soundings in Caribbean Theology* (Kingston, Jamaica: Golding Printing Service, 1981).

9. Lowe Ching, "Women Doing Theology," 18.

10. Theresa Lowe Ching, "Women and Spirituality," *Jamaica Observer*, October 23, 1996.

11. Many Jamaican Chinese are descendants of the Han people, who describe themselves as "Children of the Dragon." See, for example, Easton Lee, *Heritage Call: Ballad for Children of the Dragon* (Kingston, Jamaica: Ian Randle Publishers, 2001.

12. Lowe Ching, "The Role of Women in the Society and in the Church," 2.

13. Ibid., 10.

14. Jagdeo, "The Power of Woman in Caribbean Life."

15. Gerald Boodoo, "Theology in a Forced Context," Presentation at the Annual Meeting of the Catholic Theological Society of America, Minneapolis, Method in Theology Group, 1997.

16. Jagdeo, "The Power of Woman in Caribbean Life."

17. Jagdeo, "Women's Contribution in Transforming the Caribbean Church," 35.

18. Jagdeo, "To All My Dominican Sisters and Brothers," 88.

19. Jagdeo, "Women's Contribution in Transforming the Caribbean Church," 31.

20. Anansi is the trickster folk hero who crossed the Atlantic with the enslaved Africans brought to the Caribbean. He is an ambiguous figure who it is often claimed has shaped the moral character of many Jamaican/Caribbean people. See Barry Chevannes, *Betwixt and Between: Explorations in an African-Caribbean Mindscape* (Kingston, Jamaica: Ian Randle, 2006).

21. Diane Jagdeo "Fostering Intra-Disciplinary Dialogue: Facing the Challenges, Reaping the Benefits," *Caribbean Journal of Religious Studies* 20, no. 1 (April 1999): 60–62, at 61.

22. Jagdeo, "Fostering Intra-Disciplinary Dialogue," 61.

23. Ibid., 62.

24. Jagdeo, "The Power of Woman in Caribbean Life.

25. Theresa Lowe Ching, *Jamaica Observer*, October 14, 1996.

26. Theresa Lowe Ching, *Jamaica Observer*, October 23, 1996.

27. Theresa Lowe Ching, *Jamaica Observer*, May 20, 1996.

28. Ibid.

29. Jagdeo, "The Power of Woman in Caribbean Life.

30. Theresa Lowe Ching, *Jamaica Observer*, June 3, 1996.

31. Ibid.

32. Theresa Lowe Ching, Jamaica Observer, November 19, 1996.

33. Lowe Ching, "The Role of Women in the Society and in the Church."

34. Lowe Ching, "Women Doing Theology," 26.

35. Lowe Ching,"The Role of Women in the Society and in the Church," 4.

36. Ibid., 3.

37. Jagdeo, "To All My Dominican Sisters and Brothers," 89.

38. Ibid., 85.

39. Ibid.

40. Jagdeo, "The Power of Woman in Caribbean Life: Implications for Ecclesiology.

41. Jagdeo, "To All My Dominican Sisters and Brothers," 86.

42. Jagdeo, "The Power of Woman in Caribbean Life: Implications for Ecclesiology.

43. Lowe Ching, "Women Doing Theology," 28.

44. Jagdeo, "The Power of Woman in Caribbean Life: Implications for Ecclesiology.

45. Lowe Ching, "The Role of Women in the Society and in the Church," 3.

Magisterium, Margaret Farley, and the Ecclesial Role of Feminist Moral Theology: Discerning the *Ecclesia Discens* Today

Gerard Mannion

Introduction

In a brief article in the revised 1986 *New Dictionary of Christian Ethics*, a moral theologian spoke of the particular contributions of feminist approaches to ethics. She defined feminist ethics as "any ethical theory that locates its roots in feminism, and especially in the contemporary feminist movement," with feminism being understood as "a conviction and a movement opposed to discrimination on the basis of gender," aiming toward "equality among persons regardless of gender." Those particular and distinct contributions of feminism in general listed included the "critique of sources of sexism . . . retrieval of women's history and pro-woman myths; reconstruction of theories of the human person and the human community." It acknowledged a pluralism among feminist approaches and perspectives, including those that explore ethics and moral dilemmas, with the corpus of feminist ethics incorporating "varying combinations of, for example, liberal, socialist and radical perspectives."[1]

Those particular *achievements* of feminist ethics listed (and acknowledged as not exclusive to feminist ethics), being areas concerning which differing approaches held much in common, included "the meaning of human embodiment (especially issues of human sexuality); the nature of the human self (including possibilities for the development of character); the value of the world of nature; patterns for human relationships (both personal and political)."[2] Further contributions include the importance of women's experience, pushing the boundaries of traditional ethical theories, an assertion of the value of women as fully human, with the requisite principles of equality and autonomy, alongside that of mutuality that follow, an emphasis upon equitable sharing in (and so one presumes distribution of) the goods and services "necessary to human life and basic happiness,"[3] the implications of an embodied understanding of personhood for relationships and communities, a critique of racism and classism alongside that of sexism, and opposition to domineering power and "hierarchical gradation," as well as, for some feminists, an advocacy of the principle of nonviolence.[4] The author then denotes some particular areas of focus for *Christian* feminist ethics, including the opposition to the inferiority of women being justified by a male/female oppositional distinction analogous to mind/body, reason/emotion, activity/passivity, and so on, as well as a rejection of the notion that women will naturally be more virtuous than men ("pedestalism"). Rather, Christian feminist ethics takes on board the critique of the patriarchal failings of Christianity itself, alongside some predominant themes and concepts in that faith, as well as seeking to develop "a theory of moral and religious development and a feminist theory of virtue or character" as well as that of widely inclusive justice.[5]

Feminist thought and practice, then, and especially feminist ethics, have offered much to modern and postmodern societies. They have also contributed enormously to the church, its proclamation, teachings, and mission in these same eras.[6]

A great irony emerged in June 2012, for the moral theologian who penned that 1986 article was none other than Margaret Farley, the very same moral theologian whose book, *Just Love*, an embodiment of the very fruits of creative feminist moral theology that have brought so much to the postconciliar call for the renewal of moral theology in general, was condemned in a "Notification" from the Congregation for the Doctrine of the Faith (CDF) that same month.[7]

Lisa Sowle Cahill has said that "[v]irtually by definition, feminist theology is 'moral' theology or ethics. It emerges from a practical situation of injustice and aims at social and political change."[8] This fact sharpens the critical and hermeneutical focus that is demanded when one attempts to try and understand the thinking and agenda behind documents such as the Notification against Margaret Farley's book. The Notification focuses on the most headline-grabbing issues, despite the fact that the actual book in question did not focus solely or even in the main on these issues—indeed, one such issue merited only a very limited degree of attention in Farley's book. Rather, the book was seeking to shape a dialogical framework for exploring questions about human sexuality today. Cahill's words equally sharpen our focus when exploring the contribution of women's voices of authority to the church, that is, their exercise of magisterium.

In this essay, Farley's situation will serve as a case study to illustrate some questions and considerations pertaining to the role of women, here primarily as moral theologians, in contributing to the exercise of the church's magisterium.

"Official" Moral Teaching and Moral Theological Discernment

Two passages will help indicate the nature of the discussion that the remainder of this essay will focus upon:

> The author does not present a correct understanding of the role of the Church's Magisterium as the teaching authority of the Bishops united

with the Successor of Peter, which guides the Church's ever deeper understanding of the Word of God as found in Holy Scripture and handed on
faithfully in the Church's living tradition.[9]

As theologians know well, the term "magisterium" denotes the exercise of
teaching authority in the Catholic Church. The transfer of this teaching
authority from those who had acquired knowledge to those who received
power was a long, gradual, and complicated process, the history of which
has only partially been written.[10]

The Notification contains many problematic statements and perhaps none more
so than the first paragraph, shown above. Not only does it fail to make sense with
regard to what Farley's book is supposed to be about (it certainly is not about
the exercise of official magisterium), but this statement also overlooks the much
varied history and development of Catholic interpretations of the understanding
and exercise of magisterium itself.

The CDF said it launched an "urgent" investigation of the book (which seems
to have taken nearly two years), "Because the matter concerned doctrinal errors
present in a book whose publication has been a cause of confusion among the
faithful."[11] But the evidence suggests that if anything in recent years is causing
confusion among the faithful of the Roman Catholic Church, it is an understanding and exercise of magisterium that does not sit well with the history of
the church. Nor, the evidence equally suggests, does it serve the church well. The
Notification helps points toward many areas where such confusion is generated.
The CDF Notification continues to unfold in just as problematic a fashion:

> In addressing various moral issues, Sr. Farley either ignores the constant
> teaching of the Magisterium or, where it is occasionally mentioned, treats
> it as one opinion among others. Such an attitude is in no way justified,
> even within the ecumenical perspective that she wishes to promote. Sr.
> Farley also manifests a defective understanding of the objective nature of
> the natural moral law, choosing instead to argue on the basis of conclu-
> sions selected from certain philosophical currents or from her own
> understanding of "contemporary experience." This approach is not consis-
> tent with authentic Catholic theology.[12]

What these words appear to suggest is that a context-bound understanding
of the church's teaching authority, its teaching and tradition themselves, one that
privileges certain perspectives and theological methods and opinions, is being
presented as if there were timeless, eternal truths that have somehow dropped from
heaven and have been preserved without alteration for over two thousand years.
But the basis for such an assessment appears not to be theology, nor is it ecclesiology, or even canon law. It appears rather to be that ecclesio-political rhetoric that

has taken over the substance of far too many "official" church pronouncements in recent times. Furthermore, the Notification appears to imply that all teachings of the church should carry equal weight, which contradicts Catholic tradition about the church's own teaching. Even if the Notification does not mean to communicate such an opinion, it can easily be taken by the faithful as offering such an opinion.

For example, both the opening statement of § 1, cited above, and its continuation here seem to imply that there has been a seamless and unproblematic "constant" teaching emanating from the church's central authorities on the moral issues that the Notification brings up. There has not. Hence, moral theologians throughout history have sought to try to help the church discern and issue guidance. Farley is an exemplary moral theologian in a long line of tradition here. In fact, her book, *Just Love*, helpfully demonstrates the fluctuations that have taken place in the church's understanding and teaching on a number of the moral issues in question.[13] Second, these statements imply that "magisterium" equates to those same central ecclesiastical authorities. It does not. The teaching function of the church has, for a large part of the church's history, *involved* their participation, but that is only part of the story, albeit a very important part. The teaching function of the church, that is, what has since been termed magisterium, has involved those who have devoted themselves to the formal study of the faith since the earliest times of the church; theologians were, in fact, originally called "teachers" in terms of their ecclesial ministry, a ministry that ranked among the very highest in the early church, before being subordinated, along with all ministries, to that of the *episcopus,* later in the second century.

Farley's book explores a range of moral issues, dilemmas, and challenges. Her approach is a comparative one that is attentive to changing contexts, scientific, intellectual, and cultural situations. She attempts to explore how such issues and dilemmas are discerned from the perspective of different philosophical, social, psychological, and human scientific perspectives, as well as from different religious and sociocultural perspectives and contexts. In parts, she understandably privileges the Catholic Christian approach of moral theology in terms of the amount of attention given to this tradition (which is, itself, a collection of many traditions), because that is her own "home" context as a Roman Catholic woman religious and moral theologian. Her intention is not to try and resolve all the difficult questions and dilemmas surrounding human sexuality and relationships in our times; rather, it is "to propose a framework for thinking about these questions."[14] In doing so, she remains more true to the Catholic theological tradition, including that of the medieval disputation, than the more absolutist style of issuing definitive pronouncements and conclusions on moral issues that has increasingly come into vogue in recent times. The very opening of Farley's study reminds us that "[t]here is nothing new about questioning the meaning of human sexuality or the criteria for its incorporation into a moral view of human life." Nonetheless, she equally states the obvious fact that the context and resources for such questioning is very different today to what it was at different stages of the human story in the past.[15]

Three further important points are relevant here. The first is that it is significant that the Notification cites frequently from the *Catechism* in order to illustrate
presumed official Catholic stances on the moral issues in question. The authoritative status of the *Catechism* in and of itself is not that of the "final word" on all
teachings—far from it. It is, in effect, a compendium of other teachings, interpretations, and opinions of various authoritative degrees. If anything, the wide
doctrinal reach of the content of the *Catechism* demonstrates the fruitfulness of
theological enquiry down through the centuries and the collaborative nature of
magisterium, as involving multiple groups of persons in the church and not one
set of officeholders alone.

According to Joseph Ratzinger at the time of its release, the authority of
any given statement made in the *Catechism* is entirely dependent on that of the
teaching sources and documents it refers to—nothing more and nothing less.[16] So,
when the Notification draws together differing statements from the *Catechism*, it
is mixing and matching teachings of varying degrees of authoritative status that
demand varying degrees of assent or other responses from Catholics. Essentially,
these statements pertain to the heart of the faith in qualitatively different ways.
This blurring of the distinctions between the differing gradations of teaching
authority is one of the most lamentable developments in relation to the official
exercise of magisterium in recent decades.

Second, the *Catechism* itself illustrates how Catholic understandings of and
teachings concerning particular moral issues go through significant change and
development. The nature and form of the 1993 *Catechism*, in and of itself, was
something of a novel way for the Roman Catholic Church to bring together its
teachings. But the text and interpretations of certain teachings, including those
on moral issues, continued even after the text was initially published. Refinements
were made, changes inserted.

Third, and related to both of the foregoing considerations, the Notification
proceeds as if there is universal agreement in the church concerning how and when
the church should teach in relation to matter of moral issues and the authoritative
status of its various teachings when it chooses to do so. A particularly contested area
in recent times is whether or not the church can and should teach "definitively"[17]
on specific moral issues (as opposed to broader moral principles and existential
aspirations and orientations such as choosing good over evil). Many experts in the
fields of moral theology, canon law, and ecclesiology believe it cannot, due to the
imponderables and changing circumstances and social and intellectual developments involved in ethics, and therefore it should not.[18] In particular, debates in
recent decades have especially centered upon the understanding of "natural law"
and how church teaching pertains to such.[19] I consider the significance of such
developments in a little more detail below.

A number of the concerns considered here relate to the fact that the Notification appears to be guilty of an increasing tendency in a number of "official" church
documents and pronouncements for proof-texting official documents, sometimes

indiscriminately, as a means of trying to close debate. Assertion, rather than persuasion through reasoned argument, seems to be the method adopted. But in relation to moral dilemmas, the church's own rich theological tradition demonstrates that this cannot be the most fruitful way to proceed. Even where it contains more reflective and loving passages from church teaching, the Notification neuters their effectiveness through the tone and style of the document as a whole.

Whatever the case, one could also argue that the tone, character, and overall impression communicated by the Notification risks weakening the necessary nuanced reasoning that ethical discernment demands. If this proves to be the case, such might constitute not only rhetorical manipulation, but also possibly run the danger of further misrepresenting the teachings of the church, and so do the church an actual disservice. The overall tone of the Notification suggests a harsh, stern, and absolutist approach to moral issues and dilemmas, where the church's teaching and traditions, going back to scripture itself, suggest something very different is characteristic of the Christian approach to ethics. Compassion is "constant" in the entire story of the church and its teachings, and this compassion is found throughout scripture itself. One might call it, in terms of its many human manifestations (which, in themselves mirror the compassion of the divine love), "just love." Stern absolutism is not "constant" in the story of the church's teachings on moral dilemmas and discernment—rather it is an interloper that rears its ugly head at various junctures of the Christian story, most often when the church's leadership has somewhat lost its way for a continued period of time and perceives the need to fight a perceived battle against the world around the church.

When one explores the Notification's treatment of particular moral issues in Farley's work, a range of further problems emerge. For example, aside from the fact that Farley's book mentions masturbation only briefly (a page and a half in her penultimate chapter that outlines a framework for a just sexual ethic, with no mention in her concluding chapter), it is of concern that the Notification criticizes her in relation to the very little she does say. Although the criticism of Farley for allegedly not following the church's teaching on masturbation mentions the more humane qualification from § 2352 of the *Catechism*, that "To form an equitable judgment about the subject's moral responsibility and to guide pastoral action, one must take into account the affective immaturity, force of acquired habit, conditions of anxiety, or other psychological or social factors that lessen or even extenuate moral culpability," the tone of and the inferences drawn by the Notification suggests that the perspective behind the document risks ignoring important aspects of the Catholic tradition and even, possibly, the official teaching of the church in the *Catechism* itself.

In fact, that humane qualification was a later insertion into the *Catechism*, one of those moments of compassionate moral theology winning the day over stern and intransigent absolutism in certain quarters of the church that have proved less common in recent times. But it is also an acknowledgment that the medical and psychological sciences have helped deepen an understanding of this aspect of human sexuality. Farley's more nuanced approach acknowledges this. In fact, many ethicists would conclude that her judgment is not significantly different to that of the *Catechism*'s qualification of its own more stern judgment, when she states, "Masturbation is more likely to be considered morally neutral, which could mean that it is either good or bad, depending on the circumstances and the individual."[20]

When the Notification turns to the moral issues pertaining to homosexuality, it fares little better. It cites the condemnatory section of the *Catechism*, alongside other CDF documents—and even prefaces its comments with a section of the compassionate and pastoral part, which again mirrors gospel values and church tradition across the centuries much more consistently and transparently.[21] But the Notification entrenches the very distinction "between persons with homosexual tendencies and homosexual acts" that leads to confusion about recognizing and upholding the "respect, compassion and sensitivity" that the *Catechism* states Catholics are obliged to afford such persons. Farley's own explorations were an attempt to try to address some of the most pressing and contentious moral concerns in societies today. She argues that the church cannot ignore these because they impact the lives of individual Christians and entire church communities, and include issues of continued tolerance of widespread discrimination in many societies today: "they are questions about real persons—questions about identity, place in community, relationship, and callings."[22] One could argue, then, that Farley's approach tries to look at the reality and considers how the church's teaching concerning the duty to afford "respect, compassion and sensitivity" to homosexual persons should look in practice. Again, her book is seeking to do something very different from the assertion of absolutist moral precepts that appear to sit ill at ease alongside other church teachings.

On the indissolubility of marriage, the Notification again headlines the stern absolutism but negates to mention the (albeit very limited) compassionate understanding of the *Catechism*'s §§ 1648 and 1649. The same applies to the Notification's treatment of divorce and remarriage—it neglects to mention § 1651 of the *Catechism*,

> Toward Christians who live in this situation, and who often keep the faith and desire to bring up their children in a Christian manner, priests and the whole community must manifest an attentive solicitude, so that they do not consider themselves separated from the Church, in whose life they can and must participate as baptized persons.

Rather, the Notification again states only absolutist moral reasoning that, in itself, flies in the face of the broader Catholic moral tradition of discerning the right choice along the continuum of a moral good and evil, which makes clear that the starting fundamental principles become all the more difficult to apply the closer one gets to real-life dilemmas and situations. This, if anything, is a "constant" in the Catholic moral tradition. Instead, the Notification chooses to highlight only the most insensitive aspects of an ecclesially exclusionary perspective that so many pastors, bishops, and theologians have contradicted through their own ministry and wisdom, following their conscience as the faithful involved in such situations are called and counseled to do by the church's teaching also. What impression is given of the church and its teaching by omitting the compassionate and pastoral qualifications of even some of its most stern recent doctrinal formulations?

Because the Notification's main text brings together different church documents on these issues, it creates the impression that the church's teaching on such dilemmas *has* been seamless, whereas the footnotes of this document and, especially, the *Catechism* itself actually reference different places of origin. But the manner in which the Notification presents these teachings does not really offer most Catholics an opportunity to appreciate that, as with so much church teaching, these statements come from different places and would have been formed under different moral theological methods, approaches, and perspectives. Therefore the nuanced and ongoing nature of moral discernment is again not communicated.

The Notification concludes by stating its regret that Farley "affirms positions that are in direct contradiction with Catholic teaching in the field of sexual morality." Fundamental questions that emerge are whether Professor Farley is guilty as charged; whether her accusers are qualified or even have the right to determine such; and whether due process and justice have, respectively, been fully observed and served in this investigation. It continues: "The Congregation warns the faithful that her book *Just Love: A Framework for Christian Sexual Ethics* is not in conformity with the teaching of the Church." Farley herself acknowledges that her book explores approaches, viewpoints, and traditions other than *recent* church teaching on some of the issues in question. So, if the book makes clear that she explores alternative perspectives to those set down in certain official church perspectives of recent times, the Notification becomes somewhat redundant. Any Catholic reading the book will learn such from the book itself. The book was never intended to be a presentation of official Catholic teaching—it appears the Notification is another example of a theologian being condemned, not for what they have actually said or done, but for what they have not said, done, or sufficiently emphasized.

The moral matters involved are much more complex than such a brief, unnuanced, and unqualified statement as the Notification can, literally, do justice to. One of the most important question that requires attention here concerns the definite article thrown around with seeming abandon in such documents in these troubled ecclesial times. "The" magisterium? But this is an increasingly common category mistake of the modern era. "The" teaching of the church? "The" natural law? (Another category mistake.) "*Constant*" teaching of the church? Anyone with the most basic understanding of church history, of doctrinal development and change, as well as of the nature and responsibilities of theology, would lament such misleading and unqualified statements and lament the ecclesiological perspective that gives rise to such. Perhaps one *could* speak, with accuracy and in a carefully qualified manner, of "the" teaching of the church *as understood* in document *x*, *y*, or *z*, or by pope or bishops *a* or *b* and *c*, in accordance with the moral theological school of thought of *d* or *e*, prevalent in official church circles in recent times. But to state what the Notification states in so blunt and sweeping a manner would, once again, appear to risk contradicting other aspects of the moral tradition of the church.

With regard to this "category mistake," the Notification exhibits a further misunderstanding of magisterium. Not only does it confuse magisterium—the act of teaching with authority—with a group of actors who, among others, are charged with carrying out such an action, but it also confuses the main product of such activity with the actual thing that the activity and its product is designed to serve and explicate, namely, the Catholic faith. As John McKenzie stated in the 1960s, "There must be a clear distinction between faith and doctrine. Faith is the response to revelation; doctrine, the product of theology, is an understanding and an application of the faith . . . theology and doctrine . . . are the means by which the Church evolves with the world and with history. Faith never becomes antiquated; doctrine very easily does."[23]

The Notification's understanding of the nature and reach of magisterium, as well as its implied understanding of the role of the Catholic theologian as being merely to explicate and justify the official teachings of the church at any given time, do not sit well with the reality of the church's history and its tradition.

As Anne Patrick has reminded us, "Moral theology, that branch of theology concerned with the practical implications of Christian faiths for ideals, values, and behaviour, was identified by the Second Vatican Council as in particular need of renewal."[24] Despite the many contributions toward renewing this theological discipline, many of which have borne much fruit, it is Patrick's contention that "this renewal of moral theology still stands in need of fulfilment."[25] For Patrick, the church requires "no less than a revolution of Catholic consciousness. What is required is a profound conversion, a shift of attention, a turning from certain questions and preoccupations to new topics and new ways of regarding old ones."[26] Theologians such as Farley took up the call of Vatican II with great energy and tireless commitment to the church and human communities alike. Does the Notification risk setting back the cause of the renewal of moral theology further still?

Method and Moral Theology

The Notification on Farley's book and the narrow and, it would seem, confused or at least incomplete and ahistorical understanding of magisterium (and, therefore, potentially also of the church) that it displays, point toward a significant division in the approach to human individual and collective existence, and so to moral theology, which has grown ever wider since even before the time of the Second Vatican Council. Essentially, for a long period of time in so many parts of the church, there has been a shift away from absolutist and legalistic moral thinking that served the earlier manualist tradition of the nineteenth century and first half of the twentieth century, which grew out of an approach to moral

theology aimed at serving the training of confessors. The trajectory is toward a
more person-oriented and community-enhancing approach, aimed at retrieving a
great deal from earlier periods of Catholic moral theologizing.[27] At the same time,
however, a new approach to natural law theory has begun to gain momentum
in certain universities and subsequently in parts of the church, including at the
official level.

These different approaches, and the vociferous opposition of proponents of
the latter developments to the work of those who explore the former new directions in moral theology, are at the heart of many divisions in relation to morality
that beset the church today. They are captured well by Anne Patrick's study. Here,
she sums up the previously predominating approach in many Catholic circles and
especially at the official level where the focus on the confessional brought about a
juridical emphasis, highlighting rules,

> with less attention to education in discernment of situations and in
> weighing conflicts of values and principles. As a result, many Catholics
> grew up confident that there was a simple method to assure correct moral
> discernment: find what "the Church" teaches about a moral question and
> follow it. The only decision seemed to be whether or not to keep the rules;
> the goal was to have no transgression to confess."[28]

Although this emphasis on the intermediaries who would offer "expert" opinions
in the form of judgments continued to affect many Catholics and the post–Vatican
II church in general, Patrick also points out the evident and liberating fact that
Catholics are "increasingly . . . recognizing that it is a mistake to think that others
have certain knowledge of our moral obligations and it is immature to abdicate
total responsibility for our lives to external authorities."[29] The corollary to such
"negative insights" are the positive ones that "include instruction that will render
moral agents both competent and confident in their skills or moral reasoning,
guidance in the cultivation of their powers of imagination and creativity, and,
above all, encouragement in the spiritual discipline of attending preferentially to
the suffering and oppressed."[30]

These differences of approach to moral dilemmas also lie at the heart of the
differences between the Notification on Farley's book and the approach to human
relationships and sexuality exemplified by that very book. As James Keenan notes,
drawing his own extensive survey of twentieth-century Catholic moral theology
to a close, Farley's *Just Love*

> is emblematic of the development of theological ethics over the last
> century and highlights well its accomplishments. First, a work by a
> woman theologian, it provides a comprehensive theological anthropology
> that resonates with people's experiences both across the globe as well as
> throughout history. Second, that anthropological vision is relational and

embodied, and, while hope-filled, it is also very realistic, appreciating the imitations, vulnerabilities, and frailties of humanity. Third, while sensitive to local claims, Farley is interested in forgoing consensus on minimal but universal standards of sexual conduct. In both the regard for the local and the global, her work is very Catholic. Fourth, Farley aims for an effective work that actually affects the way people live. . . . Fifth, as a Catholic feminist, she insists that sexuality is not a private issue but rather a public one. Sixth, while the work emerges from the best of Catholic theological ethics, it is not restrictively Catholic. Rather, Farley engages other religious traditions as well, believing the development of universal ethical standards depends in part on the way faith communities envision the human. Finally, she upholds the conscience of the person, and rather than imitating the manuals by presenting a list of prohibitive norms aimed to compel the reader, Farley offers guidelines to bring the reader to greater conscientiousness, maturity and responsibility.[31]

It thus should seem clear to any fair-minded observer that Farley is not, as the Notification alleges, somehow playing down church teaching and tradition and relegating such to the status of one opinion among all others. Rather she is following the vibrant approaches that emerge out of that tradition and that have been epitomised in church teachings, not least of all many of those emerging from the Second Vatican Council, in order to explore human relationships and sexuality in a more gospel-oriented and compassionate fashion, in a manner that is attentive to changing understandings of human nature and changing social and cultural contexts. If the Notification epitomizes one approach, then Farley's epitomizes other influential forms of a more positive and life-giving approach whereby human beings are encouraged to take greater responsibility for their own lives, actions, and development, rather than abdicating moral responsibility by handing over their decisions of conscience and discernment blindly to persons in positions of ecclesial influence and authority who may lack the knowledge, training, and experiences, let alone the understanding of the context and personal circumstances of the person who requires moral insight.

It would appear that, in many ways, the moral theological method reflected in the Notification is one that is moving the church and its teaching backward instead of forward in the direction envisioned for the church at Vatican II. As McKenzie observed in the mid 1960s,

There are at least some extreme limits of the teaching office of the Church which seem obvious. The teaching office is not empowered to control either the world of learning or the world of morality. The teaching office is not commissioned to tell people what to do, but to make it possible for people to decide what to do. That people will err must be expected, and, when they do err, the temptation to exercise control is very attractive. The damage which error works must be weighed against the damage which controls works; and this measurement has not been made often enough.[32]

The ecclesial winds of change blowing through the church in the conciliar period were clearly being applied to the understanding and exercise of magisterium itself. Among the key insights that would increasingly emerge was that the exercise of magisterium pertaining to morality had to be markedly different from its form and implications concerning other doctrines of the faith. Writing just a year after McKenzie, the Dominican Herbert McCabe was already highlighting the fault lines of an absolutist approach to natural law, but it seems many influential persons in the church, then, as later, were reluctant to listen:

> The magisterium of the Church should not be quick as formerly to see in individual rules of behaviour which either prevail in society or are laid down by itself, immutable principles of natural law valid for all times and places. It should be readier to see more of these as good guides for the time being, perhaps to be modified later. Indeed the magisterium would largely spare itself the trouble of trying to distinguish between rules which are immutable as they stand and those which are not, if in moral matters it tried to be more of a pastoral guide to men [McCabe, no doubt would also have meant women], pointing out to them, under the inspiration of the love of God in Christ, the best means of living that it now knows, instead of a legal authority laying down universal laws and sanctions for them.[33]

The Notification issued on Farley's book seems to have been composed either in ignorance or in rigid refutation of the debates that have been preoccupying an increasing number of Catholic moral theologians across the past sixty or more years. To take another example, Springer, again writing in 1967, also surveyed the changing direction in Catholic moral theology prevalent at the time, particularly with regard to a reexamination of moral epistemology which took on a threefold emphasis: "First, it suggests a broader base for the data of moral reflection. Second, it calls for a revaluation of the teaching of the magisterium. Lastly, a wider role for the empirical sciences is postulated in moral theology."[34] This sounds very much like a description of the approach subsequently taken by eminent moral theologians such as Farley.

The contribution of feminist and other women theologians to transforming the church in the light of the debates that emerged from the Second Vatican Council has been greatly significant. They have been influenced by those ecclesial winds of empowering change from Vatican II; indeed, they have often led the efforts to implement the spirit and letter of the Second Vatican Council's teaching across a wide expanse of ecclesial life, including, in a preeminent fashion, the theological sciences in the field of moral theology. Here, Margaret Farley's own contributions have been especially significant. Farley's contributions to moral theology are far from being limited to the realm of human relationships and sexuality. There is a great irony in this. For Farley has also offered an inspirational account of the heart of the church's approach to moral quandaries and how it has, at its best, taken a tentative approach to offering guidance rather than laying down fixed and immutable "laws" that pay no heed to context or circumstance. She stands firmly in that tradition, as we see illustrated by the reflections from the 1960s above.

Farley has offered inspiring thoughts concerning that "grace of self doubt," which vividly captures the nature of the struggles involved in moral discernment. She wrote of a grace that "allows for epistemic humility, the basic condition for communal as well as individual moral discernment. . . . It is a grace that is accessible to those who struggle for understanding, those who have come to see things differently from what was once seen, those who have experienced the complexity of translating convictions into action."[35] This grace does not question all our fundamental, shared moral convictions, but rather recognizes the "contingencies of moral knowledge when we stretch towards the particular and the concrete." This grace allows us to listen to others and their experiences, to acknowledge differing viewpoints and experiences to our own. "It assumes a shared search for moral insight."[36] None of this entails the slightest diminishment of the church's commitment to its most central moral values and to tackling the most pressing moral challenges.

Farley's intended multiple puns on the phrase "just love" have, then, a further application: it has a resonance with the call for the church to better harmonize its ethics and ecclesiology. Farley, like many exponents of feminist moral theology, as in feminist theology more widely, has offered much inspiration and helped to retrieve and develop old and new resources alike for more dialogical, participatory, and ecumenical forms of ecclesial discernmen,t and therefore of church teaching also. Feminist theologians in general, and moral theologians in particular, have literally contributed to the pioneering of new, liberating, and empowering ways and means of teaching with authority, that is, magisterium. Often they have done so by example. Such is certainly the case in the life and work of Margaret Farley.

They have helped the church appreciate anew that, when it comes to magisterium, the *what* and not the *who* is the important question. As in the ancient church, the *regula fidei*, the faith itself, its building up and passing on are the most important things to focus on—not who is deemed to be "in charge" of such. So many women theologians, activists, and religious have demonstrated such by example over the Christian centuries. Too often their contributions are overlooked, forgotten, or treated in-depth mostly in minority subdisciplinary studies.

So the contributions of the many women theologians, including Farley, involved in taking forward the challenging ecclesial task of living out the vision of Vatican II and helping to facilitate its reception by the *sensus fidelium*, can, and must be, taken as contributions to the church's ability to teach with authority— to its magisterium. Their contributions should be acknowledged and listened to. When, on November 20, 1964, Pope Paul VI held an audience with the council auditors (along with parish priests invited for the third session), it seems clear he recognized and acknowledged the role that women auditors were performing on the church's behalf during the council. Spotting the Australian, Rosemary Goldie, he smiled at her and said "Ah, *nostra collaboratrice*"—"our co-worker."[37] Margaret Farley, like so many feminist moral theologians, is a valued collaborator in the church's magisterium. Such as these are called to exercise magisterium, and the church is so much the better for their ministry in so doing. They have taught the church much and will continue to do so. Who today in the church is the *Ecclesia Discens*, the learning church most in need of their insight? The struggles and disputes surrounding magisterium suggest that among those most in need of such learning are members of *other* groups who exercise magisterium, especially at the official levels of ecclesiastical authority.

Notes

1. "Feminist Ethics," in *A New Dictionary of Christian Ethics,* ed. John Macquarrie and James Childress (London: SCM Press, 1986), 229. Published as the *Westminster Dictionary of Christian Ethics* in the United States (Philadelphia: Westminster, 1986).

2. Ibid., 230.

3. Ibid.

4. Ibid., 231.

5. Ibid.

6. With regard to overviews of feminist theological ethics in general, see, for example, Lisa Sowle Cahill, "Feminist Ethics," *Theological Studies* 51 (1990): 49–62; Lisa Sowle Cahill, *Sex, Gender and Christian Ethics* (Cambridge: Cambridge University Press, 1986); Lois K. Daly, ed. *Feminist Theological Ethics: A Reader* (Louisville, KY: Westminster John Knox Press, 1994).

7. Congregation for the Doctrine of the Faith, "Notification on the Book, *Just Love. A Framework For Christian Sexual Ethics* by Sr. Margaret A. Farley, R.S.M." (March 30 (released June 4, 2012), http://www.doctrinafidei.va/documents/rc_con_cfaith_doc_20120330_nota-farley_en.html, No. 1.

8. Sowle Cahill, "Feminist Ethics," 51.

9. Congregation for the Doctrine of the Faith, "Notification on the Book, *Just Love,*" § 1.

10. Jacques M. Gres-Gayer, "The Magisterium of the Faculty of Theology of Paris in the Seventeenth Century," *Theological Studies* 53 (1992): 425.

11. Congregation for the Doctrine of the Faith, "Notification on the Book, *Just Love,*" § 1.

12. Ibid.

13. Margaret Farley, *Just Love: A Framework for Christian Sexual Ethics* (New York: Continuum 2006), 37–50.

14. Ibid., 245.

15. Ibid., 1.

16. Joseph Ratzinger, "The Catechism of the Catholic Church and the Optimism of the Redeemed," *Communion,* 20, no. 3 (1993): 479, cited in Francis A. Sullivan, *Creative Fidelity—Weighing and Interpreting Documents of the Church* (New York: Paulist Press, 1996), 12.

17. Even the equivocal use of this word in recent official statements causes further confusion.

18. See the discussion in, for example, John P. Boyle, "The Natural Law and the Magisterium," in *Church Teaching Authority: Historical and Theological Studies*, ed. John P. Boyle (Notre Dame: University of Notre Dame Press, 1995), 43–62.

19. An incisive study of how more recent versions of natural law theory have impacted Catholic ethics in relation to human sexuality is offered by Todd A. Salzman and Michael G. Lawler, *The Sexual Person: Toward a Renewed Catholic Anthropology* (Washington DC: Georgetown University Press, 2008).

20. Farley, *Just Love*, 236.

21. So, for example, in the *Catechism* itself we read, "The number of men and women who have deep-seated homosexual tendencies is not negligible. This inclination, which is objectively disordered, constitutes for most of them a trial. They must be accepted with respect, compassion, and sensitivity. Every sign of unjust discrimination in their regard should be avoided. These persons are called to fulfill God's will in their lives and, if they are Christians, to unite to the sacrifice of the Lord's Cross the difficulties they may encounter from their condition," Ratzinger, "The Catechism of the Catholic Church and the Optimism of the Redeemed," § 2358. The Notification in section 2 cites the third sentence above.

22. Cf. Farley, *Just Love*, 271–95. The Notification cites Farley, *Just Love*, 295, on homosexual persons and acts, and on homosexual unions, it cites ibid., 293. Farley discusses these moral dilemmas at length between pages 271 and 295.

23. John L. McKenzie, *Authority in the Church* (New York: Sheed & Ward, 1966), 126.

24. Anne Patrick, *Liberating Conscience: Feminist Explorations in Catholic Moral Theology* (London: SCM, 1996), 11. Patrick cites the example of *Optatam Totius*, the Decree on Priestly Formation (1965), § 16.

25. Patrick, *Liberating Conscience*, 12.

26. Ibid., 13.

27. See, for example, Robert H. Springer, S.J., "*Notes on Moral Theology*, July–December 1967," *Theological Studies* 29 (*1968*): 275–300; James F. Keenan, *A History of Catholic Moral Theology in the Twentieth Century: from Confessing Sins to Liberating Consciences* (New York: Continuum, 2010); Lisa Sowle Cahill, "Moral Theology after Vatican II," in *The Crisis of Authority in Catholic Modernity*, ed. Michael J. Lacey and Francis Oakley (Oxford: Oxford University Press, 2011), 194–224; Patrick, *Liberating Conscience*, 19–39; Gerard Mannion, "After the Council: Transformations in the Shape of Moral Theology and the Church to Come," *New Blackfriars* (March 2009): 232–50.

28. Patrick, *Liberating Conscience*, 193.

29. Ibid. Cf. also ibid., 15.

30. Ibid., 193–94.

31. Keenan, *A History of Catholic Moral Theology*, 221.

32. McKenzie, *Authority in the Church*, 135.

33. Herbert McCabe, "New Thinking on Natural Law," *Herder Correspondence* 4 (1967): 347–52, at 352, cited in Robert H. Springer, "*Notes on Moral Theology, July–December 1966*" *Theological Studies* 29 (*1968*): 278. He concludes, "The earlier epistemology demanding 'religious assent' to authentic teaching has been inadequate and in need of development," ibid., 279.

34. Springer, *"Notes on Moral Theology,"* 308.

35. Margaret Farley, "Ethics, Ecclesiology and the Grace of Self-Doubt," in *A Call to Fidelity—On the Moral Theology of Charles E. Curran,* ed. J. Walter, T. O'Connell & T. Shannon (Washington, DC: Georgetown University Press, 2002), 55–76, at 69.

36. Ibid.

37. Rosemary Goldie, "Una donna nella Concilio," *Review of Religious Sciences (Pontifical Regional Seminary,* Pius IX, Maufetta) January 1989: 376, translation by Rosemary Goldie as "A Woman at the Council: Memories of an Auditor," cited in Carmel Elizabeth McEnroy, *Guests in Their Own House: The Women of Vatican II* (New York: Crossroad, 1996, revised edition Wipf & Stock, 2011), 129.

Saint Gertrude of Helfta and the Forgiving of Sins

Teresa Forcades i Vila

By your grace, I acquired the certitude that all those who, wishing to have access to your sacrament, restrain themselves because of the fear of a burdened consciousness, if they seek humbly to be strengthened by me, the smallest of your servants, on account of their humility your unlimited tenderness will judge them worthy of your sacrament, and they will truly receive the fruits of eternal life; and you added, that if your justice did not allow somebody to be justified, you will not allow that one to humble her/himself seeking my counsel.[1]

"They will truly receive the fruits of eternal life." With this sentence, Saint Gertrude of Helfta binds the most sacred and heavenly gifts with her own actions on earth. And she does so explicitly, in no ambiguous terms:

You also certified to me, most unworthy, that all those who with penitent heart and humbled spirit, come to me seeking counsel about their faults, according to the degree my word declares their faults to be more or less serious, thus will You, God of mercy, judge them more or less guilty or innocent; and that, by your grace, they will henceforth obtain your help so that their defect will not impinge on them as dangerously as before.[2]

Introduction

Dom Pierre Doyère, Benedictine monk of the Abbey of Saint-Paul de Wisques, translator and editor of the works of Gertrude in 1968, deemed it necessary to introduce a footnote right after these bold affirmations of Gertrude in order to clarify that the nun had not been granted by God "any kind of sacramental role, but the gifts of enlightenment and persuasion to help a fearful consciousness come to terms with the problems of guilt and forgiveness."[3] Was Dom Pierre right? Did Gertrude, honored as one of the greatest saints of the church, receive the sacramental power of granting the absolution of sins, or did she not? Gertrude herself seems to have believed without a shadow of a doubt that such divine favor had been granted to her:

Thirdly, the abundant liberality of your grace enriched the poverty of my merits with the certainty that whenever I, trusting in the divine piety, promised somebody the forgiveness of a crime, your benign love would consider this promise according to my word, as solid as if you yourself had in truth sworn it with your blessed mouth.[4]

It seemed that Gertrude's sisters and the many pilgrims who sought her advice believed that, indeed, she had been granted that singular favor:

Many people used quite often to ask her advice on certain doubtful points, and in particular whether they should, for one reason or another, refrain from receiving communion. She would advise those who seemed reasonably fit and ready to approach the Lord's sacrament with confidence, as God is gracious and merciful. Sometimes she almost forced them![5]

And, touching the tongue of the saint, [the Lord] said: "Hereby I put my words in your mouth and I confirm with my truth all the words that you, inspired by my Spirit, will utter to anyone from me; and all that you promise on earth on account of my goodness, will be granted in heaven."[6]

It is important to note that the forgiving of the sins was not a practice reserved to ordained priests in the medieval ages:

With the appearance of monasticism, the custom was established to confess the bad thoughts and actions to the spiritual father, even though most of the time he was a lay person. The same custom was established in women monasteries, where very often it was the abbess who heard the confession of the nuns.[7]

The task of determining and administering penance was, according to the sources, to be counted among the tasks of an abbess. As already mentioned, the degree of "sacramentality" implied thereby has not yet been determined. However, it seems appropriate at the very least to relativize a strict refusal of the sacramental character of this penance.[8]

There is no dearth of controversy surrounding the life and times of Gertrude of Helfta. This essay examines the sources in regard to her claim to a special commission of forgiving sins and its implications for understanding the relationship between human beings and God, the church of her times, and contemporary ecclesial context. While not explicitly understanding this claim as a direct contestation of the historical reservation of this sacramental function to male clerics, her history allows us to draw conclusions that touch on wider questions of sacramental ministry and theological scholarship and the participation or lack thereof of women as valid leaders. I show that Gertrude's unique experience and understanding of who God is and how God invites human beings into a relationship of mutuality and reciprocity open new innovative paths to a gender inclusive sacramental theology.

Historical Context

In 1179, Lateran Council III prohibited the abbesses to forgive the sins of the nuns in their communities. Thirty-five years later, in 1215, the Lateran IV Council forced all nuns (abbesses included) to confess their sins once a year to a priest. Seventy years after this issue was clarified in church law, Gertrude of Helfta (1256–1301/02), a saint of the church and patroness of present-day female Benedictine novitiates around the world, received from God the mission of forgiving the sins not only of other nuns in her community but to all those, women and men (priests included), who sought her as their spiritual guide. There is nothing in the writings of Gertrude or her sisters that makes us think that they were engaging in a conscious challenge against the rules of the church when they described and practiced the powers that God granted to them. It is true that their community had been founded in 1229, more than a century after church law ruled out the possibility for anyone other than an ordained priest to take on the sacramental role of forgiving sins, but it is also true that in the medieval age even more than today, the fact that a decision was taken in a council did not imply its immediate reception. It could take years, or even centuries, until such a disposition was made known to all affected by it. It is also true that the community of Gertrude is a special case with regard to its dependency on male superiors, the reason being that it was founded in 1229 by seven Cistercian nuns but was never officially accepted as a Cistercian monastery because the General Chapter of the order had resolved in the preceding year (1228) not to admit more female monasteries. This is why Gertrude is described indistinctly as being Cistercian or Benedictine.

It was in these particular historical circumstances that the so-called school of women-theologians of Helfta developed its distinctively joyful character and its originality. Together with Gertrude of Helfta, three other nuns whose names have been preserved belonged to this theological circle: the Abbess Gertrude of Hackeborn (1231–91), of whom no writings have survived; her younger sister Mechtild of Hackeborn (1241–98), author of the *Book of the Special Grace*; and the Beguine (or Beghard), Mechtild of Magdeburg (1207/10–1282/94), author, among others, of *Das fliessende Licht der Gottheit* (*The flowing Light of the Divinity*).

The nuns of Helfta wrote in Latin, and Mechtild of Magdeburg, who spent the last years of her life at the monastery where she composed her main work, wrote in the vernacular (German). Their theology had one common characteristic: it described a loving and merciful God, so close to human beings as to inhabit our very heart, and so gentle to us as to bear with endless patience our ungrateful contempt—a God able to be vulnerable in the age of the Crusades, a Christ identified with the poor and needy in the age of the Pantocrator. About Mechtild of

Magdeburg, it is known that she had a male spiritual father in her early years. The nuns of Helfta, on the contrary, seem to have been accustomed to being the source of spiritual counsel for one another. They quote the spiritual teaching of each other with respect and gratitude. Their writings are completely devoid of self-demeaning remarks on the topic of being a woman. This is particularly remarkable in Gertrude, who entered the monastery at the age of five. Despite all her explicitly erotic language, the issue of "being a woman" is never mentioned as such. Gertrude, like her sisters, seemed to assume, as a matter of fact, that her inner experiences of the radical character of human freedom are open equally to all, male or female, who care to pay attention to the depth, the width, and the joy of God's love within us.

In what follows, I will analyze what I consider to be the main insights of the theological anthropology of Gertrude of Helfta: the creaturely dependency on God, the receiving God, and the reciprocity between God and God's creature.[9]

The Creaturely Dependency on God

On Sunday "Be my protector,"[10] during mass, you woke my soul kindling my desire for the noble gifts that you wanted to give me and this you did mostly by means of two words of the response: "I will bless you" and the verse of the ninth response "to you and your descendants I will give this land" (Gen. 26). Touching during the recitation of these verses your blessed chest with your venerable hand, you showed me which one was the land that your endless liberality was promising me.[11]

Jesus' breast is revealed to Gertrude as the true Promised Land, the goal of human life in its pilgrimage on earth, the pole of attraction in difficult moments. Gertrude also experiences Jesus as the good shepherd, the one to whom we can turn in full confidence when all seems lost, the one who nourishes with his tenderness the burdened soul and gives it courage:

You grew in me the spirit of reverence in the image of a green rod so that, staying always with you and never leaving the shelter of your embraces even for a single moment, I might without danger extend my care to all the wind-ings and labyrinths in which human affection so often loses itself.[12]

In another passage, Gertrude identifies her condition of creatural dependency toward God with the joy of a young child who sees herself honored above her more able siblings. With full filial trust, Gertrude acknowledges the gifts she has received and rejoices in them:

I should consider your affection towards me under the similitude of a father of a family, who, being delighted at seeing so many beautiful chil-dren receiving admiration from his neighbors and servants, had, amongst the others, a little one who was not so beautiful as his companions, whom he, nevertheless, often took in his bosom moved by paternal tenderness, and consoled him by gentle words and kind gifts.[13]

Gertrude's theological insights cause no surprise up to this point. What could best express our relationship to God, if not *dependency*, and, consequently, what could be our task with regard to God, if not that of *receiving*? God is the *giver*, we as creatures receive life from God and live it thanks to God's loving support. But there is more. As she deepens her friendship with the God who fascinates her, Gertrude unexpectedly discovers in God a vulnerability, a need, a receptive pole that in no way contradicts God's giving pole but instead, revealing itself as simultaneous, introduces the one experiencing it into the very heart of Trinitarian life. God is not only Father; in her/his relationship with us, God has wanted to be also Son, because God cannot reveal him/herself other than He/She is.

The Receiving God:
Incarnation and Subjectivation

On one occasion, during the Mass, when I was about to take communion, I perceived that you were present, and with admirable condescension, you did use this similitude to instruct me: you appeared as a thirsty man who requested that I should give you something to drink . . . I was troubled thereat.[14]

The final sentence describes Gertrude's astonishment at this most unexpected reversal of roles. One can perceive the echo of the gospel of John, but without the irony that probably accompanied the first words that the Samaritan woman addressed to Jesus: "How is it that you, being a Jew, request a drink of me, who am a woman of Samaria?" (John 4:9). How is it that you, being God and I being human, about to receive Eucharistic nourishment from you, request a drink of me, who am your creature? From Gertrude's heart comes forth the fountain of living water that Jesus promised to the Samaritan woman:

On seeing that, no matter how hard I tried, I could not force even a tear from my eyes [Gertrude is here trying to find something in her that could be offered as a drink], I beheld you presenting me with a golden cup with your own Hand [Jesus insists in being offered a drink and hands an empty cup to her]. When I took it, I experienced a deep tenderness and my heart immediately melted into a torrent of fervent tears.[15]

Despite her not having anything to offer, Gertrude does not refuse the challenge and takes the empty cup from Jesus. Her trust in the face of the limitation and her willingness to be present despite her perplexity turn her inner being into a fountain.

The mystery of incarnation starts bearing its fruits in Gertrude, inviting her to leave behind the kingdom of childish projections in order to explore the unknown territory of God's neediness: "How is it that you, being a Jew, request a drink of me, who am a woman of Samaria?" Jesus' request invites to initiate, together with him, the path of our subjectivation or the path of our personal growth, of our human plenitude, of our christification, of our divinization: Lord, what do you want me to do? "Be perfect like your Father is perfect" (Matt. 5:48). These are Jesus' words according to the gospel of Matthew. Had they not been attributed to him, such words would most certainly have been deemed heretical: how can God's creature dare aspiring to be as "perfect" as God?

In order to grasp adequately Gertrude's discovery of God's receiving pole, it is particularly revealing to compare the inner experience she describes in chapter VIII with the one in chapter XIV. On both occasions, Gertrude is participating in the mass of the fifteenth Sunday in ordinary time. In both instances, the experience takes place after chanting the antiphon of the day: "Be my protector." But while in chapter VIII (quoted above), Gertrude comes to the inner understanding that Jesus' breast is the promised land and reposes in it, in chapter XIV the words of the antiphon "Be my protector" take a most unexpected turn, because what Gertrude comes to understand this time is the following:

> You made me understand by the words of this introit, only Object of my love, that, being wearied by the persecutions and outrages that so many people inflict on you, you looked for my heart, that you might repose therein. Therefore, each time that I entered therein during these three days, you appeared to me as if lying down there like a person exhausted by extreme languor.[16]

The experience of God's receiving pole is possible for Gertrude because of the incarnation, that most distinctive and peculiar of all Christian claims: God took flesh, and existed in time and space not partially, but in all his/her plenitude. This is the reason why the limits that our spatiality and our temporality impose on us can never be obstacles to realizing in all its fullness our potential for love; if concretely embodied, these limits are the condition of possibility of our freedom in the same way the air is the condition of possibility for Kant's dove: "The dove is convinced that without the resistance of the air, it would fly quicker."[17]

The Astonishing Reciprocity between God and God's Creature

> I have many times experienced the sweetness of your kiss; so much so that while I sat meditating, or reading the canonical hours, or saying the office of the dead, you have often, during a single psalm, placed on my lips ten or more times your sweet kiss, which far surpasses the most fragrant

perfumes or the sweetest nectar; and I have often noticed your tender look on me and felt your embraces in my soul. But though all these things were filled with an extreme sweetness, I declare, nevertheless, that nothing touched me so much as this majestic look of which I have spoken. For this, and for all the other favors, whose value you alone know, might you rejoice for ever in that ineffable sweetness surpassing all comprehension, which the divine persons communicate mutually to each other in the bosom of the Divinity![18]

The look Gertrude valued so much was an exchange of light that she experienced while looking at Jesus directly in the eye:

I felt that from your divine eyes came into mine an extremely soft light that I am unable to qualify . . . so that, according to my understanding, all my substance was no other than divine brightness . . . and this communicated to my soul the joy of serene repose.[19]

God and God's creature are present face to face, looking each other in the eye, experiencing the mystery of love of the Trinity itself, the reciprocity with which the divine persons honor each other and rejoice at each other. "That they may be all one, like you Father in me and I in you, thus shall they be in us," prays Jesus right before offering his life in exchange for ours (John 17:21). In this we find the perfection that Gertrude proposes to us: that we realize that God dwells in us, that we repose without reservations in God's breast, and that we do not scandalize ourselves when God requests to be allowed to repose also in ours.

Trust, freedom, joy, depth, intimacy, body, serenity, light, repose, kiss, and sweetness are some of the words that keep reappearing in Gertrude's writings. They express how she experienced God and how she talked about God to the many pilgrims who queued at the door of the monastery to talk to her and to her sisters. The theological circle of Helfta is responsible for having started the tradition of the Sacred Heart of Jesus, understood not as a kitsch depiction of superficial sweetness but as a taking seriously God's invitation to personal intimacy and the challenges associated with it. One of the challenges for Gertrude was to discover, after having been told and having felt herself that the most appropriate chamber for God to dwell in her was "the heart," that it actually was "the brain," and after having desired to enjoy the solitude of the intimacy with God and forget about everything else, to discover that God was expecting her to love and serve all others and most particularly the poor.[20]

These challenges brought Gertrude to leave behind her childish quest for an almighty controlling God in order to discover that God was indeed vulnerable, and was expecting and actually needing from her a unique and original act of love that only she could perform—that only each of us can perform—and that needs to be constantly renewed. This striking combination of God's majesty and God's vulnerability is the theological *novum* introduced by the nuns of Helfta, a *novum* that reflects the gospel at its purest. Gertrude described this double dimension of the unique love of God with the image of the heart and the two rays of light: golden for the divinity, rose for the flesh of the incarnation. In the incarnation, God has undergone what all classical notions of God most abhor, that is, *change*. God has changed: God has acquired a body that, by the resurrection, has been incorporated into God's self for all eternity.

The nuns of Helfta did talk to each other about these inner experiences and did help each other to take seriously the challenges they involved. But each of them was utterly alone when facing them.

Gertrude and the Nuns of Helfta: The Legacy

Upon closer examination, the theological discovery of Gertrude and the nuns of Helfta has had a lasting impact on theological traditions in the church. Quite clearly, they discovered the depths of what modern language calls "subjectivity"; they were true thirteenth-century pioneers of the discovery of subjectivity and individual freedom. They anticipated the "*devotio moderna*" and were transformed by their experience in a way that gave them authority to inspire others in the path to personal fulfillment and joy. More importantly, they are an example of female leadership that escaped patriarchal control and developed in a seemingly natural and daring way. After the extraordinary influence they enjoyed while alive, Gertrude and the circle of theologians of Helfta fell into a surprising oblivion right after their deaths. Their monastery was destroyed in 1346, less than fifty years after Gertrude's burial, and they were forgotten for two centuries. Paulus of Weida published Gertrude's writings for the first time in 1505. In the Hispanic context, they were discovered during the Reformation and were politically misused: Gertrude, characterized as a celibate nun with a life of obedience centered in the liturgy, was cast in opposition to Martin Luther, the heretical advocate of personal freedom. The opposition was favored by the fact that Helfta was located a short distance from Eisleben, the city where Luther was born and where the nuns of Helfta established their new monastery after the old one was devastated.

The reasons for the destruction of such a thriving school of female theology and monastic life as Helfta are unknown, but some historical precedents (the fate of the thriving monastery of Saint Joan de les Abadesses in Catalonia, for instance)[21] lead us to suspect that these free, loving, and highly educated nuns might have been too much of a challenge for their patriarchal social and ecclesiastical surroundings. Gertrude's canonization came very late. She was included in the Roman martyrology in 1677, and in 1738 her cult was extended to all the church. By then, her free spirit had been conveniently forgotten, and it was never mentioned that she preached or that she and her sisters claimed that God granted Gertrude the power to forgive sins in God's name (that part was even erased in some of the renderings of her writings). The depth of Gertrude's experience of the love of God and her astonishing discovery of God's vulnerability and God's quest for reciprocity were also conveniently substituted by a rather hollow spirituality of the Sacred Heart based on emotion and lacking vitality.

Yet, Gertrude's writings have survived and in them, if she has the patience to cross some rhetorical boundaries that threaten to hide the pearl, the contemporary reader can still admire and be touched by Gertrude's familiarity and joy in her dealings with God. A striking example of it is the boldness with which Gertrude requests a contract from Jesus, so that she can be sure that the favors Jesus granted to her are not a product of her imagination:

> Reflecting on my mind one day about your gifts to me, and comparing my hardness to your tenderness that I so superabundantly enjoy, I dared to reproach you that your gifts to me had not been confirmed with a shake of hands as it is customary with contracts, and your loving softness promised to satisfy this objection saying: "Let your reproaches cease, come and receive the confirmation of my commitment." Then, in my littleness, I saw you opening with both hands that arch of divine fidelity and ineffable truth that is your divinized heart, and you asked me, mean as I was having asked for a sign like the Jews did, that I place my right hand in the opening of your heart and, closing it then with my hand included, you said: "Hereby I promise to keep the gifts I gave to you, so that if temporarily, I retire their effects, I oblige myself to repay all later with a benefit three times greater in the omnipotence, wisdom and benignity of the glorious Trinity, within which I live and reign, true God for ever and ever." After these words came from your most sweet tenderness, I took my hand out and there appeared seven circles of gold as if they were seven rings, one for each finger and three in the ring-finger, a faithful witness to the fact that the gifts had been confirmed according to my desire.[22]

Gertrude's writings contain a lively theology of the Trinity, a Christology, a Mariology, and a theological anthropology, but, until recently, she had been studied under the rubric of "spirituality" rather than "theology." Such has been the fate of most (all?) the women theologians in the history of the Christian churches prior to the twentieth century. Given that women were not allowed to study at the university and were not supposed to enjoy a rational capacity comparable to that of men, when they produced a theological writing of worth, it was considered directly "inspired" by God, and the woman was described as a "mystic" and not as a "theologian." This distinction corresponds to the medieval tradition of the two sides of Jesus' breast: the right side or "official side" and the left side or "mystical side." The right side is the one that becomes pierced in the gospel of John, the one that brings forth the church, understood as the Eucharistic community of the redeemed (blood and water flow from the right side of Christ, like the blood and water of the sacrifices offered at the Old Testament altar would flow from an opening on the right side of the temple that communicated the sacred space with the people who were not allowed into it and gathered outside to partake in its holiness through the flowing water). The left side is the "mystical one," the one that allows God's creatures to have access to the holiness and the love of God not directly mediated by the institutional church and not limited by the church's distinctions between holy and unholy, sacred and profane, sacramental and nonsacramental.

Gertrude speaks of the "right side" in chapter V, while describing the light that comes from Jesus and pierces her heart,[23] but her most intimate description of the love of God has it coming from the "left side" (*ex parte sinistri lateris*).[24] Gertrude's mystical experiences reveal to her a new understanding of God's omnipotence, one that has to do not with forcing others to behave as God sees fit, but rather with freely adapting to others for their sake:

> In what should my omnipotence be extolled, if I could not contain myself within myself whatever I am, so that I am only felt or seen as is most suitable for the time, place and persons? For since the creation of heaven and earth I have worked for the redemption of all, more by the wisdom of my benignity than by the power of my majesty. And this benignity of wisdom shines most in my tolerance towards the imperfect, leading them, even by their own free will, into the way of perfection.[25]

In tolerando imperfectos, quousque illos per liberum arbitrium ducam ad viam perfectionis. God's unfailing benignity sustains the freedom (*libero arbitrio*) of God's creatures. This was how Gertrude understood her own existential situation and thus preached, in the name of God, to all those coming to her to obtain reconciliation.

Conclusion

The case of Gertrude of Helfta challenges the claim that the Catholic tradition has been consistent throughout history in excluding women from the sacramental ministries. Quite clearly, it has not. Those arguing for exclusion do so at two different levels: the theological and the historical, both of which can be easily countered using arguments from tradition. At the theological level, the fact that women have always been and are also today considered able to administer the sacrament of baptism in case of imminent danger of death, disprove the claim that there are essential impediments for women to act sacramentally *in persona Christi*. At the level of tradition, the case of Gertrude is not isolated. As the recent work by Gary Macy shows, the notion of ordination changed substantially in meaning and scope between the eleventh and the twelfth centuries.[26] It moved from a community-centered approach (the ordained person as the embodiment of the communion granted by Jesus to those gathering in his name, cf. Matt. 18:20) to a legalistic approach (the ordained person as individually possessing "sacred powers," independently of the community).

According to the new definition, one of the conditions needed to consider an ordination "valid" was that the recipient of it "be male." It is anachronistic to evaluate the ancient sources according to a later definition, and it is wrong to assume that the definitions of ordination and sacrament have not changed substantially in the Catholic tradition. There is an urgent need in Catholic studies to reinterpret the history of sacramentality while taking into account sources hitherto suppressed, misinterpreted, or ignored. In doing so, as the case of Saint Gertrude compellingly shows, we will discover a new traditional image of God and of the human being able to speak to the heart of the postmodern subject, an image that describes God as vulnerable and places freedom and desire at the center of our relationship to Her.

Notes

1. *Quod gratia tua certitudinem accepi, quod omnis qui ad tuum sacramentum accedere desiderans, sed habens timorem conscientiae, trepidans retrahitur, si humilitate ductus a me famularum tuarum minima quaerit confortari, pro hac ipsius humilitate, tua incontinens pietas dignum ipsum judicat tantis sacramentis, quae vere percipient in fructum salutis aeternae; adjungens quod si quem justitia tua non permitteret dignum judicari, nunquam permitteres ad meum consilium humiliari* (Gertrude d'Helfta. *Ouvres Spirituelles II. Le Héraut, libres I–II. Sources Chrétiennes*, 143. Du Cerf: Paris, 1968. Liber II, caput XX, § 1, at 308).

2. *Unde et addidisti me indignissimam certificare, quod, quicumque, corde contrite et spiritu humiliato, aliquem defectum mihi querulando exposuerit, secundum quod per verba mea defectum illum majorem sive minorem audierit, secundum hoc, tu misericors Deus, velles judicare eum culpabiliorem vel innocentiorem; et quod gratia tua mediante post horam illam hoc semper habere deberet relevamen, quod nunquam tam periculose premi posset ab illo defectu, sicut antea fuerat pressus* (Getrude d'Helfta, *Le Héraut*. Liber II, caput XX, § 2, at 310).

3. *Il ne s'agit pas d'un rôle sacramentel, mais de grâces de lumière et de persuasión pour mettre au point dans des consciences timorées les problèmes de la culpabilité et du pardon* (Gertrude d'Helfta, *Le Héraut*, at 310–11, note 1).

4. *Tertio etiam copiosa liberalitas gratiae tuae inopiam meritorum merorum ea certitudine, ditavit, quod cuicumque aliquid beneficium vel alicujus delicti indulgentiam ex confidentia divinae pietatis promiserim, hoc benignus amor tuus secundum verbum meum tam firmum tenere proponeret, quasi hoc tu ore tuo benedicto juraveris in veritate* (Gertrude d'Helfta, *Le Héraut*. Liber II, caput XX, § 3, at 310–12).

5. Gertrud, the Great of Helfta, *The Herald of God's Loving-Kindness, Books One and Two* (Kalamazoo: Cistercian, 1991), at 82. Cf. Gertrude d'Helfta, *Le Héraut*. Liber I, caput XIV, § 2, at 196.

6. Gertrude d'Helfta, *Le Héraut*. Liber I, caput XIV, § 4, at 198.

7. *Mit dem Auftreten des Mönchstums entsteht die Sitte, dem geistlichen Vater, wenn er auch gewöhnlich ein Laie was, ein Bekenntnis aller unrechten Gedanken und Taten abzulegen. Dieselbe Gewohnheit tritt in Frauenklöstern zutage, wo vielfach die* Äbtissinen *eine Beichte der Nonnen vor ihnen verlangten.* Georg Gromer. *Die Laienbeicht im Mittelalter. Ein Beitrag zu ihrer Geschichte* (Verlag der J.J. Lentnerschen Buchhandlung: Múnic, 1909), at vii.

8. *Diese Aufgabe von Bußfeststellung und Bußübergabe kann nach den Quellen auch die* Äbtissin *leisten. Welcher Grad von 'Sakramentalität' dann vorliegt, ist, wie erwähnt,*

noch nicht zu beantworten. Doch scheint es erlaubt, eine strikte Ablehnung der Sakramen-
talität dieser Buße zumindest zu relativieren. Gisela Muschel. *Famula Dei: Zur Liturgie in*
merowingischen Frauenklöstern (Aschendorff: Munster, 1994), at 263.

9. An earlier version of this analysis was published in Spanish in Teresa Forcades i
Vila, *Gertrudis de Helfta y Teresa de Jesús: cuerpo y subjetividad en la experiencia mística.*
(Revista Cistercium, 2012), 258.

10. Sunday XV from the ordinary time.

11. Gertrude d'Helfta, *Le Héraut.* Liber II, caput VIII, § 1, at 263.

12. Ibid., caput XIII, § 1, at 285.

13. Ibid., caput XVIII, § 1, at 301.

14. Ibid. caput XI, § 2, at 277–79.

15. Ibid., caput XI, § 2, at 279.

16. Ibid., caput XIV, § 1, at 287.

17. Kant, I. *The Critique of Pure Reason* (introduction, § 3).

18. Gertrude d'Helfta, *Le Héraut.* Liber II, caput XXI, § 4, at 327.

19. Ibid., caput XXI, § 3, at 325.

20. Ibid., caput XV, at 287–89.

21. Antoni Pladevall, *Els monestirs catalans* (Barcelona: Ediciones Destino, 1970).

22. *Nam cum die quodam ea mente revolverem et ex comparatione pietatis tuae ad impi-*
etatem meam quam tam longe superabundare gaudeo, usque ad illam praesumptionem ducta
fuissem, quod causarer te mihi ea, more pollicitantium, manu ad manum non firmasse, tua
tractabilissima suavitas his objectionibus se benigne satisfacturum promisit, dicens: 'Ne haec
causeris accede et suscipe pactu mei firmamentum'. Et statim parvitas mea conspexit te quasi
utrisque manibus expandere arcam illam divinae fidelitatis atque infallibilis veritatis, scilicet
deificatum Cor tuum, et jubentem me perversam, more judaïco signa quaerentem, dextram
meam imponere, et sic aperturam contrahens manu mea inclusa dixit: 'Ecce dona tibi collata
me tibi illibata servaturum promitto, in tantum quod si ad tempus dispensative ipsorum
effectum subtraxero, obligo me postmodum triplici lucro persoluturum, ex parte Omnipotentiae
Sapientiae et Benignitatis virtuosae Trinitatis, in cujus medio ego vivo et regno, verus Deus, per
aeterna saecula saeculorum'.

Post quae suavissimae pietatis tuae verba, cum manum mean retraherem, apparuerunt
in ea septem circuli aurei in modum septem annulorum, in quolibet digito unus et in annu-
lari tres, in testimonium fidele quod praedicta septem privilegia mihi ad votum meum essent
confirmata (Gertrude d'Helfta, *Le Héraut.* Liber II, caput XX, §§ 14–15, at 318–20).

23. Ibid., caput V, § 2, at 249–51.

24. Ibid., caput IX, § 1, at 269.

25. Ibid., caput XVII, § 1, at 299–301.

26. Gary Macy, *The Hidden History of Women's Ordination: Female Clergy in the*
Medieval West (Oxford: Oxford University Press, 2007).

CINEMATIC VISIONS OF
FEMALE LEADERSHIP:
BETWEEN AUTHORITY AND DOUBT

Stefanie Knauss

Introduction

In this essay, I will approach the question of women's religious leadership, using three films to discuss the interrelation of the sociological, theological, and ethical aspects of the matter. Films are a part of society and culture; their production and reception is embedded in, and shaped by, certain social conventions and ethical principles—in this case regarding the qualities of a female religious leader and how religious authority should be exercised and to which end. While films often reproduce these social conventions in order to be more acceptable to a wider audience, their fictional status also allows them to playfully develop new visions of social relations and ethical norms, and thus to put in question what is otherwise considered an unchangeable fact. Through their narratives of concrete individuals and situations, films are able to "give flesh" to abstract concepts or principles and to induce identification and empathy with characters, becoming a catalyst for reflection and, potentially, for change.[1] In a society that still struggles with the reality of women in leadership positions, be it in the political arena or in economy, and not least in religious contexts, the question of what films make of this is particularly fascinating. How do they represent female religious leaders, which leadership types do they use as models, and what difficulties and challenges faced by female leaders do they discuss? Do the films reflect social facts and attitudes toward women leaders, or do they use the space of their fictional narratives to develop new ideas?

The films I have chosen are all set in a Catholic context but in different times: *Pope Joan* (Sönke Wortmann, Germany/UK/Italy/Spain 2009) is set in ninth-century Germany and Rome and tells the story of the legendary female pope; *The Messenger: The Story of Joan of Arc* (Luc Besson, France 1999) is set in sixteenth-century France; and *Doubt* (John Patrick Shanley, USA 2008) is a story about a nun, the principal of an American Catholic school, in the 1960s. The films refer to similar questions (legitimacy of a woman's leadership, leadership abilities and style, social reactions to a female leader), but they do this in different ways and with different overall effects. After a brief introduction to the sociological, theological, and ethical issues relating to the question of women's leadership, the main part of the essay will be dedicated to the analysis of the films, followed by a discussion of what they achieve and how.

Theoretical Background: The "Nature Trap" of Female Leadership

A good forty years into the second women's movement, the question of women's leadership in the political, economic, and religious sphere is far from settled. The number of women in top-level positions remains low in spite of evidence of their positive impact on a company's performance,[2] and those women who make it to the top are then scrutinized with regard to their leadership style but also trivial matters such as their wardrobe or whether they do their own shopping.[3] This shows how underlying social ideas regarding a leader's (masculine) qualities and expectations of feminine behavior clash when a woman becomes a leader. As Carole Elliott and Valerie Stead underline, there is a fundamental contradiction in how societies deal with the question: On the one hand, successful female leaders become news items, are held up as models, and their "feminine" leadership style is embraced as an exemplary new form of leadership. On the other hand, the fact remains that not very many women ever make it to a leadership position because "leadership remains framed by male norms and values."[4] The authors point out that new, celebrated "post-heroic" models of leadership that emphasize equality, flexibility, community, and collaboration, can even become disadvantageous when practiced by women, because these values are not perceived as successful leadership qualities, being interpreted as selfless helping or even motherliness.[5] Paradoxically, thus, the practice of new and effective styles of participatory leadership can be detrimental to the position of leading women because of tensions between gender role expectations and old and new leadership models. Elliott and Stead therefore state, "In not recognizing the power and gender dynamics inherent in post-heroic models women may be expected to practise leadership in this way, but without it being acknowledged as leadership behaviour that expects a degree of reciprocity and has leadership capital."[6] The attempt to discover "feminine" characteristics of successful leadership, such as cooperation, reciprocity, or a more caring attitude, versus a masculine, more authoritarian, autonomous, and hierarchical leadership style, rooted in women's and men's "nature," cannot be empirically sustained. Thus, while it is important to promote more participatory styles of leadership that are ethically valuable in their emphasis on equality and democracy,[7] to identify such leadership styles with women and their "caring" nature can have a negative effect on both women, men, and the groups they lead, because it reinforces existing gender stereotypes and the power relations based upon them, which precisely counteract the processes of participation and cooperation that these leadership styles attempt to construct.[8]

Rather than trying to discover a feminine style of leadership and to limit women *qua* their nature to it, it might be useful to identify social factors that favor the positive exercise of leadership by women. Elliott and Stead point to the impact that upbringing, environment, focus on their goals, and networks and alliances play in the advancement of women leaders, and thus to the relevance of social relations and a supportive environment rather than just individual capacities of a woman.[9] This view is shared by Catherine Wessinger with regard to religious leadership; she also emphasizes the necessary precondition of social equality in order to be able to establish female leadership in a religious context.[10]

The issue presents a specific set of questions in relation to religious settings. While religious communities in general are often marked by a certain traditionalism that also extends to gender-role stereotypes, this tendency is reinforced by the institutionalization process that established religious communities undergo and in which initial charismatic leadership of women is replaced by male leadership.[11] In the Roman Catholic Church, on which this essay focuses, the issue is even more difficult because of its theology of ordination and priesthood: the priest is seen as a mediator between God and human beings, so that the act of ordination imparts a particular authority to the priest *qua* office that does not depend on his personal leadership abilities. The necessary condition for being ordained a priest is a person's male sex; women cannot be ordained priests or deacons, as Pope John Paul II declared firmly in *Ordinatio sacerdotalis* (1994). Thus, in Catholicism, women are excluded from top-level leadership positions because of their gender. Nevertheless, due to recent institutional, theological, and demographic changes, more and more women do become leaders in the Catholic Church—not as priests, but in other positions such as pastor, or educator, or in the diocesan administration.[12] In all these cases, however, they remain subordinate, at least in some respects, to the authority of male priests or bishops, and finally of a male pope. Elaine Ecklund has shown that reactions to women's leadership depend to a large degree on how church is imagined: as a flock of sheep to be guided by its shepherd (an authoritarian model) or as the people of God (a more democratic model promoted by Vatican II). Consequently, women pastors can be perceived as "second best" because of the priest shortage in the first model, or instead, their leadership is seen as a positive aspect of, and a force in, the democratization of the church in the second model.[13]

In addition to these sociological and theological aspects, the presence of women in leadership positions in religious contexts gives rise to a number of questions concerning the ethics of leadership. What type of leadership should be exercized in a religious community that is founded on the equality of all human beings before God and that aims at providing the conditions for all persons to flourish and to be able to develop fully their potential? What should the relationship between leaders of a parish, or the church, and its members be like? What is the role and function of authority? Is it a matter of carrying out one's "own will despite resistance," as Max Weber defines power and authority,[14] or "the achievement of goals by means of other people," as Guttorm Fløistad says?[15] Aternatively, is leadership "an influence relationship among leaders and collaborators who intend real changes that reflect their mutual purposes," as Joseph Rost sees it,[16] and about

empowering individuals to take over responsibility for the life of their community and furthering their own initiatives, as a woman pastor puts it?[17] Studies of
women leaders in religious communities show that the question of the leader's
gender is tied up closely with the question of how to understand and exercize
authority and leadership, and to which end.[18] While again it might be tempting
to underline the specific "femininity" of female pastors' style of leadership (cooperative, empowering, inclusive, participatory, personal, based on dialogue rather
than the authority of office, etc.), women pastors' leadership style is most likely
not the result of their female nature, but rather of their situation as women in a
patriarchal setting in which a man's word has always carried more weight, and as
nonordained laypersons with limited empowerment (not allowed to preach or celebrate the sacraments).[19] This means that the traditional, authoritarian masculine
model of religious leadership is simply not available to them, not even as a copy.
Female pastors have to develop new models of leadership and find new sources
of authority, since they cannot fall back on their ordination for legitimation or
on the distribution of sacraments as a source of power over their parishioners.[20]
Thus, the presence of female pastors provides the opportunity to question authoritarian and hierarchical structures in a parish, and in the church at large, and to
develop new forms of leadership in the administration of a parish, pastoral care,
and liturgy that can have a transformative effect not only on the female pastor's
own position but also on how parishioners view leadership in their community, on
the understanding of priestly authority, and the role of justice and equality for all
in the church.[21] In the next sections, I will analyze three feature films about female
religious leaders on the background of these sociological, ethical, and theological
aspects of the question. The central question is how each film presents female religious leadership, and to what effect.

How about a Female Pope? Pope Joan

The position of pope is the highest ranking leadership position in the Catholic Church. As women cannot be ordained priests and bishops, they are also not
eligible for the position of pope (Code of Canon Law 331–35). A film about a
female pope can therefore be an interesting thought experiment: *What if* women
were allowed into *the* leadership position in the Catholic Church?

Based on Donna Woolfolk Cross's bestseller *Pope Joan*, the fictionalization of
a medieval legend,[22] the film tells the story of Joan, the daughter of a peasant priest
born in the ninth century; she has to fight discrimination as a woman until she
takes on her brother's identity and, disguised as a man, can develop her abilities as
a theologian and a physician that allow her ascend to a position of influence, first
in a monastery in Germany, then at the papal court. After Pope Sergius's death, she
is elected pope and rules for several years for the good of the church and the people
of Rome, realizing important social and theological reforms, until she becomes
pregnant and dies from a miscarriage during an Easter procession. The story of her

ecclesial career is spliced together with a romance with Count Gerold, who has always supported her and who, as an army leader at her papal court, finally becomes her lover. A frame narrative of a female bishop, who inserts Joan's name in the *Liber pontificalis* from which she had been deleted and who continues to tell sections of Joan's story in voiceover, suggests that there might have been a hidden tradition of female leadership in the church over the centuries.

How is Joan's leadership represented? Right from the beginning, Joan is described as something special, better than her brothers and schoolmates, unusually intelligent and curious about the world, autonomous in her thinking and her critique of conventions, and unusually determined in the pursuit of knowledge. Yet knowledge is not an end in itself for her, as she is intent on using it for the good of others, as a physician who cares for the rich as well as the poor, as an administrator who works to improve living conditions in Rome and to give women access to education, but also as a politician when she is able to avoid bloodshed through her intellectual maneuvers and vast knowledge of hydraulic mechanisms through which she is able to simulate a miracle. Most importantly, the use of her rationality and intellect are, in Joan's view, not a contrast to Christian faith and piety; rather, rationality and faith seem to strengthen and motivate each other in her development: when she finally arrives at the apogee of her career, this is not only an achievement in worldly power for her but also the moment when she is closest to God. The film suggests that spirituality and the inner strength and moral integrity based on it are important and positive factors in Joan's leadership,[23] in contrast to the purely worldly ambitions that drive all others at the papal court.

It is first of all through her superior capacities that Joan is respected in her authority. Yet it also becomes clear throughout her life that this is not enough: she needs the support of men—her first teacher, Count Gerold, Pope Sergius—to arrive at the highest point of power. Curiously, the only women who help her are either helpless or staunch supporters of patriarchal power. That successful leadership depends on networks of support and also on models to emulate[24] also becomes clear from the framing narrative: Joan was a role model for the woman bishop, while herself motivated by the model of St. Catherine, whose image sustained her during her difficult early years.

Joan's style of leadership is characterized by fearless response to opposition, rationality, nonviolence, and tolerance. Strongly determined to realize her ideas, she does not rely on blind obedience or violence to enforce her views, but rather uses a mix of rational argumentation and ironical humor to rebut counterarguments. Thus, in one scene in which she announces the introduction of schools for girls in Rome, she rebuts the traditional argument that intellectual activities make a woman infertile by listing exemplary women who had had children in spite of being educated. While this strategy works well to unveil the prejudice of such arguments, it is shown to be less useful to convince another person to change his or her mind without losing face. Joan's clever argumentation certainly raises a laugh from her supporters (and the film audience), but it also creates some powerful enemies that in the end conspire to have her killed.

Reactions to her leadership are not always positive; while she has some supporters, her apparently drastic reforms also cause rejection. Her leadership style is described as weak and "feminine," unwittingly revealing her real gender. By inserting this comment, rather than a remark on her "masculine" determination, strength, or intellectual capacities, the film implicitly naturalizes her "feminine" leadership style. The film's reduction of Joan to her gender is further reinforced through its continuous references to the struggle between her feminine "nature" and masculine role. Living as a woman is represented as being irreconcilable with autonomy, knowledge, or leadership; it is only as a man that Joan can achieve this. On the other hand, love or family are possible only in exchange for her freedom. Like many women up until today, Joan has to choose between family and career.[25] Thus, the film presents Joan as an exceptional case who made her way up through the hierarchical structure of the church but without criticizing the underlying gender system: in order to ascend to power, a person has to be male, either by nature or by disguise. And yet in the end, nature will always win out. Joan is not brought down by the intrigues of her enemies but by her female nature. Her pregnancy seals her destiny as a woman, and her ambition to continue in her (masculine) office will cause her death. The film leaves it open whether her miscarriage during a procession is a punishment for her pretence at the papal throne or simply the treachery of her female nature.

The film closes on a sour note. An exceptional, able female leader is portrayed whose success is confirmed both by the positive changes she effects and by how the people love her. On the other hand, she can do this only disguised as a man and is not able to escape her nature, and thus the question is raised as to whether women, because of their nature, should simply decline to take on leadership positions.

Furthermore, the positive elements of the film (its criticism of the discrimination of women in the church, the promotion of a rational, tolerant, nonviolent style of leadership, the reconciliation between faith and reason) are compromised by its formal and dramaturgical weaknesses. While apparently criticizing stereotypes, such as women's intellectual inability, the film itself relies strongly on stereotypes in its *mise-en-scène*: the Middle Ages are dirty and unenlightened, with church dignitaries growing fat on the exploitation of the poor;[26] faith is violently intolerant, while philosophy promotes peace and equality; good people are beautiful, while a sinister character is indicated by a pinched face and ears that stick out.[27] The world of the film and its characters are divided into black and white, without any grey areas or nuances in characterization or development. While Joan's courage and suffering make her a character with whom film viewers can empathically identify and thus be drawn into the film and Joan's story, film critic Michael Kohler rightly points out that the voiceover produces a certain emotional distance,[28] reinforced by the rather pale acting (not only facial color) of Johanna Wokalek as pope that limits the audience's emotional involvement in the film and the questions it tries to raise regarding the discrimination of women in Catholicism.

The impact of the film is therefore limited: the thought experiment of a female pope fails, not because the idea is so absurd, but because the film is not able to develop it with the necessary courage and subtlety. In the end, it gives in to the nature trap it tried to challenge: women will not succeed as leaders because of their female nature. And while the framing narrative suggests a considerable tradition of women leadership in the church, one is left to wonder why, if this was the case, these women have not been able to improve the position of women in the church.

For Love of War or Love of God?
The Messenger: The Story of Joan Of Arc

Also a costume film, *The Messenger* tells the well-known story[29] of Joan of Arc, from her peasant childhood through her success as a charismatic leader of the French Army against the English to her death at the stake. Joan's authority is primarily based on her conviction that she has been called by God to save France from the English, a conviction shared by the people of France, if not by its leading elites, who coolly calculate the use of Joan's charisma for their purposes. However, doubts regarding her mission are raised early on, because Joan is established as an obsessive character, excessive in her piety and in how she relates to others. Her motivation to fight against the English may not be altogether disinterested, but instead could be nourished by a personal desire to revenge her sister's rape and murder by an English soldier, which Joan had witnessed and feels guilty for all her life. Her (cinematographically somewhat unimaginative) visions of a male figure, growing with her in age, giving her instructions, of strange winds and voices, enormous bells, and flashes of light, can easily be believed to be the fruit of her own traumatized mind, rather than a message sent by God—nothing else but an excuse to lead her very own—not God's—war against the English.

As a charismatic leader,[30] validated by extraordinary, supernatural powers (she recognizes the Dauphin among his followers without having seen him before and is healed quite miraculously from an arrow wound) and apparently sent by God, Joan holds an authority that is not based on any objective ability of warfare or statesmanship, but only on her own belief in her mission, on the recognition of her charisma by her army, and on its initial confirmation through military success. As film critic Janet Maslin writes, Joan's leadership abilities are "noticeably dubious,"[31] with her commands being intuitive, based on what her voices tell her, rather than a clear view of the situation or the advice of more knowledgeable officers. She is impatient, ruthless, imperious, and negligent toward the needs of her soldiers, political strategies, or financial considerations, and she is driven only by her goal to expel the enemy of God's country. The attempt to blame her gender for not being acknowledged as their leader by the other officers is therefore not quite convincing, since she commands in a way that is inconceivable for an officer and is irresponsible toward her men. Joan's blindness to the real and material consequences of a war raises the deeply ethical question as to the relation between the end of her mission and the means by which to achieve it: when she sees the rows of dead and maimed bodies after a battle (displayed in gory detail by the camera that pans across them after the battle scene), and her own bloody face and hands, she (and the viewers) awakes from the trance of battle to the reality of its bloodshed, becoming horrified by what God has asked her to do. Can this really be God's will? Or has she mistaken her own wish for revenge as a divine commandment? Also problematic is the fact that Joan identifies so much with her mission that her call to follow God in this war becomes a call to follow her: the distinction between her followers' veneration of her and the God who sent her becomes blurred, and it is not altogether clear whether she herself maintains this distinction, or whether her campaign is driven primarily by her own vanity, as her conscience accuses her at the end.

Not surprisingly, her charismatic leadership is successful only in the exceptional situation of a great crisis but fails the test of everyday political business. The Dauphin's mother-in-law, a coolly calculating stateswoman, is depicted as a kind of contrasting character to the impulsive Joan, who does not pursue a long-term strategy in her actions. Rather than contrasting male and female leaders, the film seems to focus on the difference between a charismatic, emotional type of leadership and a more traditional, rational type.[32] Yet while Joan is established as the main female protagonist and thus her leadership style is central, and the Dauphin's mother-in-law and her rational style of authority remains marginal, Joan's obsessive character and her eventual failure add some critical undertones to the type of leadership she represents.

The overall question that the film raises from the beginning is whether Joan's visions are truly visions, or the fruit of her own imagination, and thus whether the authority attributed her by the people is legitimate or simply based on their superstition and despair. In contrast to Joan's followers within the film, who believe in her even after her imprisonment and who collect the ransom to free her, the audience is led to doubt her sanity from early on such as in the sequence when the girl sneaks into a church at night and, in order to feel closer to God, gulps down Eucharistic wine until it drools down her chin while thunder and lightning rage outside. At first, enthusiasm about her success silences doubts regarding the divine origin of her mission, but the final blow comes when, in prison, her personified conscience appears and starts questioning her visions, the sense of her mission and her own role in it, weakening her—and the audience's—trust in her voices and in Joan. The more-than-justified ethical questions concerning the legitimacy of a bloody warfare in the name of God for the sake of worldly power, and Joan's pride in a success and popularity based on pure violence, unfortunately remain marginal in comparison to the question of her personal credibility.[33] The fact that her conscience torments her with these extremely relevant questions is thus less disturbing than the ease with which she gives in to her doubts: where is the strength of character that the girl showed standing alone before the English Army or defending her mission in court? Why would she believe this voice more than the other voices she had heard? With the film suggesting that her conscience might be correct—although some ambiguity remains—this ending is doubly disappointing, not only because her mission is portrayed as simply motivated by revenge and pride, but also because Joan is shown to be so easily manipulated and weak. An inspiring female leader? The film closes on a contradictory note: while, on the one hand, it suggests that Joan was simply a schizophrenic, on the other hand, its reference to her canonization 500 years after her death also points toward her real, continuing importance for many women and men.

Certainty in Uncertainty: *Doubt*

Doubt differs from the previous films discussed here in several ways. While it is also a costume drama, it is set in a time much closer to ours (in 1964), and in contrast to the other two films, it has no ambitions at representing a historical or even legendary character. Based on a play by the director, it is entirely a piece of fiction, and it uses the liberty of narrative development this allows. The story it tells, however, is one that could happen every day—and most likely has happened, in a more or less similar form. Sister Aloysius, principal of a Catholic school, sees a boy during recess shrink back from physical proximity to the school's chaplain, Father Flynn. She communicates her doubts about the priest to the other sisters, and sure enough, a younger colleague, Sister James, comes forward to tell her about the close, personal attention Father Flynn pays to Donald, the only black pupil of the school. Determined not to let him have his way, and aware that none of Father Flynn's (male) superiors will support her in this, Aloysius sets off on an investigation of the matter in which Father Flynn's guilt is very soon assumed as a given. With no further proof, Aloysius confronts him, pretending to have heard similar stories from a nun of his former parish, and forces him to ask for a transfer. Although certain that Flynn is guilty, in the end, Aloysius breaks down and admits to her doubts.

Unlike *The Messenger*, *Doubt* maintains the tension of uncertainty regarding Flynn's guilt or innocence all through the film and beyond. Did he, or did he not, pay undue attention to Donald and to the boy who shrinks back several times from him? Tilted images and symbols, like the cold, strong wind that in several occasions blows into Sister Aloysius' office and around the school, underline the sense of uncertainty, loss of balance, and the impression that both protagonists might be moved by powers beyond their control, as Flynn says in his farewell sermon. But the question here is not Flynn's guilt or innocence, but rather how the female protagonist acts as a principal and leader of her school and community, and how she manages this situation of crisis. Sister Aloysius is a leader from the old school: authoritarian and severe, both in her official role as principal and in her private relationships. When Sr. James remarks that the students live in absolute terror of her, Aloysius sees nothing wrong in this; fear is her primary source of authority and discipline her instrument of power. Yet the subtle acting of Meryl Streep and the film's nuanced representation show that her authoritarian regime is informed by a profound knowledge of human nature, and not least by a compassionate heart that shows rarely, but leads her to negotiate the principles of authority and discipline with the individual needs of her pupils. While her leadership style is focused on the strict obedience of rules, it is not entirely lacking human warmth and understanding. This aspect, however, is hidden so well under Sister Aloysius's rigid, authoritarian behavior that a rare, unexpected flash of humor simply confuses her fellow sisters or students.[34]

Flynn is introduced as a contrasting character and, as such, draws considerable sympathy: jovial, open-minded, with a sense of humor and a love for the good life (the contrast between a lively, rich dinner at the rectory and the simple, sober meal at the sisters' community speaks volumes). While Aloysius relies on an impersonal, rule-based style of authority, Flynn tries to establish a close personal relationship with his pupils and parishioners in his general attempt to make the parish and the school a more welcoming place with a less hierarchical structure and a more equal leadership style. Interestingly, however, as the crisis unfolds, Flynn gives up his attempts at democratic leadership and resorts to the safety of traditional hierarchies, demanding from Aloysius that she follow the ecclesial chain of (male) command rather than taking matters in her own hands.

In the situation of crisis the film centers on, Aloysius reacts without hesitation and without doubt. As a woman in an ecclesial, patriarchal environment, she is on her own, as she explains to James, knowing apparently from experience that in these issues, men will always protect each other. Taking the necessary steps of talking to Flynn and to the boy's mother (although not to the boy himself) without results, she resorts to a lie, admitting to James that the prevention of wrongdoing might require stepping away from God's commandments. Although Aloysius pursues Flynn relentlessly, she does not get pleasure out of it; for her, it is a distasteful, but necessary task to punish the wrong that had been done, rather than trying to cover it up or turn her head the other way, as Donald's mother does—not because she is not worried about her son, but because she prioritizes other values (his successful graduation and relations with his father). Aloysius's ethical orientation on objective categories of right and wrong is thus put into question by Donald's mother, who introduces other criteria, such as the future of her son, his vulnerable situation as the only black boy in school, and his homosexual interests. Her worries induce Aloysius to negotiate her strict, abstract reasoning with Donald's individual needs, putting the boy's well-being first in her resolution of the situation without letting Flynn, of whose guilt she is absolutely convinced, go unpunished. However, in the end, Aloysius's efforts at punishing the wrongdoers and protecting the victims are futile. Her warnings go unheard by the monsignor, and Flynn is transferred to yet another parish and another school.

Sister Aloysius is shown to be a character of strong convictions, acting resolutely and with certainty, although facing nothing but uncertainty; and yet, at the very end, when everything seems resolved, and Father Flynn's resignation apparently proves what she had only suspected, the strong, unemotional woman breaks down and cries on Sister James' shoulder about the doubts she continues to have of having done wrong. It is this moment of weakness, admitting to her own doubts and wrongdoings, that truly establishes Sister Aloysius as a strong, mature character and able leader in the end. The film does not approve or disapprove of her handling of the situation, but it sympathizes with its protagonist, a woman who, within the limits that her gender and her position within ecclesial hierarchies impose and in spite of persistent doubts, resolves a crisis in a way that is consistent with her own character and convictions of good and bad, without losing sight of the needs of the weakest party, the boy.

Discussion: The Strength of Doubt

With only minor variations, the films represent the three models of leadership described by Max Weber: the charismatic type is clearly represented by Joan of Arc, while Sister Aloysius impersonates the legal-bureaucratic type, whose authority is founded on the obedience of rules and laws, and Pope Joan might be considered a traditional leader, with her leadership being supported by the framework of ancient traditions and customs.[35] What role, then, in the representation of the films, does gender play in the depiction of these three leaders? In the case of the charismatic leader Joan of Arc, gender plays the least important role; more important than social gender roles is her charisma, her divine legitimation (which the film, however, puts in question). In the case of Pope Joan and Sister Aloysius, on the other hand, as leaders who are inserted into a system of traditions and norms from which they also derive part of their authority, their gender becomes a problem because it contradicts social and ecclesial expectations of ideal leadership. As a pope, Joan has to hide her gender, and Aloysius's rigidity might also have to do with the fact that she knows herself to be fighting not only individual men but a whole (patriarchal) system.

Yet the contrast between the protagonists' gender and social leadership ideals serves as a focal point to highlight some questions concerning leadership and authority in religious settings: the relationship between means and their end (in *The Messenger* and *Doubt*); the conflation of the leader's person with her position and her mission (in *The Messenger*); the involvement of church leaders in politics (as in *Pope Joan* and *The Messenger*); the importance of social relationships of support (in *Pope Joan*); the balance of absolute principles with the situational needs of a person (in *Doubt*); and the (inevitable?) correlation between the hierarchical system of the church and an authoritarian leadership style (important to all three films). Because of the nature of the films—aiming at dramatic action rather than ethical speculation—these questions are not discussed in detail, yet their inclusion in the dramatic narrative can evoke critical reflection in viewers who are open to such challenges.

Overall, however, the films appear doubtful as to whether a woman's leadership in a religious setting is possible at all (in spite of positive developments in the wake of Vatican II) and can truly be successful. In *Pope Joan*, the film falls back onto the idea that their female nature prevents women from living an autonomous life and filling a position of authority. While the film seems to suggest that women leaders practice a particular, "feminine" style of leadership, characterized by integrity, justice, tolerance, and equality, it is nevertheless only by denying their female nature that women can become leaders.[36] Regarding leadership styles, *The Messenger* does not so much focus on its protagonist's gender, but rather on her (in)ability to sustain inner psychological stress and stand up to her own doubts. It is at this point that Joan fails and lacks inner strength, while she had been able to resist external pressures. Sister Aloysius in *Doubt*, on the other hand, shows resistance both to internal and external pressure, insisting on her certainty, even though she can have none. While she shows remarkable consistency and strength of character, even more so for admitting to her doubts without being paralyzed by them, her behavior raises the question of when such determination is necessary for a leader and when it becomes simple stubborness. The film stands out in comparison with the other two in showing its female protagonist as a nuanced and complex character, with both negative and positive aspects that equally influence her leadership style. This gives her the possibility to change and grow in the course of the film. Even more importantly, without closing its eyes before the real problems that Aloysius' gender causes in the patriarchal context of the church, the film does not reduce its protagonist to naturalized gender stereotypes regarding her leadership abilities or style, accepting her instead as a unique, complex individual with her very own capacities. While the film closes on doubt, and thus also implies doubt in its protagonist, it does so in a way that does not weaken her as a character or in her authority—quite unlike Joan of Arc's doubts or Pope Joan's being betrayed by her female nature, which leave the viewer with the idea that women are unable to be leaders in religious settings.

Thus doubt—in both its constructive and destructive forms—is what remains from these three films on women religious leaders: doubts regarding their leadership qualities, and doubts regarding traditional forms of authoritarian leaderships and the relationship between means and their ends. Finally, regarding the social contexts of each narrative, the films raise a fundamental doubt as to whether societies are, even now, unwilling to give women the space to develop their capacities, without trapping them in gender-role stereotypes. While such stereotypes remain dominant in church and society, the cinematic portrayal of women's leadership exposes underlying social assumptions and raises ethical and ecclesiological questions in regard to how power and authority are perceived, constructed, and exercised.

Notes

1. Jolyon Mitchell, "Ethics," in *The Routledge Companion to Religion and Film*, ed. John Lyden (London: Routledge, 2011), 491. See also John Lyden, *Film as Religion: Myths, Morals, and Rituals* (New York: New York University Press, 2003).

2. Ginka Toegel, "Disappointing Statistics, Positive Outlook," Forbes.com, February 18, 2011; http://www.forbes.com.

3. German chancellor Angela Merkel recently made headlines for buying her own vegetables and even carrying her shopping bag herself, as reports *Bild* on March 2, 2012; http://www.bild.de—a piece of news considered to be important enough to be picked up by *Die Zeit* and other German newspapers.

4. Carole Elliott and Valerie Stead, "Learning from Leading Women's Experience: Towards a Sociological Understanding," *Leadership* 4, no. 2 (2008): 161.

5. Ibid., 164.

6. Ibid.

7. See, for example, Lisa Bass, "Fostering an Ethic of Care in Leadership: A Conversation with Five African American Women," *Advances in Developing Human Resources* 11, no. 5 (2009): 619–32.

8. Elliott and Stead, "Learning from Leading Women's Experience," 163–65.

9. Ibid., 175–76.

10. Catherine Wessinger, "Women's Religious Leadership in the United States," in *Religious Institutions and Women's Leadership: New Roles Inside the Mainstream*, ed. Catherine Wessinger (Columbia: University of South Carolina Press, 1996), 6.

11. Wessinger, "Women's Religious Leadership in the United States," 5.

12. Ruth A. Wallace, "The Social Construction of a New Leadership Role: Catholic Women Pastors," in *Gender and Religion*, ed. William H. Swatos, Jr. (New Brunswick, NJ: Transaction Publishers, 1994), 16–18. The decisive factors Wallace mentions are Vatican II's theology of the church as people of God and its call for inclusion of women in the apostolate; changes in the Code of Canon Law that allow women to act as parish administrators; demographic changes, namely, the shortage of priests versus a growth in numbers of parishioners as well as the more general impact of the women's movement on women's education and their own self-perception as religious subjects. One could also add the effect of the Council's opening of theological studies to women, which allows them to acquire the necessary knowledge and theological qualifications to question certain exclusive traditions and negative views of women, for example, their responsibility for the fallenness of humankind. See also Wessinger, "Women's Religious Leadership in the United States," 6.

13. Elaine Howard Ecklund, "Organizational Culture and Women's Leadership: A Study of Six Catholic Parishes," *Sociology of Religion* 67, no. 1 (2006): 81–98. As Ecklund shows, "Those parishes that had an ideological commitment to women in leadership may be more likely to survive in the midst of a continuing decline in the number of priests when compared to those that viewed women merely as placeholders until more priests were found." Ibid., 96.

14. Max Weber, *The Theory of Social and Economic Organization*, trans. A. M. Henderson and Talcott Parsons (New York: Oxford University Press, 1947), 152.

15. Guttorm Fløistad, "Community Culture, Ethics, Professionalism and Human Values: A View from Norway," *Journal of Human Values* 1, no. 1 (1995): 13.

16. Quoted in Peter Gilmour, "Leadership and Religion in the 21st Century," *Journal of Leadership & Organizational Studies* 4, no. 4 (1997): 34.

17. Ruth A. Wallace, "Women Administrators of Priestless Parishes: Constraints and Opportunities," *Review of Religious Research* 32, no. 4 (1991): 300.

18. Gilmour, "Leadership and Religion in the 21st Century," 36–38; Wallace, "The Social Construction of a New Leadership Role," 19.

19. Wallace, "Women Administrators of Priestless Parishes," 291–92.

20. Wallace, "The Social Construction of a New Leadership Role," 19.

21. Gilmour, "Leadership and Religion in the 21st Century," 37–38; Wallace, "Women Administrators of Priestless Parishes," 301–02; Ecklund, "Organizational Culture and Women's Leadership," 93–95; Tony Watling, "'Leadership' or 'Dialogue'? Women, Authority and Religious Change in a Netherlands Community," *Sociology of Religion* 63, no. 4 (2002): 535.

22. On the development of the legend, see Max Kerner and Klaus Herbers, *Die Päpstin Johanna: Biographie einer Legende* (Cologne: Böhlau, 2010).

23. Bass, "Fostering an Ethic of Care in Leadership," 627–28.

24. As pointed out in the study by Elliott and Stead, "Learning from Leading Women's Experience."

25. Interestingly, the wise Alexandrian philosopher Hypathia faces a similar choice in Alejandro Amenábar's film *Agora* (Spain, also 2009) and also has to pay for her love for knowledge and autonomy of thought with death.

26. Some reviews have applauded the film for the historical verisimilitude of its setting; however, it does not seem enough to simply depict medieval life as dirty and rough in order to achieve historical realism; cf. Marco Lucchino, "*La Papessa*: Papa Giovanna," http://35mm.it; however, compared with *The Messenger*'s idyllic scenery and reimaginations of medieval weaponry, *Pope Joan*'s *mise-en-scène* does indeed seem quite realistic.

27. Michael Kohler, "Die Päpstin," *film-dienst* 62, no. 23 (2009); http://cinomat.kim-info.de.

28. Ibid.

29. Françoise Meltzer mentions more than forty films, without counting TV series, about Joan of Arc; cf. her study "Joan of Arc in America," *SubStance* 31, no. 1 (2003): 92.

30. Cf. Weber's description of the charismatic leader in his *The Theory of Social and Economic Organization*, 358–63.

31. Janet Maslin, "Joan, Medieval Warrior Princess," *New York Times*, November 12, 1999.

32. Weber, *The Theory of Social and Economic Organization*, 341–42.

33. Some viewers take up these and other questions reflecting more in depth on them than the film itself; cf. Mercian, "Inspired by . . . ?," Reviews and Ratings on imdb.com; http://www.imdb.com.

34. The complexity of Aloysius' character and Streep's acting escapes numerous reviewers, too, who seem to find it easier to reduce her to her authoritarian, fear-inspiring side; cf., for example, Stephanie Zacharek, "Doubt," *salon.com*, December 12, 2008; http://www.salon.com.

35. Weber, *The Theory of Social and Economic Organization*, 329–63.

36. Elliott and Stead, "Learning from Leading Women's Experience," who find similar contradictions in how society perceives women leaders and tries to establish a supposedly "feminine" style of leadership and yet makes it difficult or impossible for women to achieve such positions.

The Gallant: A Feminist Proposal

James Keenan

"It's been hard ever since the trial, ever since we the jurors came to the verdict that Sandusky is guilty." Barnes said she's haunted by the memories of Sandusky's young victims and their emotional testimony in the trial for the longtime football coordinator, who was convicted of abusing ten boys. "I go to bed at night and I end up falling asleep, and I wake up and think about the victims," she said. "They didn't need to go through this. It should have been stopped years ago and it wasn't."[1]

There is something different happening in the sexual abuse cases, usually involving boys, making the news in the United States these days. Probably, more than any other case, the Jerry Sandusky case highlights the change. This change, in my estimation, is the more assertive role of women in prosecuting predators.

On June 5, 2012, the trial against Jerry Sandusky began. Sandusky, the assistant football coach of Pennsylvania State University, was accused of sexually abusing up to ten boys over a fifteen-year period. Some of the instances of abuse occurred on Penn State grounds.[2] On June 22, he was found guilty of forty-five of the forty-eight allegations against him.[3] Sandusky was the assistant to the legendary Joe Paterno, who won more games for Penn State than any other college football coach in U.S. history.

It is necessary to appreciate that, in most instances, the sexual abuse of boys occurs in exclusively all-male environments; in the same environments in which male supervisors protected the predators and covered up the sexual abuse. They also assiduously kept women out of any of the deliberations about what to do with accounts of sexual abuse. There are hardly any cases where women were known to have been involved in subsequent cover-ups.

Early in the sexual abuse cases that were discovered in the Boston Archdiocese, individual women, both mothers and aunts of boys who were abused, were often the first persons to make complaints to their pastor or bishop. In most instances, these complaints were completely ignored. Women's voices were not heard. Their hearing only occurred in the depositions for the trials of some priests.

The written complaints of Margaret Gallant, whose seven nephews were among the 130 children molested by the infamous Father John J. Geoghan, provide a clear example. The *Boston Globe* reports,

The files . . . contain a poignant—and prophetic—August 1982 letter to
Law's predecessor, the late Cardinal Humberto Medeiros, from the aunt of
Geoghan's seven Jamaica Plain victims, expressing incredulity that the church
to which she was devoted would give Geoghan another chance at St. Bren-
dan's after what he had done to her family. "Regardless of what he says, or
the doctor who treated him, I do not believe he is cured; his actions strongly
suggest that he is not, and there is no guarantee that persons with these
obsessions are ever cured," Margaret Gallant said in her plea to Medeiros. "It
embarrasses me that the church is so negligent," Gallant wrote. Archdiocesan
records obtained by the *Globe* make it clear why Gallant wrote her irate letter
two years after the abuse: Geoghan had reappeared in Jamaica Plain, and
been seen with a young boy. The records note that the next month, "Another
letter from Mrs. Gallant. Why is nothing being done?"[4]

With the Jerry Sandusky case, we saw women entering the prosecution
of predators. As opposed to the male enclave of four top executives protecting
Sandusky, the women's intolerance of Sandusky's actions and his bosses' cover-up
is strikingly more in evidence than we have seen before. I believe lessons are to be
learned from the case of Jerry Sandusky. So let us return to the case.

In 1998, an eleven-year-old boy returns home with wet hair after an outing
with Sandusky. Victim #6 (each of the ten victims is only identified by numbers)
tells his mother he took a shower with Sandusky and that the coach hugged him
several times. The boy's mother contacts university police, triggering an investigation. On two subsequent dates, a police detective records the boy's mother during
a call with Sandusky. Court papers say Sandusky acknowledges that he show-
ered with the boy as well as with others. When the mother cuts off contact with
Sandusky after a second call, he tells her, "I wish I were dead." Two weeks later, an
investigator from the Pennsylvania Department of Public Welfare takes part in an
interview of Sandusky. According to the grand jury report, Sandusky admits to
hugging the boy in the shower and says he will not shower with children again. The
detective speaks to another boy who reports similar treatment to that reported by
Victim #6. But the investigation ends after the district attorney decides the case
warrants no criminal charges. The detective tells the grand jury that the head of
campus police told him to close the inquiry.

Thirteen years later, on March 31, 2011, after extensive interviews, twenty-
two-year-old Sara Ganim of Harrisburg's *Patriot-News* breaks the story of Jerry
Sandusky being subject to a grand jury investigation.[5] Ganim had heard a report
that Sandusky was being investigated for molesting a boy; she kept digging until she
had enough evidence to write the first story exposing the grand jury hearing as well
as accusations that the former coach had molested at least one boy in the university's locker room. While some readers attacked the newspaper for "printing gossip,"
other media and sports reporters ignored the news, even as Ganim continued to
report the story. "It felt like we were living in the Twilight Zone," says the *Patriot-*

News' editor, David Newhouse. Ganim adds, "Particularly with the local papers, I thought [that] was pretty irresponsible." It took a full seven months—after Sandusky was arrested and publicly charged with the sexual abuse of eight boys he met through his charity, The Second Mile—for national news media to pounce.[6]

Ganim later learns and reports that after the alleged victim came forward in 1998, adults allegedly witnessed sexual assaults by Sandusky in 2000 and 2002. Ganim reports that it was not until 2008 that Victim #1 came forward and was believed, and it was not until 2010 when the state attorney general's office began to supervise the case that the investigation picked up.

"We expected you just arrest people who do stuff like that," Victim #1's mother told Ganim. "We didn't realize it was going to be this difficult and take this long."[7]

Finally on November 5, 2011, Sandusky is arrested. The *American Journalism Review* reports that it was then that a torrent of news began flowing. More alleged victims of child sexual abuse by Sandusky emerged. All at once, Sara Ganim and the *Patriot-News* had plenty of company on the story.[8]

On November 7, 2011, Ganim publishes a very powerful essay: "Mothers of Two of Jerry Sandusky's Alleged Victims Lash out at Penn State Officials' Handling of Scandal."[9] It is a powerful account of the mothers and their sons learning the extent of the Sandusky abuse cases and learning how long they had been making their complaints.

On the very same day, Linda Kelly steps right into her position as state attorney general and effectively makes the Jerry Sandusky case a high-profile one.[10] At the press conference announcing the charges against Sandusky, she also posts the perjury charges against two university executives, Penn State athletic director Tim Curley and Penn State Vice President Gary Schultz.

On November 9, the board of trustees fires both Penn State President Graham Spanier and head football coach Joe Paterno.[11] In response, thousands of Penn State university students take to the streets and break out into a riot to protest the firing of Paterno.[12] On January 22, 2012, Joe Paterno dies, aged 85, of lung cancer.

On April 16, 2012, Sara Ganim is awarded the Pulizter Prize for local reporting and "courageously revealing and adeptly covering the explosive Penn State sex scandal involving former football coach Jerry Sandusky."[13] In her remarks celebrating her award, she shares two moments that conveyed the relevance of her work: the first is a call from the psychologist for Victim #1 (now seventeen years old) who said that the victim felt it was all so worth it because he had seen that other older victims told of their stories of sex abuse because he had had the courage to acknowledge his story in the first place; the second is that she learned that, after the release of her March 2011 story, six of the eight victims came forward to talk with the police and report their cases of abuse. On June 22, 2012, Jerry Sandusky was convicted of forty-five of the forty-eight counts.[14]

Later, on July 10, 2012, former U.S. Attorney General Louis Freeh's study, commissioned by Penn State's board of trustees, unequivocally identifies a culture of silence orchestrated by Paterno and Spanier as well as Curley and Schultz.[15] "In order to avoid the consequences of bad publicity, the most powerful leaders of Penn State," Mr. Freeh's group said, "repeatedly concealed critical facts relating to Sandusky's child abuse from the authorities, the board of trustees, the Penn State community and the public at large."[16]

After releasing the report, Freeh does a series of interviews in which he talked, first of the 1998 incident, then of a 2000 incident, and finally one in 2001. His comments, made to ABC News, capture the depth of the depravity and the scope of the cover-up. "What's striking about 1998 is that nobody even spoke to Sandusky, not one of those four persons, including the coach, who was four steps away from [Sandusky's] office," Freeh said.

Between the 1998 and 2001 incidents, Freeh noted that there was a 2000 incident in which janitors saw Sandusky molesting a boy in the showers and decided not to report it. This incident, Freeh said, showed more than any of the others that the culture at Penn State was one where no one could question or confront the all-powerful football program.

"Take a moment for janitors," Freeh said. "That's the tone on the bottom. The employees of Penn State who clean and maintain the locker rooms where young boys are being raped. They witness what I think is most horrific rape being described, and they panic. The janitor said, 'It's worst thing I ever saw.' He's a Korean War veteran, and he said, 'It makes me sick.' The other janitors are alarmed and shocked, but they say, 'We can't report this because we'll get fired.' They're afraid to go against it. If that's the culture on the bottom, God help the culture on the top." Freeh reports then that in 2001, a graduate assistant reported to Paterno, Spanier, Curley, and Schultz that he witnessed Sandusky sexually assaulting a boy. The four eventually agreed to not report the incident.[17]

On July 23, the National Collegiate Athletic Association, levied a $60 million penalty on the university, announced a four-year ban on any postseason play, and vacated all wins from 1998 to 2011, thus taking away from Paterno his legacy as the most successful college football coach in U.S. history. In making public the fine, the NCAA president called the case the most painful chapter in the history of intercollegiate athletics.[18]

Lessons

As I was researching the Sandusky matter, I kept going back to another set of writings, this one dealing with the church's sexual abuse crisis. I recalled a collection of essays on the topic and that the three editors of the collection, *The Structural Betrayal of Trust*, were all moral theologians: Regina Ammicht-Quinn, Hille Haker, and Maureen Junker-Kenny. I recalled that they underlined that they were also women and mothers. In 2004, they wrote,

> We, the editors of this volume, are theologians. We are women. We are mothers. Often enough, from the perspective of traditional church struc-

tures, we stand on "the other side," though we are not the ones who define where the boundaries are drawn.[19]

They observed that, to date, church leaders, particularly the hierarchy, were not looking to examine and reform the structural problems that prompted the crisis in the first place. They wrote,

> We cannot avoid the impression that here a problem is being "dealt with": some procedures have been changed, but otherwise the fundamental questions are being avoided. These fundamental questions are questions about the structure of a church based on a hierarchy which cannot be questioned by "outsiders" and which as a result gives rise to structurally "appropriate" mentalities on the part of those who hold office and those who are dependent on them.[20]

Something bothered me about what they wrote. I could see mothers of the abused as outsiders, but in 2004, I wondered whether it was good for theologians to think of themselves as outsiders. Do we, when we do that, place ourselves on the sidelines? I was struck that one of the great shifts in moral theology has been the entry of laypeople into the ranks of moral theologians and that, during the sexual abuse scandal here in Boston, laymen and women who were moral theologians, notably my colleagues, Steve Pope and Lisa Sowle Cahill, were themselves parents. There was something about them being both theologians and parents that was striking.

Though the three editors underlined that they were outsiders, I saw nothing in the stance of my colleagues that made them outsiders. In 2004, the same year that Ammicht-Quinn and others published their essays, Steve Pope edited a collection in light of the sexual abuse scandal in Boston entitled *Common Calling: The Laity and Governance of the Catholic Church*. There, he laid claim to the laity's role in church governance. There was nothing about being an outsider in that collection.[21] Lisa Sowle Cahill wrote in that collection, "If the current sex abuse crisis in the Catholic Church urges a call for greater lay participation, it is the participation of women in decision-making roles that, above all, must be enhanced." She later added, "if women do possess, as John Paul II believes or hopes, a special 'genius' by which they 'see persons with their hearts [that can] ensure sensitivity for human beings in every circumstance,' then women's judgment is all the more necessary to guide the internal affairs of an organization ostensibly devoted to faith, compassion, harmony, and service—especially to the most vulnerable, including children."[22] She added, "Many observers have noted that the isolation of this leadership from women's influence—and to an extent from the influence of men who are married to women, and who together with women are parents—has contributed to an ecclesial decision-making environment likely to conceal abuse and even to create it."[23]

In a manner of speaking, in 2004, neither set of theologians was an outsider. On the contrary, both were insisting on the need for the laity and in particular for women to be involved in church deliberations, and both were insisting that the exclusion of the mothers was itself an integral step to the overall disaster of the sexual abuse scandal.

In many ways, their observations helped me to see things in the Sandusky case (set not at a church, but at a university) that I may not have noticed. One of the primary lessons I learned came from the journalistic instincts of the reporter, Sara Ganim. Her loyalty was to the story, but along the way she became convinced that the testimonies of the mothers and their sons were not being heard. The story would not be complete until their voices were heard. On the other hand, attempts to diminish the seriousness, regularity, and depravity of Sandusky's abuse ("horseplay" as the men call it) were developed by the men initially investigating and covering up for the case.

We should not miss the gender differences here. The cover-up was exclusively male, the exclusive male leadership of Penn State. The whistle-blowers were exclusively female. The first to reckon the wrongness of the sexual abuse were singularly women, both the mothers and Ganim, and eventually the new attorney general. Finally, some men, notably Ganim's editor, stood with the reporter, and the issues kept moving forward.

We also should not overlook that this is the story of rape and sexual abuse, a topic that preeminently sees women and girls as victims. It is not until women entered into this fifteen-year-old narrative that someone stood up to protect male children. No man stood up to protect a male child.

Third, the overall approach was to simply foster silence, which is a deliberate approach. Women know about the silence that is confronted in the face of sexual abuse. It is a routine default position.[24] In the instance of Sandusky, silence was maintained for fifteen years. The attempt to break through it was by mothers, not unlike Margaret Gallant here in Boston. Against this silence, women worked with one another to protect boys and to restore their dignity, while forcing the men to accountability.

In all this, we have to wonder about the environment in which men remain unchanged by stories of boys being attacked and of mothers being ignored who make evidently credible accusations. Clearly this is like a club, where such reports are not taken seriously and where women are not credible witnesses. It is a familiar setting where exclusively male leadership, in churches, athletic offices, and university chambers, has been known for stonewalling reports of sexual abuse. For some, that exclusively male life is their life.

Learning about Male Privilege and Feminism

I live that life. Like many clergy, I live in an environment where my usual common discourse is with other men, usually Jesuit priests. My meals are taken with my community, and I often socialize with my male community members. A world of men, in which women are not present, is my world.

I have found, however, that in any apostolic work that I do, I am among men and women. More specifically, in any administrative work that I do, I count on women. I co-chair the Catholic Theological Ethics in the World Church Planning Committee with Linda Hogan, of Trinity College, Dublin. The committee is made up of four men and four women. As director of the Presidential Scholar's Program, I work alongside the female associate director with whom I review all ideas, programs, and more. I have always found the specificity of a woman's perspective helpful and, in some instances, different. As groups like our planning committee develop, I recognize that I need as many women as men precisely so that there is no minority status in our way of proceeding.

Margaret Farley, in her much cited book *Just Love*, looks at length into the issue of gender and at the situations in which it is important attend to the workings of gender. Among the moments that it does matter, she writes that gender matters also in "non-sexual human relationships and human endeavors, if for no other reason than that women and men are socialized very differently. Thus they sometimes do bring different experiences to relation and action, experiences that enrich or correct one another's contribution."[25]

This has been my experience. As a member of an all men's religious community, I have found that I cannot function adequately without women colleagues participating fully in my life. I have also learned that excluding women and their voices from those occasions and locations almost always becomes problematic. Having watched my own archdiocese for so many years so deeply embroiled, day in and day out, in the all-male stonewalling of the sexual abuse crisis, I see the dangers that are wrought by the absence of women.

I have also understood that those attempts to exclude women are themselves attempts to protect and maintain what some call *male privilege*. The term "male privilege" appears in an essay by Peggy McIntosh, who was trying to develop another concept, *white privilege*.[26] In 1990, McIntosh wrote that we are "taught to see racism only in individual acts of meanness, not in invisible systems conferring dominance on my group." To illustrate these invisible systems, McIntosh wrote a list of twenty-fix invisible privileges whites benefit from.

Before doing that, she described male privilege. "I have often noticed men's unwillingness to grant that they are over-privileged, even though they may grant that women are disadvantaged. They may say they will work to improve women's status, in the society, the university, or the curriculum, but they can't or won't support the idea of lessening men's privilege."

So how do we males recognize male privilege? I want to tell two stories of my own coming to understand male privilege. Starting in the mid-1990s, a group of members within the Society of Christian Ethics in the United States tried to pass a motion at the convention's business meeting on instituting standards of professional conduct. These members were concerned about the possibility of a member's inappropriate conduct toward one another, and we thought that standards and sanctions ought to be stipulated. These procedures would take nearly five years to be approved.

As a junior member of the society, I began to note each year that the committee would report their guidelines, but invariably older, white males began to argue against the necessity of this, saying that as we were a society of colleagues, such standards might suggest that there were suspicions among members. They argued that we should not address something that is not a real issue and that the procedures themselves would alienate and breed suspicion.

At these annual business meetings, I also began to realize that most of the motion's supporters were women, who regularly assured the doubting older men that they thought these standards would only further engender trust in the society. Inevitably, however, a vote would be taken to send it back to committee for a rewrite. I remember this exchange repeating itself for about four years. At the end of the fourth business meeting, when the same dynamics occurred, I turned to my friend and colleague Margaret Farley and noted that every year the committee proposed the redrafted and amended standards of professional conduct, and that every year, the opposition came from older white men. I suggested that the impasse might be not the document but a gender issue. Margaret Farley asked me what stopped me from stating that outright.

I do not mean to suggest that what the older white men said was without merit. I simply saw a dynamic that I thought was noteworthy. But I did not publicly acknowledge it. I saw male privilege, but I did not act to counter it. My silence was complicit. I later realized that recognition is only part of the change; one has to act to divest. In the fifth year, the standards were passed and an oversight committee was established.[27] I am now one of the committee's three members.

The second occasion concerned our plans for hosting, at Padua, the first international conference of Catholic Theological Ethics in the World Church. We decided to bring forty sponsored participants from each of the three southern continents: Africa, Asia, and Latin America. The planning committee members from each of these continents were to draft a list of invitees. When I saw the lists being proposed, I realized that in Latin America, there were hardly any women. Among the Africans, there were none. I thought of four well-known African ethicists who were not trained as theological ethicists, but having studied theology, philosophical ethics, or bible, had migrated into theological ethics. I asked the African chair why their names were not included. He insisted that only moral theologians should be on the list. I noted that from the industrialized world there were a number of scholars coming who were not unlike these women, and they were being read today as Catholic ethicists. He replied that Africa had more than forty moral theologians, and we should not exclude those who were so trained. I replied that we could not have, in 2006, forty African ethicists who were exclusively male. As the chair and as the sole fund-raiser, I insisted that four of these women theologians be placed on the list, Philomena Maura, Anne

Nasimyu, Bernadette Mbuy-Beya, and Teresia Hinga. Anne was unable to come, but the other three women were present.

Four hundred people attended the Padua conference. A highlight of the conference consisted of the five continental plenary panels, which had three major speakers each. Their brief was to answer the following questions: What are the challenges on our continent? How are we addressing them? What hope do we have for the future? The first continental panel was the African one, and the packed audience was ready to listen. In the course of forty-five minutes, the three presenters spoke of African identity and self-understanding, the history of slavery, corruption, civil war, depleted natural resources, and more.[28] As the floor opened for questions, the three African women each went to the microphones. They asked how, in forty-five minutes, the speakers made no mention of HIV/AIDS, health care, or women? In those opening minutes, I realized how relevant their presence was. The presence of these women in our midst was tangibly felt.

At the end of the Padua conference, the planning committee made a pledge to the members that when we returned to the next conference (Trento, 2010), we would have established a scholarship fund for African women to do doctorates in moral theology. Four years later at Trento, we were able to introduce our seven women doctoral scholars.

Proposing a Simple Rule

These two experiences were relevant moments in my own understanding that as a theologian, an ethicist, a Jesuit, and a priest, I enjoy a great deal of privilege. As such, I need not only acknowledge my privilege; I must make sure that women are involved in decision-making activities. I am now suspicious when women are not present at any meeting in which I participate. In fact, I propose a fundamental rule that all men should embrace: no meeting of social responsibility should ever be held that does not have the participation of women in it. If women are not present, men should ensure that women participate, even if the one making the complaint has to abdicate his space to accommodate women.

I want to note that I am not emphasizing any more than this, but nothing less. I am not advancing the so-called controversial issues about reproductive rights, women's ordination, or any other hot-button issues. I am simply arguing that wherever we are, we need to have women as active participants, simply because their perspective is their perspective, and it is one that is often lost in single gendered gatherings and deliberations.

I also say this as a priest, a religious, and a senior faculty member. I know that in the church and in the university, as sexual abuse cases show, there are all-male enclaves of power, and men must work to make sure that they cease to exist as such and that women are incorporated into the structures of decision making. For this reason, the rule will need to be invoked time and again, but it will need to be men invoking it since women are not present.

I offer the following as an example. The Committee on Doctrine for the United States Conference of Catholic Bishops was established in 1988 to revisit the Ethical and Religious Directives for Catholic Healthcare. I, along with Thomas Kopfensteiner, a diocesan priest from St. Louis, was asked to sit on the committee, first as directive draftsmen and then as advisors. These directives would go through more than eleven drafts. One of the great ironies was that, aside from the staff, the committee had only its bishop members, its four advisory theologians (all men), and its two draftsmen (Tom and I). It also sent its reports out to five ethics centers, including the Catholic Health Association, the Kennedy Center, and the National Catholic Bioethics Center, each of which was headed by a male.

As everyone knows, Catholic health care in the United States was predominantly established and sustained by women religious. Despite our urging, on only two occasions were drafts sent to health care systems; only then did women actually see and respond to the directives. At the last meeting, we insisted as a matter of record that any subsequent revision would have to have women in the room as advisors for the bishops drafting the revisions.

I have now realized that acknowledging male privilege is not enough. As in working to get funding for and participating with the two editors of this volume, Linda Hogan and A. E. Orobator, in establishing the scholarship program for women in Africa, I realize that I must work for the empowering of women in the church and the academy. In the twenty-first century, women should not be outsiders.

I have finally understood that I, like other men, must become feminists. In "Why All Men Should Be Feminists," David Moscrop writes,

> If true equality is to be achieved between men and women, men are going to have to enlist as feminists. This begins with men realizing that being a "man" is complicated, variable, and has nothing to do with sports, worn jokes, and preserving unjust and unearned privilege. It proceeds when men realize that they are bound up in those social structures that obscure, oppress, and abuse many women. But the pursuit of equality never ends. Instead it remains active as a constant and critical reflection about how we engage with one another as gendered human beings and action toward remedies.[29]

In a similar vein, Mandy van Deven writes,

> For male feminists, maintaining an awareness of their own privilege in order to vigilantly disassemble male dominance is crucial. It is not enough to talk the talk; one must also incorporate principles of equality into one's daily life. This means not only treating individual women with respect (for example, sharing household and child care responsibilities, encouraging women's financial independence and economic success) and refusing to be complicit when other men demonstrate sexist behaviour, but also

taking steps to shift societal dynamics that benefit men as a group (such as raising awareness about the links between dominant constructions of masculinity and gender-based violence, promoting reproductive justice policies and rejecting unearned authority). And it means recognizing that while individual power varies, in most places around the world men receive institutional benefits and power to the detriment of women. Being accountable for the deconstruction of male privilege means men should find creative ways to undermine and disassemble patriarchy.[30]

Both Van Deven and Moscrop make clear that being a feminist means being one who is ever vigilant about the role and place of women in our society, both locally and universally. I believe that men like me ought to keep as a rule, for the many meetings that we attend and the many deliberations that we advise and/or make, that we cannot be silent when women are absent. Had Curley, Schultz, Paterno, or Spanier let women know that they had heard of Sandusky's abuse, or had the Boston archdiocese met with Margaret Gallant, I am sure the outcomes would have been otherwise. The wisdom of women is not to be discounted. Men must realize not only that a Sara Ganim will insist on her right to report but that we must also make sure that she is not the only one working to guarantee that the mothers' voices are heard.

In the church and in the academy, too many decisions are made by men only. It is as if the claims of patriarchy have not been disclosed, time and time again. There is no reason for the absence of women. The simple rule that I propose of guaranteeing the presence of women at every deliberation ought to be made known throughout the world. Men ought to insist on it at every occasion. I suggest we call it the Gallant Rule. Such a name might give us another reason for realizing what is at stake when we fail to invoke Gallant.[31]

Notes

1. Matt Carroll and Chris Rosenblum, "Juror in Jerry Sandusky trial watches removal of Joe Paterno statue," *News Observer* July 22, 2012. http://www.newsobserver.com.

2. Mark Memmott, "As Sandusky Trial Begins, a Two Minute Guide to the Case," *National Public Radio,* June 5, 2012; http://www.npr.org.

3. Bill Chappell, "Penn State Abuse Scandal: A Guide and Timeline," *National Public Radio*, June 21, 2012, http://www.npr.org.

4. Michael Rezendes, "Church Allowed Abuse by Priest for Years," January 6, 2002, *Boston Globe* http://www.boston.com. This article narrates the numerous attempts by women to get the clerical authorities to stop giving the infamous Father Geoghan access to boys. The site also provides the entire history of articles by the *Boston Globe* on the sexual abuse case in the Boston archdiocese. On Gallant, see also Pam Belluck, "Cardinal Law Says Pedophile Matter Left to Aides," *New York Times* May 9, 2002, A1.

5. Sara Ganim, "Jerry Sandusky, Former Penn State Football Staffer, Subject of Grand Jury Investigation," March 31, 2011, *Patriot-News:* http://www.pennlive.com.

6. Liz Brody, "Meet the Woman Who Exposed Jerry Sandusky," *Glamour* February 2012; http://www.glamour.com.

7. Mark Memmott, "Report: Years and Years of Missed Chances in Penn State Scandal," *National Public Radio*, November 14, 2011, http://www.npr.org. See Ganim's own account of the misses on this case, "A Patriot-News Special Report: Who Knew What about Jerry Sandusky? There were many missed chances to investigate as early as 1995, November 11, 2011, *Patriot-News*, http://www.pennlive.com.

8. George Solomon, "Slow to React," *American Journalism Review*, December, 22, 2011, http://ajr.org.

9. Sara Ganim, "Mothers of Two of Jerry Sandusky's Alleged Victims Lash out at Penn State Officials' Handling of Scandal," November 7, 2011 *Patriot News*, http://www.pennlive.com.

10. "Who Is Linda Kelly? New Pennsylvania Attorney General Steps into Spotlight," November 7, 2011, *Patriot News,* http://www.pennlive.com.

11. Mark Viera, "Paterno Is Finished at Penn State, and President Is Out," *New York Times* November 9, 2011.

12. Sarah Maslin Nir, "Penn State Students Take to the Streets after Paterno Is Fired," *New York Times* November 10, 2012.

13. Mathew DeLuca, "Reporter Sara Ganim, Who Won a Pulitzer for Breaking Sandusky Story," *Daily Beast*, April 17, 2012, http://www.thedailybeast.com.

14. Joe Drape, "Sandusky Guilty of Sexual Abuse of 10 Young Boys," *New York Times,* June 22, 2012.

15. Sara Ganim, "Analysis: FBI Director Louis Freeh, State's Results Differ Greatly. Why?" *Patriot-News* July 12, 2012, http://www.pennlive.com.

16. Ken Belson, "Abuse Scandal Inquiry Damns Paterno and Penn State," *New York Times* July 12, 2012.

17. Colleen Curry, Penn State Board Slams Former President Spanier, Questions Future Honors for Joe Paterno," *ABC News* July 12, 2012, http://abcnews.go.com.

18. Pete Thamel, "Sanctions Decimate the Nittany Lions Now and for Years to Come," *New York Times* July 23, 2012.

19. Regina Ammicht-Quinn, Hille Haker, and Maureen Junker-Kenny, eds., "Post-script," in *The Structural Betrayal of Trust* (London: SCM Press, 2004), 133.

20. Ibid., 131.

21. Stephen Pope ed., *Common Calling: The Laity and Governance of the Catholic Church* (Washington, DC: Georgetown University Press, 2004).

22. Lisa Sowle Cahill, "Feminist Theology and a Participatory Church," *Common Calling,* 127–49, at 127. Cahill is referring to John Paul II, *On the Dignity and Vocation of Women* (Washington, DC: United States Catholic Conference, 1988) 30, 112.

23. Cahill, "Feminist Theology and a Participatory Church," 128.

24. Beth Crisp, "Silence and Silenced: Implications for the Spirituality of Survivors of Sexual Abuse," *Feminist Theology* 18 (2010): 277–93.

25. Margaret Farley, *Just Love: A Framework for Christian Sexual Ethics* (New York: Continuum, 2006), 158.

26. See the excellent collection on this topic, Laurie M. Cassidy and Alex Mikulich, eds., *Interrupting White Privilege: Catholic Theologians Break the Silence,"* (Maryknoll, NY: Orbis Books, 2007).

27. http://www.scethics.org.

28. James F. Keenan, ed., *Catholic Theological Ethics in the World Church: The Plenary Papers from the First Cross-cultural Conference on Catholic Theological Ethics* (New York: Continuum, 2007).

29. David Moscrop, "Why All Men Should Be Feminists," *Vancouver Sun*, March 29, 2012.

30. Mandy van Deven, "Is Feminism Men's Work, Too?" *Horizons* 23, no. 2 (2009): 16–21, at 19–20.

31. I want to thank Katherine Dullea, Sahil Angelo, and Nicole Benevenia for their assistance with this essay, especially in their research of the Sandusky event.

The Personal Is Political: Toward a Vision of Justice in Latina Theology

Nichole Flores

Introduction

Theology arising from Latina contexts has envisioned a robustly relational account of the human constitution, derived from the integral role that social relationships play in Latina/o cultures. While justice is frequently referenced in Latina theology, this concept demands greater conceptual definition from within this particular discussion. This essay suggests a starting point for elaborating a positive account of justice in Latina theology, one that undergirds ethical references to right relationship in this particular conversation. Employing Latina anthropological insights—along with supporting evidence from feminist and Latino anthropology—and the Thomistic conceptions of justice and the common good, I will begin the process of developing a notion of justice that emphasizes intersubjectivity in the pursuit of political justice or the connection between the personal and the political dimensions of justice.[1] These anthropological insights inspire a notion of relational justice that resonates with Latina experience.

This essay contains four movements. First, I explore the theological foundations of relationality that influence Latina theological anthropology as synthesized in the constructive anthropological work of Latina theologian Michelle González, which identifies both personal and political elements of human relationship. Next, I engage with *mujerista* ethicist Ada María Isasi-Díaz's foundational insights for connecting the personal and political elements of human relationship in a comprehensive understanding of the reality of suffering and resistance in the lives of Latinas. Third, I interface this account of relationship with the conception of justice articulated by Thomas Aquinas in his *Summa Theologiae*. Engagement between Latina and Thomistic theologies catalyzes a new interpretive perspective on Thomistic justice, revealing the profoundly relational and communal implications of his thought. Finally, I demonstrate how the Thomistic account of general and particular justice, as connected through his common good framework, serves as a resource for elaborating the Latina insight of justice as right relationship in community that seeks survival and flourishing for all people. I argue that a vision of justice emanating from Latina theology asserts the integral connection between personal and political aspects of justice grounded in the fundamental anthropological assertion of human relationality.

The Personal and the Political: Relationality in Latina Anthropology

In this section, I explore the theological foundations of relationality that influence Latina theological anthropology as synthesized in the constructive anthropological work of Latina theologian Michelle González, revealing Latina contributions to developing a relational Christian theological anthropology. González's constructive work emphasizes both the interpersonal and public facets of human relationship and thus lays the groundwork for the connection between personal and political justice in Latina theology.

U.S. Latina/o theologians, according to González, "ground their contemporary scholarship in the lives, struggles, identity, and, most importantly, faith of Latino/a people."[2] With this goal in mind, Latina theological anthropology aims to articulate an understanding of human identity that affirms the fundamental dignity of Latinas and other people for whom humane treatment cannot be taken for granted. Several prominent Latina theologians have made significant contributions to the field of theological anthropology, including *mujerista* theologian Ada María Isasi-Díaz and Latina feminist theologian María Pilar Aquino, in the late twentieth and early twenty-first century, and Mexican philosopher and theologian Sor Juana Ines de la Cruz in the seventeenth century. González synthesizes the rich anthropological insights of these theologians to reveal their contribution to broader anthropological discourse. She identifies four major anthropological themes emanating from Latina theological inquiry: (1) *mestizaje/mulatez* (difference), (2) community and family, (3) relationship and the Trinity, and (4) grace and culture.[3] Among these themes, González gestures to community and human relationality as the heart of Latina anthropology.

While González acknowledges the basic reality of human difference, she argues that human beings are fundamentally relational creatures by virtue of our reflection of God's Trinitarian nature.[4] She argues for a "justice-infused understanding of the Trinity,"[5] which is the paradigm of right relationship: "The relational nature of humanity is grounded in God's Trinitarian nature as relational and our reflection of this nature through the *imago dei*."[6] If the Trinity is fundamentally constituted by relationship, then human beings, as ones created in God's image, are also fundamentally relational.

The centrality of relationality in Latina/o accounts of anthropology is evident in the prominence of family, church, and community in our theology. As González explains, "The relationship between the individual and the community is dialectical. Linked to this communal understanding of the self is an emphasis on *familia* as a defining dimension of who we are."[7] Latinas/os perceive individual identity as being codetermined, but not subsumed, by our families and communities. Latino theologian Gary Riebe-Estrella attributes the primacy of community and family to the Latina/o social worldview:

> Latino cultures, by and large, are "sociocentric organic" in nature. In other words, the fundamental unit of society is envisioned as a group, primarily the family. The identity of an individual emerges from his or her membership in the group. In this cultural perspective, human persons mature by recognizing their place within the group and by refining to some extent the mutual obligations and rights which that place entails. But who they are is always bounded by the group.[8]

Riebe-Estrella reemphasizes the centrality of relationality, through family and community, in Latina/o culture. The robust Latina/o conception of relationality yields a strong emphasis on interpersonal relationships through marriage, immediate and extended family, *compadrazgo*, neighborhood, and church. Given the prominence of interpersonal relationships, an articulation of a Latina/o vision of justice would be remiss to neglect the implications of right relationship in these contexts.

Sociality is not a static element of human existence; it demands active engagement in relationship across human difference. Latino theologian Roberto Goizueta explains the energetic demands of this relational existential: "The human person is defined, above all, by his or her character as a relational being. Yet this relationality is not merely some static 'essence' of the person, but an *active* relating in and through which the person defines him or herself, in interaction with others."[9] In other words, "Relationship is an action. We recognize each other as individuals only when we encounter another."[10] If relationship calls for action, then *right relationship* requires participation also. As theologians have emphasized throughout Christian history, right relationship is *achieved* through God's grace alone. Still, as those created in God's image, humankind is called to *participate* in creating a more just reality, pursuing right relationship in cooperation with God's will.

The active demands of human relationality have important implications for justice in both public and interpersonal contexts. Feminist theologian Mary Catherine Hilkert emphasizes the political implications of Trinitarian theology: "If the Trinitarian model offers the ideal paradigm for social and political relations, then unity-in-diversity and radical equality become ethical and political mandates."[11] God calls humanity to seek reconciliation with all of creation, including the racial, sexual, religious, and political other, especially "the least of these" (Matt. 25:45) or those who have suffered most severely from *wrong relationship*. González elaborates Hilkert's point:

> In a world marked by the systematic degradation of other human beings, the image of God is found in the crucified people who image the crucified Christ. Only through our protest and action against that which violates

the image of God in all of humanity is the image as "compassionate love in solidarity" revealed. The image of Christ is a vocation we are called to fulfill. Hilkert's dynamic notion of *imago Dei* presents the image as something we embody through our ethical actions, a challenge we must meet in order to truly reflect our intended nature. We are called to image God through our actions and relationships with one another.[12]

González and Hilkert reveal a foundational aspect of justice emerging from both Latina and feminist theological insights: if relationship is central to our anthropology via an understanding of the *imago Dei* and Trinitarian theology, then the public pursuit of justice, or right relationship as revealed in the Trinity, is an integral aspect of Christian discipleship.

Relationality is central to an understanding of justice. A theological vision of human relationship as analogous to the Trinity is foundational for both interpersonal and political justice. This insight is helpful for identifying a vision of justice arising from Latina theological inquiry. It is necessary, however, to investigate the relationship between these elements and the implications of this relationship for the pursuit of right relationship in communities. This is the task of the next section.

The Personal Is Political: Struggle and Resistance

Here, I develop González's and Hilkert's insights into the interpersonal and political implications of human relationality, engaging them with Isasi-Díaz's *mujerista* conception of relational anthropology. I will employ Isasi-Díaz's articulation of *la lucha* (the struggle) to illustrate how the interpersonal and political aspects of justice are connected in Latina theology.

Isasi-Díaz's *mujerista* theology emerges from engagement with a specific group of women, a context that allows her to attend to the everyday struggles of these particular "grassroots Latinas."[13] Isasi-Díaz identifies three phrases, frequently employed by the women with whom she works, which constitute *mujerista* theological anthropology: (1) *la lucha*, (2) *permítanme hablar* (allow me to speak), and (3) *la comunidad/la familia* (the community/the family).[14] These phrases, she claims, arise from Latina's descriptions of their everyday life, or *lo cotidiano*, emphasizing their daily struggle for survival, their unique contributive voices, and their relational understanding of the self. These phrases serve as "both a source and a framework for *mujerista* theology."[15] While each of the three phrases gestures to an integral theme in Latina theology, I will focus on *la lucha* as a source for revealing the integral connection between the personal and the political in Latina and *mujerista* theology as this theme lends insight into the vital connection between personal and political justice in Latina theology.

Mujerista theology, according to Isasi-Díaz, is concerned with the everyday struggles of Latinas. She writes, "The daily ordinary struggle of Hispanic Women to survive and live fully has been the central element of *mujerista* theology from the very start because it is, I believe, the main experience in the lives of the majority of Latinas."[16] *La lucha Latina* describes the reality of economic, political, and social suffering endured by grassroots Latinas. While unjust suffering is a part of Latina experience, *la lucha* is concerned with resisting suffering rather than romanticizing it.[17]

Resisting suffering, for Latinas, is a social activity. The *fiesta*, or celebration, then, is a central event in Latina/o communities. Goizueta argues that the *fiesta* is a central concept in Latina/o theological anthropology, suggesting that "the *fiesta*, as a thanksgiving for having received life, reflects and expresses a profound sense of the human in relationship to the sacred."[18] Similarly, Isasi-Díaz identifies the *fiesta* as a site of social resistance for grassroots Latinas:

> I have gotten the best clues for understanding how Latinas understand and deal with suffering by looking at Latinas' capacity to celebrate, at our ability to organize a *fiesta* in the midst of the most difficult circumstances and in spite of deep pain. The *fiestas* are, of course, not celebrations of suffering but of the struggle against suffering. The *fiestas* are, very often, a way of encouraging one another to not let the difficulties that are part of Hispanic Women's daily life overcome us.[19]

During *fiestas*, Latinas come to realize that they are not alone in their daily struggles. These gatherings present opportunities to name suffering in community, and further, to develop creative strategies for responding to this suffering. It is in this relational venue that Latinas start to make the concrete connection between the personal problems they face in everyday life—poverty, violence, exploitation, marginalization—and the broader social implications of these problems.

Isasi-Díaz thus surfaces the connection between the personal and the political in Latina theology and ethics. Both interpersonal and public relationships are integral to the development of a Latina approach to justice. She asserts, "*Mujeristas* denounce the split between the personal and the political as a false dichotomy used often to oppress Hispanic Women."[20] The false bifurcation of these spheres does harm to Hispanic women by reinforcing oppressive conditions that perpetuate suffering. The private and public spheres mutually condition one another. This insight is foundational for an understanding of justice that acknowledges and responds to Latina experiences of injustice.

One can observe the connection between interpersonal and political justice in the lives of many Latinas and other people for whom survival is a daily struggle. The economic and social problems of the family bear on the common good; war and governmental politics profoundly affect the family, especially families on the economic, political, and social margins of society. The connection between personal and political issues of justice is illustrated by a recent public policy decision in Massachusetts. In April 2011, state lawmakers proposed a 20 percent cut to funding for the Women, Children, and Infants (WIC) program, which provides basic nutrition for low-income mothers and their children, including healthy food and formula. Despite serious concerns expressed by program administrators and poverty advocates about the detrimental effects of these cuts on the most vulnerable members of society, the Massachusetts Department of Public Health claims that the cuts are necessary to sustain the state budget: "Massachusetts, like all states, continues to feel the impact of the global economic crisis . . . no agency wants to have to make these decisions, but sound fiscal management has required tough choices."[21] In response to the cuts, poverty advocates emphasize the adverse effect of budget cuts on the poorest of the poor, "This would just make it harder for poor families . . . it would undermine our efforts to make sure low-income families have access to healthy food."[22] In addition to the short-term struggles of the particular women and children affected by this decision, this policy negatively affects broader society, hindering the healthy development of future generations of citizens who can contribute to the flourishing of society as a whole. Here we can see plainly the effect of national and global political and economic problems on the life and flourishing of Massachusetts's poor mothers and their children. For this reason, a vision of justice emanating from Latina theology aims to reaffirm the feminist claim that "the personal is political," revealing the connection between personal struggle of marginalized people with politics and public policy.

For Isasi-Díaz, theology begins, but does not end, with the particular experiences of Latinas in the United States. She couples *mujerista* theology's concern for particular, everyday experience with a firm commitment to social activism.[23] Thus, Isasi-Díaz does not simply propose a panacea for the daily struggles of Latinas; she argues that these struggles are the source of social and political activism that seeks justice for marginalized people, starting with Latinas. In this way, she contributes to developing a conception of justice that responds to Latina experience.

Thomas Aquinas:
Justice and the Common Good

I now consider the conception of justice in the works of Thomas Aquinas. His account provides resources for further elaborating a positive articulation of justice in Latina theology. Upon examination of Aquinas's understanding of justice in light of Latina contributions to theological anthropology, one sees parallels, and even affinity, between the two discourses. The Latina theological concerns with personal and public relationality illuminate the relational implications of Aquinas's conception of justice. The Thomistic contribution can help shape, define, and support Latina articulations of justice by providing a framework for our relational anthropology as an integral facet of building and sustaining right relationship in community.

Aquinas's discussion of justice occupies sixty-five of 148 articles in the *secunda secundae* of his *Summa Theologiae*. In the first question, he defines justice as, "the constant and perpetual will to render to each one his right."[24] In the subsequent questions, he addresses matters of both political and interpersonal justice, including just rule (government), war, usury (money lending), and backbiting (gossiping). His most noteworthy question for our inquiry, however, is his treatment of the relationship between general justice, which refers both to the comprehensive virtue of justice and legal justice, and to particular justice. Here, Aquinas explains the distinction between general/legal justice and particular justice:

> Legal justice is not essentially the same as every virtue, and beside legal justice which directs man immediately to the common good, there is a need for other virtues to direct him immediately in matters relating to particular goods: and these virtues may be relative to himself or to another individual person. Accordingly, just as in addition to legal justice there is need for particular virtues to direct man in relation to himself, such as temperance and fortitude, so too besides legal justice there is need for particular justice to direct man in relation to other individuals.[25]

Aquinas thus distinguishes between matters of public justice, pertaining immediately to the common good, and matters of private, interpersonal justice, pertaining immediately to other particular goods. Aquinas asserts that there is a fundamental difference between these two types of justice:

> The common good of the realm and the particular good of the individual differ not only in respect of the *many* and the *few*, but also under formal aspect. For the aspect of the *common* good differs from the aspect of the *individual* good, even as the aspect of the *whole* differs from that of *part*. Wherefore the Philosopher [Aristotle] says that *they are wrong who maintain that the State and the home and the like differ only as many and few and not specifically.*[26]

General/legal and particular justice differ in their primary object and thus are not explicitly connected. Aquinas's distinction between general and particular justice thus appears to run counter to the claims of Latina and feminist theologians that the personal and political spheres are integrally connected.

Yet, if we read Aquinas's understanding justice through the lens of his approach to the common good, we see a stronger connection between general/legal and particular justice. This relationship is revealed in his understanding of the relationship between the whole and the part: "we call those legal matters just which are adapted to produce and preserve happiness and its parts for the body politic."[27] The parts of the body politic, or the members of society, are not an afterthought in his conception of justice. The parts do not eclipse the whole, but the whole is nothing without its parts. While legal justice concerns the social body in general and particular justice concerns the members, neither part could function without the other. Examining Aquinas's understanding of justice through the lens of the common good, we can see that the interpersonal interactions that constitute particular justice have a significant effect on the good of society as a whole. The connection between general/legal justice and particular justice supports the argument that public and interpersonal actions mutually condition each other. In other words, our interpersonal actions affect the common good, and it is therefore appropriate to consider the implications of daily practices and experiences, *lo cotidiano*, on the development of the common good. This interpretation of Aquinas's treatment of justice surfaces a useful structure for relating the personal and public aspects of justice through concern for the common good of society. Societal justice demands justice at the level of interpersonal relationships. I develop this claim in the next section.

Toward a Vision of Justice in Latina Theology

Aquinas's understandings of the relationship between general/legal and particular justice is fertile ground for enhancing the conception of justice that arises from Latina relational anthropology. Like Aquinas, the aforementioned Latina theologians observe an integral connection between interpersonal and public, particular and general, justice. Interpersonal relationships are codetermined by our public relationships, and vice versa. To be in right relationship, then, means that human life, dignity, and flourishing are promoted in both spheres. Indeed, flourishing in one sphere is made quite difficult without support from the other. Returning to the situation of WIC funding in Massachusetts, cutting funding is a public and political choice that affects the physical and mental development of particular poor children who do not have access to proper nutrition during their formative years. We see that justice cannot truly be served for the whole without serving justice for the constitutive parts. Thus, a vision of justice emanating from Latina theology asserts the integral connection between personal and political aspects of justice grounded in the fundamental anthropological assertion of human relationality.

The encounter between Thomistic justice theory and Latina theology reveals three important facets of a Latina vision of justice. These implications are a continuation of an on-going conversation on justice, as well as a starting point for a more focused and intentional pursuit of this question in Latina theological ethics. First, interpersonal relationships are foundational for all types of justice. Right relationship is cultivated at the "grassroots" level. We learn the virtue of right relationship through interpersonal contexts—marriage, parenthood, siblinghood, friendship, church, community organization, etc. Forged from the lessons we learn in our lives together, often through offense, error, and misunderstanding, our interpersonal relationships teach us how to recognize and pursue justice on a particular level.

The second implication is that our interpersonal relationships serve as the foundation for public justice. Through our pursuit of right relationship on the level of particular justice, we learn the importance of justice in the general/legal sphere. Further, through public engagement we learn that our own struggles are not isolated from the struggles of other people. We learn that the pursuit of right relationship is a pervasive human characteristic, yet another aspect of our reflection of the *imago Dei*. While the public square is often the site of seemingly intractable conflict and disagreement, it might also serve as a pathway toward concern for the social, economic, and political other. Revealing the breadth and depth of human suffering, the public sphere demonstrates the necessity for righting relationships the level of general/legal justice.

Finally, through analysis of interpersonal and public justice, we can discern the mutual conditioning of these spheres in the pursuit of right relationship. Drawing on the insights of Latina approaches to theological anthropology, we observe that justice (or injustice) in one sphere has an immense effect on the other through the relationship of private justice to the common good. The codetermination of the public and interpersonal spheres ought to influence our concrete ethical practices, moving us to advocate for policies, programs, public officials, and laws that recognize the relationship between *lo cotidiano* and the common good. The "justice-infused" Latina approach to relational anthropology, therefore, forms a strong basis for creating a community characterized by equality, respect for difference, and the perpetual pursuit of right relationships that are the true source of human dignity.

In light of these three implications, how can we begin working toward justice? Drawing on the connection between the personal and the political, Isasi-Díaz suggests that justice is best understood as a reconciliatory process, where conflicting groups move toward right relationship by building and strengthening relationship across difference.[28] The *telos* of this process is not a particular product or outcome; the relationship itself is the goal:

> The work of reconciliation has to recognize that those who have been apart and opposed to each other need to move together, one step at a time, willing to accept that risk, ambiguity, and uncertainty are part of the process. The work of reconciliation asks above all for a commitment to mutuality, to opening possibilities together even if one might never see them become a reality—this over and above a desire for tangible changes.[29]

Here, Isasi-Díaz emphasizes the necessity of relationship in the work of justice. If the Latina emphasis on rich interpersonal relationships has anything to contribute to justice discourse, it is that transformation and reconciliation are possible through building interpersonal bridges. Personal encounter initiates relational transformation with family and community, with nation and world.

Conclusion

Employing Latina anthropological insights and Thomistic conceptions of justice and the common good, I identify a starting point for a positive vision of justice in Latina theology. I outline key contributions to justice from a Latina theological perspective, including the centrality of relational anthropology and the association between personal and political justice. I argue that a vision of justice in Latina theology asserts the integral connection between personal and political aspects of justice grounded in the fundamental anthropological assertion of human relationality. This vision of justice emphasizes intersubjectivity in the pursuit of political justice. I invite Latina theologians, ethicists, activists, and allies to join me in the pursuit of the deep justice insights contained in this particular theological conversation, bringing them to bear on a global pursuit of justice in the twenty-first century.

Notes

1. Cf. Carol Hanisch, "The Personal Is Political," http://www.carolhanisch.org.

2. Michelle A. González, "Who We Are," in *In Our Own Voices: Latino/a Renditions of Theology*, ed. Benjamín Valentín (Maryknoll, NY: Orbis Books, 2010), 64.

3. Ibid., 71–78.

4. Ibid., 75.

5. Ibid., 76.

6. Michelle A. González, *Created in God's Image: An Introduction to Feminist Theological Anthropology* (Maryknoll, NY: Orbis Books, 2007), 118.

7. González, "Who We Are,"73.

8. Gary Riebe-Estrella, "Pueblo and Church," in *From the Heart of Our People*, ed. Orlando O. Espín and Miguel H. Díaz (Maryknoll, NY: Orbis Books, 1999), 173.

9. Roberto Goizueta, *Caminemos Con Jesús: Toward a Hispanic/Latino Theology of Accompaniment* (Maryknoll, NY: Orbis Books, 1995), 72.

10. González, "Who We Are," 75.

11. Mary Catherine Hilkert, "Cry Beloved Image," in *In The Embrace of God: Feminist Approaches to Theological Anthropology*, ed. Ann O'Hara Graff (Maryknoll, NY: Orbis Books, 1995), 199.

12. González, "Who We Are," 76.

13. Cf. Ada María Isasi-Díaz, *En La Lucha: Elaborating a Mujerista Theology* (Minneapolis: Fortress Press, 2004), 23. As defined by Isasi-Díaz, "a *mujerista* is a Hispanic Woman who struggles to liberate herself not as an individual but as a member of the Hispanic community . . . a *mujerista* understands that her task is to gather the hopes and expectations of the people about justice and peace and to work, not for equality within oppressive structures, but for liberation." This definition derives from the engagement of Isasi-Diaz in theological discourse with grassroots Latinas, as well as both feminist and womanist scholars, including Letty Russell and Katie Cannon, who encouraged her to define a particular approach to Latina theology. (Cf. Isasi-Díaz, *La Lucha Continues: Mujerista Theology* (Maryknoll, NY: Orbis Books, 2004), 21. It is noteworthy, however, that few Latinas, including Latinas in academic theology, explicitly identify as *mujerista* theologians. Others identify themselves as Latina feminists or with no particular label at all. *Mujerista* theology is a vital and meaningful movement in Latina theology, but it is inaccurate to identify all Latina theology as *mujerista* theology.

14. Isasi-Díaz, "Elements of a *Mujerista* Anthropology," *In the Embrace of God,* 90.

15. González, "*Nuestra Humanidad*: Toward a Latina Theological Anthropology," *Journal of Hispanic/Latino Theology* 8, no. 3 (2001): 53.

16. Isasi-Díaz, "Elements of a *Mujerista* Anthropology," 91.

17. Ibid.

18. Goizueta, "Fiesta: Life in the Subjective," in *From the Heart of Our People*, 84–99.

19. Isasi-Díaz, "Elements of a *Mujerista* Anthropology," 91.

20. Isasi-Díaz, *En La Lucha*, 24.

21. David Abel, "Child Nutrition Program Faces Cuts," *Boston Globe*, April 16, 2011. http://www.boston.com.

22. Ibid.

23. González, "*Nuestra Humanidad*," 53.

24. Thomas Aquinas, *Summa Theologica*, IIaIIae, q. 58, a. 1.

25. Ibid., IIaIIae, q. 58, a. 7.

26. Ibid., IIaIIae, q. 58, a. 7 (emphasis in original).

27. Ibid., IaIIae, q. 90, a. 2.

28. Isasi-Díaz, *La Lucha Continues*, 219–36.

29. Ibid., 224.

Feminist Contributions to Traditional Moral Knowledge: Rhetorical (Inter)Play of Clerics and Women

Elizabeth Bucar

Introduction

This essay challenges the assumption that authoritarian structures are detrimental to feminist thought by demonstrating the manner in which papal rhetoric provides opportunities for feminist social and political ethics. I look at two women, Diana Hayes and Helen Hitchcock, both of whom are recognizable public intellectuals in the U.S. Catholic context and on different ends of the spectrum of liberal to conservative feminism. I show how they each leverage John Paul II's teachings to make feminist claims unanticipated by the former pope. I identify specific tactics of intellectual engagement—symbolic and embodiment—through which these women redefine the moral conversation for the twenty-first century.

In the twentieth century, the magisterium, particularly John Paul II, addressed women's moral lives with new frequency. While Catholic feminists may not agree with the benefits of the content of this teaching, the rhetoric increased the visibility of women in the World Church, made women's moral lives a legitimate topic of moral debate, and called attention to women's lived experiences as significant sources of moral knowledge. This essay seeks to understand how religious women work within the parameters of clerical rhetoric and yet still produce innovative moral discourse. I use rhetorical analysis, drawing categories from rhetorical studies such as claims, grounds, warrants, and backings.[1]

Rules of the Game

The metaphor of a game is helpful for conceptualizing the moral life within a religious community.[2] Picture a soccer field on which the moral life of the community is "played." The assumptions of many secular feminists is that, given the authority structure of Catholicism, male clerics set the rules for play and act on the field as referees. This would mean that what counts as off-sides, penalty shots, out of bounds, goals, and more in the tradition are conveyed through clerical rhetoric. To some extent then, a Catholic woman's "play" is expected to depend on the clerics' ability to convey the rules, and her success in the moral life will depend on her ability to put the clerical rulebook into practice.

But in fact, upon closer rhetorical inspection, we find this is not a simple story of men creating a game and women playing it out. John Paul II's rhetoric does not turn out to be something that women have to overcome in order to engage in feminist politics. Instead we find an effective feminism that is operating within the parameters of official religious teachings.

Case One:
The Symbolics of Moral Exemplars

The virtues of exceptional women are important for the moral life of ordinary believers in religious communities. Consider how often women in scriptural narratives are referenced in contemporary communities when women's proper roles are discussed. What these various women have in common is that their piety is remembered and retold. The content of their exemplarity is dynamic and evolving, insofar as it is remembered in different ways, in different places, at different times, and by different people. In this way, it is not only the actions of an exemplar, but also how these actions are used discursively to affect our visions of what makes a good woman.

I explore how clerical rhetoric about a role model becomes recast into feminist politics by creating new functions for role models, even while maintaining some of the clerical epistemologies related to exemplarity. Questions considered include the following: How are role models transformed when they are engaged by women versus male clerics? What additional resources do women bring to understanding the politics of exemplarity? What happens when different models are chosen or different attributes of models emphasized?

Mary in Official Rhetoric

Mary is a powerful rhetorical exemplar for John Paul II. He felt he had a special connection to her through his own physical and emotional sufferings,[3] and produced numerous mediations on her role as the Mother of God. For the sake of rhetorical analysis, I consider one section of John Paul II's apostolic letter, *Mulieris Dignitatem* (The Dignity of Women).[4] Published in 1988, this document covers many themes relating to the moral life of women, including Eve, Christ's relationships with women, the reconcilability of virginity and motherhood, and the role of love in a mother's moral life.

This letter was written on the occasion of the Marian Year, and John Paul II devoted the first section to "Woman—Mother of God (*Theotókos*)." He makes two claims related to the moral life. First, Mary's representation of all humankind in the salvific event makes her an exemplar for all people.[5] Although Mary's union with God is not, for John Paul II, merely spiritual, but rather has an embodied component, he describes the physical aspect of the union metaphorically in order to warrant his claim that she is a model for all kinds of gendered bodies. The virgin womb becomes a metaphor for readiness to be filled with God's grace.

At the same time, John Paul II forwards a second claim specific to women in this section of the letter: Mary is an especially important model for women, the "essential horizon of reflection on the dignity and vocation of women."[6] Here, John Paul II argues that Mary's message for women is that motherhood is central to their dignity.

The Bible and the magisterium are the central backing for both claims about Mary as exemplar. John Paul II relies on Genesis for a gendered moral anthropology and the record of Christ's birth in the New Testament (Letter to the Galatians 4:4). In addition, the Second Vatican Council, Pius XII, and John XXIII are mentioned by John Paul II in his introduction to the Apostolic Letter, as having similar concern for the dignity and vocation of women. In terms of John Paul II's understanding of Mary as *theotókos*, the Third Ecumenical Council at Ephesus in 431 is specifically cited.

Refocusing on Hagar
as the Hope of Black Women

In the late twentieth century, efforts from the right and left have tried to make Mary, respectively, more and less important in church teaching. Prominent conservative Catholics, including New York's Cardinal John O'Connor, petitioned John Paul II to declare Mary, in cooperation with Jesus, co-redemptrix of humanity. Although John Paul II had referred to Mary as co-redemptrix, he refused to make this belief dogma. At the same time, some women stepped up their critiques of Mary as an unobtainable model of moral perfection. What both these actions have in common is a strategic attempt to change the logic of Mary's exemplarity: either elevating her status theologically beyond a moral exemplar or eradicating it. In contrast, my concern in this section is how women remain within the logic of clerical use of moral exemplars and still recast what this exemplarity means.

An example of an expositor of this tactical middle ground is Diana Hayes, currently a professor of systematic theology at the Jesuit-run Georgetown University and the first African American woman to receive the Pontifical Doctor of Sacred Theology degree from the Catholic University of Louvain, Belgium. Hayes is well known for her pioneering work as a womanist theologian. "Womanist," a term originally coined by Alice Walker, is used by black feminists and feminists of color as an alternative to the term "feminist." According to Hayes, a womanist's goal is more expansive than a feminist goal. A womanist seeks liberation, "not simply for herself but for all of her people and, beyond that, for all who are also oppressed by reason of race, sex, and/or class."[7] Womanists are interested in oppression and understand oppression to arise out of a matrix of origins and to take a variety of forms.[8]

In addition to being a womanist, and thus locating herself within black feminist theology, Hayes is Catholic, and situates herself within the history of the American Catholic Church. She gives special attention to the church's historical role in justifying slavery.[9]

I consider two claims made by Hayes, which serve as responses to John Paul II's vision of Mary as a moral exemplar for woman. The first claim is that a womanist perspective changes the moral exemplarity of Mary. In her 1998 essay, "And When We Speak," Hayes makes the claim, similar to John Paul II's, that Mary is a role model,[10] but her grounds are very different. It is not Mary's role as *theotókos*, God bearer, which makes her a moral exemplar for women, but rather (1) her status as oppressed, poor, marginalized, and an unwed pregnant woman; and (2) the strength of her faith, which breaks through the limitations put on her by society. Instead of John Paul II's use of the warrant that God's grace perfects her nature, Hayes' claim is warranted by the fact that aspects of Mary's life resonate with black women's experiences. In Hayes' reading, Mary becomes a vision of hope in the context of struggle and a model for black women as the vessel, quite literally, for the future black church.

When Hayes was asked to give the Saint Mary's College Madeleva Lecture in 1995,[11] it was Hagar, and not Mary, whom Hayes chose as a model for black Catholic women. In this lecture, entitled "Hagar's Daughters: Womanist Ways of Being in the World," Hayes claims, "We are the daughters . . . of Hagar, the rejected and cast-out slave, mother of Ishmael, concubine of Abraham and threat to Sarah, his barren wife."[12]

Hagar, which sounds like the Hebrew ha-ger or "the outsider," is the Egyptian slave-woman of Sarai, wife of Abram, whose story is found in Genesis 16 and 21.[13] When Sarai has difficulty conceiving a child, she suggests that Abram use Hagar as a surrogate. When Hagar does become pregnant, Sarai feels her position in the household is threatened. Sarai begins to treat Hagar very poorly until Hagar decides to run away from her masters. At this point, an angel visits the pregnant Hagar and commands her to return to Sarai and Abram,[14] which she does, and gives birth to her son Ishmael. Years later, Sarai also conceives and bears a son, Isaac. She comes to perceive Ishmael as a threat to her son, and urges Abram to banish Hagar and Ishmael. Hagar and Ishmael are cast out into the desert without adequate provisions but saved from death by a direct intervention by God, who proclaims a great future for Ishmael: "Arise, lift up the boy, and hold your hand on him, for I will make him a great nation." (Gen. 21:18). Ishmael goes on to found a community in Mecca.[15]

Hayes anticipates her audience's confusion over Hagar as a role model: "Why Hagar, you ask?"[16] Hayes acknowledges that, in the biblical account, Hagar is in many ways passive, and that her story is often read as one of surrogacy.[17] Nevertheless, she provides three reasons for Hagar as moral exemplar. First, Hagar is triply oppressed.[18] As a slave, she is oppressed for her race. As a concubine, she is oppressed for her gender. Hayes gives particular attention to Hagar's oppression based on her class at the hands of Sarai, who "lost sight of the reality that she and Hagar had more in common as women in that society than 'that which divided them as Hebrew master and Egyptian slave woman.'"[19] In this way, Hayes reminds us of how white women have exploited black women through our historic "inability to recognize our shared commonalities and rejoice in our differences."[20] Models that do not account for differences among women in the same way can be exploitative.

A second ground for Hagar as a womanist model is that she has suffered. Hagar is enslaved, forced to serve as concubine, mistreated by Sarai, and finally abandoned in the desert by her masters. For Hayes, this abandonment is shared by Catholic African Americans, who are disregarded by the church, where they are invisible "outsiders-within,"[21] and neglected by white feminists and black Protestants. When Hayes speaks about her background and experience, she makes clear that she feels this abandonment on a very personal level.[22]

The final ground for Hagar as a moral exemplar is the fact of her survival and manner in which she survives. Hayes argues, "God reaches out to Hagar in her abandonment and provides her with 'new vision to see survival resources where she had seen none before' . . . and as Hagar learned how to survive and acquire an 'appropriate quality of life' for herself and her son, so also did the African slaves."[23] Not only does Hagar not perish in the desert, through what Hayes calls "direct contact" with God, she gains new hope and is able to realize a full life, in a context when the ability to flourish seemed impossible. This is similar to the experience of African Americans, according to Hayes:

> It is our experience, not as victims, but as survivors, that is the foundation for the renewal of the Black community. Like Hagar, we have been harshly used in this world yet we have found strength in ourselves and in our faith in a God who fights on the side of the oppressed and we have continued to "move on up a little higher."[24]

The move from these three grounds (Hagar as oppressed, abandoned, and yet a survivor) to Hagar as a womanist model is warranted on a number of levels. For example, Hayes implies that there is a difference between white and black values, a statement she has made explicitly elsewhere.[25] So while Mary, as a model of moral perfection, might work for some women, African American women need a model that provides hope for survival within difficult, externally imposed, circumstances. Hayes suggests that it is not the heroines, but rather the tragic figures of the Bible who may provide better models of women's moral lives. The warrant that moral exemplars must reflect contemporary experience is also operative in Hayes' rhetoric. Hagar is a role model because her story resonates with black women. The concrete, particular experiences of women, and not biblical stories, are the starting point of Hayes' ethics. This leads to another warrant operative in Hayes' rhetoric: the Roman Catholic Church has something to learn from the experience of black women. Black women's authenticity as Catholics is "worthy not only of being preserved but also of being shared with the Church as a whole."[26]

In addition to the biblical story of Hagar, Hayes backs her claim with the black literary tradition, especially the work of Alice Walker and Toni Morrison, "as a source for discovering and recovering the spiritual values and voice of Black women."[27] This is very similar to the way literature has been a central source for Protestant womanists such as Katie Cannon.[28]

Hayes' discursive performance can be considered as citational of John Paul II in several ways. They share the claim that Mary is a significant moral exemplar for women, grounded by her place at the center of the major Christian salvific event. But, in terms of the components of informal argumentation, that is where the similarity ends. Ignoring John Paul II's additional ground of Mary as the bearer of God, Hayes provides two of her own: Mary's status as an oppressed, unwed mother, and her ability to do more than society thought she could. In contrast to the facts about Mary that John Paul II invokes, which are highly theological, Hayes relies on Mary's concrete actions. The emphasis on Mary's role as mother is also shifted from a literal bearer of God to a mother who struggles to pass on tradition under difficult circumstance. If John Paul II is concerned with conceiving and birthing the child, Hayes focuses on Mary's survival, the survival of her child, and the survival of the new Christian community.

Another major shift in Hayes' rhetoric is her trumpeting Hagar as the quintessential female biblical exemplar. Both John Paul II and Hayes look to the Bible for a moral exemplar, but the choice of Hagar requires radically different grounds (Hagar as oppressed, abandoned, and a survivor). On a general level, picking a moral exemplar like Hagar, instead of Mary, recasts the goal of the role model, and by extension the moral life, in a different light. While Mary is perfection, Hagar is resourceful under difficult circumstances. The selection of Hagar as a model implies a vision of the moral life that stresses realistic goals under difficult circumstances rather than perfect piety.

The warrants that authorize this shift are where we can most clearly see what is at stake for Hayes in her response to John Paul II's rhetoric. While John Paul II is concerned with speaking to all of women, Hayes insists on differences between women, especially based on race: Hagar is the model for black women. This complicates John Paul II's vision of women as a cohesive group, as defined by natural law. Hayes' emphasis on the difference between women means not only will the Roman Catholic Church have to work hard to acknowledge and include black women but also black women's exemplars, so long neglected, which, according to Hayes, have something to teach the magisterium about womanhood.

Case Two:
Women's Bodies in Public Spaces

The issue of ordination has been a concern of a number of Catholic reform movements in the United States, and there are various types of responses to clerical rhetoric on the issue, including two direct rebuttals. One rebuttal argues for entry of women in the priesthood based on gender equality (confirmed through baptism) and on the recuperation of support for women's ordination in church tradition (historically, women have been ordained into the deaconate, most recently during the Communist period).[29] A second response moves beyond ordination to a new understanding of the church, emphasizing what Elisabeth Schüssler Fiorenza calls "the discipleship of equals."[30] This rhetoric aims to change the hierarchy of the Roman Catholic Church, not merely to inject women into the level of priests, citing that ordination of women in other denominations has not removed all barriers to women's equal participation or prevented sexist teachings on moral matters. Some women in this camp have focused on establishing alternative women's liturgy groups.[31] I find both these arguments rich, but as direct responses they are strategic rather than tactical, insofar as they try to refute, rather than work within, clerical logic. Here, I focus on a different sort of response to the ordination from the right, one that affirms a male-exclusive priesthood. I argue that even this tactical response reworks some of the clerical logic of the ban on women's ordination, even if not intentionally. At stake are the public conceptualization, display, and work of women's bodies.

Women's Exclusion from Priesthood in Official Rhetoric

In 1994, John Paul II issued *Ordinatio Sacerdotalis*,[32] in which he claimed (1) the Roman Catholic Church does not have the authority to ordain women[33] and (2) women's exclusion from the priestly vocation is not a form of discrimination.[34] With the first claim, John Paul II shifted the focus of the conversation about ordination from "should women be priests?" to "could the church ordain women, even if it wanted to?" John Paul II articulated three primary grounds that he called "fundamental reasons" for this first claim, drawing from Paul VI's earlier statement on the issue: (1) the first apostles were all men; (2) the Roman Catholic Church has always exclusively ordained men; and (3) the Roman Catholic Church has always taught that only men can be ordained. In addition to these three grounds found in Paul VI's statement, John Paul II added a fourth: the Eastern churches do not ordain women.

A number of warrants helps connect these grounds to the claim. For example, the Roman Catholic Church has only the authority to do what it has done before: what Christ has done, what the church has practiced and taught. Therefore, since the priesthood is a continuation of the Apostolic Tradition, what the apostles were in the beginning (male), as well as the tradition of ordaining priests to serve the function of apostles, becomes evidence for why women cannot be ordained. Another warrant implied is the importance of Catholic unity, since the Eastern churches' nonordination of women is used as a ground for why the Roman Catholic Church has no authority to ordain women. A final warrant John Paul II explicitly offers is that his grounds indicate some of the contours of "God's eternal plan"; a plan must be followed to the extent it can be understood.

A second claim in the letter is that women's exclusion from the priesthood is not a form of discrimination against women by the Roman Catholic Church. This is grounded, like the first claim, in the fact that Christ selected only male apostles and in the presumption that Christ's example is an egalitarian one. If Christ did not select female apostles, such exclusion cannot be discriminatory.[35]

John Paul II's backing for these warrants is located in the scriptural record of Christ's selection of only men as his apostles, the writings on Paul VI,[36] the statements of the Congregation for the Doctrine of the Faith,[37] and the Catechism of the Catholic Church,[38] as well as his own moral teaching in *Mulieris Dignitatem* and *Christifideles Laici*.

Implementing Moral Leadership
beyond the Pulpit

This section focuses on the rhetoric of "Affirmation for Catholic Women," a statement of "fidelity to church teachings,"[39] which Helen Hitchcock, along with six other women, drafted in 1984, and on Hitchcock's essay "Women for Faith and Family,"[40] which describes the process of turning this statement into a petition, and the activities of the organization that resulted.

Hitchcock is a former Protestant journalist who converted to Catholicism in 1984,[41] the same year she founded Women for Faith and Family and helped to draft the Affirmation. In this statement Hitchcock and others pledged their "wholehearted support to Pope John Paul II" and affirmed "his apostolic teaching concerning all aspects of family life and roles for men and women in the Church and in society."[42] Hitchcock formed the organization Women for Faith and Family (WFF) to collect signatures of support for this statement. In 1985, 10,000 names were presented to John Paul II. This number doubled by 1986 and is currently at 50,000, although all references to John Paul II were changed to Benedict XVI in 2005.[43]

The Affirmation includes a paragraph supporting the Roman Catholic ban on women's ordination, which is the first claim I consider. The relevant paragraph reads in its entirety as follows:

> We therefore also reject as an aberrant innovation peculiar to our times and our society the notion that priesthood is the "right" of any human being, male or female. Furthermore, we recognize that the specific role of ordained priesthood is intrinsically connected with and representative of the begetting creativity of God in which only human males can participate. Human females, who by nature share in the creativity of God by their capacity to bring forth new life, and, reflective of this essential distinction, have a different and distinct role within the Church and in society from that accorded to men, can no more be priests than men can be mothers.[44]

Although issued ten years before John Paul II's apostolic letter, the claim is nevertheless the same: women cannot and should not be ordained. But unlike John Paul II, who draws to a large extent on Paul VI's argument for women's exclusion from the priesthood, Hitchcock focuses on two different grounds in the Affirmation. First, there is the ground that ordination is not a right based on competence or merit, but rather a vocation bestowed by God. Women do not have a right to any vocation. This is an implicit critique of some feminists' use of rights-based language in attempts to reform theological issues, an enterprise Hitchcock finds inappropriate. The second ground she provides is that a priest must be a man because only a man can represent the "begetting creativity of God." In contrast, women represent the "birthing creativity of God." This draws on a strict vocational gender distinction based on the embodied physical differences between the sexes.

Hitchcock relies on two warrants in her rhetoric. One warrant is the general importance of conserving Catholic tradition in a current atmosphere of dissent.[45] A second warrant is the necessity of supporting John Paul II's moral teaching as a good Catholic. Her argument is backed by the sheer number of women who signed her petition. She writes, "No petition of dissent in the postconciliar era, including the highly publicized statement of dissent from *Humanae Vitae* in 1968, has attracted comparable response."[46] Her claim is also backed by John Paul II's acceptance of the statement and petition. In her organization's newsletter, Hitchcock writes that she delivered the Affirmation and petition to John Paul II during a 1985 papal audience, and upon receiving the packet, John Paul II said, "God bless the women of the United States."[47] It is noteworthy that John Paul II is rhetorically invoked both as warrant and backing.

Before demonstrating how Hitchcock, perhaps unintentionally, shifts John Paul II's rhetoric on ordination, I want to consider a second claim in Hitchcock's essay about her organization, WFF. This claim can be found in the organization's mission statement: "to serve as a channel through which questions from Catholic women seeking guidance or information can be directed."[48] Although Hitchcock uses the word "channel" to describe WFF's activities, its actual work makes it more of a source than channel: WFF answers letters and mail directly, organizes volunteers to conduct any necessary research, and only occasionally consults with other individuals or organizations for their expertise.[49] It is intriguing that, in Hitchcock's description about this dimension of her organization's work, there is no attempt to link it to papal or other magisterial teachings about women. The reason why WFF began offering direct responses to Catholic women on moral issues is the fact that women approached WFF and asked them for such advice. Hitchcock writes,

> What began as a way to show support by Catholic women for church teachings about women and family quickly grew beyond this relatively limited goal; response to the needs of women led to a continually expanding set of initiatives. It soon became apparent to Women for Faith

and Family's organizers that its original aim—to communicate information from Catholic women to the bishops—was only one means of
serving the church and women. . . . Women for Faith and Family receives
many letters and telephone calls from women requesting assistance and
information of various kinds, as well as advice and encouragement. These
communications typically ask for help in addressing problems with religious and/or moral education affecting their children in Catholic schools
or raise questions about church doctrine and discipline which affect the
life and worship of every Catholic; but there are also many requests for
help on matters such as family, marriage, or spiritual problems.[50]

The move from the ground (women asked us) to the claim (so we needed to
respond) is warranted by the assumption that laywomen are responsible to serve
as resources to other laywomen and backed by the practical need for a direct service
that WFF is able to provide. In Hitchcock's words, "we are sensitive to the deep
desire on the part of many Catholic women for a doctrinally reliable and spiritually
nourishing source of companionship and mutual support."[51]

Given the organization's other activities in regards to the *Affirmation,* Hitchcock appears to think that simply providing advice to women on moral matters
is equivalent to supplying reasons why women cannot be ordained. This suggests
that there is something distinctly male about priestly leadership and something
distinctly female about a community of "companionship and mutual support."
Note how similar this is to Schüssler Fiorenza's more radical claim from the left:
a discipleship of equals (women in sisterly solidarity) is an alternative and better
model to the present hierarchy. My point is not that Hitchcock is making a similar
claim, but rather that she promotes the benefit of women-centered communities,
especially on moral matters.

Hitchcock affirms the same claims made by John Paul II: a Catholic ban on
women's ordination and a critique of the interpretation of this ban as gender discrimination. Her goal in the Affirmation is to perfectly reiterate John Paul II's teachings,
and she uses John Paul II as a warrant and backing in her rhetoric. But this reiteration
is creative and shifts the logic of John Paul II's rhetoric in significant ways.

One major shift is in the grounds Hitchcock provides for the ban on women's
ordination. She does not link priesthood directly to the original twelve apostles as
John Paul II does, but instead, she focuses on priesthood as a vocation bestowed
by God and the theological rationale for why only men can represent the begetting of creation. If John Paul II's grounds are primarily historical, Hitchcock's are
theological. While John Paul II's statement on ordination is made chronologi-
cally after Hitchcock's, the source for his grounds, Paul VI's 1975 statement on
the issue,[52] was available to Hitchcock. The fact that she does not use Paul VI's
historical grounds could be considered an implicit critique of John Paul II's later
rhetoric. Perhaps she finds these grounds inadequate or believes they are vulnerable to rebuttal. Even if a shift is not intended by Hitchcock, she moves the game

of debate onto a different field and opens up new opportunities for theological responses to Catholic ban on women's ordination.

A second shift from John Paul II in Hitchcock's rhetorical performance is her slide from the ordination issue to a need to respond directly to women's moral concerns. Hitchcock's organization, founded to affirm papal teachings, evolves into a direct service organization (WFF), where volunteers read, assess, research, and respond to women's moral inquiries. This is an implicit critique of clerical moral guidance. WFF does this work because there is a need for it; women are not getting adequate advice from the official pastoral activities of the Roman Catholic Church to live fully moral lives. Through this work, they have also bypassed the need for ordination by creating a women-centered practice of ethical reflection. In some ways, this can be seen as a more radical move than ordaining women, because it moves ethical work from the clergy class to laywomen who have no formal training and who base their advice on their own experiences as Catholic women. In this way Hitchcock uses the clerical logic of institutional hierarchy to make an argument about the moral guidance that is not hierarchical at all.

Conclusion

In this essay, I have juxtaposed John Paul II's and women's arguments about moral exemplars and ordination in order to isolate feminist contributions to moral knowledge. In doing so, it has become clear that these women employ some components of clerical rhetoric and shift others in new ways. Some of these women argue for the same claims (Mary is a moral exemplar, women have no right to be ordained). Some of the clerical grounds are deployed by these women (the role of Mary in the salvific event, hierarchy is not discriminatory), and they use similar backings (biblical and clerical authority).

Even as women conform to some of the components of clerical rhetoric, they demonstrate creativity by shifting the arguments. I identity this creativity as Catholic feminist ethics. These feminist contributions can be grouped into three categories. First, women recombine logical components of papal rhetoric to make claims unanticipated by papal teachings. Second, women engage in rule making for judging proper moral action, especially when they determine that clerical teachings create obstacles for their moral lives. Finally, feminists change the very nature of ethical knowledge in the modern church by using the physical experience of womanhood to gain traction in debates about counts as ethical knowledge. In these ways, leading Catholic feminists work within the tradition (versus rebelling against it). In fact, they guarantee the survival of the tradition by integrating new ideas and experiences.

Returning to the metaphor of the game, while initial assumptions may have been that male clerics determine the game of the moral life for women in the Catholic tradition, in fact, both laywomen and male clerics participate in deciding the parameters of the field (what counts as ethical knowledge), the rules of play (how to judge ethical action), and even the very nature of the game itself (how tradition informs contemporary action). This is an important insight into the production of ethical knowledge within the community. While one might initially assume that clerics are producing moral rhetoric and women merely responding, in truth the situation is more complicated that a simple hierarchy. Both engage in the rhetorical augmentation aimed at persuading the community about the moral life. Both interpret the tradition. Both construct and respond to discourse; and the clerics do not merely observe from the sidelines, since they are also on the field engaged in rhetorical exchange about the moral life, getting muddied shoes and grass-stained knees.

This can be pushed even further. We can assert that what counts as morality is a social invention and that authority is merely the agreed-upon normative apparatus of the group. This is not to say that there is no ethical truth. In fact, the members of the group who care about moral knowledge (the soccer players or the religious believers), "treat inquiry into the truth-value of such claims as an objective affair, to be settled by the testimony of trustworthy eyewitnesses, the evidence of instant-replay videos, and so forth."[53] Rhetoric, then, becomes the way the truth status of normative claims gets worked out.

Notes

1. For an accessible introduction to informal argumentation, see Stephen Toulmin, Richard Rieke, and Allan Janik, *An Introduction to Philosophy* (New York: Macmillan, 1984).

2. Jeffery Stout shows how the game metaphor demonstrates that ethics in a democracy is a social practice, aims at objective truth, and involves a symmetrical relation between moral agents. Robert Brandom, whom Stout draws on, uses the metaphor of a game throughout his work to show how the meaning of an expression is determined by how it is used in inferences. Jeffrey Stout, *Democracy and Tradition* (Princeton, NJ: Princeton University Press, 2004), 270–86. Robert Brandom, *Making It Explicit: Reasoning, Representing, and Discursive Commitment* (Cambridge, MA: Harvard University Press, 1994).

3. John Paul II felt that his experience with illness, accidents, an assassination attempt, and loss of close friends and family connected him in an intimate way to the Virgin Mary. One of John Paul II's biographers, Tad Szulc, writes, "John Paul II is convinced, in a most mystical fashion, that he, too, has been chosen for suffering and martyrdom. He believes that the Virgin Mary, whom he deeply venerates...has saved his life on many occasion as well as having taught him how to suffer." Tad Szulc, *Pope John Paul II: The Biography* (New York: Scribner, 1995), 30. This seems to be confirmed by the Pope's own statements. For example, after a month long hospital stay for broken hip his first public comments are "through Mary I would like to express my gratitude today for this gift of suffering." Ibid.

4. John Paul II, *Mulieris Dignitatem*.

5. Ibid., paras. 3–4.

6. Ibid., para. 5.

7. She continues, "Sexism is not the only issue; rarely is it the most important issue. Rather, it is the intertwined evil emanating from the multiplicative effect of all of these which act to restrict her and her community that are the cause for her concern." Diana

Hayes, *And Still We Rise: An Introduction to Black Liberation Theology* (New York: Paulist Press, 1996), 140.

8. Hayes identifies Delores Williams, Jacquelyn Grant, Katie Cannon, Emilie Townes, Renita Weems, Cheryl Saunders, and Kelly Brown Douglas as Protestant womanists, and Shawn Copeland, Jamie Phelps, Toinette Eugene, and herself as Catholic womanists. Ibid., 141.

9. In 1452, Nicholas V gave permission to the Kings of Spain and Portugal to enslave pagans. Alexander VI extended this to the Americas in 1493. As late as 1866, the magisterium declared that slavery was not contrary to natural law. It was not until 2002 that John Paul II made a public apology for the church's role in justifying the slave trade. The ordination of black men and their leadership in other forms was not encouraged until the twentieth century, demonstrating internal institutional racism. Cyprian Davis, *The History of Black Catholics in the United States* (New York: Crossroad, 1990).

10. Diana Hayes, "And When We Speak," in *Taking Down Our Harps: Black Catholics in the United States*, ed. D. Hayes and C. Davis (Maryknoll, New York: Orbis Books, 1998), 113–14. Hayes has made similar statements elsewhere about Mary, most recently in Diana Hayes, "Black Catholics in the United States: A Subversive Memory," in *Many Faces, One Church: Cultural Diversity and the American Catholic Experience*, ed. P. Phan and D. Hayes (New York: Rowman & Littlefield, 2005), 57.

11. "The Madeleva Lectures series annually commemorates the opening of the Center for Spirituality of Saint Mary's College, Notre Dame, Indiana, and honors the memory of the woman who inaugurated the college's pioneering program in theology, Sister Madeleva, C.S.C." Front matter, Diana Hayes, *Hagar's Daughters: Womanist Ways of Being in the World* (New York: Paulist Press, 1995).

12. Ibid., 6.

13. My understanding of the account of Hagar in Genesis 16 and 21 is greatly informed by Tikva Frymer-Kensky and the biblical translations I use in this section are hers. Tikva Frymer-Kensky, "Hagar, My Other, My Self," in *Reading the Women of the Bible* (New York: Schocken Books, 2002), 225–37.

14. "The angel of YHWH said to her, 'Return to your mistress and be oppressed under her hand'" (Gen. 16:10).

15. Hagar is a particularly interesting role model because Hagar also holds an important place in Islamic narratives. Hagar, or Hajār in Arabic and Persian, founds the Islamic civilization in Mecca by bringing Ishmael there and finding him a wife. Muslims consider Ishmael a fully legitimate son of Abraham who inherited his line of prophethood; the Prophet Muhammad is a direct descendent of Ishmael and Hajār.

16. Hayes, *Hagar's Daughters*, 6.

17. Ibid., 6–7.

18. Ibid., 8.

19. Ibid., 7.

20. Ibid., 6.

21. Hayes writes, "Black Catholics have been invisible both to those inside and outside the Roman Catholic Church." Hayes, "And When We Speak," 108.

22. "All too often in that struggle [to find myself], my greatest challenge came from my own—Black men and women or white women—who distrusted my efforts and sought to impede my self-emancipation for reasons of their own. Thus, my struggle was two-sided. It involved the white world, that dominant structure which sought to label and thereby

suppress my voice and my own world, that of African-Americans, who often saw me as a traitor to the race, as well as to Protestant Christianity." Hayes, *Hagar's Daughters*, 43–44.

23. Ibid., 60.

24. Ibid.

25. See Hayes, "And When We Speak," 113; Diana Hayes, "To Be Black, Catholic, and Female," *New Theology Review* (May 1993): 52–62; and Diana Hayes, "My Hope Is in the Lord: Transformation and Salvation in the African American Community," in *Embracing the Spirit: Womanist Perspectives on Hope, Transformation and Salvation*, ed. E. Townes (Maryknoll, NY: Orbis Books, 1997).

26. Hayes, "Black Catholics in the United States: A Subversive Memory," 55.

27. Hayes, *Hagar's Daughters*, 33–34.

28. Katie Cannon, *Black Womanist Ethics* (Eugene, OR: Wipf & Stock, 1988).

29. Women who make this type of argument include Joy Barnes, Mary Ramerman, and Joan Chittister. For further background, see Angela Bonavoglia, *Good Catholic Girls: How Women Are Leading the Fight to Change the Church* (New York: ReganBooks, 2005), 239–52, and Mary Jo Weaver, *New Catholic Women: A Contemporary Challenge to Traditional Religious Authority* (Bloomington: Indiana University Press, 1995), 109–18.

30. Elizabeth Schüssler Fiorenza, *But She Said: Feminist Practices of Biblical Interpretation* (Boston: Beacon Press, 1992), 20.

31. Ibid.

32. John Paul II, *Ordinatio Sacerdotalis*.

33. Ibid., para. 1. John Paul II is here quoting Paul VI, "Response to the Letter of His Grace the Most Reverend Dr. F. D. Coggan, Archbishop of Canterbury, concerning the Ordination of Women to the Priesthood" (November 30, 1975).

34. John Paul II, *Ordinatio Sacerdotalis*, para. 3.

35. Note that this was not explicitly part of the argument in the earlier *Inter Insigniores* justification for the ban on women's ordination.

36. Ibid.; Paul VI, "Address on the Role of Women in the Plan of Salvation (Jan. 30, 1977)," *Insegnamenti*, 15 (1977).

37. Congregation for the Doctrine of the Faith, *Declaration Inter Insigniores on the question of the Admission of Women to the Ministerial Priesthood* (Vatican City: Vatican Polyglot Press, 1976).

38. *Catechism of the Catholic Church*, no. 1577.

39. Helen Hull Hitchcock, "Appendix A.I: Affirmation for Catholic Women," in *Being Right: Conservative Catholics in America*, ed. M. J. Weaver and R. S. Appleby (Bloomington: Indiana University Press, 1995), 177–78.

40. Helen Hull Hitchcock, "Women for Faith and Family: Catholic Women Affirming Catholic Teaching," in *Being Right: Conservative Catholics in America*, 163–76.

41. Hitchcock's conversion story is published as part of a larger collection in Robert Baram, *Spiritual Journeys* (Boston: Daughters of St. Paul Press, 1987).

42. Hitchcock, "Affirmation," 178.

43. The number of signers is according to the Women for Faith and Family website, http://www.wf-f.org/.

44. Hitchcock, "Affirmation," 178.

45. Ibid., 166.

46. Ibid., 168.

47. Helen Hitchcock, "Ten Thousand Names Presented to Pope John Paul II," *Women for Faith and Family Newsletter* 1, no. 1 (August 1985): 4.

48. Hitchcock, "Women for Faith and Family," 166.

49. Hitchcock describes the work of WFF as follows: "The volunteer staff responds to these requests. In 1994, at this writing, three volunteers spend one day a week in the 'mailroom' in one woman's home, answering letters and fulfilling routine requests for WFF publications . . . occasionally a request may involve research and/or consultation with or referral to other individuals or organizations with appropriate expertise. Most research, when necessary, can be done in the office library or nearby university libraries, or via computer-accessible resources." Ibid., 169.

50. Ibid., 168–69.

51. Ibid., 171.

52. Paul VI, "Response to the Letter of His Grace the Most Reverend Dr. F. D. Coggan."

53. Stout, *Democracy and Tradition*, 272.

Getting Ready for Voice Lessons: Toward a Catholic Feminist Ethics of Spirituality

Anne E. Patrick

This is not an easy time to be a Catholic. It is an easy time to be discouraged and to withdraw from the community fully or partially, to exercise the option of "exit" in response to disillusionment with the institution. And it is a very easy time in which to exercise an angry and resentful "voice." Both of these responses are understandable. Neither is a particularly constructive option, consistent with our baptismal calling or with the long-term good of the Christian community. Instead, I believe we need to be developing a loyal voice, imagining and bringing into being the church that God would have us live in, in this place, in these times.[1]

Just as human relationships are or ought to be governed by certain norms or ethical principles—in particular, norms of justice; so also, institutional frameworks for commitment in human relationships ought to be subject to norms of justice. If they are not, we challenge or forsake them, or we shrivel up within them.[2]

Introduction

These passages from eminent U.S. Roman Catholic thinkers frame the considerations I will raise here about the tendency to compare "religion" unfavorably with "spirituality," thereby justifying the relinquishment of church involvement. Social policy expert Mary Jo Bane (quoted first), a professor at Harvard University's Kennedy School of Government, recognizes the appeal that withdrawal from Catholicism has for many Americans, but instead she advocates developing a "loyal voice." Such a voice, she maintains, is "attentive to revelation and respectful of tradition but also confidently prophetic and visionary and as radical as the voice of the One who lives in the church forever."[3] Theological ethicist Margaret A. Farley, for decades a professor at Yale University Divinity School, wrote the words quoted above (second) about the institution of marriage, but they are applicable as well to other institutional contexts in which Catholics discern what God is calling us to do, including the church itself. Farley summarizes the options well: challenging injustice in our institutions, leaving these institutions, or "shriveling up" within them.

In what follows, I advocate developing an "ethics of spirituality," something that is preliminary to the construction of an "ethics of church participation," a project too large to begin here.[4] Such new foci for ethical reflection are, I believe, important for the well-being of Catholicism in the United States and perhaps elsewhere as well. As a first step, I object to the tendency to oppose spirituality to religion, which may be contributing to the diminishment of one of the chief resources of our tradition, namely, the idealistic and energetic young persons who were raised as Catholics but are easily disillusioned by the ineptitude, sins, and scandals that abound in our leaders, members, and structures. It cannot be a matter of indifference to theological ethics, especially in a World Church, if the next generation of American Catholics lacks the loyal, prophetic voices that Bane advocates, or opts for leaving the church or shriveling up within it instead of calling Catholicism to live up to its ideals, as Farley's words suggest is preferable. Below, then, I first describe the sociological context in which I object to the uncritical opposition of religion and spirituality. I then critique a popular articulation of this opposition and argue that, instead of idealizing spirituality at the expense of religion, it is important to ask the same moral questions of both secular and religious forms of spirituality. Finally, I propose several qualities of character that both types would do well to foster and commend perspectives that value both religion and spirituality.

The Rise of the "Nones" and the
Spirituality-Religion Dichotomy

In the last half-century, the shift of emphasis from an ethic of obedience to an ethic of responsibility has meant that contemporary Catholics are generally more willing to look critically at the institutional contexts of their lives than were believers of the mid-twentieth century, at least in the United States.[5] Indeed, many have been critical enough to leave the church entirely, so that by 2007, "former Catholics" comprised 10 percent of the U.S. population, outnumbering nearly all religious denominations except the groups that still identified themselves as Catholic or Baptist. Nearly half of these former Catholics joined Protestant groups, a small number joined other religions, and about half claimed no religious affiliation.[6]

There is every indication that the trend toward disaffiliation will increase, as a 2012 study by the Pew Research Center has shown. In their report, "'Nones' on the Rise: One-in-Five Adults Have No Religious Affiliation," researchers found that 34 percent of Americans born during 1990–94 checked "none" on a survey inquiring about religious affiliation, in contrast to only 5 percent of the generation born during 1913–27. The 2012 survey also showed that for the first time in U.S. history, Protestant Christians comprise less than half of the adult population, and while Catholics have remained "roughly steady" at about one-fourth of the population, an influx of immigrants from Latin America has masked the loss of many U.S.-born Catholics. Although the United States remains a "highly religious" country in comparison with European democracies, the recent survey indicates that it is becoming markedly less so, and Catholicism is rapidly losing members, especially younger ones. It is important to note that the decline in religious affiliation among Americans is happening mainly among *white* adults, while Americans of African and Hispanic-Latino descent are generally remaining religiously affiliated, though whether this will continue to be the case is uncertain.

The overall trend is clear. According to the 2012 study, the number of Americans who declare "none" when asked about their religious identity has risen to 46 million, nearly 20 percent of the adult population, compared to just over 15 percent in 2007, and "below 10% from the 1970s through the early 1990s." Current statistics for adults younger than thirty are even more striking, with one-third of them "religiously unaffiliated." Nevertheless, although they do not identify with a religion, "many of the country's 46 million unaffiliated adults are religious or spiritual in some way," with 68 percent saying they believe in God, 58 percent affirming feelings of "deep connection with nature and the earth," and 21 percent acknowledging they pray daily. Of particular interest here are the facts that 37 percent of the 46 million religiously unaffiliated Americans "*classify themselves as 'spiritual' but not 'religious'*" and "*74% of them were raised in a religious tradition*" (emphasis added).[7] What factors allow, encourage, or justify this trend? Is it a trend that Catholic ethicists should be doing anything about? As interpreters of our moral tradition, should we merely observe or lament the loss, perhaps regarding it as inevitable given the state of church governance today, or should we be asking what can be done about it?

When I consider this trend toward disaffiliation of U.S. Catholics from the perspective of the World Church, I am deeply troubled. Despite its problems, institutional Catholicism has been a vessel of the gospel for our culture, and I do not see other institutions capable of challenging our racism, individualism, and consumerism, or calling us to love our different and distant neighbors as ourselves, with anything like the power that the church, at its best, can exert. Undoubtedly the reasons for the decline in Catholic affiliation are many and complex, but two factors are especially important for feminists, whether women or men. One involves the situation of injustice that Farley emphasizes, since church practice has not kept pace with the rhetoric of women's equal human dignity used in recent decades by popes and bishops. A second factor involves the anti-institutional bias that has been a recurrent theme in American culture and is especially pronounced today. Catholics discerning what God is asking of them today conduct this discernment within a social context that regards both government and religion with considerably more skepticism than prevailed at the time of the Second Vatican Council. I believe this anti-institutional bias contributes to the uncritical preference for "spirituality" over "religion" among so many Americans.

Spirituality vs. Religion:
A Misplaced Debate

For years I have heard people say, "I don't belong to a religion, but I am into spirituality." Religion, they believe, is rigid and oppressive, while spirituality is altogether creative and liberating. Small wonder that they avoid identifying with an organized faith tradition and instead affirm that spirituality is what keeps them going through life. They are happy to be independent of the ambiguous heritages that may have sustained their ancestors through poverty, war, disease, and dislocation, for something bright and free of flaws is available now. No more shoveling coal into the furnace and putting up with dust and soot, for in these enlightened times we have merely to touch a thermostat in order to reach a spiritual comfort zone.

For an extended articulation of this view, one can turn to a volume by the popular writer Diarmuid O'Murchu, *Religion in Exile: A Spiritual Homecoming*. The back cover description is telling: "Following on his earlier work, *Reclaiming Spirituality*, Diarmuid O' Murchu continues to offer some penetrating and original insights into the changing and evolving spiritual awareness of our time, one that is rapidly outgrowing the time-honored but exhausted vision of formal religion."[8] There are, indeed, original insights in this book from 2000, but we also find strong echoes of Karl Marx, Mary Daly, and Matthew Fox, and far too little critical probing of their claims, especially those of Marx and Daly. He declares, for example, that "[w]hile religion has aided the development of the human species," it has also "colluded with the patriarchal drive to exalt humanity over the rest of creation, thus breeding the ferocious anthropocentrism that reaps such havoc in our world today. . . . Religion in its essential essence is about alienation from the Earth and from the cosmos."[9]

Marx discerned that religion has functioned as an opiate and that theological emphasis on the afterlife can lead to political passivity. But while religious beliefs have sometimes legitimated oppressive systems, and inhibited women and the poor from taking action to better their lives, religion has also inspired resistance and rebellion, a fact Marx failed to recognize.[10] Likewise, Daly deserves credit for having identified the patriarchal bias of world religions, starting with her own Roman Catholicism. The challenge Daly leveled in her groundbreaking book from 1973, *Beyond God the Father*, has inspired a generation of feminist scholars.[11] They are retrieving, reimagining, and reconstructing religious thought and practice that respects women's full human dignity. Some do this work within their traditions, while others have walked away from the institutions that once nurtured their thirst for justice and for God. Finally, Matthew Fox has helped many readers see that too much stress on sin and redemption can skew the spiritual life by neglecting basic truths such as the goodness of creation and the reality of divine incarnation.[12] Fox's own retrieval of a neglected heritage of creation-celebrating mysticism, epitomized in the brilliant works of Hildegard of Bingen, has added much to contemporary life. O'Murchu does well to look appreciatively at ideas from Marx, Daly, Fox, and others, but he goes too far when he endorses the outright rejection of institutional religion that Marx and Daly advocated.

The popular view that spirituality should supplant religion is also problematic for historical reasons. Historically, movements that define themselves as the opposite of institutional religion tend to institutionalize themselves, and, although terminology may differ, functional resemblances to religion emerge. Individuals can live off the spiritual capital of their ancestors and their own youth for a while, but eventually there comes a need for shared stories and structures, and even for ritual and doctrine. The pendulum swing from heavy emphasis on institutional participation to individual autonomy is just that. One doesn't strike a balance by forgoing organized religion altogether. Indeed, the happily unchurched may in time find themselves the aging parents or grandparents of a new generation of devotees of a traditional faith, often a fundamentalist one, or of some new religious movement altogether.

What concerns me even more than the lessons from history are the moral implications of this trend. The belief that spirituality opposes or should supplant religion is elitist and dualistic, and it sometimes masks the unjust appropriation of cultural property of indigenous peoples.[13] Furthermore, it is naïve about human nature and history. Would the civil rights movement in this country have succeeded without the churches that provided the mimeographs, meeting spaces, and telephones, let alone the spiritual fire preached from the pulpits and alive in the people? What would have happened in South Africa if church leaders had not opposed apartheid policies and racist theology, as they did in the 1985 *Kairos Document*? Where would South Africa be today if religious radio had not preached the social gospel, if Regina Mundi Church had not provided a place for African National Congress members to gather in Soweto, and if black and white South Africans had been "into spirituality" instead of being involved in the churches?

Of course, organized religion can also be guilty of elitism, dualism, naïvete, and injustice, and Christianity was implicated in the evils of slavery and apartheid. My aim is to overcome the oppositional approach toward religion and spirituality, not simply to reverse the accusation that one is bad and the other good. My position is characteristically Catholic. Instead of accepting an *either/or* dichotomy, I believe a *both/and* approach to the relationship between spirituality and religion is intellectually more adequate and morally more beneficial.[14] I am *not* saying that people who claim they are religious are better than those who avoid such statements in favor of saying they are "into spirituality." Nor am I saying the opposite. Rather, I maintain that the cultural situation that fosters this way of describing things so that people feel they need to choose one or the other is problematic. Whose interests are served by opposing spirituality to religion? Who benefits when individuals sever ties with traditional communities of faith? Does it matter that often those who do this are affluent and well educated? Has "spirituality" become one more department in the aisles of today's supermarket of options for the liberally educated and affluent, a store whose wares are hardly accessible to the service workers who stock the shelves and mop the floors?

My conclusions are not as pessimistic as these critical questions might suggest, however, for I see promise in the fact that so many religiously unaffiliated Americans are willing to claim spirituality as a significant part of their identity. Perhaps this development reflects a new stage in the evolution of human religiosity, one that can benefit communities, as well as individuals, by promoting greater social justice and ecological responsibility. But, for this to happen, such secular forms of spirituality need an ethic no less than do the traditional religious faiths. Both sorts of spirituality, the traditionally religious and the avowedly secular, should be asked the same moral questions. Does this spirituality build an inclusive community of justice and care? Does it offer hope to the poor and oppressed? Does it get at the truth of things? Does it promote the acquisition of virtue in its adherents, something that is not as easy as imagining oneself innocent, or wishing to be good?

Toward an Ethics of Spirituality

As an initial step toward an ethics of spirituality, I will mention some qualities of character that both the avowedly religious and the avowedly secular forms of spirituality would do well to foster. I assume that all the virtues express and contribute to the perfection of love, and agree with Margaret Farley that justice must be the norm of love.[15] My list, which is by no means complete, describes qualities that contribute to a character capable of love that is just.

Self-care

Jesuit moral theologian James Keenan has proposed that self-care be considered a cardinal virtue.[16] In doing so, he resonates with a feminist scholar of religion, Valerie Saiving, who claimed in a groundbreaking 1960 article that the sins (and, by implication, the virtues) of women and men are affected by their differing social locations. Under patriarchy, the besetting temptations of women tend to involve not pride and self-aggrandizement, but rather failure to have a centered self.[17] The appropriate correction is to recognize that cultivating proper self-esteem and caring for one's personal well-being are essential aspects of fostering goodness, especially for those who have suffered from unjust power relationships. With regard to spirituality, self-care may entail, at times, a strategic withdrawal from religious systems or practices that are experienced as harmful, though it is a mistake to demonize these systems in the process.

Ideally, such withdrawal would not be total or permanent. Even a feminist as critical of church patriarchy as Rosemary Radford Ruether argues against indefinite separation from the tradition and opposes the idea of separatism as an end in itself. Instead, she sees the independence of women from oppressive situations as a necessary stage on a journey toward a community of Christian women and men together engaged in liberation from patriarchy. Ruether is enough of a realist to know that a widely shared conversion from patriarchy is a long way off, and in *Women-Church* (1986) she recommends "neither leaving the church as a sectarian group nor continuing to fit into it on its terms." Instead, she advocates "establishing bases for a feminist critical culture and celebrational community that have some autonomy from the established institutions."[18] She posits that, historically, the church is best understood as a dialectical interaction between two elements, namely, the "historical institution" and the "spirit-filled community."[19] In using this model, it is important to recognize the presence of the Spirit in the larger historical institution, and not to assume that all truth and goodness reside with self-proclaimed prophetic feminists, much less that the latter are immune from error and sinfulness. Certainly, the existing churches have a long way to go in the process of conversion from patriarchy, and self-care vis-à-vis existing institutions represents both a necessary virtue and a great challenge to the traditionally religious. Self-care is also important for those whose spiritual affiliations involve less traditional groups. These groups are not immune from defects and oppressive ways simply because they define themselves as different from traditional religion.

Solidarity

All the virtues are related to the ideal of charity, and, if self-care focuses on the quality of love for the self, solidarity is a way of characterizing the ideal relationship with one's neighbor. In *Mujerista Theology* (1996), the late theologian Ada María Isasi-Díaz argued that solidarity is the form that neighbor-love should take in our day. She saw it as a matter of effective, cohesive struggle, governed by a shared understanding of issues.[20] But solidarity is much easier to talk about than to practice. In a 1994 address to the College Theology Society, African American theologian M. Shawn Copeland cautioned that having common problems does not automatically lead to sisterhood. She said that Celtic-, Anglo-, and European-American feminists sometimes adopt the "rhetoric of solidarity," but nevertheless "consume the experiences and voices of the marginalized and oppressed, while, ever adroitly, dodging the penitential call to conversion—to authenticity in word and deed."[21] She advocated specific ways for white women and women of color to learn this virtue, and she enjoined all to be self-critical, honest, courageous, and willing to do the hard work of social analysis.

Courage

This virtue is essential to an ethic of "creative responsibility." Passive responsibility, embodied in duty, is important but secondary. Creative responsibility is distinguished by a willingness to think deeply and originally about the situations that confront us, and to take appropriate risks for the sake of promoting good and minimizing evil. The courage to take such risks comes from trust in God's power to act both in and beyond us, making up for what is lacking in our own efforts. Such courage also depends on the confidence that God's mercy is always there, supporting us and protecting us from the harms we fear and especially from our own limitations.[22]

Humility

The root meaning of this term involves being "of the earth," that is, being constituted of the same elements that make up soil, rocks, and trees. This is easier to affirm in the abstract than in life, as the poem "I Know Women" by Christian feminist Mara Faulkner, OSB, suggests. Faulkner addresses a different problem, but one that has some bearing on the issue of seeking to disconnect spirituality from the flaws, or flesh, of religious institutions. Faulkner writes,

> I know women and even girls who want to leap out of the boat
> of their bodies—
> that leaky skin craft
> with its fragile ribs, its clumsy opaqueness
> whose every heavy movement is ambiguous and veiled.
>
> . . .
>
> Women want to be pure mind, light
> Invisible as air
> free and beautiful like the idea of song
> that doesn't seem to need the pumping lungs
> the husky, muscled larynx
> the pink and flabby tongue.
>
> They can't believe that Jesus once set free
> would return to his body
>
> with cries of joy
> as to a long-lost friend.[23]

These lines suggest a continuing agenda for growth in the sort of humility that starts by affirming our physical bodies and also accepts our creaturely need for structures to serve the social body.

Conclusion

Having commended the virtue of humility, I must acknowledge that my thinking about the relationship between religion and spirituality is ongoing. For me, the complex picture is summed up by an image of two vast river systems, as well as many smaller streams, which can be distinguished, although their waters mingle here and there. The first, and much larger system, represents the classical spiritual traditions we associate with institutional religion, be it Buddhist, Christian, Hindu, Islamic, or Jewish, each of which carries many subsystems within it. By contrast, the second principal system is detached from traditional religion, especially of the institutionally organized and creedally demanding variety. It is often linked with the love of nature, art, and beauty; with the concern for ecology, justice, and peace; and with the pursuit of physical and mental health, including recovery from the damage caused by aspects of institutional religion. It may be that both large systems are authentic responses to the divine Spirit in history, as are the many smaller streams that represent indigenous or tribal forms of religion in this model. All of these "rivers" may be necessary in the human evolutionary process; certainly a God who loves biodiversity so much can handle religious diversity. Yet no spiritual system can hope to realize its humane ideals if its followers assume they are free from the limitations and evils that are part of being human.

Humility, being grounded in our finite, earthly condition, requires that we respect what is good in religious and secular traditions other than our own, as well as our own. It also requires that we acknowledge the problems of both institutional religion and secular spirituality, and not idealize one at the expense of the other. Were there space I would enlarge on a secular hero of mine, the nineteenth-century author Marian Evans who wrote fiction under the name of George Eliot. After a devout girlhood as an Evangelical Christian, she chose the secular stream of spirituality for herself, for reasons that still make sense. But unlike her contemporary Karl Marx, she knew that traditional religion had value, too, especially the Jewish tradition that most of her British contemporaries did not prize. Those who espouse secular spirituality today can learn much from her example.[24]

We can all learn from an earlier spiritual leader who received very mixed reviews in his day. Jesus managed to strike the right balance between religion and spirituality. As New Testament scholar Sandra Schneiders observes, "Jesus did not oppose his personal spirituality to his religious tradition but expressed his spirituality through his religious practice, even as he freely criticized the religious institution out of his own experience of union with God." She adds, "No one controlled Jesus' access to and relationship with God, but he was able to make his spirituality a resource for the reform of the tradition rather than an alternative to it."[25]

Building on Schneiders' insights, I conclude that the right relationship between religion and spirituality comes down to this matter of *balance*. Spirituality is a resource for religion, religion is a resource for spirituality, and ethics is needed to help each realize its potential for good. The virtues I have singled out for attention can be seen as paired counterweights that contribute to the equilibrium needed on both sides. Self-care and solidarity are mutually supportive and mutually correcting qualities, as indeed are courage and humility. The world can use more of them all. It is my hope that a balanced ethics of spirituality will encourage

Catholics, especially the young, to develop the sort of "loyal voice" recommended by Mary Jo Bane, one that helps transform the church into the community "that God would have us live in."

Notes

1. Mary Jo Bane, "Voice and Loyalty in the Church," in Steven J. Pope, ed., *Common Calling: The Laity and Governance of the Catholic Church* (Washington, DC: Georgetown University Press, 2004), 181.

2. Margaret Farley, *Just Love: A Framework for Christian Sexual Ethics* (New York: Continuum, 2006), 260.

3. Bane, "Voice and Loyalty in the Church."

4. Preliminary work toward an ethics of church participation is found in Anne E. Patrick, *Conscience and Calling: Ethical Reflections on Catholic Women's Church Vocations* (London: T&T Clark/Bloomsbury, 2013).

5. See Albert R. Jonsen, *Responsibility in Modern Religious Ethics* (Washington, DC: Corpus Books, 1968) for discussion of the post–World War II shift of emphasis from "obedience" to "responsibility" among Protestant and Catholic thinkers.

6. Pew Forum on Religion & Public Life, "U.S. Religious Landscape Survey," February 25, 2007. According to the survey, "While nearly one-in-three Americans (31%) were raised in the Catholic faith, today fewer than one-in-four (24%) describe themselves as Catholics. These losses would have been even more pronounced were it not for the offsetting impact of immigration. . . . Approximately one-third of the survey respondents who say they were raised Catholic no longer describe themselves as Catholic. This means that roughly 10% of all Americans are former Catholics." Quoted from http://religions.pewforum.org/. In an article commenting on this study, Thomas J. Reese, S.J. noted that if these ex-Catholics "were a separate denomination, they would be the third largest denomination in the United States, after Catholics and Baptists." See Reese, "The Hidden Exodus: Catholics Becoming Protestants," *National Catholic Reporter,* April 15, 2011, 1.

7. Pew Forum on Religion & Public Life, "'Nones' on the Rise: One-in-Five Adults Have no Religious Affiliation," October 9, 2012, http://pewforum.org.

8. Diarmuid O'Murchu, *Religion in Exile: A Spiritual Homecoming* (New York: Crossroad Publishing Company, 2000). O'Murchu is a social psychologist and member of the Sacred Heart Missionary Order who has worked as a counselor in London, who travels internationally to give workshops on adult faith formation, and who has recently published books that include *In the Beginning Was the Spirit* (2012), *Jesus in the Power of Poetry* (2009), and *Consecrated Religious Life* (2005). I infer from his website that his 2000 polemic against religion is not his full position on the subject. Indeed, *Religion in Exile* is not listed among his books "currently in print" at http://www.diarmuid13.com. Nevertheless, *Religion in Exile* remains available at Amazon.com, with the description: "O'Murchu offers penetrating and original insights into the changing spiritual awareness of our time. He believes that we are rapidly out-growing the time honored but exhausted vision of formal religion."

9. O'Murchu, *Religion in Exile*, 66.

10. For a solid presentation and critique of Marx's position, see Daniel L. Pals, *Eight Theories of Religion*, 2nd ed. (New York: Oxford University Press, 2006), 118–48.

11. Mary Daly, *Beyond God the Father* (Boston: Beacon Press, 1973).

12. See, for example, Matthew Fox, *Original Blessing* (Santa Fe, NM: Bear & Co., 1983), and Matthew Fox, *Creation Spirituality* (San Francisco: HarperSanFrancisco, 1991).

13. See Ronald L. Grimes, "Forum: American Spirituality," *Religion and American Culture* 9 (1999): 145–52. Grimes paraphrases the observation of a Native American colleague thus: "Every time . . . I hear a white person use the term 'spirituality' rather than 'religion,' I worry, because I know that person is in the process of packaging for export the very practices I grew up with and continue to revere" (ibid., 150).

14. Eminent among various others who take this position is Sandra M. Schneiders, who probes the relationship between spirituality and religion in many writings, including "Religion vs. Spirituality: A Contemporary Conundrum," *Spiritus* 3 (2003): 163–85.

15. Margaret A. Farley, "New Patterns of Relationship: Beginnings of a Moral Revolution," *Theological Studies* 36 (1975): 627–46.

16. James F. Keenan, S.J., "Proposing Cardinal Virtues," *Theological Studies* 56 (1995): 726–28.

17. Valerie Saiving, "The Human Situation: A Feminine View," *Journal of Religion* 40 (1960): 100–12.

18. Rosemary Radford Ruether, *Women-Church: Theology & Practice of Feminist Liturgical Communities* (San Francisco: Harper & Row, 1986), 62.

19. Ibid., 11.

20. Ada María Isasi-Díaz, *Mujerista Theology* (Maryknoll, NY: Orbis Books, 1996), 86–104.

21. M. Shawn Copeland, "Toward a Critical Christian Feminist Theology of Solidarity," in *Women and Theology* (Maryknoll, NY: Orbis Books, 1995), p. 3.

22. See Anne E. Patrick, *Women, Conscience, and the Creative Process*, ed. Mary Ann Hinsdale and Phyllis H. Kaminski (New York: Paulist Press, 2011), 67–72.

23. Mara Faulkner, OSB, "I Know Women," *Hedgebrook Journal*, August 2000, 6. Used with permission of the poet.

24. See Bernard J. Paris, *Experiments in Life: George Eliot's Quest for Values* (Detroit: Wayne State University Press, 1965), and also George Eliot's final novel, which is concerned with Jewish identity and traditions, *Daniel Deronda* (1876).

25. Sandra M. Schneiders, *With Oil in Their Lamps: Faith, Feminism, and the Future* (New York: Paulist Press, 2000), 101.

A Feminist Ethical Perspective on Women/Girls as Oppressors: The Cycle of Oppressor-internalized Oppression

Shawnee M. Daniels Sykes

Introduction

In this essay, I maintain that when communities of women and girls have lost their memory, hope, and practices of commitment[1] to each other as human beings created by God and social beings integrally connected, there persist also women and girls who are oppressors.[2] Despite the fact that, in many places in the world, women and girls live in traditional patriarchal systems, still the propensity exists for the cycle of women and girls as oppressors that leads to internalized oppression in other women and girls. In patriarchal systems, for example, "Male dominance has been historically tolerated and manifested in intra-familial power relations between men and women."[3] Indeed, these relationships are stereotypically characterized by male domination and women's subordination, as men are/were able to advance their ability to dominate through violence or threat of violence toward women and girls.[4] Women and girls can be heavily influenced by the patriarchs' dominant ways of being in direct relationship to women and girls. Further, they can also be heavily influenced by the invisible or indirect hand of patriarchy. Hence, women and girls already may be internally oppressed as the result of living in traditional patriarchal systems of domination that degrade, dehumanize, and objectify them. From this male dominating ethos, I maintain that the cycle of women and girls as oppressors is generated, a cycle that, in turn, may evoke internalized oppression in other women and girls.

Paulo Freire, in *Pedagogy of the Oppressed*, characterizes internalized oppression as "[t]he oppressed, having internalized the image of the oppressor and adopted *his*[5] guidelines, are fearful of freedom."[6] The oppressed accept their fate, their vulnerability, their exploitation, done unto them at the hands of their oppressors. In essence, once oppression has been internalized, little force is needed to keep people in a subordinate or submissive position. They are paralyzed to the point that even thinking about what it means to strive for freedom brings terror and trepidation to their psyches. Freire echoes this sentiment in that, for those who are internally oppressed, they harbor deep inside themselves the pain and the memories, the fears, the confusions, and negative attitudes that were drilled into them by their oppressor(s).[7] Of course, it is possible that the internally oppressed can turn into the oppressor, continuing the cycle of oppression—internalized oppression. And the issue of internalized oppression is continued as a result of the concrete existential situations where many women and girls live in hostile and oppressive environments. Hopelessness, despair, powerlessness, poverty, marginalization, depression, even death, among other social, economic, and psychological dispositions emerge.

I will illustrate such instances of this oppression and internalized oppression dynamic not only in the Sarah, Abraham, and Hagar biblical story of rivalry and tension, which I draw on as a point of departure for this essay, but also in discussions concerning women at the forefront of the human and sex trafficking of other women and girls, women and girls being bullied, and women at the helm of female genital mutilation of girls. I note that in order to transform this cycle of oppressor-internalized oppression, the persons involved must understand that a glimpse of the living God requires a profound rebirth. Nonetheless, these four moral issues run counter to a major argument that feminist theologian Elizabeth A. Johnson posits, in *Friends of God and Prophets: A Feminist Theological Reading of the Communion of Saints:*[8]

> Genuine communities of hope, although not quickly formed, are those communities that contain the ideas about character and attributes of a good person. Some carry reminders of corporate achievements and also of shared suffering endured in the past; some, too, painfully remember sufferings the community has inflicted upon others, with the call to remedy ancient evils.

She asserts that these memories found in genuine communities carry a vital élan that inspires and energizes action for the good. That is, the past turns us toward the future as perpetual genuine communities of hope are revealed in the symbolic relationship of the communion of saints.[9] Obviously, Johnson's observations speak antithetically to those women and girls who knowingly or unknowingly are entrenched in their roles of oppressors, inflicting emotional, psychological, spiritual, and/or physical pain and suffering onto other women and girls. Unfortunately, too many internally oppressed women and girls have lost their lives and/or livelihoods as a result of enduring the wicked and inhumane assaults from women and girls who act as oppressors. Instead Johnson would insist upon dispositions and behaviors that halt the cycle of oppressor-internalized oppression and that illuminate respectful relationships, while exuding faith, hope, and love in God, self, and others.

Freire admonishes that we must unlearn or dismantle the cycle of oppressor and internalized oppression so that individuals are able to move into relationships of goodness, beaming with social justice and love. Johnson offers that, in the communion of saints as friends and prophets of God, a profound relationship exists between the living and the dead. For her, the communion of saints as friends of God and prophets comprises *all* living persons of truth and love and those who have died leaving behind this same legacy: all who respond to the promptings of the Holy Spirit and follow the words and actions of Jesus Christ. Indeed, it is a profound relationship of goodness. Thus, I believe that this kind of relationship cannot be the result of the living inflicting pain and suffering on others, as a result of their oppressive acts that destroy the body, mind, and spirit. This represents the mark of evil. As Johnson maintains, internally oppressed women and girls need to be connected to memories, hopes, and practices of commitment as the communion of saints demonstrates for us. This same need also must be attributed to women and girl oppressors. In other words, as oppressors, degraders of others, they, too, must be redeemed and become a part of the communion of saints as friends of God and prophets. In this, they are transformed into a profound relationship of goodness; this goodness enhances human life rather than diminishing or destroying it.[10] This goodness is enveloped inside a community for the living and the dead as illumined in the "communion of saints as friends of God and prophets."

To further illustrate the complexities around male patriarchy, women oppressors, and internalized oppression, let us first take the example of Abraham, Sarah, and Hagar, as narrated in Genesis 16:1–16 and Genesis 21:1–21.[11]

The Cycle of Oppression to Internalized Oppression in Action: Abraham, Sarah, and Hagar (Genesis 16:1–16, 21:1–21)

The patriarch Abraham was the man of God chosen to begin Israel's social, cultural, national, and religious legacy.[12] The matriarch Sarah lived in a world where "bearing children upheld a woman's status as opposed to childlessness which was regarded as a virtual sign of divine disfavor."[13] In this story, we find the matriarch Sarah, the first wife of the patriarch Abraham, and Hagar as the lonely Egyptian slave girl of Sarah and Abraham. More specifically, Hagar is held in bondage by Sarah, dehumanized by the oppressive ways of Sarah (who, herself, also has internalized oppression), stripped of her personhood, and removed from the memory of her heritage, ancestors, and tradition. Barren, Sarah forces Hagar to have sexual intercourse with Abraham, and Hagar becomes pregnant. Sarah starts to act disingenuously, inhospitably, and with meanness toward her slave girl after she was impregnated by Abraham. Refusing to endure this type of despicable treatment, Hagar runs away from Sarah into the desert near a spring on the road to Shur. Pregnant and desolate in the desert, God appears to Hagar questioning where she was coming from and where she was going.[14] God instructs her to return to Sarah and to submit to her authority. Hagar was also told by God that she would have a son to be named Ishmael.[15] After Hagar returned home, Sarah became pregnant by Abraham too, and bore a son, Isaac.

In the meantime, as Isaac grew older, Sarah accused Hagar and Ishmael of ridiculing him. Upset by their offensive behavior toward Isaac, contemptuous Sarah becomes adamant, declaring that Hagar and Ishmael would never share in the family inheritance. Sarah banishes Hagar and Ishmael into the wilderness. Arguably, this could be another concrete instance of how Sarah, the oppressor, acted against Hagar. Hagar, however, has a second encounter with God. According to Johnson, "God gives her a new vision to see resources for survival where she had seen none before; a well of water in the desert for herself and her wailing, dying child to drink."[16] Marginalized Hagar and Ishmael, graced and protected by God in the wilderness without water, ultimately find their special place among the communion of saints.

Sarah, of course, is a product of her time, social location, and condition. Since the issue of barrenness thwarted Sarah's liberation and covenant relationship with God, one can argue, that she, too, was oppressed as a result of the patriarchal worldview in which she found herself: as subordinated and subjected to a propertied man, Abraham. She is in an antagonistic, contemptuous relationship with her slave girl named Hagar. Hence, one can make the case that Sarah, as an oppressed woman, had taken on the ways of the patriarchal oppressive environment in which she lived; she has adopted *his* way of thinking, ruling, and behaving toward Hagar.[17]

Freire would concur that any matriarch who is involved in inflicting pain and suffering onto another (i.e., one who is subordinate to her) through degrading or demeaning acts appears to "have adapted to the structure of domination in which [she is] immersed, and [has] become resigned to it."[18] I would argue that the behavior of the matriarchal oppressor, Sarah, results in the cycle of gender prejudice and oppression in the context of Hagar's situation. Essentially, the Sarah and Hagar rivalry speaks of a disingenuous relationship that needs to be transformed through the conversion of minds and hearts in order that memory, hope, and practices of commitment abound in their relationships. Space does not allow me to recount other stories of the matriarchs Rachel and Leah, who engaged in similar types of behavior with their maidservants, Bilhah and Zilpah, respectively, in order to have them bear children for Rachel and Leah.[19] These stories also exemplify women who have been heavily influenced by the traditional patriarchal system of oppression that has persisted throughout the millennia. Thus, they embody the cycle of women and girl oppressors who have internalized the oppression that they inflict upon other women and girls.

In essence, the ethical issue of oppressor-to-internalized-oppression has an extensive history that is found in patriarchal traditions, not only exemplified within the confines of the Abraham, Sarah, and Hagar story. Other instances exist wherein the destructive behavior of women oppressors results in the internalized oppression of other women and girls. Women and girls bullying other women and girls, especially in the workplace or in the school or playground setting, are other examples.

Bullying Women at Work, Girls at School, and the Playground Settings

We like to believe that women and girls are in solidarity with one another in our society, but it is a myth and a stereotype in so many circumstances. It does not mean that female solidarity does not exist; it means that not all women and girls are authentic in their relationships with one another. In terms of bullying, it is important to note that statistics reveal that workplace bullying exists, and it is not gender free. Men bully men, and men bully women, and women bully other women. "In a nutshell, the concept of bullying refers to repeated mistreatment against another individual manifested in either verbal abuse, or conduct that is threatening, humiliating, intimidating, or sabotage that interferes with work."[20] The act of bullying can be viewed as a way to maintain inequality—positions of authority and positions of subordination. Bullying may ensue for many different reasons—jealously, a workplace threat, power-plays, dislike, and retaliation, among others.

On the one hand, in male-dominated organizations, societies and/or professions where men hold all the executive or top-level positions, women may tend to adopt male sex-type dominating and oppressive behaviors to survive and succeed in their employment or social status. "Feminists argue that adherence to patriarchal ideology of male dominance has been the single most significant risk marker of violence against women."[21] A key finding from *The 2007 US Workplace Bullying Survey* was that "57% of those employees targeted for the bullying abuse are female."[22] For women (and men), a result of participating in this type of environment day in and day out, arguably, can lead to their becoming oppressors. For these women (and men), they may tend to bully or treat other women with disgrace, disdain, and/or disrespect, resulting in the other women's internalized oppression.

In a similar way, when women are in positions of influence and authority, often in female-dominated professions or organizations, it happens that female bullies target women simply because they are the ones present. "*The 2007, U.S. Workplace Bullying Survey* found that with respect to targets, female bullies target female employees in 71 percent of the reported situations."[23] One woman described workplace bullying among women in this way: "it was almost like she had to have a woman to pick on and, at different times in the years that I was there, she would choose one woman to direct her anger at, and she would do that for a year or so. Then she would pick on somebody else and leave that person alone."[24] Again, this consistent type of oppressive environment can result in other women's internalized oppression. Reiterating Freire's sentiment, hence, "the oppressed, having internalized the image of the oppressor and adopted her guidelines are fearful of freedom."[25] In other words, the internally oppressed might feel a lack of freedom to engage in the struggle for liberation because to do so requires risk taking that could result in a loss of employment, harassment, defamation of character, inability to find other meaningful work, among others.

Besides being a very serious workplace problem with real consequences, bullying also occurs in school or playground settings. The situation of girls bullying girls, boys bullying boys, girls bullying boys, and boys bullying girls is happening in epidemic proportions in the United States, to the point where President and Ms. Obama have recently stepped up to speak out against this life-threatening issue.[26] For them, bullying is psychologically and physically damaging to our children, and it needs to stop. In most cases, the person bullied ends up alienated, threatened, afraid, and marginalized, which, in turn, can lead to her becoming extremely fearful and despondent, mistrustful, and in the worst case scenario committing suicide.

In essence, reports reveal that girls (and boys) in these settings have become depressed due to overwhelming fear and anxiety. For example, they may fear going to school or the playground, become despondent, develop a health condition(s), fail classes, and/or commit suicide because of the horrific amount of pressure from being bullied. Children need healthy and understanding adults, parents, and/or guardians to assist them in regaining the confidence to transform the situation instead of allowing the perpetuation of the cycle of oppressor-internalized oppression to destroy them.

Although a different form of mistreatment from bullying, the cycle of oppression and internalized oppression in respect to human trafficking works in a similar way. In the next section of this essay, we find that reportedly, more women are engaged in perpetuating trafficking in human persons today, than men.

Trafficking: Women Organizing and Executing Human Trafficking

The phrase "trafficking in human persons" involves any type of human exploitation—psychosexual, physical (forced labor, forced marriage, domestic bondage or servitude), or otherwise that occurs day after day, sometimes for years on end by an oppressor or someone in a dominant role. For many, it is a modern form of human slavery that occurs in cities, towns, rural communities, suburbs, streets, and highways. According to the February 2009 Executive Summary Report from the United Nations, *Global Report on Trafficking in Persons,*[27] women, otherwise known as madams, play an unexpectedly large role in perpetuating human or sex trafficking.

> It might be assumed that human trafficking, where violence and threats are key to the business, would likewise be overwhelmingly male dominated, but surprisingly, the data on gender of those convicted for trafficking in persons do not support this premise. The gender of offenders in 46 countries suggests that women play a key role as perpetrators of human trafficking.[28]

In other words, in the global system of human trafficking, women enter various villages, cities, and towns to talk to economically poor people about opportunities for women and girls to make honest money by becoming secretaries, domestic servants, executive assistants, and/or professionals.[29] Women and girls are tricked and taken into captivity for the purpose of human or sex trafficking. This example illustrates one way that "[w]omen commit crimes against women, [and girls] and in many cases the victims become the perpetrators . . . [t]hey become the matrons of the business and they make money."[30] Although trafficking in human persons is a global and economic enterprise, in numerous countries in Europe, women make up a large share of those convicted for trafficking in persons.[31] Women, engaged as oppressors in egregious inhumane treatments such as trafficking women and girls, perpetuate the cycle of oppression and internalized oppression. As discussed in the next section, women engaged in female genital mutilation of other women and girls for the benefit of men also, arguably, perpetuate this cycle.

Female Genital Mutilation (FGM): Women, Girls, and the Invisible Hand of Patriarchy

FGM is a common cultural practice in certain regions of Africa and Asia.[32] A cultural practice often performed by women on other women and young girls, it has a history of more than 2,000 years.[33] FGM is the term used for the nontherapeutic partial or complete removal of the female genitalia. According to the World Health Organization, "100 to 140 million girls and women worldwide have endured this horrific non-anesthesia surgical procedure. Annually, about 300 million more girls are at risk."[34] It is performed mainly to lessen female sexual desire. Although men tend to be far removed from the procedure itself, the practice of FGM is not an isolated traditional cultural practice thought up by and executed only by women. Rather, the invisible hand of patriarchy lurks somewhere behind the process of FGM, even as women are engaged in performing the surgical procedure.

According to Musimbi R. A. Kanyoro, "women in Africa are the custodians of cultural practices. In many cases, women themselves are the objects of these cultural practices and are also diminished by them."[35] In other words, the invisible hand of patriarchy creates women oppressors. Women oppressors become the visible female technicians or clinicians of FGM. These women have identified with and have taken on the rules and thinking of patriarchal society through a process of enculturation; they have become the oppressors of other women and girls. As a consequence, it could be argued that women who engage in the oppressive practices of FGM inflict trauma, pain, and suffering on other young girls and women, which, in turn, results in their internalized oppression. As oppressors, these women violate the right to health and to freedom from torture or cruel, inhumane, or degrading treatment of other women and girls. FGM survivors carry a multitude of untold long-term consequences, both medically and psychologically. Studies reveal that women and girls who have experienced FGM "show various degrees of psychological morbidity, such as loss of trust, prevailing lack of bodily well-being, post-traumatic shock, low self-esteem, anxiety and depression . . . and sexual or reproductive problems."[36]

As mentioned above, the invisible hand of patriarchy has played a strong and dominant but indirect role in the cycle of women oppressor-internalized oppression issue, especially in FGM. Not only does FGM harm those women and girls who are directly affected, it negatively impacts women and girls all over the world. Johnson's notion of the communion of saints as friends of God and prophets stands in sharp contrast with those practices that deface and destroy what God has created. Freire would affirm Johnson's insights.

A Glimpse of the Living God Requires a Profound Rebirth

Beginning with the Sarah and Hagar rivalry, I have presented concrete ways in which women oppressors inflict pain and suffering on other women and girl, as well as through bullying in the workplace and in school and playground settings, women trafficking of women and girls, and FGM. Along with these ethical concerns, we must remember that the invisible hand of patriarchy remains operative in all of these issues.

Johnson argues that "where memory, hope, and practices of commitment disappear, the empty-self proliferates and society degenerations."[37] I believe that her insights are quite *apropos* when applied to the cycle of oppressor-internalized oppression and as exemplified in the previously discussed ethical issues. Moreover, Johnson holds that the communion of saints who are the friends and prophets of God serves to always remind us of the constant need to restore and keep memory alive, keep hope alive, and maintain practices of commitment to one another. Johnson's observations point to the need for goodness in relationships. This implies that the dehumanizing behavior of women oppressors must stop. Women and girls who are internally oppressed, despondent, muted, and dismissed into the wilderness, for example, are the least among us, as demonstrated in the biblical narrative of Sarah, Hagar, and Ishmael, as well as for those three additional contemporary global ethical issues previously discussed. The restoration of human dignity and a preferential option for the poor, vulnerable, and marginalized is due to the conversion of women who are oppressors as well as those who are internally oppressed.

Johnson's insights also challenge women who have taken on patriarchal thoughts and behavior, who, as oppressors, destroy the God-given lifeforce in other women and girls leaving them, in turn, internally oppressed. Freire affirms Johnson, adding that, "the [internally] oppressed as objects, as 'things,' have no purposes except those their oppressors prescribe for them."[38] Afflicted with much pain and suffering, they may succumb to the oppressors' abusive ways and die.

Still, for Johnson, the communion of saints symbolizes the fact that human beings are called to be relational, existing in an all-inclusive community, where everyone is of equal value, equal dignity, and equal worth in God's view. Everyone is called to create and sustain relationships of goodness. All are called to engage in words and actions that promote the dignity and flourishing of human life. Every woman, as a result of her particular social location and social conditioning, who has taken on patriarchal mind-sets and proceeded thoughtlessly to hurt or traumatize other women and girls, may in her process of conversion, "glimpse the living God." In essence, conversion toward goodness in relationships, for Freire, "requires a profound rebirth."[39]

For this glimpse of the living God and for a profound rebirth to occur, no single human being should stand dominant over another, and no single human being should be situated in a permanently submissive role where she is made vulnerable to malice or abuse by an oppressor(s). In fact, women and girl oppressors who "proclaim devotion to the cause of liberation yet are unable to enter into communion with other [women and girls] whom they have continued to regard as totally [subordinate] are grievously self-deceived."[40] However, when this ethical issue is positioned within the context of the communion of saints, then, and only then, will there be no more bullying, no more FGM, no more human or sex trafficking of women and girls, and the direct and indirect invisible hand of patriarchal mind-sets will disappear. Created in the image and likeness of God, and claimed for Jesus Christ, "the redeemed become the locus of God's saving intent and action."[41]

Conclusion

Beginning with the Sarah and Hagar rivalry and drawing on the argument from Elizabeth Johnson in *Friends of God and Prophets: A Feminist Theological Reading of the Communion of Saints* and Paulo Freire's *Pedagogy of the Oppressed,* I sought to examine a cycle of gender prejudice and oppression from the perspective of women as the oppressors, inflicting pain and suffering on other women and girls that can result in their being internally oppressed. Further, I drew attention to Freire's demand to unlearn the cycle of the oppressor-internalized oppression dynamic. In other words, it is understood that a glimpse of the living God really does require a profound rebirth for both the oppressor and the internally oppressed. I believe that Johnson would concur that the communion of saints who are the friends and prophets of God is also manifested in this process of rebirth. Then, and only then, will the empty self no longer proliferate; society and the world will, instead, produce women and girls who discover and engage in relationships of goodness that glow with peace and harmony.

Notes

1. This notion of "lost their memory, hope, and practices of commitment," is taken from Elizabeth A. Johnson, *Friends of God and Prophets: A Feminist Theological Reading of the Communion of Saints* (New York: York: Continuum, 1999).

2. For Paulo Freire, "The oppressor consciousness tends to transform everything surrounding it into an object of its domination." See Paulo Freire, *Pedagogy of the Oppressed: New Revised 20th-Anniversary Edition* (New York: Continuum, 1994), 40.

3. Seed Ahmad Watto, "Conventional Patriarchal Ideology of Gender Relations: An Inexplicit Predictor of Male Physical Violence against Women in Families," *European Journal of Scientific Research* 36, no.4 (2009): 561–69.

4. See Elisabeth Schüssler Fiorenza, *The Power of Naming: A Concilium Reader in Feminist Liberation Theology* (Maryknoll, NY: Orbis Books, 1996), xx–xxii.

5. For this essay the notion of accepting *his* guidelines is also viewed as accepting *her* guidelines—the oppressive behaviors and attitudes of women and girls that can lead to internalized oppression of women and girls.

6. Paulo Freire, *Pedagogy of the Oppressed* (New York: Herder and Herder, 1970), 31.

7. Ibid., 29.

8. Johnson, *Friends of God and Prophets,* 22.

9. Ibid.

10. See Desmond Tutu and Mpho Tutu, *Made for Goodness: and Why This All Makes a Difference* (New York: HarperCollins Publishers, 2010).

11. Johnson, *Friends of God and Prophets,* 142. It is important to note, here, that the lost memory, hope, and practice of commitment for Hagar and Ishmael remained until God communicated and intervened a second time and provided them with some refreshment in the form of living water.

12. Lauree Hersch Meyer, "Hagar's Holiness: Genesis 16 and 21,"*Brethren Life and Thought* 37 (Summer 1992): 145.

13. Susan Niditch, "Genesis," in *The Women's Biblical Commentary* (Louisville, KY: Westminster Knox Press, 1992), 17–18.

14. Toba Spitzer, "'Where Do You Come From, And Where Are You Going': Hagar and Sarah Encounter God," *The Reconstructionist* (Fall 1998): 8–18.

15. Genesis 16:1–16 (NAB).

16. Johnson, *Friends of God and Prophets,* 143; see also Genesis 21:1–21 (NAB).

17. In this case, one can also argue that Sarah, living in a patriarchal traditional system, is not only the oppressor, but she is also internally oppressed.

18. Freire, *Pedagogy of the Oppressed,* 32.

19. Renita J. Weems, *Just a Sister Away: A Womanist Vision of Women's Relationships in the Bible* (San Diego,: Lura Media, 1988), 4; Susan Niditch, "Genesis," 17.

20. *U.S. Workplace Bullying Survey* (2007), http://bullyinginstitute.org. At the time, this was the largest scientific survey of workplace bullying that has been conducted in the United States. Zogby International for the Workplace Bullying Institute conducted a poll.

21. Watto, "Conventional Patriarchal Ideology of Gender Relations: An Inexplicit Predictor of Male Physical Violence against Women in Families," 561–69.

22. Teresa A. Daniel, *Stop Bullying at Work: Strategies and Tools for HR and Legal Professionals* (Alexandria, VA: Society for Human Resource Management, 2009), 20.

23. Ibid., 20.

24. Ibid., 71.

25. Freire, *Pedagogy of the Oppressed,* 31.

26. President Barack and First Lady Michelle Obama call for a united effort to address bullying on March 10, 2011, http://stopbullying.gov.

27. Antonio Maria Costa, *Global Report on Trafficking in Persons: Executive Summary* (New York: United Nations Office on Drugs and Crimes, 2009).

28. Ibid., 4.

29. Liz Conn, "International Justice Mission Combats Human Trafficking," *UWIRE: The College Network*, http://uwire.com.

30. Associated Press, "Female Role in Human Trafficking Spurs Shock," http://newsok.com.

31. Maria Costa, *Global Report on Trafficking in Persons*, 4.

32. Sharmon Lynnette Monagan, "Patriarchy: Perpetuating the Practice of Female Genital Mutilation," *Journal of Alternative Perspectives in Social Sciences* 2, no.1 (2010): 160–81.

33. Ibid., 160.

34. Taghreed Adam, Heli Bathija, David Bishai, et al., "Estimating the Obstetric Costs of Female Genital Mutilation in Six African Countries," *Bull World Health Organization* 88 (2010): 281–88.

35. Musimbi R. A. Kanyoro, "Engendered Communal Theology: African Women's Contributions to Theology in the Twenty-first Century," in *Hope Abundant: Third World and Indigenous Women's Theology*, ed. Kwok Pui-lan (Maryknoll, NY: Orbis Books, 2010), 20.

36. James Whitehorn, Oyedeji Ayonrinde, "Female Genital Mutilation: Cultural and Psychological Implications," *Sexual and Relationship Therapy* 17, no.2 (2002): 165–66.

37. Johnson, *Friends of God and Prophets*, 23.

38. Freire, *Pedagogy of the Oppressed*, 40.

39. Ibid., 43.

40. Ibid.

41. Johnson, *Friends of God and Prophets*, 220, 223.

CONCLUSION:
LOOKING BACK, LOOKING FORWARD

Linda Hogan

Forty years on from the publication of Mary Daly's groundbreaking *Beyond God the Father*,[1] the theological landscape has been transformed. Whereas in the early years feminist theologians were only beginning to articulate the depth of the misogyny inherent in the traditions and practices of Christianity, today we are more clear sighted about the nature and extent of the problem. Through the 1960s and 1970s, feminist scholars excavated the biblical and theological canon, unearthing the ideologies of subordination that had become embedded in the tradition. The early inspiring works like Rosemary Radford Ruether's *Religion and Sexism*[2] and Kari Elisabeth Børresen's *Subordination and Equivalence*[3] highlighted how thoroughly and energetically ideologies of subordination were adopted, developed, and promoted within the Christian tradition. Very quickly this critical mode was supplemented with the determination both to retrieve the neglected antecedents of women's equality and to reconstruct the tradition in a manner that is more consonant with the original egalitarian vision of Christianity.

Feminist theology did not evolve in a vacuum but developed alongside the critical perspectives of political, black, and liberation theologies. The Second Vatican Council, which encouraged theologians to respond to the "signs of the times," the turn to politics in the writings of Jürgen Moltmann, Johannes Baptist Metz, and James Cone, and the efforts of liberation theologians to "do theology from the underside of history" each provided important resources for feminist theologians. Moreover, particularly in the United States and Europe, the women's movement, with its all-encompassing critique of patriarchy, provided both practical and theoretical resources for this fledgling discipline. However, the early advocates of feminist theology in no way anticipated the diversity of women's experience. Viewed with the benefit of hindsight, these initial attempts to theologize from women's experience now seem extraordinarily naïve. Yet once women began to engage in theological reflection, the differences among women came to the fore. Whereas initially the racial, ethnic, economic, and geographical differences between women were neglected, in the last three decades this precise issue has become a dominant theme in feminist theological discourse.

Particularly since the mid-1980s, the differences among women have been foregrounded in theological reflection. Womanist theology, pioneered by Delores

Williams and Katie Cannon, that emerged out of the African American community attempted to tackle the sexism within that particular theological and cultural context, while simultaneously challenging the sexism and racism of the dominant society. Hispanic women in the United States, too, named their distinctive theological perspective *mujerista* theology, a neologism coined by the late Ada María Isasi-Díaz, who sadly passed away before she could complete her essay for this volume. The 1980s and 1990s also saw the emergence of postcolonial feminist theological voices, particularly from the global South. Mercy Amba Oduyoye from Ghana, Virginia Fabella from the Philippines, and Ivone Gebara and Elsa Tamez from Latin America were pioneers, each attending to the symbiotic relationship between Christianity and indigenous traditions in the maintenance of sexist beliefs and practices. Forged from these multiple voices, contemporary feminist theology is now a pluralistic and intercultural enterprise, although for many the struggle to be heard continues.

This collection represents a coming of age of another phase in the evolution of feminist theological voices, one in which the intersections of gender, race, and class are further complicated by the cultural diversity embedded in local Catholic Church contexts. Indeed, as the essays in this collection demonstrate, the impact of this cultural diversity is highly significant in the articulation of a critical feminist theological voice within Catholicism. Moreover, as these intersections become more visible, the diversity of Catholicism comes ever more clearly into view. However, what many of the essays also suggest is that in addition to the diversity of the cultural contexts from which these feminist voices emerge, these cultural contexts themselves are evolving and therefore display a degree of internal diversity that has previously not been fully appreciated. Indeed, in many of the essays, the dynamism of contemporary cultural formation is brought to the fore, so that one can see very clearly how cultural identity is formed in a continuous process of engagement and exchange. We see in the essays of Lilian Dube and Agnes Brazal that culture is a performative activity rather than a static entity.[4] Moreover, we see in these postcolonial contexts (Zimbabwe and the Philippines, respectively) that culture is not only a site of exchange, but it is also a liminal space in which cultural differences not only narrate but also produce new constructions of cultural and religious identity. These new forms of religious and cultural identity challenge and disrupt the traditional markers and practices of religious identity in important ways, as is evident in Brazal's essay on postcolonial female leadership in the Philippines. In addition, they bring to the fore inherited inequities that have tended to be justified with reference to the traditional markers of religious identity, but which demand to be addressed in light of new understandings. The essays of Shawnee Daniels Sykes and Shaji George Kochuthara in particular highlight this important dimension of such renegotiations of religious and cultural identities today.

These and other essays also highlight the manner in which globalization has changed irrevocably the shape of religious and cultural identities. There is no doubt that radical disparities of power abound within this globalized world, and religious communities are no more immune to the impact of such disparities than are any others. The force of these disparities and their consequences is a constant theme throughout the collection but is especially emphasized in the essays of Alison Munro, Mary Yuen, and Maria Clara Lucchetti Bingemer. Nonetheless, whether one's life is lived in the midst of poverty and violence or of luxury and privilege, we all now have multiple allegiances and affiliations. Kochurani Abraham's essay, which focuses on the construction of womanhood in India, captures well the complexities inherent in these multiple allegiances. He discusses how class, caste, and religion intersect with gender to construct Indian women's identities. From her vantage point in the Anglophone Caribbean, Anna Perkins also underscores the complexities and challenges of such multiple affiliations in a globalised world.

In addition to the malleability of culture and the hybridity of contemporary belonging, these essays also highlight the dynamism of tradition. Highlighting the issue of gender equality, Anne Arabome, Sharon Bong, Aloysius Lopez Cartagenas, and Veronica Rop each demonstrate how the traditions of Catholicism evolve along a trajectory of continuity and change. As has been previously discussed, notwithstanding the fact that religious traditions are frequently characterized as static and unchanging, Catholicism, like other religious traditions, is dynamic and evolving.[5] With respect to the moral tradition of Catholicism, the historian John Noonan has demonstrated that this idea of a fixed and unchanging tradition is a fiction. He characterizes the Catholic Church's moral tradition thusly: what was forbidden became lawful (the cases of usury and marriage); what was permissible became unlawful (the case of slavery); and what was required became forbidden (the persecution of heretics).[6] Thus, not only has the church's position on the equality of women and men changed, so, too, has its stance on divorce, abortion, slavery, religious freedom, and human rights. Previously unquestioned positions have frequently been abandoned, and substantial innovations have occurred. Additionally, not only have the conclusions about the morality of certain practices changed, but the ethical frame within which many practices are evaluated has also been transformed. Within this context of continuity and change, the essays of Arabome, Bong, Cartagenas, and Rop each suggest that, although the church's position on gender equality has improved, nonetheless there is much still to be done to uproot the ideology of subordination that still pertains in much of its theology and practice. This is confirmed moreover in the essays of Bucar, Cuda, Forcades i Vila, Keenan, Knauss, and Mannion, since each demonstrates in different ways how ambivalent both church and society continue to be about the exercise of women's agency. Although the tradition is evolving, the pace of change is disappointingly slow.

Recent years have seen a transformation in feminist theological discourse, particularly with the emergence of new generations of women from the global south. The diversity of the economic, political, cultural, and religious contexts from which they speak has had a significant impact on the substantive issues with which feminist theology has traditionally been concerned. More than just the issues, however, it has also expanded the approaches and methodologies that are deployed in the pursuit of a theology that is more reflective of the diversity and dynamism of the tradition. There is no doubt that this broadening of the conversation partners has added significantly to the richness of the interactions; however, it has also challenged further the tradition's capacity for inclusive engagement. In recent decades, the space for inclusive engagement within the church has shrunk further. Indeed, the absence of hospitable spaces for theological conversations has led many to leave the institution and to find refuge in various secular forms of spirituality. Anne Patrick's essay cautions against such an approach, suggesting that secular forms of spirituality, too, face similar challenges in promoting an ethic of social justice in the context of its absence. Patrick's ultimate concern, however, is to develop an "ethics of church participation," the parameters of which many of the essays herein will undoubtedly help clarify.

The last forty years have certainly seen important milestones in the pursuit of gender equality in the Catholic Church. The ideology of female subordination is no longer in the ascendency but is challenged whenever it surfaces, as invariably it still does. The critical perspectives of feminist women and men are now articulated more clearly, although they struggle to be heard where decisions are made. Greater attention has been given to the gap that exists within the church between the language of equality and the practice of inequality. Yet the disparity between the rhetoric and the reality continues to grow. The authors writing herein are deeply aware of these challenges and do not underestimate the task ahead. They are clear sighted about the task ahead and are determined to pursue a vision and praxis of mutuality.

Notes

1. Mary Daly, *Beyond God the Father: Toward a Philosophy of Women's Liberation* (Boston: Beacon Press, 1974).

2. Rosemary Radford Ruether, *Religion and Sexism: Images of Woman in the Jewish and Christian Traditions* (New York: Simon & Schuster, 1974).

3. Kari Elisabeth Børresen, *Subordination and Equivalence: The Nature and Role of Women in Augustine and Aquinas* (Kampen: Kok Pharos, 1995 [1968]).

4. Homi Bhabha, *The Location of Culture* (London: Routledge, 1994), 2.

5. Linda Hogan "Mixed Reception: Paul VI and John Paul II on Sex and War" in *The Papacy since 1500 from Italian Prince to Universal Pastor*, ed. James Corkery and Thomas Worcester (Cambridge: Cambridge University Press, 2010), 204–22.

6. John T. Noonan Jr., "Development in Moral Doctrine," in *The Context of Casuistry*, ed. James F. Keenan and Thomas A. Shannon (Washington, DC: Georgetown University Press, 1995), 194.

CONTRIBUTORS

KOCHURANI ABRAHAM is a senior fellow of the Indian Council of Social Sciences Research (ICSSR) with affiliation to Mahatma Gandhi University, Kerala, India, and is currently engaged in a research on gender education. She holds a doctorate in Christian Studies from the University of Madras, India, a MSc in Child Development from the University of Kerala, India, and a Licentiate in Systematic Theology from the University of Comillas, Madrid, Spain. She has taught in the Department of Christian Studies, University of Madras and served earlier as the coordinator of *Streevani's* (The Voice of Women) project for the empowerment of women religious in India. She is a member of the Indian Theological Association (ITA), the Indian Women Theologian's Forum (IWTF), Ecclesia of Women in Asia (EWA), and the Indian Association of Women's Studies (IAWS). Her research interests include gender, Indian feminism, ecology, and interreligious questions. She teaches Feminism and Feminist Theology and Feminist Spirituality in various institutes of formation, and conducts gender sensitization programs. She has published several articles on feminist concerns in journals of theology and sociology. She is also involved with grassroots women's movements and is committed to bridging the gap between academia and these fields to achieve a liberative praxis.

ANNE ARABOME, a Sister of Social Service (Los Angeles, USA), holds a Doctor of Ministry degree in spirituality from the Catholic Theological Union in Chicago. She is presently working on a second doctoral degree in Systematic Theology at Duquesne University in Pittsburgh, Pennsylvania. She is the author of "Woman, You are Set Free! Women and Discipleship in the Church" in *Reconciliation, Justice, and Peace: The Second African Synod*, ed. Agbonkhianmeghe E. Orobator (Maryknoll, NY: Orbis Books, 2011), and "Gender and Ecclesiology: Authorities, Structures, Ministry" in *Gender in Theology, Spirituality and Practice*, ed. Lisa Sowle Cahill, Diego Irarrazaval, and Elaine M. Wainwright (Glen Rock, NJ: Concilium 2012/4).

MARIA CLARA LUCCHETTI BINGEMER is associate professor in the Theology Department at the Catholic University of Rio de Janeiro, Brazil. She graduated from the Gregorian University in Rome. Her major areas of research include Christian mystics in the contemporary era and the theology of God. She is author of many books and articles in Portuguese, Spanish, Italian, and French. English publications include *Mary, Mother of God and Mother of the Poor* (with Ivone Gebara) (Maryknoll, NY: Orbis Books, 1989), and two forthcoming books, *A Face for God?* (Convivium Press) and *The Mystery and the World* (Cascade Books). A more complete list of works is available at http://lattes.cnpq.br/8374950313063279.

SHARON A. BONG is senior lecturer in Gender Studies at the School of Arts and Social Sciences, Monash University, Malaysia. She is author of *The Tension between Women's Rights and Religions: The Case of Malaysia* (2006) and editor of *Re-imagining Marriage and Family in Asia: Asian Christian Women's Perspectives*. Her ongoing research interests include feminist standpoint epistemologies; women's human rights and genders and sexualities in religions; and qualitative researching and analyses using ATLAS.ti (Computer-Assisted Qualitative Data Analysis Software). She is currently completing a project that examines the ways in which GLBTIQ (gay, lesbian, bisexual, transgender, intersex, queer or questioning) persons negotiate fully living out their religiosity and spirituality in same-sex partnerships in Malaysia and Singapore. Future research projects include religious discourses in cyberspace, asexuality, and queering time and space. She is involved in the Forum for the Study of Sexuality, Gender, Race and Religion as a research associate, is a forum writer and member of the Asian Regional Committee of the Catholic Theological Ethics in the World Church, and is former coordinator of the Ecclesia of Women in Asia.

AGNES M. BRAZAL is director of the Office for Research and Publications and coordinator of the Graduate program (PhD/MA) at the St. Vincent School of Theology-Adamson University, Philippines. She was past president and founding member of the DaKaTeo (Catholic Theological Society of the Philippines) and one of the first coordinators of the Ecclesia of Women in Asia (association of Catholic women theologians in Asia). She has been a planning committee member of the Catholic Theological Ethics in the World Church since 2007 and editorial board member of the journals *Asian Christian Review* and *Budhi*. She obtained her STD/PhD in Theology at the Katholieke Universiteit Leuven. Among her various publications are her coedited books *Transformative Theological Ethics: East Asian Contexts* (2010), *Faith on the Move: Toward a Theology of Migration in Asia* (2008), and *Body and Sexuality: Theological-Pastoral Reflections of Women in Asia* (2007; finalist, National Book Award, Philippines). She was also awarded the 2003 MWI (Institute of Missiology, Missio, Aachen) prize for the international academic essay contest on Contextual Theology and Philosophy, on the theme, "Religious Identity and Migration."

ELIZABETH BUCAR is associate professor at Northeastern University and works within the Shi`a and Catholic traditions on issues of gender, politics, and emergent technologies (new media and medical advances). Her books include *Does Human Rights Need God?* coedited with Barbra Barnett (Eerdmans, 2005); *Creative Conformity: The Feminist Politics of U.S. Catholic and Iranian Shi`i Women* (Georgetown University Press, 2011); *The Islamic Veil: A Beginner's Guide* (Oneworld, 2012); and *Religious Ethics in a Time of Globalism: Shaping a Third Wave of Comparative Analysis*, coedited with Aaron Stalnaker (Palgrave, 2012).

Aloysius Lopez Cartagenas is a native of Loon, Bohol in the Philippines. He did his theological studies at the Loyola School of Theology (Ateneo de Manila University) and the Katholieke Universiteit in Leuven (KUL) where he earned a doctorate in Theology. His dissertation on the foundations, method, and discourse of church social teaching received an award from the KUL Foundation for the Advancement of Church Research in 2002. He served the Archdiocese of Cebu from 1998 to 2006 as rector of San Carlos Major Seminary and from 1996 to 2010 as professor of its Graduate School of Theology. He is a member and past president of the *Damdaming Katoliko sa Teolohiya* (DaKaTeo), a society of Catholic theologians in the Philippines. He is also a member of the International Association for Catholic Social Thought and serves on the editorial board of the *Dharmaram Journal of Theology* (Bangalore). He is coeditor of *Politics and Christian Tradition* (2010) and *Transformative Theological Ethics: East Asian Contexts* (2010), and author of *Unlocking the Church's Best Kept Secret: Principles for the Interpretation, Communication, and Praxis of Catholic Social Teaching* (2012). He resigned from the clerical priesthood in 2011 and moved to Ireland, where he now lives.

Emilce Cuda is associate professor at Universidad Nacional Arturo Jauretche, Buenos Aires, Argentina, and invited professor at Universidad de Buenos Aires y Pontificia Universidad Católica, Argentina. Her specialties are Theology and Politics, and she teaches courses in Culture History, Ethics, Political Philosophy, and Aesthetics. She also investigates the relationship between Catholicism and democracy, particularly in her book, *Catholicism and Democracy in the United States* (Buenos Aires: Agape, 2010). She has written numerous articles and book chapters on topics including social equality, populism, union workers, work migration, democracy, and a theology of the people.

Shawnee Daniels Sykes, SSND, is an associate professor of Theological Ethics at Mount Mary University, Milwaukee, Wisconsin, and adjunct associate professor for the Institute for Black Catholic Studies at Xavier University of Louisiana. She is also a volunteer faculty member at the Center for the Advancement of Underserved Children at the Medical College of Wisconsin/Children's Hospital of Wisconsin, where she works as a bioethicist with an attending pediatric physician and a health lawyer to examine ethical issues. Dr. Daniels Sykes earned a PhD in Religious Studies from Marquette University, Milwaukee, Wisconsin. She holds an MA in Pastoral Studies from Saint Francis Seminary, Saint Francis, Wisconsin, and two undergraduate degrees: one from the University of Wisconsin-Milwaukee in nursing and another from Spelman College, Atlanta, Georgia, in biology/biochemistry. Her research interests include the intersection of philosophical normative ethics with Catholic Social Teaching; beginning, middle, and end of life issues; health care disparities; the pandemic of HIV/AIDS; and examining social bioethical issues from the perspective of the poor, vulnerable, marginalized, and communities of color. Currently, Dr. Daniels Sykes is the first and only African American female Catholic bioethicist in the United States.

LILIAN DUBE is an associate professor in the Theology and Religious Studies Department at the University of San Francisco. She graduated from Stellenbosch University as the first black African woman to earn a Doctor of Theology in 1999. Her teaching and research is focused on how religion, gender, and sexuality are affected by the reality of HIV/AIDS in different contexts. Lilian Dube developed and leads "USF in Zambia Today," an international service-learning program focused on the community's response to HIV and AIDS.

NICHOLE FLORES is a Margaret O'Brien Flatley Fellow in theological ethics at Boston College and Graduate Research Assistant at the Boisi Center for Religion and American Public Life. Her research interests include Catholic ethics, ethics and aesthetics, public theology, theories of justice, and U.S. Latina/o theology and ethics. She is currently writing her dissertation on U.S. Latina/o public theology and the role of religious aesthetics in U.S. public life. Nichole is a North American contributor to the Catholic Theological Ethics in the World Church Forum. She earned an A.B. in government from Smith College and a MDiv from Yale Divinity School. Nichole joined the faculty at Saint Anselm College in Manchester, New Hampshire as Instructor of Moral Theology in August 2013.

TERESA FORCADES I VILA is a physician, theologian, and Benedictine nun in the mountain monastery of Sant Benet de Montserrat (Catalonien, Spain). She holds a Master of Divinity degree with a dissertation on the philosophical underpinnings and the pitfalls of multicultural dialogue apropos of the work of C. Taylor and H. G. Gadamer (Harvard, 1997), a doctorate in Public Health with a dissertation on alternative medicine (U. Barcelona, 2004), and a doctorate in Sacred Theology with a study of the notion of person in classical Trinitarian theology and its relationship to the modern notion of freedom as self-determination (Facultat de Teologia de Catalunya, 2007). Her publications in English include "Crimes and Abuses of the Pharmaceutical Companies" (*Cristianisme i Justícia*, Booklet 124, 2006) and in Catalan or Spanish: *La Trinitat, avui* (PAMSA, 2005), *La Teologia Feminista en la Història* (Fragmenta, 2007) and *Ser persona, avui* (PAMSA, 2011). In 2009–10, she taught for two semesters at the Theology School of Humboldt University in Berlin. At present, she lives and teaches at her monastery in Montserrat and is preparing a book on the critique of medicalization.

LINDA HOGAN is vice-provost and chief academic officer and professor of Ecumenics at Trinity College, Dublin. As vice-provost/CAO, she has overall responsibility for education and research at the university and deputizes for the provost as required. She is a theological ethicist whose primary research interests lie in the fields of theological ethics, human rights, and gender. She has published widely on the ethics of human rights, intercultural ethics, and gender. She has also been the lead academic on a number of research projects focusing on religious pluralism and inter-religious ethics.

FR. JAMES KEENAN, SJ, is the Founders Professor of Theology at Boston College. A Jesuit priest since 1982, he received a licentiate (1984) and a doctorate (1988) from the Pontifical Gregorian University in Rome. He has edited or written sixteen books and more than 250 articles. He is the founder of Catholic Theological Ethics in the World Church and cochairs, with Linda Hogan, its "Planning Committee for the Future." Among his recent books are *A History of Catholic Moral Theology in the Twentieth Century: From Confessing Sins to Liberating Consciences*; *Paul and Virtue Ethics* (with Dan Harrington), and *Ethics of the Word: Voices in the Catholic Church Today*. He also edited the papers from the Conference of Theological Ethicists that was held in Trento, Italy, in 2010, *Catholic Theological Ethics, Past, Present, and Future: The Trento Conference*. He is presently working on two manuscripts on ethics and the university as well as a history of moral theology.

STEFANIE KNAUSS studied Theology and English Language and Literature in Germany, the United Kingdom, and Austria. After postdoctoral studies at the Fondazione Bruno Kessler (Trent, Italy) and a research fellowship at Köln University and Humboldt University Berlin (Germany), she worked as assistant professor of theology and culture at Villanova University. Her main research interests are the relationship between theology and media, in particular film; gender and queer studies in theology; and body and sexuality in religion. Recent publications include: *La saggia inquietudine: Il corpo nell'ebraismo, nel cristianesimo e nell'islam* (2011), *Gendered Ways of Knowing in Science: Scope and Limitations* (with Th. Wobbe and G. Covi, 2012), and an issue of *CrossCurrents* on theological aesthetics (with D. Zordan and S. B. Plate, 2013).

SHAJI GEORGE KOCHUTHARA, CMI, is associate professor in Moral Theology and the head of the Department of Moral Theology at Dharmaram Vidya Kshetram (DVK), Bangalore. He also serves as the editor in chief of *Asian Horizons*: *Dharmaram Journal of Theology* and as the chairperson of the Institutional Ethical Review Board of St John's Medical College, Bangalore. He was director of the Centre for Women Studies, DVK (2006–11). He is a member of the Asian Regional Committee of CTEWC and the "capo" of the Asian Forum Writers of CTEWC. He completed his licentiate and doctorate in moral theology at the Gregorian University, Rome. He is the author of *The Concept of Sexual Pleasure in the Catholic Moral Tradition* (Rome: Editrice Pontificia Università Gregoriana, 2007). He has edited two books and has published research articles in journals and collection of essays. He took initiatives to organize a national workshop on "Moral Theology in India Today" at DVK from July 12–15, 2012 (The papers will be published shortly).

GERARD MANNION is professor of Theology and director of the Frances G. Harpst Center for Catholic Thought and Culture at the University of San Diego, California. Educated at the Universities of Cambridge and Oxford, his academic career has included posts in Oxford, Leeds, Liverpool (all United Kingdom) and Leuven (Belgium). He has held visiting research fellowships at Union Theological Seminary/Columbia University, New York City and the Fondazione Bruno Kessler, Trento (Italy) as well as visiting professorships at the Universities of Tübingen (Germany) and Chichester (United Kingdom). He has published widely in the fields of ecclesiology and ethics as well as in other aspects of systematic theology and philosophy. Recent books include *Ecclesiology and Postmodernity: Questions for the Church in Our Time* (2007), *Moral Theology for the Twenty-First Century: Essays in Celebration of Kevin Kelly* (2008, ed. with Julie Clague and Bernard Hoose), *The Routledge Companion to the Christian Church* (2008, ed. with Lewis Mudge), and *The Art of Magisterium: a Teaching Church that Learns* (2013). He serves as chair of the Ecclesiological Investigations International Research Network, and as editor of the Continuum Series, "Ecclesiological Investigations." He is an Irish citizen and passionate about social justice, rugby union, and music.

SR. ALISON MUNRO is the director of the AIDS Office of the Southern African Catholic Bishops' Conference, based in Pretoria, South Africa, and supporting the home-based care, ARV treatment, and orphan care response of the church in Botswana, Swaziland, and South Africa. She is a Dominican Sister and holds master's degrees in Counseling Psychology and Education as well as Theology. She has worked in high school education, in psychological services for novices and seminarians, in a land reform program of her congregation, and on the Congregational Council of the Dominican Sisters of Oakford.

FR. AGBONKHIANMEGHE E. OROBATOR, SJ, is a Nigerian Jesuit, the provincial of the Eastern Africa Province of the Society of Jesus (Jesuits), and lecturer in theology at Hekima College Jesuit School of Theology in Nairobi, Kenya.

ANNE PATRICK, SNJM, is William H. Laird Professor of Religion and the Liberal Arts, *emerita*, at Carleton College in Northfield, Minnesota, USA. Her books include *Liberating Conscience: Feminist Explorations in Catholic Moral Theology* and *Conscience and Calling: Ethical Reflections on Catholic Women's Church Vocations*. She is a past president of the Catholic Theological Society of America and a founding vice president of the International Network of Societies for Catholic Theology.

ANNA PERKINS is a former Dean of Studies of St Michael's Theological College, Jamaica. She holds degrees from the University of the West Indies, Mona, Jamaica; Cambridge University, United Kingdom; and Boston College, United States. She is currently Senior Programme Officer, Quality Assurance Unit, UWI, Mona;

adjunct faculty at St Michael's Theological College; and editor of the college journal, *Groundings*. Her first book is entitled, *Justice as Equality: Michael Manley's Caribbean Vision of Justice*. She has a jointly edited publication entitled *Justice and Peace in Renewed Caribbean: Contemporary Catholic Reflections* in preparation for publication.

Veronica Jamanyur Rop is a member of the Assumption Sisters of Eldoret, a local congregation based in Kenya. She is a doctoral student (PhD/STD/MT) in the Faculty of Theology, Department of Moral Theology at the Catholic University of Eastern Africa. She is also a recipient of a CTEWC Scholarship for African women. She presented an earlier version of this essay at the CTEWC Conference in Trento.

Mee-Yin Mary Yuen, from Hong Kong, China, received her MA in Theology (Ethics and Social Theory) from the Jesuit School of Theology-Santa Clara University. She is currently a Ph.D. candidate of the Graduate Theological Union in Berkeley, California, focusing on Christian ethics, Chinese Confucian ethics, and Asian theology. She was a researcher and guest professor of social ethics at the Holy Spirit Seminary College of Theology and Philosophy in Hong Kong, and also taught Catholic social thought in the Chinese University of Hong Kong. She is the former executive secretary of the Justice and Peace Commission of the Hong Kong Catholic Diocese. Her research interests include social ethics, ethics and spirituality, Asian theology and Asian feminist theology, globalization, economic justice, and Confucian ethics.

Index

abortion, 109, 116, 118, 153, 282
Abraham, 246, 270, 271–72
Abraham, Kochurani, 3, 5–6, 10,
  11, 97–107, 282, 284
Addelson, K. P., 101
Aeneas, 169
"Affirmations for Catholic Women"
  (Hitchcock), 250–53
African Independent Churches (AIC), 36
agency of women, 102–3
AIDS
  African women infected
    with HIV, 29, 45
  antiretroviral (ARV) treatment of,
    in South Africa, 3–4, 54–63
  beginnings of PEPFAR-funded ARV
    treatment program for, 54–55
  care for people with, 34, 39
  challenges to treatment for, in
    South Africa, 59–60
  condom use for prevention of, 61–62
  drug and laboratory services
    for treatment of, 57–58
  ethical questions concerning
    treatment of, 60–62
  expansion and consolidation of ARV
    treatment program for, 55
  foreign nationals and South
    African treatment of, 58
  in Hong Kong, 132
  public-private partnership models
    for treatment of, 56–57
  statistics on, 44–45
  sustainability of ARV treat-
    ment program for, 56
Ammicht-Quinn, Regina, 222–23
Amorsolo, Fernando, 74–75
Anansi model, 170
Anna (Mary's mother), 34–35
antiretroviral (ARV) treatment of AIDS, 54–63

Aparecida conference, 145
apartheid in South Africa, 62, 262
Aquinas, Thomas, 12, 232, 237–39
Aquino, Corazon "Cory," 74
Aquino, María Pilar, 154, 233
Arabome, Anne, 2–3, 11, 14–25, 282, 284
Arendt, Hannah, 156
Argentina, 151–53, 160, 162, 163
Aristotle, 99, 156, 163
Arokiasamy, S., 114, 119
ARV treatment. *See* antiretroviral
  (ARV) treatment of AIDS
Azcuy, Virginia, 154, 155

Bachelet, Michelle, 7, 151–52
Banana, Canaan, 36–37
Bane, Mary Jo, 258, 267
Bansikiza, Constance, 51
barkada (social bond between males),
  87–88
Base Ecclesial Communities (BEC), 89
BEC. *See* Base Ecclesial Commu-
  nities (BEC)
Beena (name changed), 99–100
Beguines and Beghards, 160
Benedict XVI, Pope, 93, 153, 250
Beyond God the Father (Daly), 261, 280
Bible. *See specific persons and books of the
  Bible*
BILA. *See* Bishops' Institute for the Lay
  Apostolate (BILA) on Women
Bilhah, 272
Bingemer, Maria Clara Lucchetti, 7,
  137–49, 154, 155, 161, 282, 284
Bishops' Institute for the Lay Apostolate
  (BILA) on Women, 128–29, 130
Body and Sexuality, 65
Bong, Sharon A., 4, 5, 7, 64–71, 125, 282,
  285
Boodoo, Gerald, 168
Børresen, Kari Elisabeth, 280

291